# Governing Environmental Flows

# Governing Environmental Flows
## Global Challenges to Social Theory

Edited by Gert Spaargaren, Arthur P. J. Mol, and
Frederick H. Buttel

The MIT Press
Cambridge, Massachusetts
London, England

MIT Press books may be purchased at special quantity discounts for business or sales promotional use. For information, please e-mail <special_sales@mitpress.mit.edu> or write to Special Sales Department, The MIT Press, 55 Hayward Street, Cambridge, MA 02142.

This book was set in Sabon by SNP Best-set Typesetter Ltd., Hong Kong. Printed on recycled paper and bound in the United States of America.

Library of Congress Cataloging-in-Publication Data

Governing environmental flows : global challenges to social theory / edited by Gert Spaargaren, Arthur P. Mol, and Frederick H. Buttel.
  p. cm.
  Includes bibliographical references and index.
  ISBN 0-262-19545-3 (alk. paper)—ISBN 0-262-69335-6 (pbk. : alk. paper)
  1. Environmental policy. 2. Environmental policy—Social aspects. I. Spaargaren, Gert. II. Mol, A. P. J. III. Buttel, Frederick H.

GE170.G684   2006
333.7—dc22

                                                            2005057674

10 9 8 7 6 5 4 3 2 1

For Fred

# Contents

# Preface

In 2004, John Urry visited the Wageningen University circle of social theorists (also known as the "Giddens circle," as Anthony Giddens was its first visitor back in 1984) to discuss his "new rules for sociology." The debate was friendly, but vibrant and rather passionate. Urry seriously questioned a number of long-cherished notions and basic concepts in the social sciences, asking for nothing less than a fundamental new outlook for social theory. To live up to the tasks and challenges of today, social theory must be made less static, more fluid, and more directed toward flows and networks, instead of social systems and in particular the nation-state.

The debate on the reformulation of social theory goes beyond Urry, and includes, among others, scholars such as Manuel Castells, Arjun Appadurai, and Ulrich Beck. The environmental sociologists and political scientists who make up this book share an interest in exploring what such a reformulation means for the environmental social sciences—especially since the new rules for sociology have been rather superficial in regard to environmental questions. How should environmental flows be governed under conditions of globalization? How should the changing role of the environmental state be defined in Europe, the United States, and elsewhere in the global network society? How should one conceptualize agency and technology when analyzing environmental flows as well as the networks and scapes that "govern" them? And how far does one go in lifting the borders between the social and the natural, between society and nature? In short, how should one evaluate from an environmental perspective the revisions put on the agenda by the sociology of networks and flows?

Several of the chapters here find their origin in, and profited from, the International Sociological Association's RC–24 regional conference we organized on this central theme at Wageningen University. The ideas in these chapters have been further sharpened by follow-up conferences, such as the one organized at the University of Wisconsin, Madison, by Frederick H. Buttel.

We want to express our thanks to all the colleagues participating in the debates during the conferences, to the anonymous reviewers who helped to further improve this volume, and to Clay Morgan at MIT and Corry Rothuizen at Wageningen University who, by doing their jobs in a careful and qualified manner, made it a pleasure for us to be involved in this book project. Finally, we want to thank the Department of Social Sciences at Wageningen University, the Wageningen University Fund, and the province of Gelderland for their financial support of this project.

Fred took his full share in the making of this book, until his very last moments. He did not want to be treated different. He never ceased to think and write about the future challenges facing our world, and about the best way to respond as (environmental) social scientists—until nature forced him to. We dedicate this book to an irreplaceable colleague and friend.

Gert Spaargaren and Arthur P. J. Mol
Wageningen, fall 2005

# Abbreviations

ANT   Actor Network Theory
BEC   Binational Executive Committee
BECC   Border Environmental Cooperation Commission
BSE   Bovine Spongiform Encephalopathy (mad cow disease)
CBD   Convention on Biological Diversity
CBO   Community-Based Organization
CI   Conservation International
CILA (IBWC)   Comision Internacional de Limites y Aguas
DPSIR   Drivers, Pressure, State, Impacts, Response
ECNC   European Centre for Nature Conservation
EPZ   Export Processing Zone
EU   European Union
FAO   Food and Agricultural Organization of the United Nations
FLO   Fair-trade Labeling Organization
FSC   Forest Stewardship Council
GATT   General Agreement on Tariffs and Trade
GCR   Global Competitiveness Report
GEP   Global Environmental Politics and Governance
GINs   Global Integrated Networks
GM(O)   Genetically Modified (Organisms)
GNP   Gross National Product
GWP   Global Water Partnership
HACCP   Hazard Accident Critical Control Point

HEP   Human Exemptionalist/Exceptionalist Paradigm

IBWC (CILA)   International Boundary and Water Commission

ICA   International Coffee Agreement

ICC   International Criminal Court

IISD   International Institute for Sustainable Development

IJC   International Joint Commission

ILO   International Labor Organization

IMF   International Monetary Fund

I(N)GO   International (Non)Governmental Organization

IPCC   International Panel for Climate Change

IPPC   International Plant Protection Commission

ISO (14000)   International Standards Organization

IUCN   World Conservation Union

IWC   International Whaling Committee

LCA   Life Cycle Analysis

LPI   Living Planet Index

MEA   Multilateral Environmental Agreement

METI   Ministry of Economy, Trade, and Industry (Japan)

MIT   Massachusetts Institute of Technology

MNC   Multinational Corporation

MSC   Marine Stewardship Council

NACEC   North American Commission on Environmental Cooperation

NADB   North American Development Bank

NAFTA   North American Free Trade Agreement

NEP   New Ecological/Environmental Paradigm

NGO   Nongovernmental Organization

OECD   Organization for Economic Cooperation and Development

OIE   International Office of Epizootics

PEEN   Pan-European Ecological Network

R&D   Research and Development

RTB hypothesis   Race to the Bottom hypothesis

SBSTTA   Subsidiary Body on Scientific, Technical, and Technological Advice

SPS Agreement   Sanitary and PhytoSanitary Agreement

TBT Agreement   Technical Barriers to Trade Agreement

TNC   Transnational Corporation

UK   United Kingdom

UN   United Nations

UNCED   United   Nations   Conference   on   Environment   and Development

UNCTAD   United Nations Convention on Trade and Development

UNEP   United Nations Environment Program

UNESCO   United   Nations   Educational,   Scientific,   and   Cultural Organization

UNFAO   United Nations Food and Agriculture Organization

USEPA   United States Environmental Protection Agency

WB   World Bank

WBCSD   World Business Council for Sustainable Development

WEF   World Economic Forum

WHO   World Health Organization

WST   World-System Theory

WTO   World Trade Organization

WWAP   World Water Assessment Program

WWF   World Wide Fund for Nature (originally World Wildlife Fund)

WWII   World War II

WWV   World Water Vision

# Contributors

**Hans Bruyninckx** is an associate professor of international environmental politics in the political science department at the Catholic University Leuven, Belgium. His main research interests are the political economy of global environmental relations, the functioning of governance arrangements under the pressure of globalization, and the linkages between environmental degradation and violent conflicts.

**Frederick H. Buttel** (1948–2005) was a professor of rural sociology and environmental studies at the University of Wisconsin, Madison. He was president of the RC-24 Environment and Society network of the International Sociological Association from 1998 to 2002. Buttel was coeditor in chief of the international journal *Society and Natural Resources*, and published numerous books and articles in the field of environmental and rural sociology. He is the coauthor and editor of such recent books as *Environment, Energy, and Society* (2002), *Environment and Global Modernity* (2000), and *Sociological Theory and the Environment* (2002).

**Itay Fischhendler** is a lecturer in the geography department at the Hebrew University, Jerusalem. Fischhendler's research interests focus on environmental politics and environmental conflict resolution with particular emphasis on international water resources decision-making processes. He has been a research fellow at the University of California, Berkeley, the University of Texas, Austin, and the University of London, and published in *Political Geography, GeoForum, Environment and Planning C*, and *Water Policy*. His most recent work, on the geographic scale of management as a decision-making variable in resolving water conflicts, is scheduled for publication as a book.

**Zsuzsa Gille** is an assistant professor of sociology in the sociology department at the University of Illinois, Urbana-Champaign. Her field of study includes environmental sociology, the sociology of knowledge, globalization, cultural studies, and Eastern Europe. She has a book forthcoming, titled *From the Cult of Waste to the Trash Heap of History: A Social Theory of Waste*.

**Martin Jänicke** is a professor of political sciences at the Free University, Berlin, and has been head of its research group in environmental policy since 1986. He has served on numerous committees and boards both at the national and international level, and is connected as an editor, adviser, or initiator to a series of leading journals in the fields of environmental sciences, politics, and law. Jänicke has published a great number of monographs, and edited volumes on the role of the state in environmental politics and on structural environmental change in industrial societies.

**Mette Jensen** is a senior researcher in environmental sociology in the policy analysis department at the National Environmental Research Institute, Denmark. Her main research themes are in the fields of mobility, modernity, risk perception, and environment. She is a member of the steering committee for the Danish social sciences environmental research network Misonet, and a member of the Nordic sociological research network Environment and Risk of the Nordic Sociological Association. She teaches environmental and risk sociology in the sociology department at the University of Copenhagen.

**C. S. A. (Kris) van Koppen** is a senior lecturer with the Environmental Policy Group at Wageningen University and a professor of environmental education by special appointment at the University of Utrecht. His main research interest concerns the relationship between environmental policy and social learning, with a focus on nature valuation and nature policy. He is coordinator of the Environment and Society Research Network of the European Sociological Association.

**Arthur P. J. Mol** is chair and a professor of environmental policy in the social sciences department at Wageningen University. He chairs the Board of Mansholt Graduate School for Research at Wageningen University, and is the current president of the research committee on Environment and Society of the International Sociological Association. He has published widely in the fields of social theory and the environment, environmental transformations and reform, globalization, and social movements, including the book *Globalization and Environmental Reform: The Ecological Modernization of the Global Economy* (2001). He coordinates a series of research programs on environmental reform in Southeast and East Asia.

**Peter Oosterveer** is a senior lecturer with the Environmental Policy Group at Wageningen University. His main research interests and publications are in the fields of the globalization of food production and consumption, sustainable food consumption, and environmental sociology. He is coordinator of a research program on the transformation of agro-industries in Southeast Asia.

**Luciana M. S. Presas** is a Post-doctoral Fellow at the University of São Paulo, Brazil who specializes in sustainable building and urban development. She is author of a number of publications in the fields of urban ecology, globalization, and corporate environmental policy. Presas is currently carrying out research on poverty-environment linkages in major cities.

**Gert Spaargaren** is a professor of environmental policy for sustainable lifestyles and consumption with the Environmental Policy Group at Wageningen University. His main research interests and publications are in the fields of environmental sociology, sustainable consumption and behavior, and the globalization of environmental reform. He is chair of the Dutch national network on social sciences and the environment, and coordinator of an international research program on sustainable consumption.

**Dimitris Stevis** is a professor of international politics at Colorado State University. His research focuses on the social regulation of global and regional integration, with an emphasis on environment and labor. He has served as chair of the Environmental Studies Section and the Sprout Award Committee of the International Studies Association. Stevis is the coeditor (with Valerie Assetto) of the book *The International Political Economy of the Environment: Critical Perspectives* (2001), and is currently completing a book titled *Globalization and Labor: Democratizing Global Governance?* (with Terry Boswell) and researching the views of labor unions toward global environmental issues.

# Governing Environmental Flows

# 1

## Introduction: Governing Environmental Flows in Global Modernity

Gert Spaargaren, Arthur P. J. Mol, and Hans Bruyninckx

Global warming and the policy efforts undertaken at different levels to alleviate this problem can be used as a metaphor for a number of hotly debated issues concerning interdependence, globalization, and transformations in environmental governance. For some, global warming illustrates the irrelevance of state sovereignty, given the tension between the inherently global nature of the problem and the relative insignificance of a single state's actions. For others, it demonstrates the importance of new policy arrangements that assign new roles to different policy actors, such as industrial sectors or scientists (e.g., IPCC), or an increased emphasis on cooperation between states and industry. Still others place the debate in the conceptual framework of governance and institutional analysis, pointing to the emerging norm and rule-setting context of global warming in the absence of clear and effective state action (Young 1994).

A similarly illustrative example can be found in the international trade in waste. What do we learn from the fact that not only shiploads of waste but also ships that have become waste are moved around the globe in increasingly significant numbers? By moving waste around, national borders and—at the same time—boundaries of sovereignty, regulation, and governance are crossed. This moving around of waste between "environments" with very different rule-setting contexts provides incentives for economically efficient specialization in waste management and trade. Some interpret this as a painful instance of the absence of national and international regulations. Others interpret this development as a search for economic efficiency in the areas of reuse and recycling. The globalization of all aspects of production and consumption, even waste, could be offered as an explanation as well. A more explicit North-South interpretation emphasizes the geographic externalization of the environmental costs of the Western growth model.

There is clearly no lack of possible conceptualizations of such environmental issues, as different disciplines and authors are offering various explanations for the globalization of what we will call *environmental flows*. The notion of environmental flows is put forward in this volume as the key unit of analysis. This concept accommodates well with some branches of the environmental sciences like material flows analysis, industrial ecology, and so-called footprint analyses. The concept of environmental flows as it is used here, however, is given a thoroughly social dimension as well since we discuss material, environmental flows with the help of some recent sociological and political science–based theories that focus on networks, scapes, fluids, and flows. In particular, the works of Manuel Castells, John Urry, Arjun Appadurai, and Saskia Sassen have contributed in the last decade to a better understanding of the dynamics of (environmental) flows in modern societies. One of the core features determining the dynamics of environmental flows and making the "behavior" of these flows in the present really different from preceding periods is the globalization of social and environmental relations. Both examples of environmental flows ($CO_2$, shipwrecks) discussed above illustrate rather well the fact that the transnational and global character of environmental problems is radically changing our conventional ideas of policymaking, government, and governance. Individual, independent, and autonomous (nation-)states for a long time have been regarded as the single most important actors in environmental politics, and have been treated also as the theoretical cornerstones in many sociological and political science analyses of environmental policies. In the last decade, though, the nation-state has lost its position as the key "power-container" (Beck and Willms 2004) in environmental politics. The changes in the role and function of nation-states in environmental politics have been framed and emphasized by social and political scientists in discourses on globalization and governance in many different ways. This book will contribute to that debate by focusing on the relationships between globalization, the environment, and the state. Consequently, we stress three specific domains in the broader studies and debates on globalization and governance.

First, this volume attempts to conceptualize the changing nature of the *state* and its role in global environmental governance. The state has been crucial—or even formative—in twentieth-century social and political sciences as well as twentieth-century studies on environmental deterioration and reform. But under conditions of globalization, the state is transforming in a fundamental way. Any analysis of the changing nature and role of the state in entering the twenty-first century can of course only be done properly when interpreting the state in close relation to other actors and institutions, such as companies and markets, NGOs and civil society, and international organizations. The rather recent conceptual shift in attention from government to governance, and from organizations to institutions, has led to a stream of studies and approaches on innovative rule-setting arrangements beyond the traditional, rather dominant focus on government institutions or international organizations. While innovative and refreshing, the danger of such new approaches, however, can be a certain disregard for the state as such. The effort we make in this book is to analyze how new systems of (environmental) governance have influenced the state and what roles states still play in global governance. There are different perspectives on this issue. On the one hand, there are those scholars who claim that the state is becoming largely irrelevant because of the formation of totally different networks of power, rule setting, and principles of behavioral practices (e.g., Ohmae 1995; Castells 1998). On the other hand, there are theorists who still concentrate largely on the conventional state bureaucracy in their description and analysis of (environmental) policymaking and reform (e.g., Hirst and Thompson 1996; chapter 3, this volume).

Second, the environmental dimension is emphasized in this book as crucial to the dynamics of globalization and governance. Environmental issues are not only illustrative of state-related transformations—for example, globalization, governance processes, the formation of alternative policy arrangements and transnational networks, and the emergence of subpolitics—but are also constitutive elements in these changes. By focusing on the substantive area of (global) environmental change, we avoid the pitfall of a (dare we say sterile) debate on the relevance or irrelevance of the state. Our central goal is hence to understand and elaborate on the need and possibilities to reinvent what has elsewhere been labeled the "environmental state" (Mol and Buttel 2002) in an era of global modernity. Reinventing the environmental state does imply more than rethinking the role of statist actors with respect to different kinds of arrangements. The role of environmental states also needs to be discussed in a broader perspective. How can we redefine notions of (ecological) citizenship and legitimacy, how do we delineate the arena for political discourse, and what is made "negotiable" and opened up for participation? In addition, who are the (new) actors to be represented in these participation processes, and what are the rules that the game players can use to organize the debate and the decision-making process?

Third, this volume shows an interest in assessing the consequences of globalization and the changing role of the environmental state for our understanding of the very notion of the *environment* itself. How can we conceptualize the environment now that the notion of the environment as a nationally defined and managed sustenance base for national economies and societies is no longer valid? The 1992 UNCED is considered by many authors as a turning point in this respect. After this world summit, the environmental agenda—whether implemented as the Kyoto protocol or local Agenda 21—is dominated by global environmental issues and policies. The prominence of environmental issues that crosscut existing boundaries and policy levels—with biodiversity, climate change, deforestation, ozone layer, and water issues being among the most well-known examples—calls for a rethinking of the nineteenth- and twentieth-century formulations of the concept of the environment itself. The nineteenth-century-based notion of the environment as "external" to societies (Beck et al. 1994), and the twentieth-century notion of the environment as something to be managed and controlled in the context of neatly delineated and defined (national) territories, are no longer valid (Spaargaren et al. 2000). They have become worn-out concepts as a result of globalization and the changing role of nation-states in environmental policies. To conclude that mainstream concepts have become obsolete is one thing; to come up with an alternative set of concepts to do the analytic job under present-day conditions is more difficult. In this book, we explore the notion of environmental flows along with the social sciences–based theories on networks, fluids, and flows as possible candidates for this job.[1]

**Environmental Flows as a Starting Point**

The conceptualization of the environment in terms of environmental flows is taken as a starting point for both the empirical and theoretical chapters in this book. In the empirical chapters, the authors base their contributions on actual "flows stories" when referring to flows of energy, water, waste, biodiversity, and genetic material, or "green" products. In the theoretical chapters, the authors focus on the definition of the flows concept itself and the theoretical issues related to the governing of environmental flows.

The notion of environmental or material flows is not new in the environmental sciences and environmental studies. There exists a rich natural-sciences-based literature on material flows analysis, industrial ecology, and "additions and withdrawals" (see also chapter 2, this volume). But by drawing heavily on the social sciences, the connotation and operationalization of the concept of environmental flows taken in this book differs significantly and fundamentally from the ones used in the environmental sciences and environmental studies. By exploring the specific characteristics of environmental flows in comparison to the flows that are discussed in the (sociological) literature on globalization—that is, the flows of money, images, investments, people, and information—this volume moves away from the technological or natural sciences–based outlook that is so characteristic of much of the environmental sciences, human ecology, and industrial ecology literature on environmental change. In other words, the aim is to analyze which sorts of new networks, arrangements, and infrastructures are constituting and governing different sorts of environmental flows, rather than the material dimensions of environmental flows as such or in isolation.

Environmental flows are environmental (in contrast to other flows) because they form a specific category of flows with a common denominator: their thoroughly material character. Nevertheless, the term *thoroughly material* can have two different meanings, both relevant to the issues at stake in this book. On the one hand, it relates to the material character of the flows of products and environmental goods, thus representing a physical reality. It is well documented that these flows of solid waste, wastewater, energy, green products, biodiversity, and the like have transformed over the last decades in quantity, quality, environmental

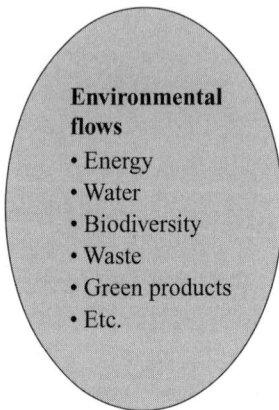

**Figure 1.1**
Environmental flows

impact, and the governance arrangements and networks "guiding" them (Jänicke et al. 1992). By selecting a number of case studies that are built around specific environmental flows, this volume sets itself the task of analyzing the ways in which changes in material flows pose new challenges for all actors involved in the environmental governance of these material flows. On the other hand, the term *material* can also be interpreted from a more structuralist perspective. It then refers to social relations and networks that give rise to, or accompany, the environmental flows. By this we refer to the relationships between actors in decision making on production and consumption processes. This material structure to a large extent defines the social dynamics of the flows and the differential social impact they have on several actors. It is obvious that the state and other (economic) actors play a role in these dynamics, and that globalization as a process is changing the material setting in the latter meaning of the term.

## Theoretical Perspective of the Book: The Governance of Environmental Flows

In the remainder of this chapter, we will further introduce and discuss the theoretical perspective used in this volume. We start, in the next section, by presenting a selective review of the existing sociological and political science literature on environmental governance and global modernity in order to substantiate our claim that most bodies of literature have a rather limited focus as well as to specify the need for a complementary integrated approach. The integrated approach to the governance of environmental flows in global modernity as put forward here has two distinct characteristics. First, when dealing with issues of governance, this approach makes use of the notion of *hybrid arrangements* for understanding the governance of environmental flows in the context of globalization. Following Beck and the growing body of literature on so-called subpolitical arrangements, we argue that the (nation-)state-based arrangements for the management and control of environmental flows have not disappeared but are joined by transnational arrangements that crosscut formerly distinct divisions of tasks among state, market, and civil society actors. A second characteristic of our approach is the emphasis on the notion of *hybrids* in terms of the complexities of social and material entities. In order to make sense of the complexity of environmental governance in global modernity we need to understand environmental governance in terms of arrangements for (global) hybrids. This is because of the fact that not just the relations, tasks, and responsibilities between policy actors or stakeholders have become more diffuse and complex but also the ways in which these social actors are (conceived to be) related to the material objects of policy-making have changed. Following Urry in this respect, we discuss in a third section the notion of hybrids in an effort to make sense of human–material flows relationships under conditions of a globalizing modernity. The concept of hybrids or hybrid systems together with the related notions of scapes and networks are used to analyze the fluid boundaries between the social and the physical, between (policy) actors and (material-flows-based) structures under conditions of global modernity.

When taken together, the emphasis on hybrid arrangements and arrangements for hybrids can be said to represent a new integrated approach to the issues of governance, globalization, and the environment. In the fourth section, we further situate our approach and discuss its central aims and objectives by reviewing the contributions it delivers for environmental sociology and the environmental sciences, and by looking at its relation with some existing theories of environmental change, notably ecological modernization theory and WST. The chapter concludes with an outline of the argument and an overview of the different chapters contained in this book.

## Environmental Governance: A Selective Review of the Literature

Some of the most pressing questions with respect to flows, and especially regarding environmental flows, are related to their management, governance, and control. How to design and direct environmental flows so as to limit environmental deterioration? From the early start of the environmental debate in the 1970s, the crucial role of the state in preventing (or curing) environmental deterioration has been acknowledged. Throughout the last three decades, different schools of thought in social and political sciences have documented how national states formulated, formalized, and tried to implement the environmental agendas as being pressed by especially civil society actors. In more recent environmental (policy) discourses, the emphasis has switched to the challenges national state authorities face, first by the (supposed) supremacy of the market and subsequently by the dynamics of globalization.

One way to look at the different and diverging theoretical contributions to this debate is to place them in the state, environment, and globalization triangle (figure 1.2). In reviewing the relevant literature on the governing of environmental flows, we contend that most contributions in sociology and political science should be placed in one of the corners of the triangle since they provide theoretical refinement and insight on only one or two of the elements represented in the figure. They are either strong on environmental issues (Conca and Lipschutz 1993), the state (Evans 1995), or globalization (Castells 1998). Sometimes they focus on the interplay between two elements of the triangle, such as Giddens (1998) on state-globalization relations, and Wapner (1998), Dryzek and colleagues (2003), and Eckersley (2004) on the state-environment linkages. Rare, however, are significant contributions that link and relate all three edges of this triangle, and thus provide theoretical views on the environmental state from a globalization perspective. By outlining a selection of the theoretical contributions that make up the triangle, we

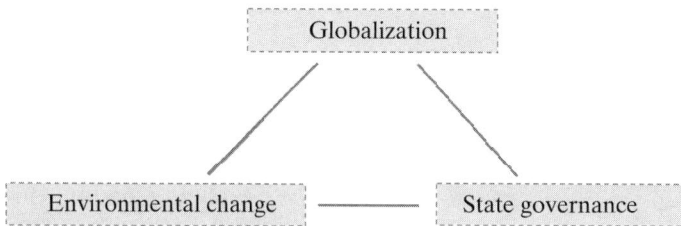

**Figure 1.2**
Making sense of the triad: Evaluating different theoretical perspectives

identify the contours of the playing field as a start for a search toward new syntheses between so far largely separated scholarly traditions in (environmental) sociology and political science.

*Globalization scholars* have described and analyzed in great detail global and local processes of social change, as can be observed during the last two decades. The increasing transboundary nature of social processes strongly driven by the enhanced possibilities of information and communication technologies, the emergence of global networks next to states as organizing principles of globalization, and the flows of money, information, capital, and persons between the nodes of these global networks characterize many of these contributions to globalization (Castells 1998; Giddens 1998; Held 1995; Held et al. 1999; Urry 2003). Global networks, in which norms and rules are less and less set by traditional loci of authority such as states, prevail prominently in this body of literature. Most of the time, authors within this tradition refer to environmental deterioration and reform as useful illustrations of the sort of broader dynamics they attempt to analyze, understand, and explain. They do not, however, offer an elaborate view on the specific contribution of environmental flows to the issue of global governance.

In the relation between internationalization/globalization and the environment, the field of *international environmental politics* has contributed significantly to our understanding of how different actors and institutions deal with environmental problems at a transnational level. The most prominent (if not dominant) theoretical framework—namely, regime theory—focuses on the dynamics of actors in designing, managing, and implementing international agreements and institutions (Young

1994; Haas et al. 1993). Others have used slightly different explanatory frameworks for analyzing the rise and relevance of different actors such as (I)NGOs, CBOs, banks, TNCs, or scientists (e.g., Wapner 1996, 1998). Arguably, most studies and theories in the field of international environmental politics remain characterized by a poor conceptualization of the state (Litfin 1998), regardless of the attention paid to, and the discourse on, sovereignty, governance, and globalization.

*State theorists* have given an explicitly historical and articulated account of the importance and role of the state (see also chapter 4, this volume). The state is interpreted as the exclusive or dominant locus of sovereignty and military power, having a direct impact on processes of societal change. The field has theorized on processes of state formation and transformation, the link between the state system and global dynamics in economic development and trade, and specific intra- and interstate (welfare) dynamics (Skocpol and Evans 1985; Jessop 1991; Evans 1995). Yet regardless of this emphasis, state theorists pay surprisingly little attention to environmental issues and their impact on state formation, dynamics, and change.

Most state studies of *environmental social scientists* are strongly empirically oriented at (transformations in) environmental policies, politics, environmental NGOs, and ideological frameworks, and have only a limited foundation in social theory. More theory-informed analyses have been related to state failures (Jänicke 1986), new state-market relations (e.g., the studies under the heading of ecological modernization; see Mol and Buttel 2002), green politics and governments (Dryzek 1997; Carter 2000; Eckersley 2004), green ideologies (Dobson 2000), and the countervailing powers of civil society (Rootes 1999; Dryzek et al. 2003). But these dominant themes from at least the mid-1980s onward have been mostly contained in a national or nation-state paradigm. Only recently has some interest emerged among environmental sociologists and political scientists to include processes of globalization into their analytic frameworks (Yearley 1996; Mol 2001; the recently established journal *Global Environmental Politics*; some studies on global environmental movements).

It is especially at the crossroads and via a cross-fertilization of these traditions that we might be able to understand the governance of envi-

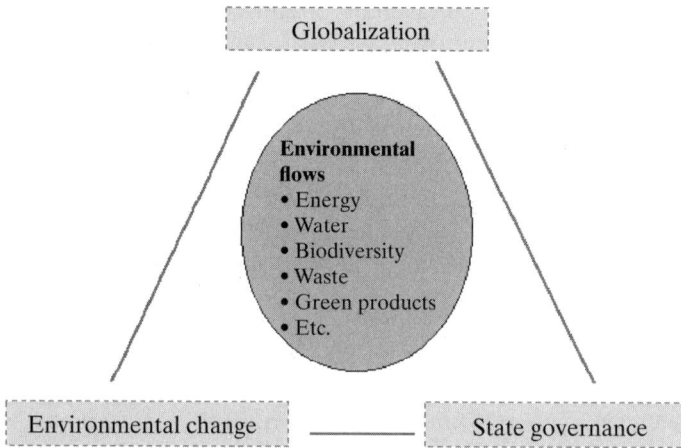

**Figure 1.3**
Studying the governance of environmental flows in global modernity

ronmental flows in an era marked by globalization (figure 1.3).[2] If there is any common denominator in the diversity of studies and analyses that concentrate on understanding the governance of environmental flows in this triangle, it might be the focus on the enmeshment of the conventional social sciences categories of state, market, and civil society.

### Hybrid Arrangements for the Governance of Environmental Flows: Beyond State–Market–Civil Society

It is crucial to realize that the study of environmental globalization and its governance arrangements does require more than just working at a higher systemic level of analysis, while using conventional social and political concepts and parameters. In some respects, the concepts and parameters themselves must be redefined. "Old" concepts—for example, the state—will have to be revisited and reinvented; conventional distinctions between the state, the market, and civil society will start to shift; instruments will have to be evaluated in light of new goals and dynamics; and social relations and networks will change.

Within what has recently become known as the (global) governance literature, there is a strong tendency to interpret some of these transformations in terms of a weakening of conventional social forces and political institutions such as the state. Theoretically, the state becomes increasingly replaced by a proliferation of governance arrangements that create new forms and institutions for "regulating" actors' behavior in the international or global arena. Governance has then an almost inherently positive undertone, based on the following mantra: away with traditional government, which is associated with command-and-control, old-fashioned statist policymaking, and onward to innovative, participatory, multilevel arrangements. This (theoretical) shift has far-reaching implications for understanding legitimate behavior in international and global settings, as it touches on the fundamental principle of state sovereignty. This transition from government to governance is based on the understanding that the political is not limited to the traditional concept of the state, in the sense of a delineated institution. Transformations of the state, new alliances between the state and other actors, and the state as only one (pivotal) element of global networks form new foci of theoretical attention in the governance literature.

In understanding the environmental state in global modernity, attention should be given to the dynamics and transformations that challenge the distinction between the state, the market, and civil society. For instance, when MNCs with a proactive environmental strategy are working in a "low-governance arena," they sometimes come to act as government-like agents, regulating flows from a broader perspective than just an economic one. We then can see market actors behaving like states. But it also happens the other way around: states buying and selling carbon dioxide sinks on international markets, competing for "green product flows," and rationalizing their green energy politics from a liberalization and privatization point of view. Finally, the sharp divisions between markets and states and their system rationalities, on the one hand, and civil society with its broader rationality, on the other (Habermas 1982), seem to have lost some of their significance too. Civil society actors are working increasingly (also) within the official system. Here we can see environmental NGOs acting as MNCs, trading in environmental liability or credibility (e.g., the WWF), and actively creating subpolitical arrangements in direct negotiations between NGOs and market actors. Sometimes nonstate actors fill the gaps that are left open by official institutions that cannot keep up with the forces of globalization.

This volume analyzes such shifting boundaries and pays special attention to these hybrid arrangements in the field of global environmental governance (see figure 1.4). Of course, the relevant questions are: Where and when do we see, expect, need, or want these kinds of hybrid arrangements? How are these hybrid arrangements related to globalization? And what are the consequences of such arrangements for regulating environmental flows in terms of, for instance, environmental effectiveness and democracy? It would be beneficial if the debate on these arrangements (Leroy and Van Tatenhove 2000) converged toward general characteristics, typologies, and modes of operation that could structure the analytic scope for further research. Analyzing existing frameworks and categorizations as well as presenting empirical research efforts on new arrangements will help us further.

In combining the flows model with the emerging new hybrid arrangements that move beyond the conventional arrangements of state–market–civil society, the debate on the transformations in the state,

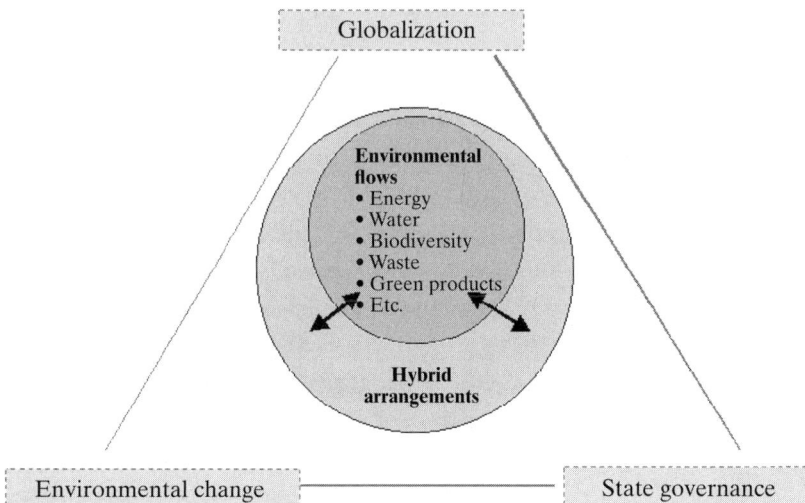

**Figure 1.4**
Hybrid arrangements in the regulation and governance of environmental flows

environment, and globalization triangle, most probably will become better focused. The range of possible hybrids or a set of ideal-type arrangements for global environmental governance could be elaborated. It also allows for distinctions between what could be called flows-specific networks and arrangements along with a number of more fundamental general characteristics of hybrid arrangements that hold across different flows, but perhaps not across different countries or regions.

The identification and understanding of hybrid arrangements in environmental governance may have major consequences for the issues of the state and sovereignty. But there is much debate and discussion on what the consequences exactly are. Some have declared the end of states and sovereignty, advocating the emergence of a stateless society. In his influential book *International Governance: Protecting the Environment in a Stateless Society*, Oran Young (1994), one of the most important theorists in international environmental politics, doesn't define clearly what a stateless society might be, or what the term stateless might mean. But at the same time, Young does suggest a fundamental change in global political and social organization, and how conventional concepts such as power and legitimacy are used in analyzing environmental reform. In a slightly different way and from a more sociological perspective, both Beck and Willms (2004) and Urry (2000, 2003) also make a plea for the dissolution of what they call zombie concepts like the state and society as analytic categories for analyzing flows in global modernity, suggesting a more networklike definition of (transnational) states.

Other theorists, including some political scientists and a group of international relations scholars, are arguing for what they call more realism in the demise of the state idea (Litfin 1998; Keohane 2002; Shaw 1994). Keohane clearly states that we live in a partially globalized world, "a world of thick networks of interdependence, in which boundaries, and states, nevertheless matter a great deal" (2002, 245). Keohane and Nye (2002) have developed the idea of *networked minimalism* to describe the direction of the current trend in governance on the basis of two elements. On the one hand, networks of norm- and rule-setting actors will emerge on issues that transcend the national, traditional government institutions. Economic actors, NGOs, scientists, international organizations, and others will become increasingly constitutive partners of governance arrangements at multiple policy levels. Their role in implementation and compliance is especially interesting to observe in the future as those have been the areas in which the state has been the (near-)exclusive actor for a long time. On the other hand, these governance arrangements will be inherently minimalist because traditional states still keep a major check on the depth and width of governance.

All these scholars share the idea that the nature, position, and role of the (environmental) state is changing, and that we have to look for new concepts to analyze these transformations where they relate to environmental challenges in a global world order. The degree of state transformation and the final relevance of the state in environmental governance remain open to debate and empirical investigation. And it is exactly this task that is taken up in this book.

### Arrangements for (Global) Hybrids?

From the review of the social sciences and political science literature on global environmental governance it can be concluded that there has been a shift in emphasis from the role of nation-states toward a perspective that includes nonstate actors operating at different policy levels and discusses new (network-based) roles for nation-states in the context of globalization. We argued for the need to rethink the role of state, market, and civil society actors in global governance because of the enmeshment and hybridization we witness between formerly distinct entities and roles. Roles and responsibilities formerly reserved for (nation-)state actors are fulfilled by market actors and civil society groups and organizations, and vice versa. This hybridization of roles and responsibilities is essential if we are to understand the basic dynamics of environmental governance in a globalizing modernity.

There is, however, also a second manner in which talking about hybridization makes sense in the context of this book. With Urry, one can assert that in sociology, some of the most commonly used and cherished dichotomies like the social and the material as well as human agency and technology need to be reconsidered and reformulated, especially when globalization adds a new dimension to the complexity of

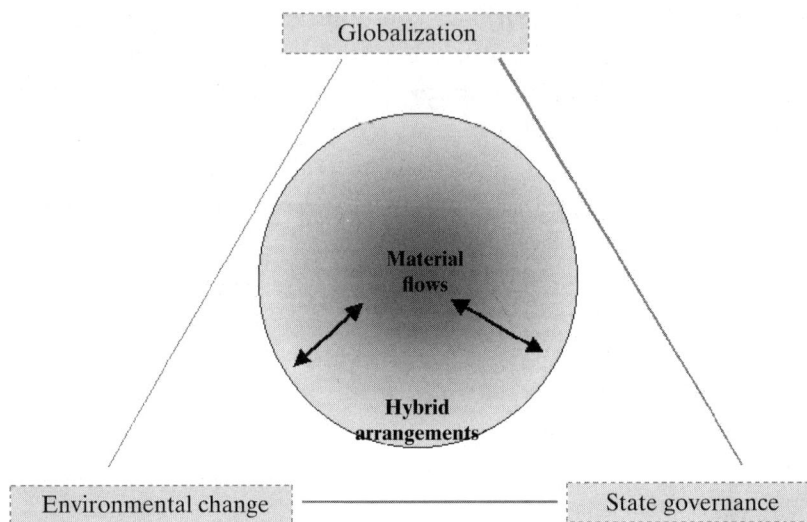

**Figure 1.5**
Hybrid arrangements for hybrid systems

human-machine or human-technology interactions. In the tradition of Michael Callon, Bruno Latour, and the by now well-established ANT school, Urry criticizes mainstream sociology—especially the structuration theory of Giddens—for emphasizing agency over (technological) structure in this respect. When, for example, the car system is at (environmental) stake, the best way to make sense of the future development of these kinds of systems is to conceive of them as *hybrid systems*.

When discussing hybrid systems, it is recognized that the interrelation between the social and the material should be analyzed with more and different kind of concepts than the agency-structure dichotomy alone. To make sense of hybrid systems, notions from systems theory and even complexity theory will have to be used, and some of the natural sciences could be put to work also in the social sciences. This challenging view could perhaps be neglected when working in thoroughly social fields like labor relations or gender, but not when working in the environmental field. Since its inception, *environmental* sociology has been struggling with society-nature/social-material interactions and the ways in which these interactions could best be conceptualized.

## Environmental Sociology on Society: Nature Interactions

A short selective review of the history of environmental sociology will serve to illustrate the permanent struggle for (conceptual) clarity in human-nature interactions. Early strands of the Chicago school's human ecology used the concepts and tools of plant ecology to make sense of settlement patterns in Chicago in the 1930s. Nelissen (1972) argued that the distinction between society and a "biotic community" was at the heart of the Chicago school's spatial-environmental research. The introduction of the biotic community concept served to emphasize the role of nonsocial or subsocial factors in shaping societies. When functionalism became the dominant school within sociology, the physical/material reality disappeared out of sight since social facts were to be explained by (other) social facts only.

When seen in retrospect, the debate between the HEP and NEP launched in the social sciences by Riley E. Dunlap and William R. Catton Jr. in the 1970s and 1980s can be interpreted as an attempt to bring back in the physical and material dimension. The NEP echoed the human ecology tradition in its plea to analyze social systems not in isolation from their material physical flows. The dependencies between human societies and ecosystems were discussed with the help of the Darwinian concept of the "web of life," and framed in the Club of Rome–inspired language of the physical limits to economic growth (Dunlap and Catton 1994). Dunlap and Catton did not discuss in any detail the epistemological issues one is confronted with when dealing with society-nature interactions in a human ecology–inspired way.

Allan Schnaiberg in his classic study (1980) on the field of environmental sociology took up this challenge, arriving at a conclusion that was strikingly different from Dunlap and Catton. Schnaiberg argued against the partial or total fusion of the material and the social as well as the disciplines designated for studying these different realms since the social—according to Schnaiberg—is different from the natural in some crucial respects. Societies are "dependent from" the sets of ecosystems they rely on for their proper functioning, but they do not function in the same (mechanistic) ways that ecosystems do. Since the social is different from the natural, the sciences of ecology and sociology should also be kept separate, so Schnaiberg contended. Sociology or the social sciences in general should not become mixed up with ecology or the natural sciences. This plea for separate tasks and identities within the social and natural sciences can also be found in Giddens's structuration theory as it became influential in sociology from the 1980s onward. When discussing epistemological issues, Giddens (1976) asserted that those looking for natural sciences–based laws and explanations in the social sciences did not just pick the wrong platform, but were also waiting for a train that is never going to arrive.

It is against this short and selective review of environmental sociology's history of conceptually dealing with human-nature interactions that one has to understand and assess the emerging discussion on sociotechnical scapes and hybrid systems in (environmental) sociology. With the arrival of the sociology of networks, hybrids, and flows—one is tempted to conclude—the ongoing debate in environmental sociology on the relationship between the social and the material has taken a new direction and become radicalized. Urry—also following Beck in this respect—argues that some of the well-defined "units of analyses" so frequently used in contemporary sociology, turn out to be valid only in relation to societies of the first or "simple modernity" phase of development. Key concepts like nation-state or environment—when used under conditions of second or reflexive modernity—seem to have lost most of their validity. The concept of environment or nature during second modernity can no longer be used in isolation from society since nature or environment is "pulled into society." The concept of nature as external to society, either in the form of a sustenance base carrying social activity (Schnaiberg) or a sink and reservoir exploited for human progress (environmental sciences), is outdated. Only when it is recognized that society and environment in reflexive modernity are intermingled in many diverging ways can one make sense of the (world) risk society as emerging right under our eyes. The formaldehyde in your kitchen, the BSE risks in your food, and the nuclear fallout of Chernobyl all offer proof of the outdated character (or at least the limited use) of the sociological concepts of nature and nation-states.

## Central Aims of the Book: Positioning the Argument

This book does not start from the radical premise that current conditions have made sociological concepts like the nation-state, agency, and environment obsolete and inadequate. But we do concur with the idea that under the present condition of global modernity, the analysis of environmental governance is in need of new analytic concepts and that some of the conventional categories miss the essence of contemporary developments. Nevertheless, revising and redesigning sociology in order to come up with new valid, precise, and illuminating concepts and categories for analyzing environmental dynamics, change, and governance in present-day modern societies is more than a day's work (or a one-book effort). The introduction of still rather broad concepts like hybrid arrangements and hybrid systems are in the end not an alternative; but these interpretations do help us as a starting point in illustrating the need for and developing such new categories and concepts. The central aim of this book is to begin discussing and designing a set of concepts (which might be developed into a theory) capable of more adequately analyzing the governance of environmental flows in global modernity. Building new syntheses between still-separate streams of thinking in (environmental) sociology, (environmental) political science, and environmental sciences is the best way to forward this project, in our view. The effort to build such new syntheses, which is undertaken in this volume, could be named in two different ways.

First, it can be seen as an attempt to develop a social sciences approach or *sociology* of environmental flows. Building on recent developments, innovative theories, and insights in the social sciences in general and sociology in particular, we develop a new perspective on understanding the governance of environmental flows, which contrasts, complements, and yet also partly links with the natural sciences perspectives on flows. When interpreted in this way, the approach suggested in this book builds on the work conducted so far under the heading of ecological modernization. The theory of ecological modernization was developed in the late 1980s and the 1990s to move beyond the technocratic models of the environmental sciences, and to analyze the changes in nation-state-based environmental politics in some European societies (Hajer 1995). From its inception, ecological modernization showed a special interest in the material dimension of environmental change. For that reason, it was labeled (and criticized by some) as being an overly materialist or realist approach, with some Eurocentric biases resulting from its geographic context of origin. While efforts have been made to meet some of these criticisms, and especially to reformulate ecological modernization theory in the context of both globalizing modernity (Mol 2001) and changing state-society interrelations (Mol and Buttel 2002), it can be concluded that the sociology of networks and flows as developed in the works of Castells, Urry, Sassen, Held, and others offers new opportunities to analyze the massive impact of globalization on the contemporary world. Environmental sociology can become a better kind of sociology when taking these new perspectives into account and by incorporating some of the key concepts developed in general sociology into the theoretical frameworks—ecological modernization theory being one of them— applied within environmental sociology for analyzing the global dynamics of environmental flows. Some of the most relevant (dis)continuities that can be said to exist between the sociology of environmental flows and ecological modernization theory are discussed in more detail in both chapter 6 and the epilogue (this volume).

Second, the approach developed and defended in this book could also be seen as an attempt to develop an *environmental* social sciences approach to flows or an *environmental* sociology of flows. Whereas most of the flows literature in the social sciences emphasizes flows of capital, information, images, ideas, and people (travel and migration) (see Appadurai 1996), and analyzes them from perspectives as diverse as economic development, governance and control, cultural diversity, or democracy, this volume aims to contribute to the development of an explicitly environmental interpretation of the flows concept. This environmental interpretation is developed in two ways: by analyzing flows of information, capital, goods, and persons from an ecological rationality point of view (by looking at environmental information, green products, sustainable management concepts, environmental certification schemes, and flows of environmental activists and their ideas); and by analyzing environmental flows as such. Neither Castells nor Urry nor Appadurai have yet developed an in-depth account of environmental change in either of the two ways. Environmental flows are mentioned in between all other kinds of flows that could become the object of socio-logical analysis, and these other flows are not assessed for their role in and (potential) contribution to environmental governance, deterioration, or reform. Nowhere, however, do these authors argue that the set of material flows as commonly addressed within the environmental sciences and some branches of environmental sociology deserve special treatment. Clouds, information, peoples, or wastes are treated in similar ways. We try to illustrate in this volume that a specific environmental emphasis on flow analysis, and especially a specific emphasis on environmental flows, has something to offer to this emerging branch of general sociology.

Where the approach taken in this book differs from existing analytic schemes becomes visible if we compare it with the theoretical perspectives in the social sciences that come arguably the closest to our approach: those loosely gathered around the WST. Are the environmental flows we describe and analyze today essentially different from the flows that figured in conventional macrohistorical accounts some decades ago? Earlier studies on imperialist extraction and exploitation, WST analyses on the environment (Goldfrank et al. 1999), and the work on the functioning of early market dynamics in natural resource flows have all linked material flows of natural resources to social and political dynamics on a global scale, and as such can be considered as precedents in this genre of analysis. What they had and have in common with the theme of this book is their claim to offer a theoretical understanding of the role of material flows in fundamental social changes on an unprecedented spatial and social scale.

Yet, these earlier studies in the WST tradition differ in two ways from the environmental flows perspective developed and applied in this volume. First, the earlier WST approaches hardly considered the material dimensions of these flows relevant (although one can witness some changes in this position recently; see Roberts et al. 2003). Material or environmental flows were similar to capital and money flows, as they all provided evidence of the same processes of unequal development, exploitation, and dependence. In fact, the materiality of the flows proved irrelevant as it was the economic dimension of environmental flows that mattered instead in their analyses. Or to put it in the perspective above:

they lack an environmental sociology of flows approach. Second, these older studies differed from the more recent flows perspectives in their account of globalization. While the earlier studies analyzed international flows between states/societies as examples of an emerging or existing international (unequal) division of labor, the recent flows theorists interpret flows as constitutive elements in a fundamentally different era of globalization. Here, we witness the differences in terms of the *sociology* of environmental flows. Linking globalization to (the governance of) environmental flows is more than a straightforward update of an existing branch of international studies. It is a genuine effort to establish the first foundations of a new theoretical approach in the environmental social sciences, building on and making use of existing traditions, insights, and scholarly debates in environmental sociology, political science, and the environmental sciences.

## The Structure of the Book

In contributing to these controversies and debates, and in developing a flows perspective to understand environmental governance in global modernity, this book is organized into two main parts. Part I includes five chapters that all address the central theme of the book from a theoretical perspective. In this part, the environmental flows perspective on (global- and national-level) governance is further elaborated from both a sociological and political science point of view. As we deal here very much with a theoretical perspective-in-the-making, the theoretical chapters show implicit and sometimes even explicit differences in accents and assessments of how to interpret and conceptualize current problems of governance and material flows. But the contributions come together in their assurance that the conventional nation-state-based interpretation schemes of environmental flows management and policy are in need of revision, and the new literature of governance and the sociology of flows provide the most interesting building block we have at the moment to start developing a new theory.

### Part I: Theoretical Perspectives and Debates

Arthur P. J. Mol and Gert Spaargaren basically work from a sociological perspective, arguing that from the work of Castells and Urry a set of concepts can be derived that enable environmental sociologists to better make sense of the governance of environmental flows in globalizing modernity. They put forward Castells's analytic distinction between the space of flows and the space of places to analyze the relationship as well as tensions between global dynamics and local characteristics and actors. They suggest that the language of flows, fluids, networks, and scapes in principle could usefully be put to work in environmental sociology, provided that some of the pitfalls in the works of Castells and Urry can be avoided or repaired. Within environmental sociology, there has been a long tradition of studying environmental or material flows. Mol and Spaargaren review these different variants of flows analysis in environmental sociology, and point to ways to redefine and improve the existing flows perspectives by incorporating some of the basic concepts from the sociology of flows. They offer definitions and discussions of key concepts like flows, fluids, networks, power, agency, hybrids, and technology, and also put forward three concrete examples of how the flows perspective could be applied in the context of future environmental research in the social sciences.

The Mol and Spaargaren chapter is followed by two chapters that take into account in an explicit way the role of the state in the governance of environmental flows. The authors of these chapters are familiar with the political science tradition along with the debates that have been going on with respect to the supposed withering away of the nation-state due to political and economic globalization—a thesis not subscribed to by the authors of these chapters.

In his chapter, Martin Jänicke makes a strong case for the role of nation-states in the governance of environmental flows. As one of the founders of ecological modernization theory, Jänicke has a strong focus on the *environmental* dimension of states and governance. He argues that the "environmental state" is at the heart of the process of modern environmental governance. The most relevant state programs and forms of environmental governance today, maintains Jänicke, have to do with the cleansing and reduction of environmental flows within industrial systems of production and consumption. Although states are and remain important actors in environmental governance—not least because of the question of the "final responsibility" for solving environmental problems—they cannot operate without good working relations with both market and civil society actors. Furthermore, the history of environmental policymaking in Europe makes us aware of the need to include in modern environmental governance sectoral target group aims and strategies, and to apply an integrated approach. Finally, Jänicke notes, we have also learned that environmental governance is manifestly and inescapably a multilayered and multiactor phenomenon. With these main characteristics of environmental governance defined, Jänicke then goes on to discuss how the features are affected by the globalization of environmental problems and policies from about the mid-1980s onward. Economic and political globalization force us to rethink the role of the state, and confront us with the need to in some respects reinvent the environmental state. Yet, this does not imply a withering away of the state, nor even a general process of the weakening of state (environmental) power in some crucial regards. To the contrary, there are a number of assertions that can support the claim that state-anchored forms of environmental governance remain important and even gain strategic significance in the context of globalization. Jänicke puts forward and discusses in some detail a number of theses on this future role of nation-states in the governance of environmental flows. His theses on globalization as creating a policy arena for pioneering countries and new lead markets for green products, as well as his (empirical research–based) conclusion that the nation-state level still seems to be the most relevant one to explain environmental innovation and stagnation, are among the challenging views explored in this chapter.

Next, Dimitris Stevis and Hans Bruyninckx start their chapter with a review of the different ways in which the state is conceptualized in the field of global environmental politics. They argue that in many contributions on changing state-market or state–civil society relations, the very concept of state is barely defined and specified. In order to make sense of the relationship between states and environmental flows, a historical perspective is crucial. The ways in which states over (long) periods of time have become embedded in networks and power relations tells us more about why certain environmental flows are regarded as strategic resources, and also managed and governed in a specific way by certain states. Oil, chemicals, wastes, and minerals matter most for powerful nation-states, and their commitment to certain governance arrangements and regimes can and must be analyzed with the help of a combined political geography and political economy perspective. Stevis and Bruyninckx claim that the governance of environmental flows at the global level should be studied primarily by "looking through the state(s)," using historically grown power relations and specific social forces to understand why "particular articulations of places and flows within the spaces of flows" arise, and how they affect future power relations in the world political economy.

In her chapter, Zsuzsa Gille explains why the flows perspective could gain popularity and should be welcomed in environmental social sciences in some respects. The flows perspective does away with overly static and mechanistic views of the human-nature interrelationship, while also facilitating a nondeterministic view of global change. Although she appreciates the flows perspective for these reasons, Gille uses most of her chapter to warn of some of the dangers that could come along with the sociology of global environmental flows. She's afraid of the flows perspective developing into a too fluid, phenomenological view of globalization that could tend to overlook issues of power and inequalities. To help prevent such a sterile and simplistic flow perspective from emerging, she proposes a bottom-up approach to the study of globalization and puts forward new key concepts like "scale-making" and "place-making projects." She lists several categories of environmental flows and discusses the political, power-bound nature of flows. With the help of a series of empirical examples from different parts of the world, she illustrates the ways in which key actors operating at the global level in reality impact local structures, identities, and power balances in a negative way. By incorporating specific concepts that help to outline the power characteristics of the global-local relationships in environmental governance, she prevents the agenda of the new environmental flows perspective from becoming a politically naive experiment.

With Frederick Buttel's contribution, the theoretical part of the book is brought to a preliminary synthesis. Buttel is familiar with both political science discussions on the role of (environmental) states (Jänicke; Stevis and Bruyninckx) as well as environmental sociology discussions on the nature of environmental flows and flows management (Mol and Spaargaren; Gille). In his chapter, Buttel welcomes the flows perspective within environmental sociology and the social sciences for two main reasons. First, it provides an alternative and more promising solution to the problem of how to conceptualize environment-society interactions. The old models—be it the bioecological solutions of the Odum type, or the Schnaibergian scheme of additions and withdrawals—no longer suffice. At the same time, however, postmodern and constructionist conceptualizations have lost most of their attractiveness. The conceptualization in terms of environmental flows could in principle do away with some of these old distinctions and perhaps even build bridges between separate research traditions, such as world-system analyses, ecological modernization theory, and some variants of the sociology of natural resources. Second, the flows perspective seems to better equip environmental social scientists with the tools to make sense of globalization and global governance. Buttel agrees with Urry that environmental sociology indeed has to go "beyond society," at least when society is conceived of in terms of sovereign nation-states with their own welfare programs as we know them from the period of early or simple modernity. Moving beyond this narrow conceptualization of the role of the nation-state, though, should not imply lapsing into a stateless view of international flows, scapes, and networks. Very much in line with the arguments of Stevis and Bruyninckx, Buttel contends that the power of the nation-state should be assessed with the help of a historical, political economy and political geography–inspired perspective. States do matter, also in a negative way, when environmental governance is at stake. The U.S. experiences with environmental policy and governance over the last two decades turns out to be really different from the European experiences as depicted by Jänicke in his contribution to the book. Buttel even goes so far as to talk about the role of the United States in the geopolitical global order in terms of the "American engine of environmental destruction." He warns some of the European scholars and also people working in the tradition of international regime theory as it became popular in the 1990s not to be too friendly with or benign toward the United States in this respect. With his concrete analyses of the selective dismantling of environmental policy arrangements by the present U.S. administration, Buttel provides a concrete example of the kind of historical, political economy–based analyses of the changing world political and economic order as asked for by Stevis and Bruyninckx.

## Part II: Empirical Perspectives

The second part consists of a number of case studies that explore the main themes of this book from different perspectives, centered around the double concept of hybridization. Either from a governance or a flows perspective, or both, the various case studies assess how under conditions of globalization, environmental flows are or can be governed. Given the status of our theoretical perspective-in-the-making, we have deliberately allowed for some eclecticism in the empirical chapters, rather than opting for a rigid theoretical scheme to be applied systematically throughout all the chapters.

Kris van Koppen rethinks nature conservation and biodiversity policies from the flows and globalization perspective put forward in the book. With respect to the flows dimension, he argues that in the language of biodiversity management as widely accepted from the Rio conference onward, there are many elements that make nature fit the (eco)modernist discourses and policy practices. With respect to the governance dimension, van Koppen maintains that nature conservation or the management of biodiversity flows always have had a kind of mixed character. On the one hand, nature conservation is a national (heritage) issue embedded in national culture and nation-state policies more than most other flows contained in the environmental discourse. Participatory strategies in nature conservation are very much organized along the logics and dynamics of the space of place. On the other hand, nature conservation is the most well-organized transnational or global phenomenon, with organizations functioning like sanguine multinationals both with respect to the central aims set at the company level as well as concerning the (huge) resources available. Van Koppen discusses the emergence of the ecological infrastructure in Europe as an example of a transnational arrangement for biodiversity management that fits very well into the language of scapes, flows, and networks. Using this new vocabulary helps one to understand the national-transnational hybrid forms as well as the meaning of nature or biodiversity itself.

In his chapter on the governance of international rivers, Itay Fis-chhendler puts forward the question of whether and in what ways nation-states take into account the long-term effects of climate change when negotiating transnational arrangements for the management of river basins. The field of river basin management is one of the areas in which the flows perspective is prominent, albeit most of the time applied in a rather restricted, technical way. Fischhendler takes a social sciences perspective to transnational river management by analyzing the risk-handling strategies of nation-states not just from a technical, engineer-ing point of view but also from a political science one. The flows, scapes, and networks involved in the transnational governance of water cannot be understood from the physical characteristics of the river basin alone: transnational arrangements and institutions that are assigned the tasks of developing sustainable water management strategies are very much governed by sociopolitical rationalities as well. With the help of three detailed case studies from different parts of the world, Fischhendler is able to show how the (non)inclusion into water treaties of certain risk-handling arrangements and institutions can be understood from the con-sequences this might have for the existing power relations between the nation-states involved in the treaty process. From the stance taken by the United States, Mexico, Canada, Israel, and Jordan when faced with climate-change-related water risks (for example, extreme droughts not foreseen in the existing treaties), Fischhendler concludes that treaties should not be analyzed only with respect to the formal mechanisms and the language used to describe the climate-change-related risks in the gov-ernance of water flows. Instead, one should be able to also "read between the lines" and analyze the hybrid arrangements that nation-states employ in such a way that they are conceived of as embedded within regional economic, political, and cultural networks that are established over the course of time, during the longer process of treaty negotiation and implementation.

Next, Peter Oosterveer addresses the changes in food chains rooted in globalization. Because of the globalization of both food production and consumption, the regulation of food-related risks and more generally speaking the environmental dimension of food production and con-sumption are much more difficult to establish. The "local arrangements" originating from nation-states regulating food issues within their national territories are challenged by the steep increase in worldwide food flows. But the transnational or global regulation of flows of food is also not (yet) able to do a proper regulatory job, since EU and WTO regulation seem to be driven primarily by economic factors and considerations. Building on the network and flows perspective of Castells, Oosterveer sets himself the task of analyzing the different dynamics within the space of places in relation to the space of flows. To understand how the regulation of food can be organized in the network society, he investigates in some empirical detail how global flows of food interact with food production and consumption at the local level. The main objects of his empirical analysis are food labels. With the help of the fair-trade label for coffee and the MSC label for fish, Oosterveer brings out the different possible arrangements, emphasizing either the need to include in global regulation the specifics of place—especially relevant of course when dealing with food—or the inclusion of global (WTO) standards and procedures in the organization of local food production and consumption. His conclusion is that food labels deal with the place-bounded social and environmental effects of global flows of food without entering into a form of de-globalization, thereby creating an innovative arrangement that fits into global modernity.

In the following chapter, Luciana M. S. Presas and Arthur P. J. Mol use the network and flows perspective to analyze the greening of transnational buildings in different parts of the world. What are the driving forces behind the greening of these transnational office buildings? Are the local (and national) governments and utility companies pushing for environmental change, or are the global standards for indoor air quality, energy consumption, and building materials more decisive? The authors analyze twelve cases of urban office buildings—situated in Amsterdam, São Paulo, and Beijing—that are constructed or at least used by four transnational corporations (ING, Andersen, ABN-AMRO, and IBM). From the case studies, they are able to show that such greening is the result of the complex interface between the local (utility) infrastructures that provide the skyscrapers with energy, water, and waste services, and the global (TNC) headquarters' environmental regulations. The office buildings in the metropolitan cities can be regarded as an interface between local and global regimes for the management of office-related environmental flows. These buildings are the meeting point between the space of places and the space of flows. When conceptualized in this way, a range of interesting questions can be raised and formulated in a precise and innovative way. Do we see similar "flow-place-hybrids" of environmental reform emerging in different global cities? Do company characteristics as formulated in the space of flows also make a difference when local environmental dynamics are weak or almost absent? Are transnational companies sensitive to local actors and infrastructures laying out the "green carpet" at the urban nodes in the network society? By discussing these kind of questions in some empirical detail, Presas and Mol help develop the future agenda for environmental flows research on local urban infrastructures in transnational space.

In her chapter, Mette Jensen agrees with Urry about mobilities being at the heart of modern life. Applying the network and flows perspective to the transportation behavior of ordinary people in everyday life, Jensen's analysis highlights some of the basic characteristics of modern societies from the microlevel perspective. She argues that the ever-expanding flows of passengers—using cars, railways, airplanes, bikes, and whatever new technologies will become available to bridge longer distances in ever-shorter times—are directly connected to environmental deteriorations of all kinds at all levels, from local air pollution up to global warming. To develop environmental policies and governance arrangements that make sense to all those people "on the move," we have to dive into the meaning of mobility to modern urbanites, and try to understand how they themselves do or do not connect environmental considerations to their ordinary mobility practices. Jensen did in-depth interviews with twenty people living in Copenhagen, Denmark, and surveyed five hundred people in the same city to get to know the meaning urban dwellers attach to mobility. It turns out that timetables as well as the coordination and synchronization of everyday life activities are key to understanding modernity and its mobilities. Time pressures, time scarcity, a lack of time, and for that reason attempts to buy or save time, or use time efficiently, are the main drivers behind the mobility explosion in modernity. Mobility and time management have become intertwined in such a way that mobility itself—moving more and more often, and faster and faster—has grown to be part of the aspiration of modern individuals, remarks Jensen. As a consequence, it seems impossible to change or solve environmental problems related to transportation without parallel changes in modern life itself. The flows perspective applied to the minutiae of everyday life can help us understand why strong environmental views and policies based on the central idea of "downshifting" mobility does not fit well into the lifestyles of modern urbanites, who tend to respond to time stresses by demanding even more (recreational) mobility.

In the epilogue, the editors of this book explore in some depth the emergence of the global environmental flows perspective in light of the sociointellectual context of the development of U.S. and international environmental sociology and—to a lesser extent—political sciences. They discuss the major intellectual sources of the approach, the (discontinuities) with respect to the existing streams of thinking in environmental social sciences, and the potential lines of convergence that arise when the flows perspective is used to organize the future agenda of research. By looking at the flows perspective in an evaluative mood and from a distance, the editors try to offer a balanced view of the potentials and pitfalls of the perspective developed throughout this book.

When situating the global governance and flows perspective in the social sciences, the editors first discuss the environmental flows perspective as being a successor to or cousin of ecological modernization. They notice that in some ways there is continuity from ecological modernization to environmental flows, while some notable departures can be detected as well. One of the overriding benefits of the flows perspective is that it can be seen as the beginning of an answer to the long-standing dissatisfaction with how environmental sociologists and political scientists have conceptualized the environment. The flows perspective transcends more or less the materialist versus culturalist perspective by talking about hybrid arrangements, sociotechnical networks, and scapes and flows that are both material and social at the same time. Finally, the environmental flows perspective should be seen as a fundamental critique of how environmental social scientists—political scientists and sociologists alike—have tended to conceptualize globalization. The changing role of the nation-state in global governance is one of the most pressing items to reconceptualize in the twenty-first century. By looking through the state at environmental flows and governance, the editors conclude from the contributions to this volume that there exist two quite different tendencies within the environmental social sciences. One tendency is to de-privilege governance, while the opposite tendency is to stress the new nature of environmental governance, given the highly interdependent twenty-first-century world that is characterized by highly structured, but often invisible, patterns of flows and fluids. The epilogue wraps up with a discussion of some of the potential shortcomings and risks of embracing an environmental flows perspective in the environmental social sciences, on the one hand, and the chances and potentialities of the flows perspective, on the other.

The book thus ends with a warning not to underscore or overlook issues of power, nation-states, distribution, and identity—a (self-)warning we wish to take seriously when suggesting the start of this new research agenda. The current shifts in global dynamics, however, are so fundamental in several disciplines that they challenge most of our established theories. New concepts are necessary because scientists in several disciplines are coming to the conclusion that the old categories are no longer adequately capturing the global environmental realities. This book is aimed at generating new theoretical insights, including concepts and analytic categories that crosscut some of the existing disciplinary boundaries. Although the flows perspective needs further development, as stressed in the epilogue, we think this perspective is a promising candidate to open up new and fruitful debates between disciplines that have traditionally used different conceptual frameworks and theoretical assumptions to describe environmental flows in the globalizing world. In that sense, the book can be seen as a deliberate attempt to build bridges between disciplines as well as between divergent perspectives on environmental change. The readers are invited to join this transdisciplinary journey.

## Notes

1. For those readers who are not familiar with the kind of social theories of networks and flows discussed in this volume, some of the most important works

will be referred to, as a matter of introduction. The subtitle of Manuel Castells's (1996) pathbreaking work *The Information Age: Economy, Society, and Culture* is *The Rise of the Network Society*. This first volume (out of three) on the network society introduces the reader to the core concepts of network and flows, and in particular the notions of "space of flows" and "space of places" that Castells uses to describe the changes in the spatiotemporal organization of modern societies under the impact of globalization. For Castells, the rise of the network society is related in a direct way to the emergence of the new information and communication technologies of our present-day (Internet) societies. Arjun Appadurai's *Modernity at Large* (1996) is from the same period, but emphasizes in particular the cultural dimension of globalization and the network society. Appadurai's notion of "scapes" (ethno-, techno-, finance-, media-, and ideoscapes are all distinguished) has been rather influential in the field, as has his vivid and colorful (anthropological) descriptions of the flows of images, peoples, machines, and ideas across the globe. Following up on Castells and Appadurai, among others, John Urry stands out as the sociologist who—together with Ulrich Beck—has written on a broad range of empirical issues to further develop the new rules for sociology for the twenty-first century. Urry and Beck argue that sociology has to move away from the static, nation-state-centered concepts and theories of the twentieth century. The jargon of flows, networks, and fluids is embraced and further detailed as well as specified in order to make the social sciences themselves more "mobile" and fit for analyzing global modernity in the new millennium. Urry's *Sociology beyond Society* (2000) provides a good introduction into his ideas, while an accessible book on Beck's basic ideas is the interview-based *Conversations with Ulrich Beck* (Beck and Willms 2004).

2. A similar exercise has been undertaken in the field of environmental politics by Karen Litfin in *The Greening of Sovereignty in World Politics* (1998), in which two distinct fields have been distinguished: global environmental politics and theories about the constitution of sovereignty. Her book attempts to construct a bridge between these two literatures.

## References

Appadurai, A. 1996. *Modernity at Large: Cultural Dimensions of Globalization.* Minneapolis: University of Minnesota Press.

Beck, U., A. Giddens, and S. Lash. 1994. *Reflexive Modernization: Politics, Tradition, and Aesthetics in the Modern Social Order.* Cambridge: Polity Press.

Beck, U., and J. Willms. 2004. *Conversations with Ulrich Beck.* Cambridge: Polity Press.

Carter, N. 2000. *The Politics of the Environment: Ideas, Activism, Policy.* Cambridge: Cambridge University Press.

Castells, M. 1996. *The Rise of the Network Society*. Vol. 1 of *The Information Age: Economy, Society, and Culture*. Oxford: Blackwell Publishers.

Castells, M. 1998. *End of Millennium*. Vol. 3 of *The Information Age: Economy, Society, and Culture*. Oxford: Blackwell Publishers.

Conca, K., and R. Lipschutz. 1993. A Tale of Two Forests. In *The State and Social Power in Global Environmental Politics*, ed. R. Lipschutz and K. Conca, 1–13. New York: Columbia University Press.

Dobson, A. 2000. *Green Political Thought*. 3rd ed. London: Routledge.

Dryzek, J. S. 1997. *The Politics of the Earth: Environmental Discourses*. Oxford: Oxford University Press.

Dryzek, J. S., D. Downes, C. Hunold, and D. Schlosberg, with H.-K. Hernes. 2003. *Green States and Social Movements: Environmentalism in the United States, United Kingdom, Germany, and Norway*. Oxford: Oxford University Press.

Dunlap, R. E., and W. R. Catton. 1994. Struggling with Human Exemptionalism: The Rise, Decline, and Revitalization of Environmental Sociology. *American Sociologist* 25:5–30.

Eckersley, R. 2004. *The Green State: Rethinking Democracy and Sovereignty*. Cambridge: MIT Press.

Evans, P. 1995. *Embedded Autonomy: States and Industrial Transformation*. Princeton, NJ: Princeton University Press.

Giddens, A. 1976. *New Rules of Sociological Method*. London: Hutchinson.

Giddens, A. 1998. *The Third Way: The Renewal of Social Democracy*. Cambridge: Polity Press.

Goldfrank, W. L., D. Goodman, and A. Szasz, eds. 1999. *Ecology and the World-System*. Westport, CT: Greenwood Press.

Haas, P. M., R. O. Keohane, and M. A. Levy. 1993. *Institutions for the Earth: Sources of Effective Environmental Protection*. Cambridge: MIT Press.

Habermas, J. 1982. *Theorie des kommunikativen Handelns, Band 1 und 2*. Frankfurt am Main: Suhrkamp Verlag.

Hajer, M. 1995. *The Politics of Environmental Discourse: Ecological Modernization and the Policy Process*. Oxford: Oxford University Press.

Held, D. 1995. *Democracy and the Global Order: From the Modern State to Cosmopolitan Governance*. Cambridge: Polity Press.

Held, D., A. McGrew, D. Goldblatt, and J. Perraton. 1999. *Global Transformations: Politics, Economics, and Culture*. Cambridge: Polity Press.

Held, D. 2004. *Global Covenant*. Cambridge: Polity Press.

Hirst, P., and G. Thompson. 1996. *Globalisation in Question?* London: Polity Press.

Jänicke, M. 1986. *Staatsversagen: Die Ohnmacht der Politik in die Industriegesellschaft.* Munich: Piper.

Jänicke, M., et al. 1992. *Umweltentlastung durch industriellen Strukturwandel? Eine explorative Studie über 32 Industrieländer.* Berlin: Sigma.

Jessop, B. 1991. *The Capitalist State.* University Park: Pennsylvania State University Press.

Keohane, R. O. 2002. *Power and Governance in a Partially Globalized World.* London: Routledge.

Keohane, R. O., and J. S. Nye Jr. 2002. Governance in a Globalizing World. In *Power and Governance in a Partially Globalized World*, R. O. Keohane, 193–210. London: Routledge.

Leroy, P., and J. van Tatenhove. 2000. New Policy Arrangements in Environmental Politics: The Relevance of Political and Ecological Modernisation. In *Environment, Sociology, and Global Modernity*, ed. G. Spaargaren, A. P. J. Mol, and F. H. Buttel, 187–209. London: Sage.

Litfin, K. T., ed. 1998. *The Greening of Sovereignty in World Politics.* Cambridge: MIT Press.

Mol, A. P. J. 2001. *Globalization and Environmental Reform: The Ecological Modernization of the Global Economy.* Cambridge: MIT Press.

Mol, A. P. J., and F. H. Buttel, eds. 2002. *The Environmental State under Pressure.* London: Elsevier/JAI.

Nelissen, N. J. M. 1972. *Sociale Ecologie.* Utrecht: Het Spectrum.

Ohmae, K. 1995. *The End of the Nation-State: The Rise of Regional Economies.* New York: Simon and Schuster.

Roberts, J. T., P. E. Grimes, and J. L. Manale. 2003. Social Roots of Global Environmental Change: A World-Systems Analysis of Carbon Dioxide Emissions. *Journal of World-Systems Research* 9, no. 2:277–315.

Rootes, C. ed. 1999. *Environmental Movements: Local, National, Global.* New York: Frank Cass.

Schnaiberg, A. 1980. *The Environment: From Surplus to Scarcity.* Oxford: Oxford University Press.

Shaw, M. 1994. *Global Society and International Relations: Sociological Concepts and Political Perspectives.* Cambridge: Polity Press.

Skocpol, T., and P. Evans, eds. 1985. *Bringing the State Back In.* Cambridge: Cambridge University Press.

Spaargaren, G., A. P. J. Mol, and F. H. Buttel, eds. 2000. *Environment and Global Modernity.* London: Sage.

Urry, J. 2000. *Sociology beyond Society.* London: Routledge.

Urry, J. 2003. *Global Complexity.* Cambridge: Polity Press.

Wapner, P. 1996. *Environmental Activism and World Civic Politics*. Albany: State University of New York Press.

Wapner, P. 1998. Reorienting State Sovereignty: Rights and Responsibilities in the Environmental Age. In *The Greening of Sovereignty in World Politics*, ed. K. Litfin, 273–297. Cambridge: MIT Press.

Yearley, S. 1996. *Sociology, Environmentalism, Globalization: Reinventing the Globe*. London: Sage.

Young, O. 1994. *International Governance: Protecting the Environment in a Stateless Society*. Ithaca, NY: Cornell University Press.

# I

## Theoretical Perspectives and Debates

# 2

## Toward a Sociology of Environmental Flows: A New Agenda for Twenty-First-Century Environmental Sociology

Arthur P. J. Mol and Gert Spaargaren

For a long time, environmental sociologists complained about the lack of attention to environmental themes and issues within general sociology. While they specialized in analyzing the (disrupting) human influences on flows of energy and materials circulating through ecosystems, their colleagues in general sociology took little notice of the results of their work. The reason for this neglect was twofold. Working in the sociological tradition as laid out by Karl Marx, Max Weber, and Émile Durkheim, general sociologists were concerned with explaining social facts by other social facts, and for that reason they did not develop any specific interest in the material underpinnings of social life. At the same time, however, environmental sociology moved away from mainstream sociological thinking by diving into biology, ecology, and other "sciences of flows," thereby undertheorizing or neglecting the social origins and dynamics of environmental flows in the first place.

There are several factors that might help explain why in recent years we witness a reapproach between general sociology and environmental sociology. First of all, this convergence can be explained by the mutual interest in the emerging debate on globalization and global (environmental) change. Within general sociology, climate change and other global environmental issues were frequently discussed as exemplary cases illustrating the new dynamics of change in global modernity, and especially the changing roles of key institutions such as science and technology and the nation-state (cf. reflexive modernization theory, risk society theory, and social constructivism). Within the environmental (social) sciences, it was especially the growing attention to transboundary air pollution (acidification) that triggered the development of the new agenda of the 1990s, often referred to as global environmental change. This agenda—pushed by the IPCC and global environmental NGOs in particular—again emphasized the important but complicated role of science and technology in the management of global environmental change, and stressed the new roles of nation-states that have to give way to actors and arrangements operating in the international/global as well as local arenas. So from the 1990s onward, both general and environmental sociology showed an interest in understanding the specific dynamics of the global vis-à-vis the local in the governance of global (environmental) change. The second—more recent—main factor contributing to the convergence of general and environmental sociology is the emergence within general sociology of a theoretical perspective in which social systems are approached in terms of networks and flows. This so-called sociology of flows seems to open up a field for discussion and research not too far away from various perspectives in environmental sociology, by focusing especially on the material, spatial dimension of social life.[1] Especially in Urry's work, as we will argue below, environmental themes and flows along with their specific characteristics and dynamics are given pride of place in the sociological analysis of complex societies.

Against this background of the growing intersection of general and environmental sociology, we explore what kind of mutual learning processes might take place at the meeting points. We investigate what the sociology of flows might have to offer in analyzing and understanding environmental flows in global modernity. And to put the matter somewhat differently, we wonder what environmental sociology could contribute to the emerging debate on the sociology of flows, of a reconstructed sociology "beyond society" (Urry 2000b). The outline of the argument runs as follows. In the next section, we provide a short and selective introduction into the sociology of flows as developed mainly in the works of Castells and Urry. We discuss this new branch of sociological thinking in relation to some of the existing perspectives—especially structuration theory—and indicate the possible relevance of the sociology of flows for understanding global (environmental) change. In the section that follows, we approach the meeting point from the other side, reviewing environmental sociology with respect to its historical engagement with flows. It is shown that in some traditions, flows are approached primarily in physical or biological terms, relying heavily on concepts and frames borrowed from the natural and eco-biological sciences, while other scholars emphasize the social actors and dynamics involved in the handling of material flows in modern societies, using general sociology as the main frame of reference. We conclude with some of the barriers environmental sociologists meet in explaining and understanding material flows in the present era of global modernity. In the subsequent section, we assess the sociology of flows from the perspective of environmental sociology, focusing especially on questions of flow definitions, hybrids, power and inequalities, and states and governance. With the lessons learned from the debate on global flows, we conclude the chapter with a "reconstructed" outline of the agenda for environmental sociology.

## The Sociology of Flows

At several points in time, sociologists claimed that the world they were studying had changed so dramatically that we were in need of radically different conceptual languages and theories to analyze, interpret, and understand the situation. Giddens, for example, made such a claim when developing his structuration theory, formalized in his influential book *The Constitution of Society* (1984). He argued extensively and in detail why nineteenth-century sociology—the sociologies of Marx, Weber, and Durkheim—was in need of being reformulated and reinterpreted to fit the study of the new constellation of the postwar twentieth century. Building on, but at the same time moving beyond, the classics, Giddens (1976) was able to show how the problems of the twentieth century could only be analyzed properly when using the "new rules of sociological method" to replace the old ones, as formulated by Durkheim (1897/1982) and his contemporaries.

In a similar way, Castells and Urry seem to claim that in the twenty-first century, we again face a new constellation, which demands a profound reconstruction and reformulation of sociology, its basic concepts, and its methods. Triggered most strongly by globalization and information technologies, a new constellation is under construction, which makes the society- and nation-state-centered sociologies of the twentieth century outdated. The suggestion put forward by Castells to label the new constellation the (world) *network society* has been received in the discipline with wide consent. When Urry sets himself the task of rethinking the consequences of this new order for the discipline of sociology, he—with apologies to Durkheim and Giddens—concludes that we are again in need of new rules of sociological method. We will explore some of these new rules, metaphors, and methods by looking in more detail at the work of both authors.

### The New Dynamics of Modernity: Space of Flows versus Space of Places

With the help of extensive empirical and historical evidence gathered all around the world, Castells in his *Network Society* (1996) tried to substantiate the claim that in the 1980s and 1990s, the network society as a new social morphology emerged. The new institutional makeup of the network society is to be understood in direct relation to a new layer or dimension emerging within and between our societies. This new layer is called the space of flows, and it should be understood not as a new layer in the geographic meaning of the word but rather in terms of a new kind of time-space organization of social practices. The space of flows refers to new social dynamics—to new concepts of time, space, and power.

To illustrate the new spatial dynamics of the space of flows, Castells uses the example of the emerging metropolitan region in the southern part of China, with a number of megacities such as Hong Kong, Macau, Zhaoqing, Huizhou, and Guangzhou in its territory, and a total population numbering somewhere between forty and fifty million. Using data with respect to the process of socioeconomic restructuring of the region in the 1990s, Castells is able to show that the megacities in this area are no longer to be understood "on their own," in terms of urban spatial units in their regional surroundings. Instead, they must be analyzed as the nodal points of global economic, cultural, and political networks. Only by seeing them as the connecting points to these global networks can one understand how they could become the most crucial "development engines" of this region, which according to Castells is due to become "the most representative urban face of the twentieth-first century" (1996, 409). Similar to the megacities in other parts of the world, those of the Pearl River Delta are the nodal points in the global network society—the new power containers of this informational age, surpassing and superseding the nation-state in many respects. Having exposed in many details the ways in which these Chinese megacities function in the global network society of today, Castells then goes on to reflect on these processes from a social theory perspective, referring to debates within the social sciences on time and space. His major theoretical conclusion from the Chinese example is that three formerly joint or interlinked processes are becoming independent or separated in the space of flows: the location of (production) functions, the appropriation of (urban) space, and the symbolic representations of space and place. Urban space becomes socially differentiated while (production) functions can be coordinated beyond physical contiguity.

We use this example to illustrate the general methodology characterizing Castells's work, indicating that next to the truly global reach of his empirical work, he combines both empirical and formal theoretical exercises in most parts of his writings. Illuminating as this methodology is most of the time, it also has its limitations when it comes to the exact interpretation of his work. Let us take the following statement as a case in point. From his discussion of the southern Chinese region, Castells concludes that these megacities function or operate in the space of flows, and this space of flows is becoming "the dominant spatial manifestation of power and function in our societies" (1996, 378). When elaborating on the meaning of this phrase, referring to the dominance of the space of flows, we run into an important feature of Castells's analysis. He does not make a sharp distinction between formal, theoretical analysis, on the one hand, and substantive, historical-empirical analysis, on the other.[2] The phrase "the space of flows" could be read and interpreted both from a theoretical and an empirical perspective, leading to different conclusions, so we would contend.

When read from a theoretical perspective, with the intention to develop a formal theory of the network society, the dominance of the space of flows is interpreted primarily in terms of the new dynamics of time and space that characterize the space of flows. In the context of this formal analysis, Castells asserts that the classical notions of clock time and real space, which characterized post–World War II (simple) modernity, are no longer the adequate tools to analyze the reproduction of social practices in the space of flows. In order to properly conduct such an analysis, these notions have to be supplemented with the new concepts of "timeless time" and "placeless space." The new formal concept of space in the space of flows refers to the material support given to simultaneous social practices." In the spatial setting of gemeinschaft, this simultaneity is restricted to physical contiguity or what Urry labels "propinquity." In the network society and more specifically the space of flows, this geographic proximity of gemeinschaft is no longer a necessary element of space since social practices in the information age can be materially supported over long time-space distances. Social practices can be supported and sustained also when lifted out of the local contexts they used to be embedded in during the earlier phases of modernity. The embedded, local meaning of time and space is used by Castells in his formal theory to depict the sharp contrast with the new dynamics of the space of flows. Where in the space of flows "time is timeless" and "space is placeless," in the space of places people organize their experience in "real" space and time. The space of places is characterized by clock time (or more specifically time organized either by nature or culture) and the "historically rooted spatial organization of our common experience" (Castells 1996, 378). When we reread the phrase on the dominance of the space of flows in the network society, from the formal theoretical perspective primarily, we can conclude with Castells that in the network society, timeless time and placeless space take on a special significance. They specify the process referred to by Giddens in terms of the increased level of time-space distanciation characteristic of late modern societies. The process of disembedding social practices and—at least when following Giddens—also their *reembedding* defines the specific nature of local-global relationships in heightened modernity.

The second way of reading and interpreting the notion of the dominance of the space of flows is to take it as an empirical fact. Then the concept is said to result from the fact that it is the social practices in the space of flows that dominate and shape the network society (Castells 1996, 412). The space of flows as a new "layer" in the network society is analyzed in terms of a specific kind of power relation, with the space of flows dominating over and disturbing as well as exploiting (practices) in the space of places. As Castells expresses this, "The power of flows takes precedence over the flows of power," and for that reason the network society is to be characterized by "the pre-eminence of social morphology over social action" (1996, 469). When reading in the substantive mode, this notion of the dominance of the space of flows refers to the power elites who operate—alternately on golf courses and in megacity centers—at the most crucial nodes of the global networks, knowing best how to handle the switches at the expense of the vast majority of ordinary people living their lives in the space of places. The only option left to the locals is protest and resistance against the disturbing and exploitative character of the space of flows. Although Castells is the first to argue that the logic of the space of flows will not be displayed in the network society without resistance, his analysis of the new constitution definitely has a deterministic ring to it, with the space of flows performing as a stand-in for a powerful class of global capitalists. From this perspective, the new social order of the network society should not be associated with the positive image of the new dynamics of "the Internet society" but instead manifests itself as a *metasocial disorder* (1996, 477), an order derived from the exploitative and uncontrollable logics of markets, genes, and technology.

Our discussion on the space of flows has been rather lengthy and detailed for two main reasons. First, by analytically distinguishing between formal versus substantive readings of the dominance of the space of flows, we want to make room for developing concepts that help analyze the reembedding of the space of flows in the space of places, with actors at the local level participating in the dialectic of control characterizing any power relation between social actors, also when these actors do operate in the space of flows. Second, the new dynamics of the space of flows have to be taken into account when developing perspectives on governance with respect to global environmental flows. We now turn to the concept of flows and its related notions, using elements of both Castells and Urry.

## A New Sociology and the Place of Human Agency

Flows and networks suggest movement, action, and mobility, and the new "sociology beyond society" should be "mobile sociology" in the first place (Urry 2000a, 2000b). In order to assess the relevance of this sociology of flows for environmental analyses, we have to look into some of the new key concepts in more detail. In this exploration of some of the central concepts of the new sociology, we draw on the work of both Castells and Urry.

One of the difficulties faced when trying to identify the theoretical kernel of the sociology of flows is the fact that neither Castells nor Urry provides a systematic overview of their formal concepts in relation to the existing sociologies. Although Urry in his *Global Complexity* sets himself the task to develop the "range of theoretical terms necessary to analyze the emergent properties of the networked 'global' level" (2003, 15), we would argue that "the constitution of flows" (cf. Giddens 1984) yet has to be written as the follow-up to the "new rules of mobile sociology." Already from the examples provided by Urry—with flows ranging from refugees to oceans to social movements to logos—it becomes clear that the author wants to disturb some of the old sociological schemes, among others, insofar as they concern the role of human agency in the reproduction of social practices. Since we think the issue of human agency to be of central importance to the debate on the governance of environmental change, we will discuss the flows vocabulary from this point of view in particular. Three aspects of human agency—"agency and technology," "agency and complexity," and the state as agent—will be considered separately. First, we discuss the relative autonomy of actors vis-à-vis objects, technologies, and the material world, paying attention to Urry's notions of hybrids, scapes, and material worlds and his plausible claim that mainstream sociology so far tends to underestimate the impacts of objects and technologies in (co)determining courses of action. Then we go on to more critically discuss his claim that the dynamics of global hybrids and material worlds demand the incorporation into the social sciences of a variant of complexity theory since otherwise social sciences lack the methodology for a proper understanding of global complexity. Finally, we turn to the question of what this means for the state and governance in the sociology of flows.

## Agency and Technology

Although he judges Castells's trilogy on the rise of the network society as the best effort so far to analyze networked modernity, Urry sets himself the task of elaborating and refining the conceptual apparatus as used by Castells. The two authors develop their analyses of time and space along much the same track, although Urry does not make use of the dichotomy of the space of flows versus the space of places, which is so central to Castells's work. Instead, Urry offers more, and more detailed, concepts to analyze the development of social practices in terms of flows and networks. He suggests that spatial patterns should be approached in three ways or modalities, distinguishing among regions (i.e., objects geographically clustered together), networks (relations between nodes or hubs, stretching across different regions), and finally fluids (spatial patterns determined neither by boundaries nor relations).

When taking up the issue of human agency in the development of networks, one set of arguments put forward by Urry has to do with human-technology interactions. To illustrate what we see as one of his main assertions, it is helpful to use the process of dwelling in a place as an example. When we look at the process of dwelling in a house, this social practice cannot be properly understood when analyzed only from the perspective of the house as region, in terms of a set of walls binding together peoples and material objects. When dwelling in the house is analyzed also from a network point of view, the house is perceived in terms of a connection made to a range of networks that provide the sets of material flows—water, energy, waste services, information, and so on—that underpin and organize our daily lives. These networks and flows are partly social and partly material or technical in character. It seems that Urry wants to employ the notion of "scapes" to refer to networks in their function as sociotechnical infrastructures. The power of these networks vis-à-vis human agents—the inhabitants of the house—are related to the size of the networks, their density, their relations to other networks, and so forth. As large sociotechnical systems, these networks display dynamics that are described in terms of path-dependencies, lock-in factors, sunk costs, momentum, and other concepts that figure prominently in the sociology of technological systems. In global modernity, the networks and flows underpinning our dwelling in the house go through massive changes, which can be labeled in terms of liberalization, privatization, and globalization. What results are networks and fluids that are powerful, yet fragmented or splintered at the same time (Guy and Marvin 1996; Van Vliet 2002). To make sense of this "local" process of dwelling in the house, Urry provides the following illuminating definition of local-ness or place:

Places can be loosely understood therefore as multiplex, as a set of spaces where ranges of relational networks and flows coalesce, interconnect and fragment. Any such place can be viewed as the particular nexus between, on the one hand, propinquity characterised by intensely thick co-present interaction, and on the other hand, fast flowing webs and networks stretched corporeally, virtually and imaginatively across distances. These propinquities and extensive networks come together to enable performances in, and of, particular places. (2000b, 140)

It is against the backdrop of this three-dimensional approach to dwelling—as region, networks, and fluids—that Urry takes up the issue of human agency and networks. His first argument is for "moderating" the role of human agency, which when compared to Giddens's struc-turation theory, for example, relates to the important—and in main-stream sociology, thus far underestimated—role of technology and material objects. In the networks and flows underpinning dwelling as social practices, human agents are very much intertwined and intricately connected with machines and technologies that through the space of fluids, literally "bring home" a range of diverse networks, flows, and fluids. The Internet connections spreading within and across our houses all over the world may serve as the best empirical example in this respect. Sometimes these global networks are so large, powerful, and unpre-dictable that it can be misleading to label them as "social" units in the first place. Following Latour in this respect, Urry states that "there are no purified social networks, only 'material worlds' (or hybrids) that involve peculiar and complex socialities with objects" (2003, 56). The development of these networks cannot and should not be analyzed as directly and uniquely connected to human intentions and action. Urry offers the concepts of global integrated networks (GINs) and global fluids (GFs) as a first step to distinguish between the many different meanings that Castells attached to the concepts of networks and flows.

In his sympathetic comments on *Sociology beyond Societies*, Leydesdorff (2002) agrees with Urry that social change does not necessarily have to refer to human agency since structures can change endogenously as a result of interactions among fluxes. In order for this to be the case, there should be imbalances between networks at their interfaces—imbalances that require a mathematical conceptualization of the subject under study (in terms of eigenvector and frequency analyses) that Urry avoids. Instead, he contends, the author replaces the methodological dichotomy of structure and action with the epistemological one of humans and nonhumans, as in ANT. When compared to the old solutions to conceptualizing actors in relation to technological structures, however, this is a step backward since the notion of agency in ANT is rather mechanical (with humans "black-boxed" as "actants") (Leydesdorff 2002, 4–5). Yet as we will see below, Urry does take up many of the key themes from complexity theory to further moderate the role of human agency in complex societies.

### Agency and Complexity

For Castells, the notion of flows is a key concept since flows are crucial elements in the network society, expressing those processes that can be said to dominate present-day economic, political, and symbolic life. Flows are to be defined as "the *purposeful*, repetitive, programmable sequences of exchanges and interactions between physically disjoined positions held by *social actors* in the economic, political and symbolic structures of society" (Castells 1996, 412; emphasis added). As can be read from the italics, with Castells the "old" notions of human agency—of social and purposeful actors involved in the programming of interactions—are still there, as is the familiar distinction between economic, political, and symbolic structures. Yet as discussed above, Castells does emphasize the fact that in the space of flows, the time-space paths seem to be much less predictable in their outcomes and less controllable when judged from the perspective of the individual actor or the single systems of a company, an organization, or a nation state.

In *Global Complexity*, Urry (2003) goes several steps further by partly substituting the concept of flows for the more volatile one of fluids, and by emphasizing the inherent unpredictability of the "space of fluids." The unpredictability of global modernity makes a conceptual reworking of human agency in the context of Urry's new sociology almost redundant since this would result only in a halfway solution. While for Castells, actors reside in the space of places, protesting against the disturbing influence of global complexity, for Urry actors seem to disappear altogether. The main reasons for the radical reassessment of many of the existing sociological debates on human agency for Urry are to be found in the extraordinary weight he thinks should be attached to the space of flows/fluids, to the new dynamics that unfold primarily at the global level. According to Urry, globalization theories as developed up to now simply have not gone far enough in their analysis and evaluation of the impacts of the global. It is the complexity that comes along with the global—that is, with the space of flows—that renders obsolete the distinctions between actor and structure, between the intended and unintended consequences of human action, and between human subjects and physical objects.

In his discussion of Giddens's positions on the duality of actor and structure, Urry concludes that within structuration theory, the recursive character of social reproduction is emphasized, while the development of social systems is also analyzed in direct connection with the intentions of human agents. The core concepts of the intended and unintended consequences of action are used to explain social transformations also at higher system levels. These kinds of "actor-oriented" perspectives on social change are rendered obsolete by the latest waves of globalization, resulting in complex cause-effect relations that are better understood through iteration rather than recurrence. Iteration is a key concept in complexity theory, referring to the "inhuman" combinations of objects and social relations as well as to social change developing in unpredictable, nonlinear directions. Making use of a butterfly-tornado example, Urry writes: "It is iteration that means that the tiniest of 'local' changes can generate, over billions of repeated actions, unexpected, unpredictable and chaotic outcomes, sometimes the opposite of what agents thought they were trying to bring about" (2003, 47). When social change is understood in this way, we can conclude that globalization "would appear to solve the problem of the relationship between structure and agency, with the former 'winning' the argument" (Urry 2003, 40).

To better make sense of the dynamics of globalization, we need a "complexity turn" in the social sciences. Urry, in a chapter on this turn in his *Global Complexity*, provides an overview of the basic concepts from complexity theory for the uninitiated in the social sciences. The comprehensive overview of concepts as used mainly in biology, ecology, and the physical sciences is necessary because, so Urry argues, "one could hypothesize that current phenomena have outrun the capacity of the social sciences to investigate" (2003, 38). Without the help of complexity sciences, the global is beyond systematic analysis and understanding. The jargon of attractors, iteration, chaos, and equilibrium, the emerging properties, autopoiesis, fluxes, and time as a nominator for dx/dt, will bring not just a sociology beyond society (as others have also claimed; see Touraine 1995) but perhaps a socionomy as the new disciplinary hybrid (Leydesdorff 2002).

**Agency, State, and Governance**

This all has consequences for the state and governance in the sociology of flows. In developing a perspective on nation-states, the sociology of flows starts from Bauman's (1987) idea of a transformation from the gardener to the gamekeeper state. Under the conditions of globalization, states have lost the ability and willingness to detail the patterns, regularities, and order of societies, and increasingly turn to regulating mobilities and ensuring the conditions for favorable interaction processes and flows. The EU is put forward by Urry (2000b) as the prototypical example of a gamekeeper state—a relatively small bureaucracy regulating activities and mobilities with computer-based information. But in developing the gamekeeping perspective, the sociology of flows moves well beyond this metaphor as far as nation-states are concerned.

States do not become irrelevant in Castells's network society, but they do become dependent on and nodes of a broader network of power. Their declining authority is placed between and dependent on networks of capital, production, communication, international institutions, crime, transnational religions, and NGOs, on the one hand, and the space of place, with communities, tribes, localities, cults, gangs, and local identities, on the other. For one, this means that states have become less and less able to act purposefully—that is, to influence the outcomes of global processes in the space of flows. Second, in the network society states have been transformed from sovereign subjects into strategic actors, who foster the productivity and competitiveness of their economies by allying themselves closely with economic interests, and structured by global rules favorable to capital flows. Urry uses Hardt and Negri's (2000) "empire" metaphor as a new attractor that draws in nation-states. Nation-states decreasingly succeed in combining the pursuit of empire with representing their constituents against the whirlwind of global flows manifested in the space of place, according to Castells. This is taken over to some extent by local states and social movements relying on the Internet communication systems.[3] Thus, nation-states seem to fall away as "mediators" between the space of flows and the space of places, which renders the concept of governance problematic.

In Urry's *Global Complexity*, the state seems to become irrelevant and is almost absent in analyses of a global modernity. GINs and especially global fluids are hardly touched by activities of nation-states, nor do the scapes seem to have any specific relation to nation-states. While in his chapter "Social Ordering and Power" Urry (2003, 109) looks briefly at the enhanced role of the state (and the EU), this is a remarkable deviation from the overall tendency of the book, and mention of the role of the state is missing in the summary chapter. Governability no longer belongs to the vocabulary of this interpretation of the sociology of flows. As with agency, the state has then turned away from the stage of global modernity, to be left to structures, attractors, and iteration.

### Environmental Sociology and Environmental Flows

In the environmental sciences and environmental sociology, flows—especially environmental flows or flows of material substance and energy—have been at the center of these disciplines from the early days onward. Carson's (1962) pathbreaking work on the flow of pesticides through food chains as well as the MIT's report to the Club of Rome (Meadows et al. 1972) on the spreading of pollutants around the globe and the depletion of natural resources are just two well-known examples of early environmental flows analyses. We will discuss and evaluate the analysis of flows as it has been (and continues to be) performed in environmental studies and environmental sociology.

**Environmental Sciences, Environmental Sociology, and Environmental Flows**

Within environmental studies and environmental sociology, there are in principle two major traditions in the study and analysis of environmental flows that can be distinguished: the classical analysis of environmental flows in physical/biological terms, and the analysis of environmental flows in relation to the institutions of modern society. While these two perspectives originated from and could easily be related to different disciplines—the environmental sciences and the environmental social sciences, respectively—more recently these distinct disciplinary roots are no longer that evident. The call for and institutionalization of multi- and interdisciplinarity research along with the demand for strong policy- and market-driven development of increasingly applied environmental research (at the expense of more disciplinary traditions) has resulted in cross-fertilization, and consequently in less distinct disciplinary boundaries, between the two perspectives. This has also increasingly led to what we could label boundary cases: studies that are not easily classified in one of the two perspectives but find themselves somewhere in between.

The origin of the classical tradition in the analysis of environmental flows lies in the ecosystem analysis and Odum's (1971) reworking of the Darwinian notion of the web of life. The complex web of life is unraveled via detailed studies of the flows of materials and energy through the ecosystem. The web of life is then to be understood as physical and biological—the complex and fine-tuned relations, interactions, and interdependencies between the physical and biological entities of ecosystems via material and energy flows. Ecosystems are defined in terms of the density of the flows within the system, this density being higher when compared to the relations with the outside world. Ecosystem studies focus on the processes of stability and change in the dynamic organization of the energy and material flows within the system. Human beings and organizations are analyzed, interpreted, and given a place in a similar "naturalistic" conceptualization: as units in the web of life that consume, process, and excrete environmental flows. This classical tradition has developed further via Daly's (1973, 1977) notions of input, throughput, and output. More recent popular perspectives such as industrial ecology, LCA, ecological footprint analysis, material flows analysis, and environmental system analysis have elaborated on this classical view of ecosystem biology.

These modern versions of the very same tradition continue to analyze environmental flows only or primarily in physical/biological terms. LCA and industrial ecology studies (e.g., Ayres and Ayres 1996; Graedel and Allenby 1995) both explore the flows of materials and energy through production-consumption chains and systems, with a main focus on input, throughput, output, system leakages, and the disturbance of the natural ecosystem.[4] These studies, however, pay little or no attention to social systems and social networks themselves (such as the social interactions, dynamics, and power relations governing these material flows, or the nonmaterial [money, information, etc.] flows that parallel these material and energy flows). Notwithstanding the periodic calls to widen the perspective with, for instance, a theory of agency (e.g., Jackson and Clift 1998) or social/industrial network analyses (e.g., Côté and Cohen-Rosenthal 1998), industrial systems and production-consumption chains remain primarily and predominantly analyzed in biophysical terms, as "industrial metabolism." Environmental system analysis, material flows analysis, and ecological footprint studies (e.g., Spangenberg et al. 1998) are equally preoccupied with material substance flows through the natural environment, especially via complex modeling on increasingly larger scales. Perhaps the IPCC models of global climate change are among the most well-known large-scale examples of environmental system analysis, consisting of numerous models of water, air, and soil pollution as well as "integrated models" of nitrogen, carbon, and phosphorus cycles. Like the material flows analysis, these models posit nominal or superficial linkages with social actors, institutions, and dynamics via either a stakeholder analysis or the introduction of the so-called DPSIR logic (see Spangenberg et al. 1998).[5]

A more sociological tradition in analyzing environmental flows could perhaps best be traced back to Schnaiberg's (1980) study on additions and withdrawals. Not unlike most environmental scholars in the classical tradition, Schnaiberg focuses on the flows of material substances (and energy), interpreting environmental problems in terms of human additions to the natural environment (leading, for example, to pollution) and human withdrawals from the natural environment (causing depletion).

But the sociological contribution to this flows analysis focuses primarily on the social practices and institutions that "govern" these additions and withdrawals, by examining the modern institutions within which the logics of unsustainable environmental flows are embedded. Many have followed Schnaiberg's influential work, and his conceptualization and analysis of environmental flows. In more or less the same tradition—but started more recently—world-system theorists (e.g., Goldfrank et al. 1999; Bunker 1996) study environmental flows primarily in an international context. The focus on larger social systems seems to give these studies a specific character when compared to the primarily national studies conducted in the tradition of Schnaiberg *cum suis*.[6] Also, world-system studies can be said to be in the sociological flows tradition because, in a manner similar to Schnaiberg-inspired studies, their emphasis is less on environmental flows as such and more on the logics of social systems that are constitutive for the specific patterns of the environmental flows under study. In a similar vein, most ecological modernization scholars take a Schnaiberg-inspired conceptualization of environmental flows when explaining disturbances of the sustenance base primarily in terms of the design faults of those institutions that govern production and consumption in modern societies. Treadmill-of-production theorists such as Schnaiberg and ecological modernization theorists work out of the same sociological flows tradition of analyzing how social dynamics, actors, institutional arrangements, and processes structure in a specific way the environmental flows—conceived of in terms of additions and withdrawals—that move between society and nature. No matter how much the conclusions from the treadmill-of-production and ecological modernization scholars may seem to differ, the starting points in their studies of environmental flows actually are quite similar (see Mol and Spaargaren 2002).

Finally, we witness the emergence of a third cluster of studies that are somewhere in between the two classic types discussed so far. In these studies, at least three types of boundary crossings can be distinguished. First, there are the "classical" technical perspectives on environmental flows, to which there is affixed some kind of soci(ologic)al analysis, most of the time resulting in rather unsatisfying analyses. This first type of scholarship is typified by the "integrated assessment studies" that have emerged out of environmental assessments. Integrated assessments aim to include economic and social analysis to complement and complete their initially restricted natural sciences perspective. In a similar way, LCA and industrial ecology studies often incorporate a so-called stakeholder analysis in order to rein in the sometimes utopian proposals for environmental change to more realistic proportions. A more successful attempt at integration can be found in Geiser's (2001) study on materials and material flows. Although Geiser begins with the classical tradition, he is able to partially transcend this approach in a constructive and productive way. Second, there are schools in environmental sociology that considerably enlarge the materialist dimensions of environmental flows in explaining social facts and developments related to these flows. In doing so, they de-emphasize socioinstitutional analysis and come close to the sociobiological school of thought. One can often detect in their studies a rather functionalist and evolutionary perspective. Fischer-Kowalski's (1997; Fischer-Kowalski and Haberl 1997) work on the materialist foundations of societies in different stages of development provides an illustrative example. Finally, we can witness various studies that strive to put material and energy flows at the core of their analyses, without falling back on a position close to sociobiology. Bunker's (Bunker and Ciccantell 1995; Barham et al. 1987) studies have a strong material foundation, but these analyses are much more careful in using material flows for explaining social conditions and developments than the ones discussed so far. In a similar manner, there exists a rich tradition on urban infrastructure that entails studies primarily focused on energy and water flows from a sociological perspective. Studies such as those of Shove (1997) and Guy and Marvin (1996, 2001) move well beyond the additions and withdrawals perspective, and come close to a sociology of flows perspective in putting material flows at the center of their sociological analysis. While starting from a material flows perspective, they explicitly ask themselves in what way the interplay between the social and the natural can be analyzed in a balanced way.

Perhaps, with the exception of this last subcategory, all three traditions of this environmental flows literature typically take three phenomena to be the central object of study: the movement of material and energy (in different forms) between the social activities of production and consumption and the natural environment; the disruption of material and energy flows within the natural environment; and/or the lack of closure of material and energy flows within the human activities of production and consumption. These flow analyses range from local studies (e.g., flow diagrams of one production process) to truly global inquiries (e.g., studies of global resource extraction, trade, and global models). In these studies, however, environmental flows are rarely combined with analyses of nonmaterial flows (with the possible exception of information flows), which assume such a central position in the sociology of flows. In addition, we might conclude that in the sociological approach, environmental flows are not often given any detailed attention—again with a few exceptions confirming the general rule (e.g., the Barham and colleagues [1987] study of aluminum, Shove's work, and the studies of Simon and colleagues on urban infrastructure). Thus, we are faced in the environmental sciences either with a choice between, first, "sociological" studies of flows taking social practices, institutions, and actors as the central unit of analysis, and second, "technical" studies that do take flows as the central unit of analysis, but leave the social dimensions—if they appear at all during the research stage—undertheorized.

### Environmental Sociology and the Boundaries of Twentieth-Century Sociology

By the end of the twentieth century, flows analyses in environmental sociology, which were so strongly put on the research agenda following Schnaiberg's (1980) influential conceptualization of additions and withdrawals, faced a number of problems and boundaries. Some of these problems can be said to be specific to environmental sociology, while others have been faced by general sociology as well, leading in the end to the emergence of the sociology of flows. But the end of the century also witnessed the emergence of several themes in sociological and social sciences scholarship that provide ways of resolving the impasse over how to think about environmental flows in a manner that is sociologically rich and biophysically meaningful.

The first theme refers to the effects of globalization on the predominantly national arrangements. This theme was articulated from the 1970s onward by several scholars who were striving to be able to address, understand, and manage environmental flows at different layers and in different segments of modern industrial society. Especially during simple modernity (Beck 1992), the flows of water, energy, waste, food risks, and so on, were not articulated as environmental flows, and were largely left invisible to the majority of the population. These flows traveled via underground pipes (sewage systems) to distant places (treatment plants or landfills), out of reach of the sensory skills. Energy and water flows, functioning as the sustenance base to household-based practices of dwelling (see "The Sociology of Flows" section above), were rendered invisible in the house, with monitoring devices hidden away in dark cellars. Due to the emerging importance attached to environmental interests and values from the 1970s onward, environmental flows increasingly were made "visible" again—much as was the case in the eighteenth and nineteenth centuries (Swaan 1988)—and were *articulated as environmental flows* in need of design, management, governing, and optimization from an environmental point of view. It is here that the ideas of ecological modernization emerge, and that monitoring, governing institutions, and organizational schemes were asked to include environmental rationalities.

Toward the end of the twentieth century, the emerging schemes for the handling of environmental flows radically changed under the processes of globalization. The nationally oriented arrangements that were predominant during simple modernity were increasingly felt to be inadequate. Among the major changes in the conceptualization and management of environmental flows were the growing recognition of the importance of transboundary movements of energy, water, waste, and risks; the phenomenon of international public and private organizations getting involved in the governing of local environmental flows; the growing significance and differentiation of global flows simultaneously affecting local conditions; the increased knowledge and reflexivity about the new conditions for the handling of environmental flows on the part of the general public; and the frequent and routine use of opinion polls, focus groups, market panels, and other "reflexive tools" to bring a citizen-consumer orientation into the arrangements for the handling of environmental flows. While initially in the 1980s and early 1990s international environmental regimes were put forward as an approach transcending the sovereign nation-state doctrine, toward the end of the 1990s it became clear that these regimes were actually extensions of that doctrine and that nation-state-oriented policies were really inadequate. With Urry, we must indeed conclude that globalization is not just a region at a higher level of aggregation.

Second, the clear-cut boundaries as they were drawn during simple modernity between the state, the market, and civil society began to shift and change (Spaargaren et al. 2000). All kinds of hybrid arrangements between and beyond these three institutions—environmental subpolitics, public-private partnerships, market actors that take on "state tasks," states that behave like market actors, private interest governments that mediate between failing states and opportunistic market actors, environmental NGOs that have begun to behave like states or even MNCs— were identified as new institutions that were supposedly or actually governing environmental flows. It seemed that concepts rooted in the traditional division among the state, the market, and civil society lost much of their adequacy for analyzing the arrangements and institutions that governed environmental flows at the turn of the millennium. There have, of course, always been in-between or hybrid institutions, but these increasingly came to be seen as the rule itself rather than exceptions to it.

Third, in the sociological study of environmental flows, the relation between the social and the natural/material/technical has recently become (again) the subject of rather intense debate and controversy. Ever since the birth of environmental sociology in the early 1970s, the issue of the natural/material versus the social was assigned a privileged position within environmental sociological analysis as a dimension that could not be reduced to social categories alone (see "The Sociology of Flows" section above). In the 1990s, social constructivism (e.g., Hannigan 1995; Yearley 1997) put the conceptualization of the material/natural on the agenda of social studies once again, as did the studies of actor networks and large technical systems in the tradition of Callon (1980, 1987) and Latour (1987) in the 1980s. ANT in particular sought to diminish the distinction between the natural/material and the social by giving the former (such as molecules and cars) equal "actor" qualities in networks combining material artifacts with human actors and organizations. Actor networks are thus seen as networks of social and material/natural entities that have interactions, interdependencies, and mutual influences. The constructivism debate of the 1990s emphasized (in different ways, to different extents, and with different conclusions) the social construction of nature and material things, trying to reduce or do away with the material dimensions of social life in sociological analysis. Although both traditions did not emerge from environmental sociology sensu stricto (but rather from the sociology of science and technology), they both had a major influence within environmental sociology, especially because both traditions touched the heart of this subdiscipline: the relation between material flows, on the one hand, and the social institutions, actors, and dynamics that governed these flows, on the other. At the end of the century, it was felt by many authors concerned that a new approach was needed, doing away with the classical dichotomies of nature and culture, the social and the natural, the realist or the constructionist, and so on.

When analyzing environmental flows in relation to society, environmental sociology runs up against the limits of twentieth-century sociological paradigms—limitations that have to do, so we argued, with the global character of the flows, questions of (science-based) management and control, and the ways in which the relationship between the material and the social is conceived of.

## Environmental Sociology and the Sociology of Flows

Although environmental flows (especially climate change, the ozone layer, and the movement of solid waste) regularly serve as illustrations of global flows and also the difficulties of the nation-state-based governance of global flows, in general it can be said that these phenomena tend to be marginalized sociologically because of the lack of profound analysis in the sociology of flows. This marginalization can take different forms—for instance, from being reduced to only social dimensions in a constructivist perspective, to being relegated to and "locked up" in the space of places, giving shape to the resistance identity against the space of flows, as in Castells's network society theory.[7]

In this section, we want to evaluate in a systematic way the potentials of the sociology of flows for *environmental flows analysis*, as we think the latter to be a serious reference for the sociological debate on the future of modernity. In this assessment, we will also make use of present-day insights, experiences, themes, and studies from environmental sociology, as we think environmental sociology's tradition in flows analysis so far also has a contribution to make to this debate. While bringing in knowledge about environmental flows into the sociology of flows, we at the same time evaluate, assess, and reformulate parts of this emerging sociology of flows perspective. We will do so around four major themes: the definition of flows, the relation between the social and the material (hybrids), issues of power and inequalities, and (global) governance.

### Definition of Flows: Changing Research Agendas in Environmental Sociology

Along with Sassen (1994) and Castells (1996, 1997a, 1997b), we agree that transactions, flows, and the space of flows are very much the privileged domain of global economics as well as information and communication technologies. It is the new constellation of these latter two that lies at the origin of flows, especially of money, information, and the related economic services. Not surprisingly, environmental flows—or more generally, material flows—are not included in Castells's flows analysis. The environment or nature enters into Castells's analysis only as negative side effects of the space of flows. In the end, Castells's view of the environment and nature comes down to being but a reformulation of the conventional point of view of environmental economics ("externalities") in combination with the traditional "protest approach" in environmental sociology (social movements organizing resistance against modernity).

When compared to Castells, Urry provides a much broader interpretation and definition of flows, widening the perspective considerably beyond just economics and information (technology). At the same time, he radicalizes the flows perspective by making flows and fluids the key units of (sociological) analysis, and the organizing principles of social systems in the twenty-first century. Fluids and flows are to be regarded as the "utterly crucial categories of analysis in the globalizing social world that have in part rendered both regions and networks less causally powerful" (Urry 2003, 61). As discussed in "The Sociology of Flows" section, the negative side of this move is the rather imprecise and arbitrary picture that results. It appears that anything that moves—from clouds to people, from vibrating atoms to transboundary solid waste—can be interpreted as a flow.

What the sociology of flows adds to—and how it might change the agenda of—environmental sociology becomes clear when one compares the additions and withdrawals that have been so central in post-Schnaiberg environmental sociology with this new sociology of flows. First, the additions and withdrawals perspective is too region focused, static, and place bound in comparison with the sociology of flows.[8] The sociology of flows is especially well developed as a response to the shortcomings of the strong region and society orientation of sociology. The clustering of objects in regions around which (nation-state) boundaries are drawn becomes untenable, especially through globalization; that is, regions can no longer be seen as mere subunits or properties of national societies. And globalization can also no longer be interpreted as just another region on a higher level of analysis or aggregation. The sociology of flows puts global fluids, global network dynamics, and the space of flows—rather than localities, static practices, and the space of places—on the research agenda. The idea of boundaries and fixed clusters, especially within a nation-state/society, is replaced by borderless global fluids. Even in the environmental analysis conducted within WST, environmental flows were situated and discussed within the concept of nation-state societies, with additions and withdrawals flowing in between rather fixed networks and scapes, following walled routes. The arguments in favor of global fluids and against local statics should be taken seriously by environmental flows analysts. But this should not result in placeless perspectives. Notwithstanding processes of disembedding, deterritorialization, delocalization, and the increasingly footloose and stateless character of global financial and economic flows, Sassen (1994), Hoogvelt (1997), and others have illustrated the fact that flows of financial capital and information have to be processed at places (the metropolitan cities), that they originate their profit from places, and that they have to "settle down" in places—for example, as (green) investments in skyscrapers and other material objects (Presas 2005). As we noted above, Castells has included the notion of the tensions between the space of flows and the space of places into the very center of his social theory, interpreting the space of places as places of resistance against the flow- and information/communication technologies–dominated global economy. While the scheme offered by Castells is not entirely satisfactory since he repeatedly emphasizes disembedding at the expense of reembedding, we think environmental sociology has a contribution to make in showing how "space of flows-based" regulatory regimes (for example, for the management of water or food systems) can be combined with equally important dynamics of the space of places (Oosterveer 2003).

Second, up until now environmental sociology rather seldom investigated or analyzed environmental flows as such. Most studies on additions and withdrawals focus on the social practices of production, consumption, mining, agriculture, and the like in terms of how they *result* in additions and withdrawals, and the concomitant changes within the sets of ecosystems making up the material sustenance base to modern societies. As the sociology of flows perspective would have it, material substance flows become the genuine unit of analysis in environmental sociology at an earlier point and in a more comprehensive way, focusing around which actors and social practices (labeled in terms of nodes and moorings, institutional developments and scapes, discourses, and networks) can be identified and analyzed in order to understand these fluids sui generis as well as the (policy) issues of management and control they bring along with them. Framed in the HEP-NEP dichotomy, which was put on the agenda so forcefully by Riley Dunlap and others in the 1970s and 1980s, this can even be interpreted as a further radicalization beyond the NEP. While from an NEP perspective, conventional sociological theories were interrogated for their "human exemptionalist" quality and their unwillingness to give ecology/environment a place, an environmental interpretation of the sociology of flows goes one step beyond the NEP by placing "material flows proper" at the center of analysis. It is this radicalization of the NEP that ultimately results in questions on whether we are to trespass the boundaries of the sociological discipline (see below).

Thus, third, while in the case of environmental flows the (larger) sociology of flows pushes material flows into the center of analysis, this also makes environmental flows inherently social. An environmental flow is not only or just material substances and technical infrastructures but also the scapes, nodes, networks, and discourses that go along with the flows or fluids in question. In this respect, environmental flows analysis distinguishes itself from the environmental sciences/studies paradigms that are the essential foundation of most of conventional material/substance flows analysis. In analyzing flows, the sociology of flows concentrates on social embeddedness while simultaneously emphasizing the material dimension. Such a perspective might be fruitful in bridging the gap between some of the environmental sciences traditions that put material flows as their core object (be it only in natural sciences terms, as noted above), on the one hand, and neo-Marxist, world-system, and other "realist" perspectives as developed in environmental sociology, on the other.

Fourth, from a sociology of flows perspective, environmental flows in terms of additions and withdrawals are to be regarded as a rather narrow and static interpretation of environmental flows since the focus is on only one aspect—that is, the *final* stage of the flows process (when it results in net additions to the environment or the net withdrawals from the environment into production/products). The dynamics of the flows themselves as displayed along the way—that is, their behavior as constantly moving, deterritorialized fluids—is left undertheorized. If we are to take the sociology of flows seriously, environmental flows, and our analyses of these flows, do not stop once they have been extracted from or added to the environment. There is *no goal, consequence, or end stage in flows*. This way of thinking about flows will have important consequences for the way we treat our object(s) of analysis. Both carbon and phosphate cycles, together with the characteristics of the automobility system on the move, would be more archetypal objects of study in a sociology of flows than would phenomena such as the extraction of ore or the emissions of heavy metals from plating industries that have heretofore been the main topics of environmental sociological studies.

Finally, the sociology of flows would reinterpret some of the environmental sociology studies that have never been identified with flows and flows analysis. In the sociology of flows, flows are not necessarily or exclusively material. They can also be for the most part social, or a combination or hybrid. Those environmental sociology studies focusing on, for instance, social movements and environmental NGOs; on environmental information, knowledge, and labeling; or on discourses, ideas, norms, and values can be reworked into an environmental sociology of flows. According to the sociology of flows, the mobility of environmental ideas, information, and interpretative frameworks flowing between networks and nodes around the globe can be interpreted in much the same way as material flows. Rather than place-bound, geographic communities, mobile placeless communities are emerging under the conditions of global complexity, each involving a particular intersection of belonging and traveling—for instance, groupings or alliances organized around food, gender, environment, spirituality, road protests, culture, and so on. These communities are to be found within, but also beyond, the nation-state. Regions, boundaries, and places become relative and permeable, and in most cases have limited relevance for understanding mobility within and between these social entities. The mobile flows themselves might not be material ones in such cases, but the infrastructures, the nodes, and the routes used certainly are material to an extent. Linking environmental issue networks with particular environmental substance flows would then become a challenging perspective.

It should be stressed and acknowledged, however, that such a widening of the flow concept within an "environmental" sociology of flows could conceivably render environmental sociology vulnerable to the same kinds of problems we signaled with respect to Urry's approach to defining flows. We must be cautious so that our commitment to the notion that material, social, and hybrid flows can be examined with similar concepts and methods does not lead to environmental phenomena being one among many types of flows on an arbitrary—and endless—list. Hence, a sociology of environmental flows is also in need of a further systematization and definition of environmental flows. In the end, though, we believe that reinterpreting and reconsidering environmental flows in the ways suggested by the sociology of flows is beneficial for environmental sociology, as it opens up new kinds of theoretical analyses, prepares the ground for new empirical research, and helps in moving beyond some of the impasses experienced within late twentieth-century environmental sociology.

## Between the Social and the Material: The Role of Hybrids in Environmental Sociology

Within environmental sociology and environmental studies, the relation between the social and the material, between society and nature, has long been subject to controversies and debates. The debates over the HEP-NEP distinction, the constructivism-realism controversy, and the debates surrounding the Latourian/Callonian ANTs all give evidence of this wrestling with the material dimensions of social theories in the context of environmental social change. Within the sociology of flows it is especially Urry who, relying heavily on the ANTs of Latour (1987) and Callon (1980, 1987) and the reinterpretation of Mol and Law (1994), tries to overcome (or do away with) the dichotomy of the social and the material. In doing so, he goes way beyond the conventional schemes of environmental sociologists, who generally speaking remain comfortable with asserting that social systems should be seen as systems having a material base, with a recognition of the fact that material conditions do matter for social practices and institutional developments.

Nevertheless, the sociology of flows does not accept the distinction of the material and the social, and argues for a merger of the natural and the social into hybrids, putting "material worlds" or hybrids at the center of analysis (see Urry 2003). The sociology of flows—as developed by Urry at least—thus moves away from the "oversocialized" analysis of classical sociology, in which social facts are to be explained by other social facts only. When it comes to the material underpinnings of social life, Urry strongly deviates from Castells, who offers what could be seen as a thoroughly HEP-based perspective on nature and the environment. For Castells, modern societies in the end have succeeded in "freeing" themselves from the constraints of nature. Only in the informational age of the twenty-first century can and must nature be reinvented and conceived of as a cultural form, independent from its material base. As Castells notes, "After millennia of a prehistoric battle with Nature, first to survive, then to conquer it, our species has reached the level of knowledge and social organisation that will allow us to live in a predominantly social world" (1996, 478).

Without fully embracing the NEP paradigm in its classical formulation, we follow Urry in his effort to construct nature not independently from the material flows that sustain social life. Also, at the conceptual level, the social and the material should be kept close to each other. Yet bringing the social and the material closer together has a number of consequences, which should be given careful attention. First, the merging of the material and the social dimension of flows leads Urry to question the adequacy of sociology as a discipline, and to call for a stronger cross-disciplinary collaboration. In his most recent works, Urry argues for the in-migration of other disciplines into sociology—especially the natural sciences. Understanding the complexity of globalization obliges sociologists to look into the other sciences for all the help they can get in interpreting and understanding global mobilities. Urry also would not hesitate to integrate various disciplines into a new (complexity) science for interpreting and understanding global modernity: "The complexity sciences seem to provide the best means of transcending such outdated divisions, between nature *and* society, between the physical sciences *and* the social sciences" (2003, 18).

Although in the environmental field periodic calls for integration and the abandonment of strict monodisciplinary scientific work are all too frequent and familiar (partly driven by funding agencies), it is remarkable to hear such a plea from one of the leading contemporary social theorists. The search for and practices of multi- or interdisciplinary collaboration have been debated vigorously already within the environmental (social) sciences and studies from the 1970s onward. At the time, there was a more or less similar claim that the complexity of environmental problems could not be understood, let alone solved, by the natural or social sciences working separately. Several attempts have been made to develop environmental studies into a new scientific discipline, with its own theories, concepts, research methodologies, and methods (Boersema et al. 1991; Leroy and Nelissen 1999). Most of these initiatives emerged from the natural or economic sciences, and tried to incorporate social sciences (e.g., integrated environmental assessment or industrial ecology). Urry's attempt at integration, however, originated from the social sciences and set the terms for the in-migration of the natural sciences, instead of the other way around as is usually the case. This makes his claim all that much more interesting. Yet it is sobering that twenty years of experiences in developing integrative methodologies and conceptual frameworks in the environmental (social) sciences have not resulted in major advancements in analyzing, interpreting, and solving problems related to additions and withdrawals. Partly, this failure can be explained by a lack of attractive, cross-disciplinary conceptual work, which manages to attract adventurers from different disciplines. With the flows perspective, this drawback perhaps could be surpassed. In the end, though, with Urry's hybrids, flows, scapes, and related formal conceptual work, the proof of the pudding will be in the eating—for example, the success will be determined to a great extent by the ability of the integrated approach to (better) analyze and understand global fluids.

Second, with considerable attention being paid by analysts such as Urry to the material dimension, the result is a much stronger emphasis on technology and technological developments in sociology and the social sciences. This stronger emphasis on technology is obvious if we compare the sociology of flows with, for instance, structuration theory. Giddens pays only limited attention to technological developments and their influence on the social order and institutional change. Both in Castells's *Network Society* and Urry's recent work on flows and mobilities, technology is brought into the core of social development and change. Technological infrastructures have always occupied a central place in environmental sociology, whether they be in the form of utility infrastructures, production plants, environmental technologies, or consumer products such as cars and computers. Environmental sociologists would feel comfortable with such a strong emphasis on technological developments in interpreting, explaining, and criticizing (late) modernity.

Third, the merging of the social and the material tends to downplay any conventional idea of agency. In line with ANTs, it is not only human agents who act within networks, fluids, and scapes. Both human agency and material objects can "act," or make a difference—hence, Urry adopts the vocabulary of "actants" without hesitation. There is no autonomous realm of human agency; there are no uniquely human societies. Societies are made up of hybrids, and when accepting the notion of hybrids, the language of actants, referring both to humans and objects or technologies, becomes inevitable. As we discussed in some detail at the beginning of this chapter, for Urry the merging of the social and the material is inextricably bound up with his turn to complexity. It is complexity science that brings him to the rather strong emphasis on the impossibility for actants to purposefully steer and control social developments, and to create and sustain structures—in sum, to act as knowledgeable and capable agents. Actants are linked up in Urry's theory of complexity with iteration. Courses of action based on local information lead to unpredictable consequences at the global level due to nonlinear processes of iteration. In the end, we are left with inherently unpredictable fluids, without a clear direction. Urry comes close to systems theory when he develops the (mechanical?) notion of attractors as the main force causing changes in fluids and their movements through scapes. The question of how far removed we are with Urry from the classical (and in the social sciences, often disputed) ecosystem perspectives as put forward by, for example, Odum (Odum and Odum 2000) becomes noteworthy.

### Power, Inequality, and Access

Within the sociology of flows, power and inequality are no longer only related to the ownership of capital, as has been the dominant view in neo-Marxist studies, or to the state, as was the mainstream conviction in most other schools of thought. In addition to these so-called old categories of power and inequality, the sociology of flows defines new inequalities in terms of having relative access to, or being decoupled from, flows. Groups, persons, cities, and regions with access to the core flows, and those located in or close to the central nodes and moorings, are the wealthy and powerful. This position comes close to that of Rifkin (2000), who stresses the importance of access rather than ownership in late modernity. It is access to the information flows via the Internet, to the flows of monetary capital and the skills of people moving around the world, that distinguishes the better-off peoples, groups, cities, and regions from their marginalized equivalents. This notion of "access to" refers to both direct access as well as the ability to structure the scapes and nodes to partially influence the fluids in terms of speed, direction, intensity, and so on.

In following this analytic pathway, a sociology of environmental flows would pay attention to the conditions for access to environmental flows and the scapes that structure the current dynamics of strategic environmental fluids, and analyze in some detail the consequences for groups, actors, and organizations to whom access is denied, or who do not manage to establish links with the relevant networks. This would reorient conventional environmental flows studies as conducted mainly from a natural sciences perspective (e.g., material flows analysis or industrial ecology) by giving priority to the social perspective in the analysis of environmental substance flows. It also would enrich conventional additions and withdrawals studies, as power and inequality are being linked to flows in a more direct way. Power is thought to reside in the additions and withdrawals themselves, and not only in the social practices of production and consumption. Environmental justice studies can be seen as a category that fits very well into such an environmental flows sociology.

Arguably, environmental sociologists interested in studying questions of inequality and power from a sociology of flows perspective would choose Castells's work over that of Urry as the most promising point of departure. This is because Castells is quite explicit and outspoken in his analysis of inequalities in the network society, especially in terms of his distinction and tension between the space of flows and the space of places. Those with access to and in (partial) control of the key economic and information flows can be said to dominate the new informational world order, at the expense of the place-bound local actors outside the core nodes of the networks. Like most political economists and neo-Marxist environmental sociologists, Castells discusses inequalities in relation to the environment primarily in the context of a rather simple dichotomy: place-bounded environmental movements resist the omnipotent actors of the space of (economic) flows. Within Castells's framework, there seems to be little room for including the environment and environmental reform within the time-space dynamics of the space of flows itself as, among others, ecological modernization scholars would have it. While Urry's notion of power is much less articulated (in part due to his notions of iteration, systems theory, and self-referentiality), and seems sometimes detached from human beings (as in the case of his notion of attractors), he provides more conceptual space for a broader, more encompassing analysis of inequality and the environment.

By interpreting the environment and nature as attached to flows rather than seeing them only as part of the space of place, and by providing an interesting new conceptual framework for analyzing the scapes, nodes, moorings, networks, and fluids determining the dynamics of flows, questions of access to and exclusion from flows make the power analyses less predetermined and more open in character. But the advantages of such an openness could disappear overnight when the concept of power is directly tied to iteration, self-referentiality, and complexity in a way that does not seem to easily fit into the social sciences tradition of dealing with inequality and power in relation to human agency. When compared to his earlier work, Urry's (2003) recent work on complexity seems to move away from power as conflict, transformative capacity, and control, to be replaced by a rather vague discussion of power in the context of iteration, chaos theory, complexity, and self-referentiality.

## State, Governance, and Regulation

Within environmental sociology and studies, the role of the state and issues of governance always have had and still have a prominent place. For one, the environment is almost always seen as an explicit or implicit collective good, the achievement of which demands state regulation and intervention in order to compensate for the externalities and other irrationalities associated with market dynamics. The state has been seen for a long time as the natural institution to take on the responsibility for regulating the consumption of collective goods, even if we grant the insights from the literature on "state failure" (Jänicke 1986). This position was only reaffirmed when international and global environmental problems arrived on political and research agendas, and institutionalists and regime theorists turned their attention massively toward the environment from the early 1990s onward. Second, most studies in environmental sociology have a strong normative undertone: environmental deterioration is often studied and analyzed with an explicit or implicit idea of improvement, management, and reform. This always entails a kind of governance, although not necessarily by the nation-state or governmental structures only. Although the notion of governance has been broadened considerably in the environmental social sciences literature, it still remains the case that notions of science and technology–based, top-down, or horizontally organized management, control, and regulation of environmental flows are prominent in most studies.

At the same time, environmental sociologists have never been naive about the capacities of and constraints on the state. Their conventional position on the state and politics is very much in line with twenty-first-century sociology: nation-state-based politics encounter formidable obstacles in controlling increasingly internationally organized capitalist markets, networks, and economies. The governance of global economic practices and flows runs counter to the specific relations between states and markets in modern, capitalist societies. The sociology of flows partly follows this line, emphasizing the changing role of nation-states, state control, and governance, but stopping short of forecasting the end of governance in a globalizing world. In analyzing what it calls GINs, the sociology of flows interprets these networks in terms of routinized behavior, predictable and calculable outcomes, and rather fixed relations between the nodes constituting the networks, and thus it sees possibilities for governance. In his earlier work on flows and mobility, Urry stressed the shift of the state's role from a gardener to a gamekeeper state (see "The Sociology of Flows" section above), seeking to identify the new ways in which states try to regulate global networks and flows (e.g., the audit state). Castells equally downplays the role of the regulating state, but emphasizes new governing agents and arrangements onstage (e.g., social movement networks and MNCs). While this is a new language and style of reasoning for environmental sociology, it can be said that it does not lie too far beyond the reformulations of the environmental state and environmental governance in some of the more recent studies and theories in the environmental social sciences, such as those on mediation, transparency, subpolitics, and global governance. All these latter interpretations have equally ambivalent evaluations of the governing powers of the nation-state in solving environmental conflicts.

But where the sociology of flows identifies the growing importance of global fluids, ideas of governance start to change dramatically. One should not be too surprised that environmental social scientists feel rather uncomfortable with Urry's stress on uncontrollable, unpredictable, nonlinear, and unmanageable fluids that move through space and time via numerous iterations and the interventions of actants. The change and chaos in these fluids have nothing to do with agents actually and deliberately seeking to change flows in size, moment, direction, or consistency. Individual agencies or countries no longer seem to be relevant categories in structuring and governing flows. In this analysis of fluids, the state appears to fade away, to become almost irrelevant. Governmentability no longer has a place in the vocabulary of this interpretation of the sociology of flows.

The abandonment of the relevance of the state in this sociology of fluids also results in abandoning the concept of unintended consequences—a notion that has always been strongly related to ideas of external effects in the environmental sciences. Due to systemic complexity, iteration, the dissolution of agency and governance, and the idea that fluids have no goal or end state, unintended consequences are interpreted as systemic features (Urry 2003, 14) rather than unwanted side effects or failures. Any normative claim or criticism thus becomes impossible; we can indeed no longer be legislators, but only interpreters (see Bauman 1987), of a changing nature and environment.

It is difficult to see what this latter perspective on (the absence of) governance would add to the existing literature on environmental flows. In moving beyond any form of governance, regulation, steering, and control, environmental sociology would move to a discipline of mere interpretation and understanding. No matter how diffuse, how widely spread among a variety of actors, and how far located outside the nation-state, ideas of governance and reform (as well as criticism on governance and failing reform) have always belonged to the very essence of the environmental social sciences. Even in more social constructionist perspectives, ideas of constructing social reality by human agents (including sociologists) remain central (Irwin 2001).

## Toward a Sociology of Environmental Flows

After analyzing and evaluating both the sociology of flows and the environmental sociology perspectives on flows, we aim to discuss the route toward a sociology of environmental flows. Such a sociology of environmental flows builds strongly on the sociology of flows, but as we have stressed at several times above, a sociology of environmental flows must necessarily deviate from the more general sociology of flows on some crucial elements. Indeed, one of the conclusions that we wish to draw here is that environmental sociologists have a key contribution to make in developing such a new sociology of environmental flows.

The sociology of flows opens various windows for environmental sociologists to update the twentieth-century perspective on additions and withdrawals to be more suitable for understanding twenty-first-century environmental flows. This perspective considerably widens the definitions of environmental flows, and it brings globalization within environmental flows analysis in a sociological way, enabling environmental sociologists to see globalization as something more fundamental than a mere scale-up of nationally based flows analysis. It also offers a new perspective on the constant wrestling of environmental social sciences and environmental studies with how to deal with the social and the material, and with how to mediate between the strong natural-sciences-based material flows analyses that continue to dominate contemporary environmental flows studies, on the one hand, and the oversocialized additions and withdrawals perspectives, on the other. Moreover, it provides concepts for bringing together environmental flows studies with other fields of environmental sociology, such as social movement studies. Finally, it offers environmental sociology new conceptualizations of power and inequalities, linking them more securely to access to material flows themselves.

In analyzing and understanding twenty-first-century environmental flows in global modernity, the key starting point should lie in the differentiation between region, networks, and fluids, and in the unraveling of combinations of specific flows and characteristic scapes that govern the flows. As a first approximation, environmental flows can continue to be categorized in conventional material and energy flows (the additions and withdrawals of waste, electricity, water, metal ore, etc.), but they also must be seen as mobile material objects that carry with them an articulated environmental profile (automobility, green products, etc.) and nonmaterial environmental flows (such as environmental information, environmental movements, environmental discourses, and environmental management concepts). Such flows can be interpreted from a region, a GIN, and/or a global fluids perspective. Analyzing the physical-technological and socioinstitutional scapes through which the environmental flows move provides further details necessary for a comprehensive flows analysis. Subsequently, the fine-tuning of such a specific flow/scape combination should lead us to the point of identifying and analyzing the nodes and moorings, access and exclusion, disembedding and reembedding between the space of flows and the space of places, and questions of governance. Below, we offer three flow/scape combinations as examples of how a sociology of flows perspective can add to conventional perspectives of environmental sociology and studies.

Within environmental sociology, the processes of dwelling in the city and the house have been discussed over recent years in terms of the infrastructural provisioning of daily social practices. When the network and flows perspective is put to work in this context, the micro-macro dichotomy as well as the human-material objects and technology dualism can be shown to lose much of their analytic sharpness and attractiveness. Instead, the interplay between the daily routines involved in handling our "local daily portion of flows" like energy, water, green products, and waste services can be shown to be connected in an intimate and direct way to the global networks and scapes that sometimes and in certain respects give these everyday flows the character of undetermined fluids. But the extra dimension that the sociology of flows perspective can add to the existing field of environmental flows studies on urban and domestic infrastructures is not restricted to this reformulation of the classical dichotomies. As Urry has argued, the process of sensual experiencing flows can hardly be underestimated in its strategic importance for the future organization of the urban and domestic flows and scapes. Especially in the field of water management, it is recognized that the quality of water (management) in the built environment is determined to a great extent by the potential to render visible, tangible, and smellable again the urban and domestic flows. We indeed try to reinvent in some respects "nature of premodern times," without, however, the (health) risks that used to come along with the traditional schemes.

The walled routes of environmental flows in an (eco-)industrial park can be interpreted from both a region and network perspective. The scapes consist of the infrastructures of waste exchange, environmental treatment facilities, and utility technologies along with the socioinstitutional settings of (national) political arrangements and (global) economic and informational networks. To understand the mobility of these environmental flows and touch on questions of governance, further analysis of the conventional contradictions between the economic space of flows and the politics of the space of places is crucial. Such a sociology of environmental flows approach would enrich the conventional sociological perspectives of industrial systems by bringing the dynamics of material flows and infrastructure networks to the center of analysis, and it would enrich industrial ecology approaches by linking their material flow analysis strongly with the scapes that govern these flows.

Analyzing the environmental flows of green products and labeling in a global economy cannot be done from a region perspective of localized production sites or localized niche markets of consumers. Increasingly, an ecological modernization perspective of environmental reform of production sites needs to be broadened to encompass the truly global nature of green products. The strong globalized nature of production and consumption, the numerous interactions within producer-consumer chains stretched around the globe, and the post-Fordist differentiation in consumption make these flows less predictable, manageable, and controllable. Here an interpretation of global fluids comes closer to the mark, pointing us to the specific characteristics of these flows and the limitations of state governance, but also to the articulation and embedding of the environment in a placeless space of flows. The scape consists of both the physical-technological infrastructures that come along with production, logistics, distribution, marketing, information exchange, consumption, and waste handling, and the socioinstitutional, economic, and symbolic landscapes through which the global fluid moves via the numerous individual decisions of political and economic actors.

McNaughten and Urry (1998) in their *Contested Natures* set out for themselves the task of illustrating that nature is not simply "out there," as suggested in some environmental discourses that rely on a rather naive realist perspective of the material versus the social. The emphasis in *Contested Natures* was primarily on deconstructing some of the absolutist views of nature and the environment as put forward by some environmental movements and policymakers. One single, objective nature is deconstructed in a multiple set of natures that are no longer out there.

When one finishes reading this book, one wonders what reconstruction is still possible after the sometimes destructive analytic work is finished. With the sociology of flows perspective, we think Urry and others got a healthy start on developing the conceptual tools for a reconstruction of different natures. As we illustrated with the three examples above, nature and the environment can be constructed in terms of different combinations of region, networks, fluids, and flows. These examples reveal not just the obvious but also the rather vague and imprecise need for the multiactor and multilevel governance of environmental change; and they show in particularly vivid analytic detail that the process of environmental construction itself is multidimensional in character. As such, the sociology of flows perspective forms a challenging perspective for the future of environmental social sciences indeed.

**Notes**

1. Urry (2000b, 2003) labels his work mobile sociology, the sociology of mobilities, or the sociology of flows. Castells (1996, 1997a, 1997b), on whose work Urry strongly builds, uses the concept of network society. Others have been influential in developing this new paradigm—such as Sassen (1994) as well as Mol and Law (1994)—using their own terminology. We will bring these studies together under the common denominator of the sociology of flows, although there are of course also differences between the various authors in this school of thought.

2. Formal theory, following Giddens's usage, refers to the new rules, the new dynamics of time, space, and power, that are not just to be represented and illustrated in empirical examples but also to be discussed in relation to each other as well as the existing "old" rules and theories. Substantive analysis refers to the empirical development of the network society as it unfolds in concrete episodes of world historical time.

3. It is especially the new social movements such as the environmental movement, religious fundamentalists, feminists, and the Zapatistas, and not the old labor movement, that form the heart of the communal resistance against the space of flows: against globalization, capitalist restructuring, organizational networking, and uncontrolled informationalism. But in their decentered activities as producers and distributors of cultural codes, they mirror the networking logic of domination in the informational society.

4. While LCA does exist in all kinds and with respect to all kinds of products, some examples that come close to the topic of this chapter are recent studies on virtual water flows between countries (i.e., the water flows that go along with

product trade), resulting in changing water balances (e.g., Hoekstra and Hung 2002; Hoekstra 2003). In terms of industrial ecology, the core idea is to study the industrial system from an ecosystem angle. This perspective basically involves two starting points. First, the industrial system itself should be interpreted and analyzed as a particular system with an "internal" distribution of materials, energy, and information flows (not unlike the ecosystem). Second, the industrial system relies on (outside) resources and services provided by the biosphere. Both the flows within the industrial system and between the system and the biosphere have to be optimized from a closed-loop perspective, as is exemplified by natural ecosystems. Several authors take the ecological analogy further and seek to apply principles from biological processes to industrial processes (e.g., the use of solar power as the sole energy source; the application of decentralized, self-organizing processes). Several industrial ecologists, however, do acknowledge that the ecosystem analogy cannot be extended to all aspects of industrial processes (e.g., Lowe 1997; Boons and Baas 1997).

5. This originates from the OECD (1991) driver-state-response trilogy, which found its way—in various modified forms—into several UN studies, to finally develop into the European Environmental Agency's DPSIR methodology.

6. In the 1990s, studies in Schnaiberg's treadmill-of-production perspective surpassed the national level, making the distinction between WST and treadmill-of-production scholars less clear (cf. especially the studies of Ken Gould). Still, the North-South relation is much stronger in the world-system studies of Roberts and Grimes (e.g., Roberts et al. 2003) and Bunker (e.g., 1996; Bunker and Ciccantell 1995).

7. At the same time, we would hasten to point out that Urry forms a positive exception among social theorists for his wide and continuing efforts to give the environment more than only a marginal place. He shares with social theorists such as Giddens and Beck the crucial role attached to the ecological discourse in processes of globalization. But as a social geographer, he details his environmental analysis much further in, among others, *Contested Natures* (McNaughten and Urry 1998) and the sections on ecological citizenship in *Sociology beyond Society* (Urry 2000b).

8. The additions and withdrawals perspective should not be seen as only relevant for neo-Marxist or political economy–inspired schools of thought in environmental sociology. As indicated earlier, this pair of concepts and related ones flourish widely in various environmental sociology traditions (including ecological modernization theory and WST), most environmental studies paradigms (such as industrial ecology and the environmental system analysis), and hands-on theories used by policymakers.

# References

Ayres, R. U., and L. Ayres. 1996. *Industrial Ecology: Towards Closing the Materials Cycle*. London: Edward Elgar.

Barham, B., S. G. Bunker, and D. O'Hearn, eds. 1987. *States, Firms, and Raw Materials: The World Economy and Ecology of Aluminum.* Madison: University of Wisconsin Press.

Bauman, Z. 1987. *Legislators and Interpreters.* Cambridge: Polity Press.

Beck, U. 1992. From Industrial Society to the Risk Society: Questions of Survival, Social Structure, and Ecological Enlightenment. *Theory, Culture, and Society* 9:97–123.

Boersema, J. J., J. W. Copius Peereboom, and W. T. de Groot. 1991. *Basisboek Milieukunde.* 4th ed. Amsterdam: Boom.

Boons, F. A. A., and L. W. Baas. 1997. Types of Industrial Ecology: The Problem of Coordination. *Journal of Cleaner Production* 5, no. 1–2:79–86.

Bunker, S. G. 1996. Raw Material and the Global Economy: Oversights and Distortions in Industrial Ecology. *Society and Natural Resources* 9:419–429.

Bunker, S. G., and P. S. Ciccantell. 1995. Restructuring Markets, Reorganizing Nature: An Examination of Japanese Strategies for Access to Raw Materials. *Journal of World-Systems Research* 1, no. 3:1–63.

Callon, M. 1980. The State and Technical Innovation: A Case Study of the Electrical Vehicle in France. *Research Policy* 9:358–376.

Callon, M. 1987. Society in the Making: The Study of Technology as a Tool for Sociological Analysis. In *The Social Construction of Technological Systems: New Directions in the Sociology and History of Technology,* ed. W. E. Bijker, T. P. Hughes, and T. J. Pinch, 83–103. Cambridge: MIT Press.

Carson, R. 1962. *Silent Spring.* London: Penguin.

Castells, M. 1996. *The Rise of the Network Society.* Vol. 1 of *The Information Age: Economy, Society, and Culture.* Oxford: Blackwell.

Castells, M. 1997a. *The Power of Identity.* Vol. 2 of *The Information Age: Economy, Society, and Culture.* Oxford: Blackwell.

Castells, M. 1997b. *End of Millennium.* Vol. 3 of *The Information Age: Economy, Society, and Culture.* Oxford: Blackwell.

Côté, R. P. and E. Cohen-Rosenthal. 1998. Designing Eco-industrial Parks: A Synthesis of Some Experiences. *Journal of Cleaner Production* 6:181–188.

Daly, H., ed. 1973. *Towards a Steady-State Economy.* San Francisco: Freeman.

Daly, H. 1977. *Steady-State Economics: The Political Economy of Bio-Physical Equilibrium and Moral Growth.* San Francisco: Freeman.

Durkheim, E. 1897/1982. *The Rules of Sociological Method.* Trans. W. D. Halls. Glencoe, IL: Free Press.

Fischer-Kowalski, M. 1997. Society's Metabolism: On the Childhood and Adolescence of a Rising Conceptual Star. In *The International Handbook of Environmental Sociology,* ed. M. Redclift and G. Woodgate, 119–137. Cheltenham, UK: Edward Elgar.

Fischer-Kowalski, M., and H. Haberl. 1997. Tons, Joules, and Money: Modes of Production and Their Sustainability Problems. *Society and Natural Resources* 10, no. 1:61–85.

Geiser, K. 2001. *Materials Matter: Towards a Sustainable Materials Policy.* Cambridge: MIT Press.

Giddens, A. 1976. *New Rules of Sociological Method.* London: Hutchinson.

Giddens, A. 1984. *The Constitution of Society.* Cambridge: Polity Press.

Goldfrank, W. L., D. Goodman, and A. Szasz, eds. 1999. *Ecology and the World-System.* Westport, CT: Greenwood Press.

Graedel, T. E., and B. R. Allenby. 1995. *Industrial Ecology.* Englewood Cliffs, NJ: Prentice Hall.

Guy, S., and M. J. Marvin. 1996. Transforming Urban Infrastructure Provision: The Emerging Logic of Demand Side Management. *Policy Studies* 17, no. 2:137–147.

Guy, S., and S. Marvin. 2001. Urban Environmental Flows: Towards a New Way of Seeing. In *Urban Infrastructure in Transition: Networks, Buildings, Plans*, ed. T. Moss, S. Guy, and S. Marvin, 22–37. London: Earthscan.

Hannigan, J. 1995. *Environmental Sociology: A Social Constructionist Perspective.* London: Routledge.

Hardt, M., and A. Negri. 2000. *Empire.* Cambridge: Harvard University Press.

Hoekstra, A. Y., ed. 2003. Virtual Water Trade. In *Proceedings of the International Expert Meeting on Virtual Water Trade*. Research report series no. 12. Rotterdam: IHE.

Hoekstra, A. Y., and P. Q. Hung. 2002. Virtual Water Trade: A Quantification of Virtual Water Flows between Nations in Relation to International Crop Trade. Research report series no. 11. Rotterdam: IHE.

Hoogvelt, A. 1997. *Globalisation and the Postcolonial World: The New Political Economy of Development.* Houdsmills, UK: Macmillan Publishers.

Irwin, A. 2001. *Sociology and the Environment: A Critical Introduction to Society, Nature, and Knowledge.* Cambridge: Polity Press.

Jackson, T., and R. Clift. 1998. Where's the Profit in Industrial Ecology? *Journal of Industrial Ecology* 2, no. 1:3–5.

Jänicke, M. 1986. *Staatsversagen: Die Ohnmacht der Politik in die Industriegesellschaft.* Munich: Piper.

Latour, B. 1987. *Science in Action.* Milton Keynes, UK: Open University Press.

Leroy, P., and N. Nelissen. 1999. *Social and Political Sciences of the Environment: Three Decades of Research in the Netherlands.* Utrecht: International Books.

Leydesdorff, L. 2002. May There Be a "Socionomy" beyond "Sociology"? *Scipolicy, The Journal of Science and Health Policy* 2, no. 1:1–11.

Lowe, E. A. 1997. Creating By-product Resource Exchanges: Strategies for Eco-industrial Parks. *Journal of Cleaner Production* 5, no. 1–2:57–65.

McNaughten, P., and J. Urry. 1998. *Contested Natures*. London: Sage.

Meadows, D. H., D. L. Meadows, J. Randers, and W. W. Behrens III. 1972. *Limits to Growth*. London: Pan.

Mol, A., and J. Law. 1994. Regions, Networks, and Fluids: Anemia and Social Typology. *Social Studies of Science* 24:641–671.

Mol, A. P. J., and G. Spaargaren. 2002. Ecological Modernization and the Environmental State. In *The Environmental State under Pressure*, ed. A. P. J. Mol and F. H. Buttel, 33–52. London: Elsevier.

Odum, H. T. 1971. *Environment, Power, and Society*. John Wiley and Sons.

Odum, H. T., and E. C. Odum. 2000. *Modeling for All Scales: An Introduction to System Simulation*. San Diego: Academic Press.

OECD. 1991. *Environmental Indicators: A Preliminary Set*. Paris: OECD.

Oosterveer P. (2003). Labeling: A New Arrangement in Regulating Global Flows of Food? Paper presented at the Governing Environmental Flows conference, Wageningen, June 12–14.

Presas L. M. S. 2005. *Transnational Buildings in Local Environments*. Hampshire, UK: Ashgate.

Rifkin, J. 2000. *The Age of Access: How the Shift from Ownership to Access Is Transforming Modern Life*. London: Penguin.

Roberts, J. T., P. E. Grimes, and J. L. Manale. 2003. Social Roots of Global Environmental Change: A World-Systems Analysis of Carbon Dioxide Emissions. *Journal of World-Systems Research* 9, no. 2:277–315.

Sassen, S. 1994. *Cities in a World Economy*. Thousand Oaks, CA: Pine Forge Press.

Schnaiberg, A. 1980. *The Environment: From Surplus to Scarcity*. New York: Oxford University Press.

Shove, E. 1997. Revealing the Invisible: Sociology, Energy, and the Environment. In *The International Handbook of Environmental Sociology*, ed. M. Redclift and G. Woodgate, 261–273. Cheltenham, UK: Edward Elgar.

Spaargaren, G., Arthur P. J. Mol, and F. H. Buttel, eds. 2000. *Environment and Global Modernity*. London: Sage.

Spangenberg, J., A. Femia, F. Hinterberger, and H. Schütz 1998. *Material Flow–Based Indicators in Environmental Reporting*. Environmental issues series no. 14. Copenhagen: European Environmental Agency.

Swaan, A. de. 1988. *In Care of the State*. Cambridge: Polity Press.

Touraine, A. 1995. *Critique of Modernity*. Oxford: Basil Blackwell.

Urry, J. 2000a. Mobile Sociology. *British Journal of Sociology* 51, no. 1:185–203.

Urry, J. 2000b. *Sociology beyond Society.* London: Routledge.

Urry, J. 2003. *Global Complexity.* Cambridge: Polity Press.

Vliet, B. J. M. van. 2002. Greening the Grid: The Ecological Modernisation of Network-Bound Systems. PhD diss., Wageningen University.

Yearley, S. 1997. Science and the Environment. In *The International Handbook of Environmental Sociology*, ed. M. Redclift and G. Woodgate, 227–236. Cheltenham, UK: Edward Elgar.

# 3

## The Environmental State and Environmental Flows: The Need to Reinvent the Nation-State

Martin Jänicke

The management of environmental flows needs new concepts of governance. What is the role of government in this context? And what is the role of the nation-state? The fact that environmental flows are typically of a global nature leads to the question of whether the nation-state is still able to fulfill its relevant functions in times of economic and political globalization. I will argue in this chapter that states remain important actors in environmental governance, although the nature of the tasks at hand and the ways in which they must be fulfilled have changed over time. I maintain that with the economic and political globalization of environmental problems and policies, there emerges the need to rethink and to some extent even reinvent the environmental state. Contrary to the thesis of the withering away of the state, it is possible to show with respect to the European situation that state-anchored forms of environmental governance even gain significance under globalization. Before developing these assertions, I would like to briefly introduce and discuss the concepts of *environmental flows* and *environmental state*.

### The Cleaning and Reduction of Environmental Flows

The concept of environmental flows in questions of governance and state regulation was introduced by Mol and Spaargaren (2003). Using this concept, they focus on both the "changing material flows in products and environmental goods" and the "social relations and networks that give origin to, or accompany," such flows (Mol et al. 2003, 5–6). This concept may be more relevant in theory than in empirical research or the field of policy consultation. As a theoretical notion, it is innovative and seems to have a high heuristic potential. It may be useful as a way to identify different institutional contexts that frame the environmentally relevant material flows (Adriaanse et al. 1997). By adopting this broader approach rather than focusing on a single emission, product, or sector, one can enlarge and possibly optimize the spectrum of intervention. This includes the identification of the main veto players in the chain of environmental flows (Tsebelis 2002).

Without discussing the concept in detail, I would propose to first focus the concept on material flows in terms of their environmental impacts, and then analyze the societal conditions that influence the flows in a second step. Material flows in terms of their environmental impacts are complex in their own right. They include not only movements of matter within space (e.g., as basic materials, goods, or emissions) but also several changes in their environmental impacts as well as different combinations with other material flows. Indeed, as environmental flows they also have a societal dimension because they are both essentially influenced by the system of consumption and production, and relevant as far as the human environment and health is concerned.

At the Free University, Berlin, we have so far used the concept of material flows in connection with a model of policy intervention (Jänicke 1995; Jänicke and Zieschank 2004). For many good reasons, the scientific debate has come to trace environmental impacts back to material flows. But it makes sense to use the more comprehensive concept of environmental flows to denominate both the material flows and the possible disturbing processes within the environment. The notion of environmental flows—if conceived of as material flows in terms of their environmental impacts—could prevent us from using a too simplistic concept of material use leading to undifferentiated postulates like "factor 10" or "factor 4."[1] This is often restricted to a "tonnage ideology," which has little to say about the various kinds of environmental impacts that tend to be quite different, and therefore require different forms of observation and control.

Instead of factor 10 postulates, I suggest one that I call the cleaning and reduction of material flows (see below). The cleaning of environmental flows (e.g., by the substitution of dangerous substances) seems to be even more important than their reduction. The paradigm for this postulate could be the new "REACH system"[2] of the EU Commission, or also the field of climate protection, where the reduction of energy consumption is of course a precondition for any success, but the cleansing of the energy mix from fossil and nuclear energies is even more important. For a long time, the paradigm for dematerialization and factor 10 (or 4) has been the area of waste management and recycling. This area, however, comprises a segment of environmental flows that is too small (less than 10 percent) and should not be overburdened by the general task of resource management.

Figure 3.1 provides a schematic model of the governance of environmental flows. As noted in figure 3.1, environmental flows typically involve four stages: the input of environmental resources; the conversion process of production and consumption (constituting the "driving forces" in terms of the well-known OECD model (<http://www.oecd.org/dataoecd/0/52/1933638.pdf>); the output of negative environmental effects (the "pressures" of the OECD model); and the resulting environmental *state* of the landscape, resources, species, or ecological functions (leading to final "impacts").

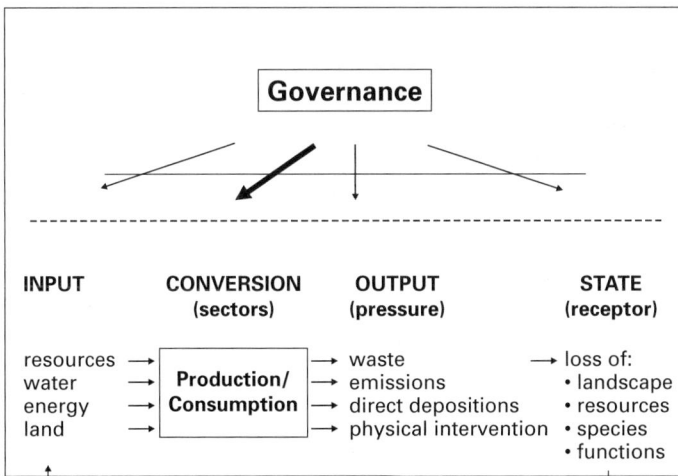

**Figure 3.1**
Governance of environmental flows
*Source*: Jänicke and Zieschank (2004)

One can similarly distinguish four stages in the development of environmental policy. The starting point in the 1970s was the visibly bad state of the environment. Initially, the main approach was the reparation and management of environmental damages, combined with some insufficient reactive interventions like the dilution of pollution ("high-chimney policy"). The next step consisted of attempts in the 1980s to reduce the level of environmental pressure. Here, the main policy approach was the use of technical prescriptions for emissions and waste, typically leading to add-on technologies. The basic idea was to separate the system of production and consumption from the environment as much as possible, essentially by technical means and technical prescriptions. For various reasons, this proved to be possible only to a certain degree. The limits to this approach can be observed, for example, in the field of agriculture or regarding dissipative losses of all kind. In the third stage, which occurred primarily in the 1990s, environmental policy was therefore shifted to bring about a conversion process within the system of production and consumption. Here, the general governance approach has so far been the broadest. The policy orientation has changed from technical standards (related to specified environmental impacts) to sectoral strategies, based on dialogue and cooperation. The debate on modern environmental governance is essentially a debate about the governance of conversion processes. The final stage—still under construction—could possibly be the reduction of the input of material flows since there is almost no environmental pressure without material flows. The taxation of the input to stimulate efficient resource use, including recycling, could be a plausible instrument for such preventive strategies. Yet the exante reduction of material flows necessarily leads to a reduced importance of powerful sectors such as mining, energy, basic industries, or construction (via the reduced input of land). For many reasons that cannot be discussed here, this approach has proven to be extremely difficult. Beyond the taxation of mineral oil, only a few input taxes exist in OECD countries.

Therefore, the environmental flows within the system of production and consumption currently are—and remain—the central challenge to modern environmental governance. This development of the environmental policy discourse has led to several proposals. The most significant is the proposed "Framework Programme on Sustainable Production and Consumption Patterns," developed by the UN Johannesburg Summit in 2002. In an attempt to implement this proposal, the EU Commission at the start of this century launched an initiative on the sustainable use of natural resources.

The sphere of production and consumption is the most important field for a strategic cleaning and reduction of environmental flows. The governance of environmental flows is necessarily multistakeholder, multisector, and multilevel governance (see figure 3.2). The traditional instruments of environmental state intervention (both standards and taxes) are still crucial—for instance, in the field of climate protection (obligatory feed-in tariffs or energy-efficiency standards like the Japanese "Top-Runner Program").[3] But at the same time, additional approaches for making better use of the existing motivation and innovation potential within society and the business sector are necessary. Hence, all kinds of modern cooperative governance have gained importance, not least to avoid complicated decision-making processes by negotiating "in the shadow of hierarchy" (Scharpf 1998). This includes sectoral strategies and environmental policy integration.

As a result of the Rio process and the experiences with environmental policy reform after 1992, patterns of governance have become more and more differentiated and complex. This is a process of trial and error, and it is still going on.

## The Environmental State

The concept of the "green state" (Dryzek et al. 2003) or environmental state (Mol and Buttel 2002; Mol et al. 2003) may be useful in this context. It has been invented and reinvented several times since the late 1980s (Kloepfer 1989). Today, it is a possible formula for the ecological dimension of modern governance in terms of the three-pillar approach to sustainable development. Beyond this, the environmental state relates to one of the three cross-sectoral metafunctions or "core interests" (Dryzek et al. 2003) that can be attributed to modern government in general—the economic, social, and ecological metafunctions, which determine more than one policy field (see also Jänicke 1990, 8–9):

• The economic metafunction—which is historically the oldest—provides the necessary regulatory framework and infrastructure for economic development and growth. The relevant policy fields (beyond economic affairs) include energy, transportation, agriculture, housing, finance, and research and education. The main political proponents are industrial organizations as well as liberal and conservative parties.

• The social metafunction comprises the provision of social security and redistribution (the "welfare state"). The relevant policy fields include social affairs, the labor market, health, education, housing, (public) transportation, and consumer protection. The main political proponents are trade unions, welfare organizations, churches, and left-wing parties.

• The ecological metafunction assures the protection of the environment (the environmental state). The relevant policy fields (beyond environmental protection) include research and education, consumer protection, and especially the environmental divisions of all those policy sectors responsible for environmentally intensive production sectors. The main political proponents are environmental NGOs, parts of the media, and the scientific community as well as green (and partly other) parties.

Already in the late 1980s, Michael Kloepfer, Ernst Forsthoff, and Hasso Hofmann had used the concept of the environmental state (*Umweltstaat*) in the context of the basic objectives of constitutional law. They distinguished the ecological functions of the modern state from the functions of the "state under the rule of law," the "industrial state," and the welfare state (Kloepfer 1989, see also Callies 2001). Later on, Dente conceived of the "ecological state" as "a broker" playing with all the involved actors "a complex set of games with the idea of decreasing resource consumption at all levels" (1998, 11). This notion is close to an understanding of the environmental state as the core of governing environmental flows (Mol et al. 2003). Typically, the environmental (ecological, green) state is also defined in the context of global governance.

The following relationships between environmental flows and the environmental state may be especially relevant. First, environmental flows not only have different effects on environmental media such as air, water, or soil but also differ from one sector to the other—for example, from energy production to the chemical industry, or from agriculture to construction. As far as environmental impacts are concerned, the management of environmental flows has therefore to deal with the inherent logic of each sector. Environmental policy integration and sectoral environmental strategies are an indispensable part of cleansing and reducing environmental flows. If one takes into consideration the cross-sectoral importance of environmental issues, the concept of the environmental state proves to be analytically useful.

Second, the management of environmental flows within the system of production and consumption is impossible without giving a strong role as well as responsibility to those actors who cause and influence such flows. Compared to governments that act in a narrower legal framework with many veto players in the decision-making process, retailers or companies are often in a better position to end the use of substances or products causing environmental stress. Also, the innovation potential of industrial actors can be activated and better used if there is a close and cooperative relationship between the government and the target group. The network could be broadened and strengthened by including environmental scientists, NGOs, or other civil society actors. The governance of environmental flows is thus commonly achieved by public and private actors.

Finally, in a similar manner, the governance of environmental flows means reaching beyond the nation-state. The flows of raw materials, (semi)goods, emissions, or waste often cross national borders. Their management, therefore, cannot be restricted to national policies. Consequently, the governance of environmental flows must be conceived of as multilevel governance and governing beyond the nation-state. This is why Dente and Kloepfer stress the role of the ecological state within the global context.

All this leads to a highly complex picture of modern multisectoral, multistakeholder, and multilevel environmental governance. Figure 3.2 aims to portray this complexity by showing graphically the different dimensions of environmental governance: social actors (civil society, government, and business), political levels (individual to global level), and environmentally sensitive economic sectors (industry, energy, transport, and so on). The situation can be even more complex if we bear in mind that the relationship between the actors involved can range from a one-sided government influence on industry (as in the beginning of environ-

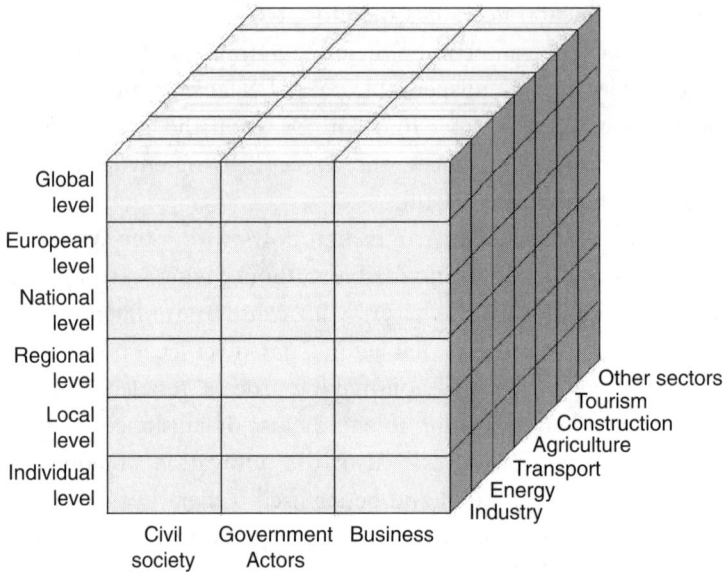

**Figure 3.2**
Dimensions of environmental governance
*Source*: Jänicke (2003)

mental policy), to a strong business influence on government (even as capture), to various forms of cooperation between the two sides.

### Reinventing Government

There are three main challenges to the role of government and the nation-state, all of which seem to contradict the postulate of a strong and more effective environmental state. The first key challenge is that of environmental governance. Today, environmental goods are produced by a large number of public and/or private actors. This leads to utterly complex actor constellations across sectors and levels, and has given rise to the concept of governance, often conceived of as a substitute for government. Political globalization—the globalization of policies (and especially that of environmental policy), which is said to reduce the role of the sovereign nation-state—is the second key challenge. Finally, there is the challenge of economic globalization; the role of international markets and MNCs is said to put pressure on the scope of action of the nation-state.

Before turning to the role of the nation-state in the process of political and economic globalization, it is worth mentioning that in the context of environmental governance the role of government in general needs to be reinvented. Even if voluntary agreements were a general solution, someone would have to make sure that the ultimate goal is finally reached (OECD 2003). These soft instruments do not work without the final say of governments, which includes the ultimate option of hard regulatory interventions (negotiation in the shadow of hierarchy). In addition, participation, "voluntarization," and consensus need to be complemented by competent moderation and professional public management. Due to market failure, environmental innovation and its diffusion also needs governmental support. Sectoral strategies and the transition management of dirty industries necessitate a strong role for government policies. The government is the main address, if there are problems such as flooding or BSE. In the late 1990s, almost 80 percent of the EU directives and regulations were still of the "command-and-control" variety (Holzinger et al. 2003).

In this context, it should also be underlined that cooperative approaches to governance need additional government capacities. The total administrative load that is required to develop such modes of government can be "surprisingly high" (Jordan et al. 2003, 222). The U.K. environment ministry, for example, recently devoted seventeen people to negotiating forty-two voluntary agreements.

There is no doubt that government as a bureaucratic rule-making machine—with its inherent tendency to expand its regulatory activity—has reached its limits. There is also the relevant potential of activated environmental self-regulation in the sphere of production and consumption. This private potential of action was the starting point for the debate on modern governance and steering beyond government. Modern governance is especially important if one turns to the difficult task of influencing environmental flows in the business sector—for example, flows along the chain of production and the life cycle of a product. Nevertheless, in the growing complexity of environmental governance, the question of final responsibility for solving the relevant environmental problems has become crucial. If everybody is responsible, nobody will be responsible. In this regard, there is no functional equivalent to national government. Its role has changed, but it has not diminished.

## The Environmental State and the Internationalization of Policies

We are faced with similar questions in relation to the nation-state and national government. Their roles have changed, and there is without any doubt a loss of national sovereignty in the context of global governance. But is this equivalent to a general withering away of the environmental state? Or has the loss in sovereignty been compensated by the new potential of collective government action? Are environmental policy and the governance of environmental flows different from other policies that have come under high pressure in the context of globalization?

There are indeed several restrictions on national environmental policy: restrictions due to WTO regulations, EU internal market regulations, or the present role of the United States in the global environmental policy arena. But the fear of a general weakening of the nation-state has so far not been confirmed by empirical research.

Regarding the role of national governments in global environmental governance, I would like to present some theses, based on different empirical studies.

*Thesis 1*    Globalization has created a policy arena for pioneer countries, at least in environmental policy. And pioneer countries play an important role in the development of global environmental governance.

Pioneering environmental policy of certain (highly developed) countries has always been possible since 1970. The influence of small, innovative countries in global policy has never before been as critical as today in the field of environmental policy (Andersen and Liefferink 1997; Jänicke and Weidner 1997; Jänicke and Jacob 2001; Andersson and Mol 2002). This influence is especially significant with respect to the development of global environmental governance as observed in Rio de Janeiro in 1992 and Johannesburg in 2002. Political globalization has created a policy arena for political competition, wherein the pioneer roles of countries are relevant (Meyer et al. 1997). International institutions like the OECD or UNEP, but also global networks of all kinds, provide a basis for benchmarking and competition in global environmental policy. Regulatory competition gives support to domestic innovative industries or protects the "national regulatory culture" against pressures to adapt to policy innovation from abroad. The present regulatory competition regarding fuel-efficient products shows signs of "green protectionism," if we take the Top-Runner Program of Japan's METI as a far-reaching example.

*Thesis 2*   The nation-state is both the subject and the object of global environmental policy learning and lesson drawing.

The national government is the subject of policy learning on how to solve environmental problems. At the same time, national governments are looking for the best practices, observing other governments (Rose 1993; Bennett 1991; Kern et al. 2001; Tews et al. 2003). Successful environmental policy innovations—the introduction of new institutions, instruments, or strategies—are thereby often adopted by other governments. This improvement by imitation can be conceived of as horizontal policy learning. It is an important mechanism of global environmental policy development and policy convergence. International institutions such as the OECD, UNEP, or special regimes play a crucial role as agents for the diffusion of environmental policy innovations. This role seems to be more important than the creation of policy innovations by the international institutions themselves. Figure 3.3 provides some examples for the process of diffusion of environmental policy innovations (such as environmental ministries or green plans) from pioneer countries to the rest of the world. The speed of diffusion increased in the 1990s, apparently due to the fact that the mobilization prior to and after Rio greatly affected the process of environmental policy diffusion. This may imply capacity building at the national level, even if the divergence of capacities (behind the convergent policy patterns) remains high.

*Thesis 3*   Globalization has very different effects on policy areas.

The international pressure on wages as well as taxes on mobile sources or social security provisions is a reality under globalization (Scharpf 1998). But environmental (as well as health or security) standards have

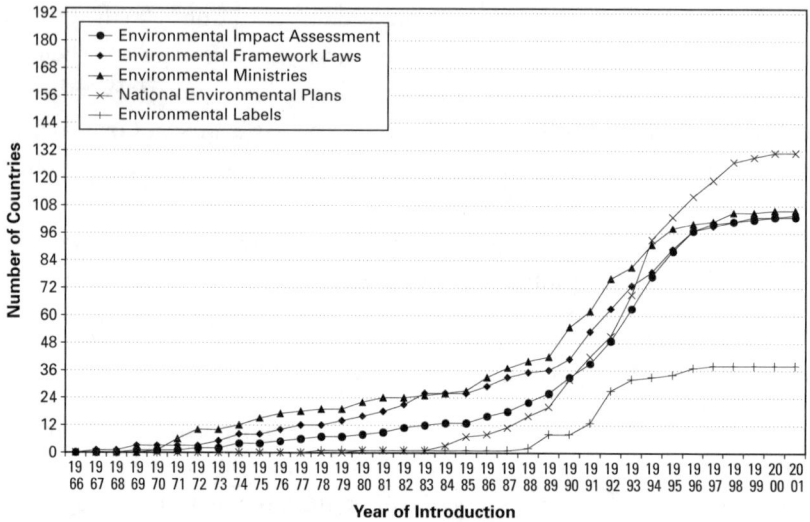

**Figure 3.3**
The global diffusion of five environmental policy innovations, 1966–2001
*Source*: Busch and Jörgens (2004)

their own rules (e.g., the WTO) and logic in international regulatory competition. It seems that the conditions for the concerted actions of environmental ministers in the global arena are at least not adverse, if compared with other policies. Environmental policy has demonstrated considerable competence in using the opportunity structure of multilevel governance.

*Thesis 4* Environmental policy innovation as well as environmental policy regression is primarily caused at the national level.

In an expert inquiry for twenty different countries, we (Jänicke and Weidner 1997) sought to identify the main sectors with environmental problems and restrictions. According to our survey, it is the energy sector—followed by road traffic, agriculture, and construction—that faces the most persistent environmental restrictions. Interestingly, these sectors do not generally face fierce global competition, and in fact, the opposite is largely the case—for example, the fact that agriculture and the power and construction industries strongly depend on domestic demand. Again, it is often the nation-state (typically influenced by domestic polluting industries) that resists international regulation. Countries such as the United States, Japan, the United Kingdom, or more recently, Denmark are examples of the double option of being either an innovator or a laggard in environmental policy. This range of options, at least for the highly developed countries, once again contradicts the argument of a general weakening of the nation-state.

*Thesis 5*    Global environmental governance strongly depends on both the competence and creativity of national governments, and on the international system as a complex mechanism of policy diffusion and coordination.

Of course, this ("horizontal") view of the role of national governments is no alternative to the ("vertical") view of international institutions. The transformation of the nation-state is a transformation *within* the context of international policy networks and institutions. And the international system is an indispensable mechanism of policy diffusion and coordination. Moreover, the international system provides the policy arena, which is important for pioneer roles and pioneering alliances in environmental policy.

The interesting question is whether international regulation or the competitive role of pioneer countries represents the main engine for global environmental policy development. At the 2002 Johannesburg Summit, the EU (strongly influenced by the German government) for the first time went beyond the (often-minimalist) global consensus by stressing its pioneer role. Together with a large group of about ninety countries, the EU decided to pursue an ambitious policy to support renewable energies (the Johannesburg Renewable Energy Coalition). This new orientation focused more on horizontal mechanisms of innovation/diffusion and competitive pressure than on global consensus at any price.

*Thesis 6*    There is no substitute for the nation-state in multilevel environmental governance in terms of financial resources, professional competence, coercive power, or the pressure for legitimation.

National governments have significantly more staff than, for example, the secretariats of international regimes (the USEPA in 2005 has eighteen hundred employees versus a few hundred in most international organizations). As a rule, the state is also the most complex nexus of relationships, being part of highly differentiated global and domestic expert networks (French 2002, 141). The state generally has the highest visibility and is the "first address" in case of complaints (Willke 1992). There is no comparable public pressure on political actors in Brussels or even at the global level. Finally, it is the national innovation system and the national lead market that play the most important role in the process of global ecological modernization.

## The Environmental State in the Global Economy

The most pessimistic arguments regarding the capacity of the nation-state focus on the presumably restrictive role of the global economy. The most popular argument is the RTB hypothesis of a regulatory downward competition between countries, in which the positions of governments in fields like environmental policy deteriorate.

*Thesis 7*    There is no RTB in environmental policy—but why?

Several empirical cross-national studies have rejected the RTB hypothesis. This discussion was extremely important and has provided many insights into the role of environmental policy in the competition between national economies. Many arguments against the RTB hypothesis are well-known today (Vogel 2001; Wheeler 2001; Drezner 2001). Countries and companies that trade with countries with strict regulations tend to have stricter policies themselves (Eliste and Fredricksson 1998; Foljanty-Jost 1997)—and the largest markets are rather strictly regulated. The globalization of environmental policy has partly changed the framework conditions of the world market (Jänicke and Weidner 1997; Weidner and Jänicke 2002; Vogel 2001). Regulatory competition with respect to the environment often creates first-mover advantages for national economies. This is part of the larger pattern of global competition (Porter and Van der Linde 1995; Wallace 1995) and is essential for the development of "environmental lead markets" (Jänicke and Jacob 2001). Multinationals tend to use the same standards everywhere (Wheeler 2001). Differences in environmental standards therefore tend to decrease; generally, they are less significant than differences in, for example, labor costs or taxes.

In addition to the preceding observations in the recent literature that cautions against the RTB hypothesis, I would like to add three arguments. First, to a certain degree, the environmental issue has become a dimension of general technological progress. Forty percent of technological innovations in 2010 are anticipated to be relevant for environmental improvement (Faucheux 2000). Second, the environmental issue has become important in light of the international competition for innovation. Finally, strict environmental regulations (within limits) remain a possibility to protect or support national industries. There have been some complaints about green protectionism—for example, when the EU Commission proposed a comprehensive regulation for chemical substances (REACH) in 2003. The ambitious Top-Runner Program of the Japanese METI noted above, with its aim of increasing the energy efficiency of even imported products, was prompted by similar protests from the U.S. administration about a violation of WTO rules (which interestingly did not prevent the METI from extending the program). All three assertions are key for convincing (at least) some OECD governments to regulate environmental flows by assuming a pioneer role that may also influence other countries.

*Thesis 8* Pioneer countries in environmental policy are highly competitive.

The *Global Competitiveness Report 2002* shows a remarkably high correlation ($R^2 = 0.89$) between the ambitiousness of environmental policy and the competitiveness of a country (Schwab et al. 2000). Other studies have revealed a similar relationship (Sturm et al. 2000). These correlations, of course, do not constitute causal proof. The causal relations can go in both directions, and third factors (e.g., GNP per capita) may be crucial in explaining both competitiveness and the ambitiousness of environmental policy. But in light of such a sizable correlation, one can no longer insist on the traditional economic argument of an immanent contradiction between competitiveness and an ambitious environmental policy. The strong intercorrelation of the third-factor GNP with environmental policy and economic competitiveness can be explained by the following formula: highly developed countries are characterized by both high perceived environmental pressure and a high capacity to react to that pressure. The interplay of both factors is the main driving force for environmental innovation.

*Thesis 9*   The open ("globalized") national economy is characterized by strong government, both in size and scope.

The fear of general economic pressure, linked to the globalization process, which would reduce the role of governments, especially in open, globalized national economies, has not been supported by empirical research. Cross-national studies have shown, for example, that public expenditures in open economies in the OECD tend to be relatively higher (see Cameron 1978; Garrett 1998; Bernauer 2000). It seems plausible to assume that countries that are highly integrated into the international economy tend to have large governments and a larger scope of government activities. Open economies: need a well-developed infrastructure for successful international competition, which in turn means more money and more public activities in fields such as education, R&D, or transport; require that there be compensational, distributional, and other effects of rapid structural changes connected, for instance, with a low degree of protection of domestic industries; and need more regulatory activities of all kinds that are necessary to adapt to international developments such as global standards.

*Thesis 10*   New environmental technologies are created within national lead markets, which are induced by government support.

The governance of environmental flows at the global level as well as the ecological modernization of the world market depends on the existence of national lead markets for environmental innovations (Jänicke and Jacob 2001; Beise 2001). The United States as the lead market for the Internet, Japan as the lead market for the fax machine, or Finland as the lead market for mobile phones are well-known examples. Empirically, lead markets are characterized by, for instance, high per capita incomes, demanding and innovative buyers, high quality standards, and pressures for further innovation (see also Meyer-Krahmer 1999).

Lead markets for environmental technologies, however, are characterized by two additional factors. First, environmental innovations relate to global environmental needs. This means that there is a global market potential. The possibility of a global market potential may help us to understand why the environmental issue is not in a hopeless situation in the global economy. Second, lead markets for environmental innovations are typically not only stimulated by the higher environmental preferences of consumers in that country; due to market failures, lead markets also depend on special promotion measures (sometimes by NGOs) or political intervention in the market. To cite an expert on the car industry: "A complex interplay has begun between regulation and competition. The regulatory drive to push down ... emissions has forced companies to compete against each other on environmental criteria" (McLauchlin 2004).

Here again, the role of the highly developed nation-state and pioneer countries is crucial. In times of economic globalization, multinational enterprises are still in need of both production locations where the risky release of a new environmental technology finds public support, and innovative buyers who are willing to pay a higher price and accept initial technological problems until the innovation becomes cheap and sophisticated enough to succeed on global markets. Regulators in Denmark and Germany created favorable market conditions, and energy consumers in both countries were willing to bear the initially high price for wind-power technology until it became competitive and profitable on the global market. Needless to say, the strengthening of wind power results in a reduction of problematic environmental flows—for example, from fossil fuels or nuclear energy.

### Reservations

The foregoing arguments should not, however, be misunderstood as an overly optimistic picture of the role of the environmental state in the global arena. In general, we are not very successful in the field of environmental protection. And the task of governing environmental flows within the system of production and consumption has proven to be even more difficult. So far, the volume of material flows has steadily increased while the environmental quality of these flows has not been significantly improved. The question, then, is whether globalization is really the main obstacle to—or also an opportunity for—far-reaching environmental progress.

Two important reservations need to be stressed. First of all, so far it is only the highly developed nation-state that has preserved or even increased its environmental capacity in the context of globalization. The situation of the less developed countries is still quite different. The second caveat is even more critical in our context. Pioneer policy in the field of the environment has proven to be successful mainly with a "technology-based" policy approach to ecological modernization (Jänicke 1985; Mol 2001). We must acknowledge that structural solutions—changes in the structure of industrial branches or lifestyles—are much more difficult to achieve. In this case, the mechanisms of the market system and those related to the competition for innovation cannot be used, thereby limiting the range of policy options.

## Conclusion

Bearing in mind these reservations, I come to the following conclusions. The (theoretical) concept of the environmental state seems to be useful to describe the role of government in a more comprehensive approach to ecological modernization, here being understood as cleaning and reducing environmental flows within the system of production and consumption. This approach requires multilevel, multisectoral, and multistakeholder governance. In this context, the environmental state may be conceived of as the core of environmental governance.

There are, however, three empirical challenges to the environmental state. The first is the new role of government within the complex set of actor constellations, referred to as environmental governance. The second is the role of the nation-state in the context of political global-ization. Finally, there is the role of the nation-state in the context of economic globalization.

The role of government has changed under globalization. But neither the increased importance of global markets nor that of global governance have weakened the role of national governments in environmental policy.

The scope of action of individual states has sometimes been reduced, but "governments in concert" have expanded and coordinated their regulatory powers. Pioneer policies, regulatory competition, and technological competition initiated by advanced industrial countries play key roles in the development of global environmental governance.

Beyond traditional forms of regulation, the governance of environmental flows in the sphere of production and consumption needs goal-oriented, cooperative, and participative approaches of all kinds. But to stress my point once again, the role of government has changed, not diminished. New management capacities are necessary to make the cooperative approaches more effective. Today, regulatory policy has often a rather latent than manifest function. But the significance of regulatory policy has not been reduced. On the contrary, new intelligent and more flexible regulatory instruments have been introduced recently (the top-runner approach, feed-in tariffs, and emission trading). There is no substitute for elected governments on different political levels when it comes to final responsibilities. It is their role to give the guarantee that the most pressing environmental problems—from climate change to the dissipation of toxic substances—are finally solved.

There is also no substitute for the nation-state in multilevel environmental governance in terms of financial resources, professional competence, staff, coercive power, or public pressure. As a rule, the state is also part of highly differentiated global and domestic expert networks. It has the highest visibility and is the first address in case of complaints.

There is no doubt that even in pioneer countries, there is reason to be dissatisfied with national environmental policies. But an ambitious approach to manage environmental flows should start from the existing national best practices. And if there is no substitute for government and the nation-state, we should finally start improving their role and capacity in environmental governance on different levels.

## Notes

1. Factor 10 and factor 4 are closely related doctrines regarding environmental protection in which the case is made that mere pollution control is inadequate; factor 10 and factor 4 proponents argue that true environmental progress requires the substantial dematerialization of production. Factor 10 and factor 4

refer to different goals for dematerialization. *Factor Four* is the title of a book (von Weizsäcker, Lovins, and Lovins 1998) in which the authors made the case that a 75 percent reduction of material throughput is necessary. Factor 10 is a more lofty goal for dematerialization. It has two assumptions: first, there is a need to reduce materials consumption globally by at least 50 percent; and second, for equity reasons—because 20 percent of the world's population consumes 80 percent of the world's natural resources—the advanced countries should aim for a tenfold improvement in resource efficiency.

2. REACH stands for Registration, Evaluation, and Authorization of CHemicals. This system—a single, integrated database on chemicals—was developed in 2003 to make possible a more progressive management of (the risks of) chemicals in the EU. It was adopted by (EU) Parliament in 2005.

3. The Japanese Top-Runner Program is a (pretty successful) government program setting energy-efficiency standards for a selected number of products that are commercially used in large quantities in Japan. Manufacturers and importers of these goods are obliged to meet these energy standards.

## References

Adriaanse, A., S. Bringezu, A. Hammond, Y. Moriguchi, E. Rodenburg, D. Rogich, and H. Schütz. 1997. *Resource Flows: The Material Basis of Industrial Economies.* Washington, DC: World Resources Institute.

Andersen, M. S., and D. Liefferink, eds. 1997. *European Environmental Policy: The Pioneers.* Manchester: Manchester University Press.

Andersson, M., and A. P. J. Mol. 2002. The Netherlands in the UNFCCC Process: Leadership between Ambition and Reality. *International Environmental Agreements* 2:49–68.

Beise, M. 2001. *Lead Markets: Country Specific Success Factors of the Global Diffusion of Innovations.* Heidelberg: Physica Verlag.

Bennett, C. J. 1991. What Is Policy Convergence and What Causes It? *British Journal of Political Science* 21:215–233.

Bernauer, T. 2000. *Staaten im Weltmarkt: Zur Handlungsfähigkeit von Staaten trotz wirtschaftlicher Globalisierung.* Opladen, Ger.: Verlag Leske + Budrich.

Busch, P.-O., and H. Jörgens. 2004. *Globale Diffusionsmuster umweltpolitischer Innovationen: Forschungsstelle für Umweltpolitik.* Berlin: FFU.

Callies, C. 2001. *Rechtsstaat and Umweltstaat.* Tübingen, Ger.: Mohr Siebeck.

Cameron, D. R. 1978. The Expansion of the Public Economy: A Comparative Analysis. *American Political Science Review* 72, no. 4:1243–1261.

Dente, B. 1998. Towards Sustainability: Instruments and Institutions for the Ecological State. Paper presented at the Concerted Action conference, Florence, May 25.

Drezner, D. W. 2001. Globalization and Policy Convergence. *International Studies Review* 3, no. 1:53–78.

Dryzek, J. S., D. Downes, C. Hunold, and D. Schlosberg, with H.-K. Hernes. 2003. *Green States and the Social Movements: Environmentalism in the United States, United Kingdom, Germany, and Norway.* Oxford: Oxford University Press.

Eliste, P., and P. G. Fredricksson. 1998. *Does Open Trade Result in a Race to the Bottom? Cross-Country Evidence.* Unpublished manuscript (World Bank).

Faucheux, S. 2000. Environmental Policy and Technological Change: Towards Deliberative Governance. In: *Innovation-Oriented Environmental Regulation: Theoretical Approaches and Empirical Analysis,* ed. J. Hemmelskamp, K. Rennings, and F. Leone, 153–171. Heidelberg: Physica Verlag.

Foljanty-Jost, G. 1997. Die Bedeutung Japans für die vergleichende Umweltpolitikforschung—vom Modell zum Auslaufmodell? In: *Umweltpolitik und Staatsversagen: Perspektiven und Grenzen der Umweltpolitikanalyse,* ed. L. Mez and H. Weidner, 314–322. Berlin: Edition Sigma.

French, D. A. 2002. The Role of the State and International Organisations in Reconciling Sustainable Development and Globalization: International Environmental Agreements. *Politics, Law, and Economics* 2:135–150.

Garrett, G. 1998. *Partisan Politics in the Global Economy.* Cambridge: Cambridge University Press.

Holzinger, K., C. Knill, and D. Lehmkuhl, eds. 2003. *Politische Steuerung im Wandel: Der Einfluss von Ideen und Problemstrukturen.* Opladen: Leske + Budrich.

Jänicke, M. 1985. *Preventive Environmental Policy as Ecological Modernisation and Structural Policy.* Berlin: Wissenschaftszentrum Berlin.

Jänicke, M. 1990. *State Failure: The Impotence of Politics in Industrial Society.* Cambridge: Polity Press.

Jänicke, M. 1995. Kriterien und Steuerungsansätze ökologischer Ressourcenpolitik. In: *Umwelt Global,* ed. M. Jänicke, H.-J. Bolle, and A. Carius, 119–136. Berlin: Springer.

Jänicke, M. 2003. The Ambivalence of Environmental Governance. In: *Environmental Governance in Europe,* ed. L. Meuleman, I. Niestroy, and C. Hey, 59–62. The Hague: RMNO.

Jänicke, M., and K. Jacob. 2001. Global Environmental Change and the Nation-State: Lead Markets for Environmental Innovations. Paper presented at the Global Environmental Change and the Nation-State conference, Berlin, December 7–8.

Jänicke, M., and H. Weidner, with H. Jörgens, eds. 1997. *National Environmental Policies: A Comparative Study of Capacity-Building.* Berlin: Springer.

Jänicke, M., and R. Zieschank. 2004. Zielbildung und Indikatoren in der Umweltpolitik. In: *Umweltziele und Indikatoren*, ed. H. Wiggering and F. Müller, 39–62. Berlin: Springer.

Jordan, A., R. K. W. Wurzel, and A. R. Zito, eds. 2003. *New Instruments of Environmental Governance? National Experiences and Prospects.* London: Frank Cass.

Kern, K., H. Jörgens, and M. Jänicke. 2001. The Diffusion of Environmental Policy Innovations. Wissenschaftszentrum Berlin, FS II 01–302.

Kloepfer, M., ed. 1989. *Umweltstaat.* Berlin: Springer.

McLauchlin, A. 2004. Car Industry Rallies to Meet Demands for Lower Emissions. *EuropeanVoice.com* 10, no. 32 (September):23.

Meyer, J. W., D. J. Frank, A. Hironaka, E. Schofer, and N. B. Tuma. 1997. The Structuring of a World Environmental Regime, 1970–1990. *International Organization* 51, no. 4:623–651.

Meyer-Krahmer, F. 1999. Was bedeutet Globalisierung für Aufgaben und Handlungsspielräume nationaler Innovationspolitiken? In: *Innovationspolitik in globalisierten Arenen*, ed. K. Grimmer, S. Kuhlmann, and F. Meyer-Krahmer, 43–74. Opladen, Ger.: Verlag Leske + Budrich.

Mol, A. P. J. 2001. *Globalization and Environmental Reform. The Ecological Modernization of the Global Economy.* Cambridge: MIT Press.

Mol, A. P. J., and F. H. Buttel, eds. 2002. *The Environmental State under Pressure.* London: Elsevier/JAI.

Mol, A. P. J., and G. Spaargaren. 2003. Towards a Sociology of Environmental Flows. Paper presented at the Governing Environmental Flows conference, Wageningen, June 13–14.

Mol, A. P. J., G. Spaargaren, H. Bruyninckx, P. Oosterveer, and S. van den Burg. 2003. Governing Environmental Flows: Reinventing the State in Global Modernity. Paper presented at the Governing Environmental Flows conference, Wageningen, June 13–14.

OECD. 2003. *Voluntary Approaches for Environmental Policy.* Paris: OECD.

Porter, M. E., and C. Van der Linde. 1995. Green and Competitive: Ending the Stalemate. *Harvard Business Review* 9/10:120–134.

Rose, R. 1993. *Lesson-Drawing in Public Policy: A Guide to Learning across Time and Space.* Chatham, NJ: Chatham House.

Scharpf, F. W. 1998. Die Problemlösungsfähigkeit der Mehrebenenpolitik in Europa. In: *Regieren in entgrenzten Räumen: Sonderheft 29 der PVS*, ed. B. Kohler-Koch, 121–144. Opladen, Ger.: Westdeutscher Verlag.

Schwab, K., M. E. Porter, and J. D. Sachs, eds. 2000. *Global Competitiveness Report 2000.* New York: Oxford University Press.

Sturm, A., M. Wackernagel, and K. Müller. 2000. *The Winners and Losers in Global Competition. Why Eco-Efficiency Reinforces Competitiveness: A Study of Forty-four Nations.* Chur, Switzerland: Verlag Rüegger.

Tews, K., P.-O. Busch, and H. Jörgens. 2003. The Diffusion of New Environmental Policy Instruments. *European Journal of Political Research* 42:569–600.

Tsebelis, G. 2002. *Veto Players: How Political Institutions Work*. Princeton, NJ: Princeton University Press.

Vogel, D. 2001. Is There a Race to the Bottom? The Impact of Globalization on National Regulatory Policies. *Tocqueville Review/La Revue Tocqueville* 22, no. 1:163–173.

von Weizsäcker, E., A. B. Lovins, and L. H. Lovins. 1998. *Factor Four*. London: Earthscan.

Wallace, D. 1995. *Environmental Policy and Industrial Innovation: Strategies in Europe, the USA, and Japan*. London: Earthscan.

Weidner, H., and M. Jänicke, eds. 2002. *Capacity Building in National Environmental Policy: A Comparative Study of Seventeen Countries*. Berlin: Springer.

Wheeler, D. 2001. Racing to the Bottom? Foreign Investment and Air Pollution in Developing Countries. *Journal of Environment and Development* 10, no. 3:225–245.

Willke, H. 1992. *Ironie des Staates: Grundlinien einer Staatstheorie polyzentrischer Gesellschaft*. Frankfurt am Main: Suhrkamp.

# 4

# Looking through the State at Environmental Flows and Governance

Dimitris Stevis and Hans Bruyninckx

About twenty years ago, a group of political scientists and sociologists sought to "bring the state back in" from the wilderness where it had been cast by mainstream social analysis, especially in the United States (Evans 1995). Just when it looked that the state was here to stay, a number of international relations analysts argued that globalization was putting its role and future into question (Strange 1996). Governing cross-border environmental flows were central in fact to this challenge to the state (Caldwell 1991; Young 1994).

It is not our intent to take an environment-inspired position on the "globalist versus statist" debate. Rather, our goal in this chapter is to understand and reframe the interface between the state and global environmental flows and their governance. We do so by making two arguments. First, we maintain that any claims regarding the changing role of states in GEP, require that the term be properly clarified. This has not been the case in GEP, as Conca (1994, 2002) has compellingly asserted over a number of years. While the term *state* is ubiquitous, it remains largely unspecified or used to mean a variety of things, even within the same work. This chapter offers an overview of the ways in which the state has been employed in GEP.

Second, we contend that any claims regarding the interface of the state and GEP cannot be based on the assumption that statehood and globality are ontologically distinct and immanently at odds with each other. Rather, the organization and rules of states (and other social entities) reflect their variable positions within the world political economy, and their strategic efforts at managing or changing that position (Bukharin [1915] 1966; Poulantzas 1974; Cox 1981, 1987; Picciotto 1990; Panitch

1996). Global environmental flows and their governance are an important component of that totality. Thus, states provide us with the vantage point through which we can view the variable interfaces of states and GEP.

Such a conceptualization is best served by a historical and sociological approach to the state, which we outline in the third part of the chapter (see Halliday 1987). In parts four and five, we explore the implications of such an approach for our understanding of the linkages between the state and global environmental politics, the basic goal of this chapter. There is no doubt that increasing global environmental flows and their governance have crucial implications for states. It is one thing, however, to consider states and environmental flows as inherently opposed to each other, and another to see them as implicated in each other's constitution and operation. A historical and sociological approach offers a number of advantages, even though it may not be as parsimonious as the atomistic approach common in mainstream international relations. In particular, it allows us to understand how the uneven constitution of states (and countries) within the world political economy leads to actions that from most mainstream international relations approaches, seem contradictory or irrational. It is only in this way that we can make sense of states advancing environmental priorities in one area, but not in another, or how a powerful state may consent to giving up its discretion in some respects—such as the United States submitting to binding arbitration under chapter 11 of NAFTA—yet not in others—such as the United States rejecting the ICC.

In all, this chapter argues that irrespective of the complexities of global flows, globalization dynamics, and ideas of shifting state sovereignty, the state is still central to understanding global environmental flow governance, even if it is no longer a separate, ahistorical, and decontextualized category. States impact on and are changed by the complex challenges environmental flows put forward in a globalizing world order. But in that transformation process, environmental states do not turn into an irrelevant category.

## The State in Global Environmental Politics

We think that bringing the state back in to environmental politics is essential for the better understanding of global environmental politics as part of the world political economy. Avoiding the issue perpetuates the unwarranted image of global environmental processes as sui generis and thus requiring a wholly different theoretical treatment. We caution, however, against a wholesale move to the state, particularly one that is based on what Buttel (1998) calls a "nomothetic" approach that draws on formal inference rather than empirical investigation. Great research has been done, and will continue to be done, on various global environmental issues that do not deal with the state. Yet if the state plays a critical role in our research, then it is incumbent on us to specify what we mean by the term (see the excellent overview in Barkdull and Harris 2002). As we will discuss below, there are many important threads of literature in GEP that are predicated on the state, yet do not specify its meaning.

With these assumptions in mind, what has the state meant in GEP? Our goal is not to provide a comprehensive review but rather to identify the major ways in which the term has been employed. In order to accomplish this, we ask two basic questions: Is the state defined in a clear way, and if so, how? Are states differentiated from each other? These questions give rise to four clusters of usage. At one end are those uses of the state without further specification. A second category differentiates among states—for example, in terms of capacities or preferences—but does not define what the institution means; it could well mean government, country, social formation, or territory. A third category involves definitions of the state that do not allow or limit differentiation among states. For instance, liberal statists (e.g., most realists) routinely argue that all states are the same in seeking power or survival. A fourth category, and the one we find more promising, involves efforts at both differentiating and defining the state.

### The Undefined and Undifferentiated State

Intensified global integration has led many analysts to cast world politics in terms of the state versus the market (Strange 1996; Reinicke

1998). According to this approach, the state can no longer perform its traditional roles, as global processes displace power and authority to market mechanisms and entities. The state-market contrast has been brought into international environmental politics by the more libertarian among the "new institutionalists" (e.g., some regime theorists), who have also launched a strong critique against the command-and-control regulation associated with the state (Young 1994). The basic argument here is that institutional arrangements can deliver environmental goods without strong organizations, whether state agencies or IGOs.

Contrasting an unspecified state to an, interestingly enough, equally unspecified market produces three problems. First, it accentuates the tensions among them at the expense of their synergies. Markets shape states, but states also shape markets. Second, it downplays the significance of variations within these two categories. As Jacobs (1995) has pointed out, market-based mechanisms vary greatly in terms of their higher-order principles and thus should not be equated. Environmental trading permits with caps, for instance, are dramatically different from trading without caps. Third, and related, it displaces the debate from one of public and democratic governance versus private and nondemocratic governance, to one of inefficient, top-down state policies versus efficient, bottom-up corporate policies. While such a move is often presented as an almost inexorable force of nature (or at least recent history), it clearly implies the rise to hegemony of a particular type of state—the liberal state—certainly different from an environmental state that values both sustainability and democracy.

Similar problems occur in relating the state to civil society. Ever since the 1980s, there has been a great deal of discussion regarding the role of national civil societies in bringing about democratization in South America and Eastern Europe. With the growth of global environmental issues, a number of analysts have taken the concept to the global level. Some of them have argued for the emergence of a global civil society (Lipschutz 1992; Wapner 1996). Others have disputed this assertion, claiming instead that what we observe are societal networks, alliances, or movements well short of constituting a global civil society (Keck and Sikkink 1998). Both approaches share the same axiology of societal politics as the source of emancipatory politics.

The state in this view becomes an undifferentiated locus of all that is anti-emancipatory and environmentally destructive. There is no doubt that much that is hopeful comes from civil societal politics. Yet as we dare to emphasize, much that is not so hopeful also comes from civil societal politics. The undifferentiated treatment of societal politics can be subjected to serious and persuasive criticism on two grounds. First, the state may be much more fluid and contested than it has been portrayed (Cox 1987). Second, and related, societal politics itself ranges across the whole spectrum of the political economy—something that has been highlighted by analysts who see world politics from a southern perspective (Petras 1997; Kamal Pasha and Blaney 1998). Examples of "global civil society" under the form of, say, Greenpeace or Friends of the Earth International behaving as a rhinoceros in a porcelain store when it comes to environmental actions in the South are well-known.

Focusing on other social entities and institutional arrangements (an element central to governance debates) broadens our theoretical and empirical horizons, and liberates us from the stultifying obsession with the state, particularly when this serves to obscure variability in the constitution and social purpose of the state. The research on societal environmental politics has produced important insights and enriched our thinking. There is also growing work on the role of corporations that recognizes both common patterns and interesting differences (Levy and Newell 2004). A political economy approach to states, markets, and societies, however, is better suited to capturing their internal dynamics as well as the interactions across these categories.

### The Differentiated but Undefined State

Many analysts, particularly those who deal with North-South relations, differentiate among states (generally meaning countries) on the basis of capacities/resources, and contend that variable capacities can explain the state's impacts on the environment or its ability/obligation to help solve environmental problems (for an incisive overview, see Jacobsen 1996; for an example, see Beckerman and Pasek 2001). There are in fact good reasons to believe that unequal resources do affect the ways in which states adopt environmental priorities. Such an aggregate categorization, however, can be misleading when it implies that environmental politics are solely or even primarily the product of unequal capacities, and hence independent of social volition. For instance, unequal resources and state capacities cannot explain the variation of environmental policies among industrial countries both comparatively and across the last thirty years. Research into various policy areas has demonstrated important variations within the South (Evans 1995). Growing research on environmental policy further underscores that similarities and strong differences coexist in the South, as they also do in the North (Desai 1998). Greece's decision to tear up its tramways in the 1950s, for example, reflected a particular developmental choice—not the only developmental choice. There is ample evidence that southern developmentalist elites and northern liberals frequently share the same (anti)environmentalist positions in global negotiations. This suggests that more attention to the domestic politics of less industrialized countries has much to contribute to our understanding of GEP.

The role of domestic politics in the formation of foreign environmental policy has received more attention in recent years (see review in Barkdull and Harris 2002; see also Underdal and Hanf 2000). The role of domestic politics in explaining the implementation of and compliance with global environmental policies has also been the subject of important research (Brown Weiss and Jacobson 1998).

Focusing on domestic politics allows us to identify significant variations among countries. It does not necessarily focus on the state as an institution, though, and may in fact use the term to mean country or domestic politics in general. In a key contribution, for instance, Schreurs (2002) examines the variation in the environmental policies of Japan, Germany, and the United States. While the nature of the state is central to the explanation of how environmental priorities become institutionalized, the term remains rather underspecified. Nevertheless, such work points us in the right direction to the degree that the role of the state as an institution is better recognized. Additional research that focuses on the role of states in a more explicit fashion can enrich our understanding of how domestic politics affect the formation and implementation of global environmental policies.

## Toward Definition and Differentiation

The rise of global integration, including the globalization of environmental problems, has led many analysts to argue that the territoriality/ sovereignty of the state is under siege (Young 1994; for a review, see Philpott 2001). Assuming that states have exclusive authority over incursions and excursions involving their territory renders any infractions a challenge to state authority. There are various problems with this approach. One serious problem has to do with its historical accuracy (Stavrianos 1981; Miller 1998). Although international relations theory mostly assumes the formal equality of sovereign states, the majority of the world's states have not enjoyed either operational or legal sovereignty. A review of the production of the contemporary world of states at four key points over the last 120 years—the Berlin conferences of the 1880s, the Treaty of Versailles in 1919, the establishment of the Soviet and U.S. empires after WWII, and the conditions that contemporary third world states must fulfill in order to operate internationally—would clarify that states, as institutions, are created different both legally and operationally.[1] A second problem is more theoretical. Sovereignty and territoriality are concepts that are better suited to conveying individuation and difference among similar units rather than historical relations that view these units as the unequal elements of a larger totality.

A number of GEP analysts have sought to rethink the concept of sovereignty over the last ten years. In an important work, Litfin (1997, 1998) and her collaborators have sought to get out of the conundrum of formal equality and operational inequality by unbundling sovereignty into a variety of dimensions that can accommodate the empirical variability of states. This project has moved us a long way toward making the principles of sovereignty and territoriality the product of world-systemic processes—in the sense that these rules require exchange and agreement among various countries. It does not, however, transcend the ahistorical and nonrelational nature of the concept of sovereignty itself. The idea of "sovereignty trading," which aims to move us away from assumptions of immutable and invariable sovereignty, implies ontologically distinct entities. In this, it is similar to saying that employers and employees are engaged in wage bargaining as if they were constituted through separate processes. Thus, while it may acknowledge that there are differences in power, it obscures the fact that these two categories cannot exist independent of each other. In our view, this same type of internal relations (Ollman 1993) applies to states within the world political economy as world historical analysts have long argued. Some states play the role of employers and some the role of employees.

## Defining and Differentiating

The definition of the state and the differentiation among various states have both had strong followings in the more historicist quarters of international relations and sociology. Historical materialists (Bukharin [1915] 1966; Poulantzas 1974; Cox 1987), dependency theorists (Cardoso and Falletto 1979), historical institutionalists (Evans et al. 1985), and historically minded liberal institutionalists (Ruggie 1992) have all defined and differentiated among states, and have employed their insights to deal with international politics. For these authors, the nature of the state, particularly of dominant states, has direct implications for the world order as a whole and the formation of other states more specifically.

With respect to international environmental politics, we can identify two clusters of literature that specify the state. Earlier literature sought to explain environmental policies in terms of the nonenvironmental characteristics of states (and domestic politics). This line of analysis continues. Some, for instance, have compared democratic and nondemocratic state responses to external influences—for instance, India's and China's responses to external pressures, and with respect to their energy sectors (Sims 2000). The common characteristic of these analyses is that the environment is taken as the explanandum, since the environmental dimension of the state is either not examined or not there. The second strand focuses more explicitly on the environmental state. Much of that research is comparative (Dryzek et al. 2002), but the interface of global processes and the environmental state are increasingly receiving attention (Mol and Buttel 2002; Eckersley 2004). A number of authors, for instance, have emphasized the role of environmental lead states in shaping EU and global environmental policies.

That the nature of the environmental state is significant for understanding international environmental politics makes sense if we look at the social welfare state. According to Rieger and Leibfried (2003), the social welfare state is a prerequisite for globalization as it provides a sense of security for those most likely to be affected by the transition to a more open world political economy. On the other hand, it is not possible to talk about a single social welfare state, opening the arena for interesting comparative research. Recent work in international environmental politics (Barkdull and Harris 2002; Schreurs 2002; Eckersley 2004) suggests that the nature of the environmental state—ranging from the liberal environmental state to the more corporatist and precautionary one—can also provide crucial insights into the interface between the state and global processes.

Our goal in this section has been to show that while the state is ubiquitous in the study of GEP, it is not clear whether those using the term mean the same thing or are even involved in the same discourse. These are not differences over what the state is or how to differentiate among states. Rather, the term is so frequently used in a casual fashion that it has no identifiable meaning. That would not be a major issue except that many analysts invest the term with important descriptive, explanatory, and axiological qualities. The concept, therefore, is not simply used in an ambiguous fashion; it is also used in a multivalent one—it means different things even within the same bodies of work. Our critique, however, does not imply that we should adopt an idiographic approach. Rather, any generalizations should be based on the historical evidence rather than an atomistic ontology, explicit or implicit in much of international relations. Again, it is not our aim to engage in a protracted debate over the definition of the state but to instead argue that the state, and all other social entities, must be investigated empirically and placed within the broader political economy.

## Toward a Historical and Sociological State

Our goal is to outline an analytic approach to the state that recognizes its significance without reifying it. In order to do so, we ask three questions: What does the state consist of? What are states embedded in? How are they embedded?

## What Are States Made Of?

States are both organizations and institutions, in the institutionalist sense. What does a state, as an organization, include, and what are the implications of its organizational characteristics? Broadening the organizational scope of the state can produce important results (Evans 2000). In addition, it can offer a richer view of intrastate conflicts and alliances as a crucial descriptive and explanatory factor. The state as an institution refers to the connection of the state with societal forces, establishing both what the state can do and within what parameters it can do so.

The organizational and institutional components of the state, then, are in dynamic relationships. An overemphasis on organizational intrastate politics, a common practice by many U.S. scholars, often serves to obscure the relations between the organizational and institutional characteristics and politics of the state in a variety of ways. First, intrastate conflicts may be more or less profound. Competition between agencies as to who will regulate a particular environmental activity may be largely bureaucratic or about institutional rules. For example, the Bush administration is using state agencies to undermine the environmental state. Yet it has also met with formidable resistance from various quarters of the state, particularly if we define the state to include subfederal units. Second, the locus of power within the state is not purely an organizational issue. Hegemonic agencies reflect social balances as well as struggles over social balances. It is for this reason that states often split down the middle, as is the case with civil wars, in the extreme, or federal arrangements, more commonly. Third, the organizations of the state are not vessels that can be filled and emptied of people and expectations whenever someone comes to power. In addition to reflecting overall social balances, states also have their own immediate constituencies— that is, people who work for or depend on states for their livelihood (often not admitting to it, as is the case with western farmers in the United States). These constituencies also have significant implications for state policies. Changing environmental or natural resource policies must also deal with these constituencies.

## Embedded in What?

Drawing on insights from Cox (1987) and Evans (1995), Buttel (1998) has argued that states are not only embedded in domestic politics but also in world politics. It stands to reason that states are embedded in those societal forces with which they have shaped the country or the social formation over which they rule. Even weak and dependent states have special connections with domestic societal forces or take the lead in creating them. Placing states within the world political economy does not deny their significance or the frequent primacy of domestic politics. It asserts, however, that external factors play an important role in the constitution (organizational and institutional) and the calculations of most states. Moreover, numerically speaking most contemporary states are directly dependent on foreign states and societal forces or global organizations. These states must take into account the impacts of their policies on the external balances that guarantee their legitimacy and operation. Lest one think that we are talking only about states in the South, we suggest taking a closer look at the cold war and the current imperial policies of the United States.

While establishing the range, there are all kinds of interesting permutations. Quite frequently, for instance, states are embedded in "domestic" societal forces that are in turn more embedded in the world political economy than the local one. For example, Greek shipping magnates depend more on the world political economy than the Greek political economy. In the same way, the state in Papua New Guinea depends to a great extent on the mining elites who are more embedded in global networks on copper or gold. Although these kinds of "hybrids" are now gaining prominence in global network theories, one can easily argue that they have long been recognized by historical structuralists, such as dependency theorists.

In addition to being embedded in some combination of domestic and foreign forces, states are also embedded in time. The particular moment in history that states emerged from has left its imprint. The organizational and institutional characteristics adopted at that specific formative moment cast a long shadow over the future of the state and the country. The decisions over competition institutionalized in the early twentieth-century United States have shaped the relations between the state and capital as well as within capital in the United States. On the other hand, German and Japanese routes to late industrialization have produced intimate organizational relations between the state and capital, and have encouraged intracapital relations that would be illegal in the United States. The same applies to the environmental state. Institutional arrangements carry a great deal of power and an enduring longevity. At the very least, they shape the attacks against them. Even the Reagan and Bush administrations were/are not willing to totally deny the role of the state in land protection and management. Rather, they have tried to modify it by shifting the locus of power and the means for management.

The ways in which states are embedded have direct implications for their organizational and institutional characteristics. States that depend extensively on global environmental flows, for instance, are shaped organizationally and institutionally to service and negotiate those flows, as would be the case with oil exporters or any monocroppers. Here we must be cautious of diffusionist accounts that tend to homogenize organizational similarities (Frank et al. 2000b). The seeming functional organizational equivalence among states can be misleading.[2] Just because many states have environmental ministries does not mean that they are the same. We are not referring here to the well-known fact that many state environmental programs lack the resources or commitment to deal adequately with environmental issues. We are saying that even strong environmental ministries may be "consumers" of others' environmental policies. New members of the EU, say, have to reorganize themselves to meet EU standards that they have no role in shaping.

## Looking at Flows through the State

Our discussion of the state has sought to underscore both the historicity and variability of states. On that basis, we now move toward an exploration of some actual relations between flows and states. The basic point here is that the space of flows and the space of places that Castells sees as the central poles of our contemporary world are not a totally new development, unless one privileges the speed of exchange. Particular cities and groups of people played nodal roles for the space of flows as far back as imperial expansions and long-distance trade. While the speed of communication was slower by comparison to the almost simultaneous exchanges of the present, the networks involved were strong and persistent. More important, Castells's (1996, especially chapter 6) space of flows involves two places—one that is part and parcel of the space of flows, and one that is independent of it. It seems to us that from a world historical perspective, the flows and places components of the space of flows are dialectically related with the balance fluctuating over time. The major challenge at present is whether social and environmental regulations will prevent hyperliberal flows from continuously "churning" places—or rather, their inhabitants.

### Historicizing Environmental Flows

By all accounts, the absolute amount of flows—environmental or not—has increased over the last century and even more so since the end of post-WWII reconstruction. By the late 1960s, oil had surpassed coal as a source of energy, making sea transport both more prominent and more environmentally risky. Nuclear energy has become increasingly globalized, starting with the U.S. "Atoms for Peace" plan in the 1950s, and continuing with the trading of nuclear wastes for reprocessing or storage in our time. The economies fueled by these sources have in turn spewed increasing amounts into the ecosphere. We think that the sheer density and speed of environmental flows has a dynamic all its own. Yet we also think that flows, whether local or global, reflect particular social choices and power relations—a fact that Castells also highlights. Most economic flows, for instance, remain within the triad of the North (Mol 2002). Most production- and consumption-related environmental flows are also concentrated in the North. Most deposits, which may spread throughout the globe, do come from the industrial world.

While the speed and density of flows are central dynamics, they are not the only ones. To begin with, environmental problems are the product of social choices. There remains a strong tendency, however, to emphasize the impacts of outcomes on the environment, such as the impacts of climate-changing substances rather than the political economy that produces them. While many analysts and activists have highlighted the structural role of the political economy, there are those who see political economic choices as so intractable as to make addressing them a lost cause.

Second, it is important in our view to distinguish those flows that reinforce existing global divisions of labor from those that change them. Increasing amounts of energy exports from the South to the North, for example, are significant but largely reproduce the existing global division of labor. On the other hand, China's emerging oil demands will transform the geography of the energy industry.

Third, any political geography of flows will be well served by identifying both the quantity and the quality of environmental flows. In fact, small amounts of flows involving key technologies and knowledge, and the environmental flows attached to them, can tell us more about the future than large amounts of existing flows. Think of the specific resources needed for the information and communication technologies (chips) industry—resources that are geographically scarce.

Finally, we must take into account the social impacts of flows. Starting with the Bengali famine of 1943, Sen (1981) observed that famines were not caused by absolute scarcities but rather by people's ability to get access to the flows of food. As a result, deaths exhibited a clear pattern, starting with the socially weak. The arrival of a few Europeans in the Americas led to a demographic crash at the same time that these few conquistadores reorganized areas that up to that time had been administered by sophisticated bureaucracies.

In short, the impact of environmental flows is not solely a function of speed and density alone. An exclusive focus on them obscures the momentous impacts of small flows. It also downplays the increasing ability of states and countries to absorb as well as monitor more flows now than in the past, largely due to the greater resources that can be marshaled as a result of the "great transformations" of the twentieth century.

## States and Flows: Flows before States

World historical accounts have made a persuasive case with respect to the existence of the global divisions of labor that underlie the pace and direction of global flows. Environmental historians are increasingly illuminating the environmental components of these dynamics (Grove 1995;

Chew 2001; Williams 2003). Some flows, such as those caused by defor-estation, the mining of precious metals and minerals, and plantation agri-culture, predate almost all modern states (and countries). More recent flows, such as those involving oil, nuclear technology, agricultural chem-icals, and other industrial practices, also predate many states. Even though the amounts may have increased, the global divisions of labor underlying these flows have remained the same. States, in turn, have been shaped by these global divisions of labor, as analysts have argued since the turn of the past century (Bukharin [1915] 1996). As anyone who is familiar with development politics knows well, changing these divisions of labor is not an easy process.

If we accept that some flows exist before the formation of countries and states, then the relationship between flows and states becomes more variable. In some cases, the primary question will be how flows were created and by whom. In other cases, the question will concern the impacts of flows on the organizational and institutional characteristics of states, such as West Asian oil exporters, whose existence is largely due to the flows of oil. More recently, the attempts to gain control over the natural resources in Central Africa are preceding the new formation of the state in the territory that is known as Congo. Complementarily, we will have to ask how states have adjusted to increasing dependence on particular products, as would be the case with oil importers in the core. Finally, we should also investigate the ways in which state agencies along the commodity chain or flow have actually marginalized alternative flows or state agencies, even as they are competing among themselves over control of the existing flow.

There is, in short, every reason to believe that the increasing density and speed of flows will exert its own influences on states (and other social forces) regardless of whether flows predated states or not. Nevertheless, we think that by taking into account the fact that flows can be histori-cally prior to states, or formative of completely new state arrangements (Weinthal 2002), we are forced to look at the state as a variable histor-ical edifice produced within the world political economy. Such an approach, in turn, can provide us with richer accounts of the structural and instrumental reasons behind state policies vis-à-vis existing and emerging flows.

## States and Flows: States before Flows

The interface of flows and states can be further enriched by examining how states deal with their sovereignty and territoriality. Whether in environmental or nonenvironmental affairs, there is abundant evidence that states are often the primary disrupters of their own boundaries.[3] We think that such practices are contradictory only if one starts from the assumption that states are wedded to exclusive sovereignty—that is, if one uses an "ideal type" to measure all states. As we have suggested, from a historical and sociological point of view uneven sovereignty claims are part and parcel of the individuation of states within the world political economy. We can also see this in the flows related to the environment. For a long time, for instance, the United States promoted (and promotes) nuclear power, but it also spent (and spends) a great deal of energy preventing the proliferation of nuclear weapons. Similarly, it has made intellectual property rights, including those involving agricultural technology, central to its global economic negotiations, but refuses to stop agricultural subsidies domestically (as do the EU and Japan).

While the state is considered the guarantor of place, in the sense of territorial exclusivity, some societal forces are considered its main challengers, also improperly in our view. It is true that some social movements, such as nativists or ecoregionalists, protect place, in the sense of Castells's space of places. Others, however, consider local responses inadequate to the nature of many environmental problems. As a result, their aim is to transform the space of flows, including the particular configuration of flows and places that create it.

More indicative of the seemingly contradictory constitution of boundaries, though, is the behavior of transnational capital. In the view of many analysts, transnational capital is the major force for and carrier of flows. Some critiques have contested this view, arguing that corporations are still the products of their countries of origin. Yet we think that TNCs reinforce territoriality in another way. Generally speaking, the globalization espoused by TNCs is contingent on countervailing forces that do not manage to establish effective control, not being able to follow them (Streeck 1998). In short, they are predicated on the selective opening and closing of national boundaries. Corporations will vehemently argue in support of domestic rules that respect private property rights and the repatriation of profits—thus increasing flows in that regard—but will claim that national laws disallow certain superior environmental and labor practices—thus limiting flows in that respect. Or they may employ global or national policy fora and rules on the basis of strategic calculations rather than doctrinaire attachments to the global over the domestic (Egan and Levy 2001). Stated differently, the conflict is among competing articulations of places and flows within the globalizing elements of the world political economy.

### States and Flows: How Do States Enable Flows?

Without aiming to be complete, we feel that states enable and reshape environmental flows in a variety of ways, through policies ranging from extreme unilateralism to global governance. The main point that we want to make is that either unilateral and multilateral routes can produce positive or negative environmental flows, reflecting the variability of state policies as well as the significance of strategic interactions. While multilateral practices may be less conflictual than unilateral ones, it is not necessarily the case that the latter will produce superior environmental or other results. Global governance, for instance, may enhance global liberalism or developmentalism while unilateral actions may be the major sources of resistance against pollution or ecological degradation.

The earliest literature on environmental flows focused on individual countries externalizing environmental harms regardless of what others did. Major industrial countries would allow the spewing of pollutants into the atmosphere or refuse to require double-hull oil tankers. Such unilateral practices can come from a wide variety of states, including environmental ones. For example, the United States has allowed the export of certain pesticides that cannot be used within its own borders. Sweden and other Scandinavian countries have an admirable domestic environmental record, but have not always been sensitive to the footprints of their furniture manufacturers.

Is it possible that unilateral measures can result in more environmentally sound flows? Vogel (1995) has made the argument that global trade flows can have positive environmental impacts. Accordingly, "the California effect" refers to the positive environmental impacts of local regulations while the "Delaware effect" refers to the negative environmental impacts of environmental regulations. In the case of the California effect, more stringent environmental rules, such as California's automobile emission standards, can force the automobile industry into an upward spiral. Since no car company wants to be excluded from the California market and since companies try to avoid multiple production processes, the environmental standards will be raised not only for California but for all the markets that the company wants to remain active in.

Not every "state" can have the same impact as California. The fact, however, that California can move to a different tune than the rest of the United States further underscores the need to pay closer attention to the composition of the state. Yet the fact that there are also clear limits to what California can do within the parameters of the United States and the world political economy should remind us that such variability exists within identifiable limits.

As much as these kinds of unilateral practices play an important part in shaping the political geography of flows, competitive unilateralism fills an increasingly crucial role as two or more states adopt policies to redirect flows in their direction. Some of these policies may aim at attracting dirty industries, such as the disassembling of vessels or noxious but effective agricultural chemicals, leading to downward harmonization. Others may aim at ecotourism or clean industry, leading to an upward spiral.

A second, less conflictual way in which flows can be engendered and modified involves consciously complementary policies without, however, some degree of international or supranational governance. Many countries have established EPZs with largely inferior environmental and social standards, when compared to those of the country of origin of the investor, in order to attract foreign investment. Quite often, EPZs are created as a result of competitive unilateralism, mentioned above. Yet they can also be established as a result of implicit commitments. The U.S. African Development Agency, for instance, rewards African states that facilitate the formation of EPZs. Such complementary rules therefore set up direct and intended flows between the parties. Quite possibly, then, the dominant state could attach environmental and labor provisions. Gross environmental and labor violations in a number of EPZs were in fact instrumental in giving rise to the corporate social responsibility movement, a business attempt at forestalling environmental and union demands for binding regulation.

A third way in which environmental and other flows can take place is through global policies—we are using governance in a broad sense here and return to it in our last section. Global rules allow and enable the movement of goods or environmental practices across boundaries. Some of these flows may be beneficial to the environment, such as the prohibition of waste dumping abroad. Others may put additional stress on the environment, such as rules enabling long-distance trade, which demands more infrastructure and energy.

## Implications

Looking at global flows in general and environmental flows in particular "through the state" as a historical and sociological institution enables us to do a number of things. First, we can look back in time in order to find out how existing states have been constituted within history and to what degree they are still constrained by these path dependencies. Second, such a perspective can help us make sense of the implications of their current strategies for existing and emerging flows. Finally, and more broadly, it can allow us to recognize that the relations of states and flows vary historically rather than ontologically.

## States and Global Governance

Over the last fifteen years, international relations analysts have sought to understand how international or global governance can take place in the absence of government (for overviews and discussion, see Hewson and Sinclair 1999; Prakash and Hart 1999). The proliferation of environmental agreements has been a major source of inspiration in this endeavor (Biermann 2002; French 2002; Gupta 2002). There is strong evidence that there has been an increase in formal global governance with some supranational attributes over the last ten years, particularly manifested in the WTO, the ICC, and some of the MEAs, such as the Montreal Protocol. Yet it would be inaccurate to suggest that there was no governance in the past. It would also be impetuous to assert that the move toward supranationality is inexorable and balanced. We will discuss some characteristics of governance in general and environmental governance in particular and then suggest how global (or international) governance looks "through the state."

### Historicizing Governance

As with the globalization of flows, many analysts have sought to identify a clear break between the organization and management of world politics, with the turning point evident around the late 1980s or early 1990s. Starting in the mid-1980s, the member countries decided to move from a weak GATT to a more powerful WTO. During the 1980s, the Montreal Protocol also heralded the arrival of strong, supranational MEAs. Parallel to these global processes we have also witnessed the deepening of regional governance, particularly in North America and Europe. It is our view that the transfer of authority to supranational entities and rules is an important development. Yet as the examples of many federal countries suggest, the allocation of authority between federal and subfederal units is quite contested and fluid over time. The addition of supranational authority in the mix of authorities operating in today's world is a critical development, but does not by itself signify a wholesale transformation.

We should pay close attention to the reasons and functions of governance as well. The basic assumption is that the increase in flows raises demands for governance. As we have noted, however, governance does not simply regulate flows in the sense of dealing with their adverse impacts and disputes among participants. It also engenders more or different kinds of flows. The WTO, for instance, aims at managing the higher flows of products, while immigration policies by industrial countries attempt to attract certain categories of workers and exclude others.

Finally, the social purpose of governance (Latham 1999; Stevis 2002) is as important as its strength and scope. What kind of social order is established when authority moves from one level to another? The move of authority from the states to the federal government—in the United States, for example—was also a shift in terms of the powers of particular social forces. Global or international governance also reflects certain social arrangements and priorities.

## Governance before States

Most modern states were in existence before the emergence of global environmental policies. Yet there are important environmental flows that are governed by rules, such as phytosanitary standards, that were put in place during the interwar period or shortly thereafter, well before most states came into existence. Such governance mechanisms have important implications for states (and countries) that have to trade in animals and plants. Similarly, the rules of nuclear proliferation and trade were put in place before many contemporary states came into existence. In general, we can identify two governance rules that were established before most modern states came into existence: colonial or imperial governance and IGO governance.

The majority of the world's states are the products of the national policies of specific countries, whether these were formal colonizers or not (Stavrianos 1981). As we have indicated in the discussion of flows, a number of countries and their states came into existence within global flows. The role of the colonial powers in shaping these flows and the state institutions to keep them operating is well-known. So is the role of noncolonial imperial countries, such as the United States and the Soviet Union, in shaping the states or the countries under their control. The majority of the world's states have come into existence via either of these two routes.

Additionally, crucial aspects of formal global governance with indirect and increasingly direct environmental impacts were already in place when decolonization took place. Organizations such as GATT, the WB, and the IMF were set up as instruments of northern hegemony, which the South failed to modify during the "New International Economic Order" debates of the 1960s and 1970s. As a result, the IMF and the WB have played a significant role in shaping the political economy of the South during the post-WWII era. Since the early 1980s in particular, the environmental implications of their structural adjustment policies have been profound. They did not simply change the environmental policies of states; they also changed the nature of those states, as the abandonment of import substitution strategies in favor of more liberal policies makes apparent (see also the WB's [1997] vision of the state). In the case of newly independent countries, such as those that resulted from the disintegration of the Soviet Union, the constitutional role of global economic organizations has been profound.

### States before Governance

The move toward global multilateral organizations should not obscure the fact that many environmental flows are not subject to global governance (e.g., energy), or are subject to more or less imperial governance (e.g., nuclear and space technologies). With that proviso, how can we look at contemporary multilateral governance in general and environmental governance in particular though the state? We touch on this question with respect to the formation and implementation of multilateral global governance.

One of the major debates of the last ten years or so has to do with the lack of democracy in the negotiation and operation of global governance organizations, such as the WTO (O'Brien et al. 2000; Verweij and Josling 2003). A number of social movements have called for various reforms, ranging from simple transparency to global corporatism. For some, the major problem is the monopoly that states hold in these organizations. For others, it is the preponderant influence of *some* states. And for still others, it is the dominant role of certain state agencies and their societal allies. We think that all of the above are valid, but that the latter concern allows for a more refined approach to the role of the state in global governance.

The major issue is not that environmentalists cannot participate in the negotiation and implementation of formal policies. In fact, one could make the case that this would create more problems for democratic representation than it would solve (on global democracy, see Shapiro and Hacker-Cordon 1999; Anderson 2002). The major problem is that environmental ministries and priorities in key states have been subordinated to non- or less environmental agencies. Environmental or labor ministries in liberal states have limited access to the negotiation of economic agreements. On the other hand, they play a more important role in democratic corporatist states. While there is no guarantee that they will seek to produce the best environmental or labor rules, their exclusion is much more difficult to accomplish.

A close examination of global governance negotiations, whether concerning the environment or labor, shows the variations among states—variations that reflect the sociology of the particular states (van Roozendaal 2002). The issue, therefore, is not one of the state versus global governance but of competing state (and societal) visions of global governance.

In turning our attention from formation to implementation, it should be noticed that during the years after the Stockholm conference of 1972, there was a proliferation of national environmental ministries. A number of analysts have noted, however, that many of them were symbolic. Thus, figuring out how environmental governance modifies individual states requires emphasis on the empirical record rather than formal organizational arrangements.

The formation of domestic environmental agencies will only be the tip of the iceberg. Modifications of other agencies to deflect or reinforce environmental priorities may actually play a more critical role. In the case of Greece, for instance, the environmental agency is part of the Ministry of Public Works. In the best of cases, it can help ensure that the large public works being built are environmentally sound. In the worst of cases, the minister of public works can directly constrain the undersecretary of environmental affairs. In the United States, the USEPA employs thousands of people and administers a large budget, but its administrator may or may not be a cabinet member.

In addition to the organizational translation of environmental governance there is also institutional translation. On the positive side, a commitment to environmental governance will result in the modification of the rules connecting the state to society and the environment. The environmental state can well be the result of global governance. The impacts of global governance are more profound, though. A number of authors have argued that there is a clear bias in favor of dealing with northern environmental issues (Jacobsen 1996). If that is the case, global environmental governance does not simply create an environmental state to deal with an existing environmental problem but defines and prioritizes the problems, as it were. In short, the state is embedded in a global process in a particular way, possibly at the expense of more relevant alternatives.

## Implications

Looking at global governance through the state means that global or international governance is not necessarily a break from the alleged full autonomy of the state. Some authors have contended that the proliferation of global environmental agreements has in fact enhanced the role of the state—compared to imperial governance policies. We think that there may be some merit to that perspective. Equally important, however, if we combine the historical/sociological approach to the state with the social purpose of governance, we can view global environmental governance as an arena of contestation involving various social forces, some participating through states and some excluded. While environmentalists may enjoy institutionalized participation in some states, they may be completely voiceless in others. Treating the state as an undifferentiated whole and overemphasizing the formal similarities among states will, in our view, deprive us of more nuanced and realistic accounts of the relations between state politics and the governance of global environmental flows. In turn, treating any engagement of societal entities with the state as a fall from grace further reinforces the reification of societal and state politics that we pointed to in the second part of this chapter.

## Conclusions

We started this chapter by highlighting the need for a more specified approach to the state in order to understand its role in governing global environmental flows. Our argument was that the term state is both broadly used and underspecified. It was not our goal to suggest that research on the state should displace existing research on societal agents or corporations and so on. Rather, we maintain that when the concept of the state is employed, its meaning needs to be described and clarified. Only after it has been clarified can we pass judgment on its role with respect to global environmental flows and their governance.

After reviewing the existing literature, we stressed the need for a more historical and sociological approach to the state in general and the environmental state in particular. According to such an approach, states are not immanently antagonistic to global processes but rather their interface with the world around them varies depending on their history and social composition. When working within such a perspective, richer accounts can be obtained of the causes behind state practices and preferences, and most important, one is able to make better sense of the many seemingly contradictory behaviors that are evident in world politics.

In employing a historical and sociological perspective on relations between states and flows we have addressed critical framings of their interface. Both flows and governance have constitutive and instrumental impacts on states. States, however, also affect the formation and impacts of flows. Their encounters are not those of alien forces but of forces that have emerged together in particular historical configurations. One way to view these configurations, therefore, is through the state rather than as ontologically at odds with each other. From such a vantage point, the major contrast is not that between the space of flows and the space of places but between the particular articulations of places and flows within the space of flows, or stated differently, over the social purpose of global environmental integration.

In addition to a richer reading of flows, looking through the state also allows us a richer reading of governance. As the editors of this book suggest, there is a great deal of hybridization between "formerly distinct entities and roles. Roles and responsibilities formerly reserved for (nation-)state actors are fulfilled by market actors and civil society groups and organizations and vice versa" (chapter 1, this volume). There is no doubt that the last fifteen years or so have witnessed an apparent move to private authority, devolution of state policies, and the rise of civil societal politics. More research on the subject will allow us to determine whether this proliferation also reflects profound changes. As it stands now, some of the strongest hybrids are a number of years or decades old—for example, sports associations, the ISO, the IUCN, and the ILO. Equally important, however, a historical and sociological approach to the state will allow us to determine whether, in years past, these hybrids existed, albeit obscured by and legitimated through state agencies that, for all practical purposes were controlled by societal forces. That this was the case is immediately evident to anyone who deals with most countries in the South. Yet private governance has also been prominent in industrial countries (Lakoff 1973). The key question, then, is whether what has taken place in recent years is a change in form rather than purpose. Or perhaps, and formulated in a somewhat provocative way, are what we think of as hybrids simply a projection of U.S.-type regulatory governance arrangements over the whole globe. In either case, it is our sense that a closer look at governance arrangements from a statist perspective can only enrich the research agenda proposed by the editors of this volume. Given that much of the governance and flows literatures tend to be located in the demise of the state discourse, we think it is crucial to advance a historical and political economy perspective on the linkages between the state, flows, and governance.

## Notes

1. Note, for instance, that the transfer of sovereignty to the new government of Iraq is conditioned on it extending an invitation to U.S. troops to remain stationed in the country, as has been the case with Germany and Japan.

2. The U.S. Department of the Treasury, for instance, can circulate an international currency. The Mexican treasury, on the other hand, is a consumer of that currency. These are only formally similar agencies.

3. Neoliberal and vocally parochial administrations such as those of Thatcher and Reagan, for instance, were at the forefront of the move to unregulated hyper-liberalism while also at the forefront of the move toward the stronger governance provided for by the WTO. In fact, this seemingly contradictory bundle of policies is part and parcel of the behavior of all states and most social forces.

## References

Anderson, J., ed. 2002. *Transnational Democracy: Political Spaces and Border Crossings*. London: Routledge.

Barkdull, J., and P. G. Harris. 2002. Environmental Change and Foreign Policy: A Survey of Theory. *Global Environmental Politics* 2, no. 2:63–91.

Beckerman, W., and J. Pasek. 2001. *Justice, Posterity, and the Environment*. Oxford: Oxford University Press.

Biermann, F. 2002. Strengthening Green Global Governance in a Disparate World Society: Would a World Environmental Organisation Benefit the South? *International Environmental Agreements: Politics, Law, and Economics* 2: 297–315.

Brown Weiss, E., and H. K. Jacobson, eds. 1998. *Engaging Countries: Strengthening Compliance with International Environmental Accords*. Cambridge: MIT Press.

Bukharin, N. [1915]. 1966. *Imperialism and World Economy*. New York: Howard Fertig.

Buttel, F. H. 1998. Some Observations on States, World Orders, and the Politics of Sustainability. *Organization and Environment* 11, no. 3:261–286.

Caldwell, L. 1991. International Response to Environmental Issues: Retrospect and Prospect. *International Studies Notes* 16, no. 1:3–7.

Cardoso, F. H., and E. Falletto. 1979. *Dependency and Development in Latin America*. Berkeley: University of California Press.

Castells, M. 1996. *The Rise of the Network Society*. Vol. 1 of *The Information Age: Economy, Society, and Culture*. Oxford: Blackwell.

Chew, S. 2001. *World Ecological Degradation: Accumulation, Urbanization, and Deforestation, 3,000 B.C.–A.D. 2000*. Walnut Creek, CA: Altamira Press.

Conca, K. 1994. Rethinking the Ecology-Sovereignty Debate. *Millennium: Journal of International Studies* 23, no. 3:701–711.

Conca, K. 2002. Imagining the State. In *Encountering Global Environmental Politics*, ed. M. Maniates, 71–84. London, MD: Rowman and Littlefield Publishers.

Cox, R. 1981. Social Forces, States, and World Orders: Beyond International Relations Theory. *Millennium: Journal of International Studies* 10, no. 2: 126–155.

Cox, R. 1987. *Production, Power, and World Order: Social Forces in the Making of History*. New York: Columbia University Press.

Desai, U., ed. 1998. *Ecological Policy and Politics in Developing Countries: Economic Growth, Democracy and Environment*. Albany: State University of New York Press.

Dryzek, J. S., C. Hunold, D. Schlosleng, D. Downes, and H. Hernes. 2002. Environmental Transformation of the State: The USA, Norway, Germany, and the UK. *Political Studies* 50:659–682.

Eckersley, R. 2004. *The Green State: Rethinking Democracy and Sovereignty*. Cambridge: MIT Press.

Egan, D., and D. Levy. 2001. International Environmental Politics and the Internationalization of the State: The Cases of Climate Change and the Multilateral Agreement on Investment. In *The International Political Economy of the Environment: Critical Perspectives. International Political Economy Yearbook*, ed. D. Stevis and V. Assetto, 63–83. Boulder, CO: Lynne Rienner Publishers.

Evans, P. 1995. *Embedded Autonomy: States and Industrial Transformation*. Princeton, NJ: Princeton University Press.

Evans, P. 2000. Sustainability, Degradation, and Livelihood in Third World Cities: Possibilities for State-Society Synergy. In *The Global Environment in the Twenty-First Century*, ed. P. Chasek, 42–63. Tokyo: United Nations University Press.

Evans, P., D. Rueschemeyer, and T. Scocpol, eds. 1985. *Bringing the State Back In*. Cambridge: Cambridge University Press.

Frank, D. J., A. Hironaka, and E. Schofer. 2000a. Environmentalism as a Global Institution. *American Sociological Review* 65:122–127.

Frank, D. J., A. Hironaka, and E. Schofer. 2000b. The Nation-State and the Natural Environment over the Twentieth Century. *American Sociological Review* 65:96–116.

French, D. A. 2002. The Role of the State and International Organizations in Reconciling Sustainable Development and Globalization. *International Environmental Agreements: Politics, Law, and Economics* 2, no. 2:135–150.

Grove, R. 1995. *Green Imperialism*. Cambridge: Cambridge University Press.

Gupta, J. 2002. Global Sustainable Development Governance: Institutional Challenges from a Theoretical Perspective. *International Environmental Agreements: Politics, Law, and Economics* 2:361–388.

Halliday, F. 1987. State and Society in International Relations: A Second Agenda. *Millennium: Journal of International Studies* 16, no. 2:215–229.

Hewson, M., and T. Sinclair. 1999. The Emergence of Global Governance Theory. In *Approaches to Global Governance Theory*, ed. L. Hewson and T. Sinclair, 3–22. Albany: State University of New York Press.

Jacobs, M. 1995. Sustainability and "the Market": A Typology of Environmental Economics. In *Market, the State, and the Environment: Towards Integration*, ed. R. Eckersley, 46–70. Melbourne: Macmillan.

Jacobsen, S. F. 1996. *North-South Relations and Global Environmental Issues: A Review of the Literature*. Copenhagen, Denmark: Center for Development Research.

Kamal Pasha, M., and D. Blaney. 1998. Elusive Paradise: The Promise and Peril of Civil Society. *Alternatives* 23:417–450.

Keck, M., and K. Sikkink. 1998. *Activists beyond Borders*. Ithaca, NY: Cornell University Press.

Lakoff, S., ed. 1973. *Private Government*. Glenview, IL: Scott, Foresman, and Company.

Latham, R. 1999. Politics in a Floating World: Toward a Critique of Global Governance. In *Approaches to Global Governance Theory*, ed. L. Hewson and T. Sinclair, 23–53. Albany: State University of New York Press.

Levy, D., and P. Newell, eds. 2004. *The Business of Global Environmental Governance*. Cambridge: MIT Press.

Lipschutz, R. 1992. Reconstructing World Politics. *Millennium: Journal of International Studies* 21, no. 3:389–420.

Litfin, K. 1997. Sovereignty in World Ecopolitics. *Merson International Studies Review* 41, no. 2:167–204.

Litfin, K., ed. 1998. *The Greening of Sovereignty in World Politics*. Cambridge: MIT Press.

Miller, M. 1998. Sovereignty Reconfigured: Environmental Regimes and Third World States. In *The Greening of Sovereignty in World Politics*, ed. K. Litfin, 173–192. Cambridge: MIT Press.

Mol, A. P. 2002. Ecological Modernization and the Global Economy. *Global Environmental Politics* 2, no. 2:92–115.

Mol, A. P., and F. H. Buttel, eds. 2002. *The Environmental State under Pressure: Research in Social Problems and Public Policy.* London: Elsevier/JAI.

O'Brien, R., A. M. Goetz, J. A. Scholte, and M. Williams. 2000. *Contesting Global Governance: Multilateral Economic Institutions and Global Social Movements.* Cambridge: Cambridge University Press.

Ollman, B. 1993. *Dialectical Investigations.* London: Routledge.

Panitch, L. 1996. Rethinking the Role of the State. In *Globalization: Critical Reflections*, ed. J. Mittelman, 83–113. Boulder, CO: Lynne Rienner Publishers.

Petras, J. 1997. Imperialism and NGOs in Latin America. *Monthly Review* 49, no. 7:10–27.

Philpott, D. 2001. Usurping the Sovereignty of Sovereignty? *World Politics* 53:297–324.

Picciotto, S. 1990. The Internationalization of the State. *Review of Radical Political Economics* 22, no. 1:28–44.

Poulantzas, N. 1974. *Classes in Contemporary Capitalism.* London: Verso.

Prakash, A., and J. Hart. 1999. Globalization and Governance: An Introduction. In *Globalization and Governance*, ed. A. Prakash and J. Hart, 1–24, London: Routledge.

Reinicke, W. 1998. *Global Public Policy: Governing without Government?* Washington, DC: Brookings Institution Press.

Rieger, E., and S. Leibfried. 2003. *Limits to Globalization: Welfare States and the World Economy.* Cambridge: Polity Press.

Ruggie, J. G. 1992. Multilateralism: The Anatomy of an Institution. *International Organization* 46, no. 3:561–598.

Schreurs, M. 2002. *Environmental Politics in Japan, Germany, and the United States.* Cambridge: Cambridge University Press.

Sen, A. 1981. *Poverty and Famines: An Essay on Entitlement and Deprivation.* Oxford: Clarendon Press.

Shapiro, I., and C. Hacker-Cordon, eds. 1999. *Democracy's Edges.* Cambridge: Cambridge University Press.

Sims, H. 2000. States, Markets, and Energy Use Patterns in China and India. In *The Global Environment in the Twenty-First Century*, ed. P. Chasek, 22–41. Tokyo: United Nations University Press.

Stavrianos, L. S. 1981. *Global Rift: The Third World Comes of Age.* New York: William Morrow and Company.

Stevis, D. 2002. Agents, Subjects, Objects, or Phantoms? Labor, the Environment, and Liberal Institutionalization. *Annals of the American Academy* 581: 91–105.

Strange, S. 1996. *The Retreat of the State.* Cambridge: Cambridge University Press.

Streeck, W. 1998. The Internationalization of Industrial Relations in Europe: Prospects and Problems. *Politics and Society* 26, no. 4:429–459.

Underdal, A., and K. Hanf, ed. 2000. *International Environmental Agreements and Domestic Politics.* Aldershot, UK: Ashgate.

van Roozendaal, G. 2002. *Trade Unions and Global Governance: The Debate on the Social Clause.* London: Continuum.

Verweij, M., and T. Josling, eds. 2003. Special Issue: Deliberately Democratizing Multilateral Organization. *Governance: An International Journal of Policy, Administration, and Institutions* 16, no. 1:1–21.

Vogel, D. 1995. *Trading Up: Consumer and Environmental Regulation in a Global Economy.* Cambridge: Harvard University Press.

Wapner, P. 1996. *Environmental Activism and World Civic Politics.* Albany: State University of New York Press.

WB. 1997. *World Development Report 1997: The State in a Changing World.* Oxford: Oxford University Press.

Weinthal, E. 2002. *State Making and Environmental Cooperation: Linking Domestic and International Politics in Central Asia.* Cambridge: MIT Press.

Williams, M. 2003. *Deforesting the Earth: From Prehistory to Global Crisis.* Chicago: University of Chicago Press.

Young, O. 1994. *International Governance: Protecting the Environment in a Stateless Society.* Ithaca, NY: Cornell University Press.

# 5

# Detached Flows or Grounded Place-Making Projects?

Zsuzsa Gille

Scholars in the field we may call globalization and the environment have conducted research in three main directions: the expansion and proliferation of international environmental treaties, the adoption of northern environmental policies in the South, and the greening of supranational organizations; the creation of a global civil society and the spreading transnational networks of environmental NGOs; and the environmental effects of neoliberal, corporate globalization, free trade, and supranational financial institutions, usually evaluated negatively. Until recently, this field has been impervious to social theories of globalization, which not only led sociologies of globalization to ignore environmental issues but also made the field irrelevant to political debates, whether implicit or explicit in polemics about globalization.

It is therefore timely and relevant to explore in this book what theories of globalization imply for how we study environmental change. In doing so, one must be aware of the causal link between globalization and environmental change as a two-way street. One should be interested not only in the ways in which social phenomena, change processes, and institutions affect the environment but also in the reverse—namely, how environmental changes are themselves "constitutive elements" of the transformations associated with globalization. In this regard, the flows concept seems particularly well equipped to synthesize the social and the natural, first, without implying their separateness, and second, without a mechanical and cybernetic understanding of how nature impacts society. With the help of some key concepts (e.g., hybrids) from ANT, it becomes possible to capture nature's agency with the concept of flows and to a lesser extent with the related concept of networks, in which the social and the natural intertwine in an undetermined dance of agency, to use Pickering's (1995) term. Looking at the nature-society interaction through this dynamic and almost phenomenological conceptual framework, one is well prepared to overcome a long-standing paradigm in environmental sociology: Schnaiberg's additions and withdrawals view. Materials are not simply added to nature (as in emissions and wastes) or withdrawn from it (as in resource extraction) but circulate the globe in socially determined ways, and these materials then themselves remake social relations and organizational configurations. To put this in rather simplistic terms, an addition in one place and at one time shows up as a withdrawal in another place at another time. This dynamic can be nicely captured when working with the concepts of disembedding and reembedding—notions I will revisit below.

A promising aspect of the conceptual framework as discussed by Mol and Spaargaren (chapter 2, this volume) refers to what the flows concept implies about globalization. In contrast to views of globalization as simply an assemblage of forces bulldozing their way across the globe, when social relations are imagined through the less deterministic metaphor of flows, our research can be more open-minded about power and agency because flows imply multidirectionality. Flows also project an image of the world as dynamic and fluid, which if applied properly in research, can provide a much-needed account of change, both social and environmental.

In all of the senses discussed so far, the concepts of networks and flows have much to offer. In order for that promise to be realized, I recommend complementing these ideas with some others coined in different definitions of globalization. I will primarily second Sassen's (1995, 2000) critique of globalization theories ignoring local material infrastructures, and will invoke Tsing's (2000) and other anthropologists' and geographers' reworkings of "territoriality" as well as my earlier work on "global ethnography." I will describe globalization as an economic and political project imagined, promoted, maintained, and endured by specific social actors in specific places and call for a research agenda that studies the relationship between globalization and environmental change through the concept of place-making projects. I will elaborate the methodological implications such as the unit of analysis and the role of scales, and argue for an ethnographic, bottom-up approach.

## The Concept of Flows and Networks in Sociological Theories of Globalization

Social scientists proposed the concept of flows and networks in large part because in globalization they saw the end of a certain simple, mono-structural hierarchy in the world, whether conceived of in terms of world systems or imperialism. In world systems and a global society described as colonial or imperial, certain flows only went in one direction, and a predictable one at that. Usually, labor and natural resources went from the periphery/colonies to the core, while capital flowed in the opposite direction. A society's position in the respective global hierarchy could predict with great certainty at what receiving end of which flows it found itself. To the extent that these transfers of labor, natural resources, goods, and capital were based on and reinforced inequality and exploitation, the political implication of such theories was that these transfers must be made more multidirectional, thereby making them more just. With globalization, as Appadurai (1990) claims, we now have former colonial entities owning giant media corporations, producing high-tech goods formerly only produced in the West/North, and money (in whatever form) moving in all directions, thereby belying previous global hierarchies. Appadurai hoped to remedy the implicit hierarchical view of global connectedness by proposing a new conceptual framework that saw the circulation of capital, money, goods, labor, and culture not only as much more vague but also as much more independent of each other's movement. His concepts of ethnoscapes, mediascapes, technoscapes, financescapes, and ideoscapes capture this disjuncture as well as emphasize that the new global relations are not objectively given but look different from different geographic places and social positions. Sociologists Urry and Castells place less emphasis on imagination than anthropologist Appadurai, but they both agree with him on multidirectionality and the relative disconnect among various circuits. Urry goes as far as debating the merits of the concept of society, not just as a well-bounded territorial and functional unit, but also as a sociological concept. Social relations not only reach exceedingly across borders, as Albrow (1995) argued, disembedding the social from place; they are far too fluid for traditional sociological thinking to be able to capture them for analysis.

No matter how fluid this new world is, Castells still sees power and inequality at its center. Yet he contends that power now increasingly emanates from certain networks, replacing well-grounded centers and agents of power. Furthermore, inequality is increasingly the consequence of one's connectedness to networks. Being switched off dooms a locality to poverty and disenfranchisement because of its inability to access the relevant networks. To the extent that this new power of flows is out of local control, Castells's flows act like global forces, and as such, render his perspective on globalization more deterministic than Appadurai and Urry would prefer. All in all, however, Urry's (2000) sociology beyond societies, Appadurai's (1990) scapes, and Castells's network society (1997) all provide a powerful argument against unidirectional concepts of the world.

For the sake of putting into context the perspective of networks and flows as laid out in this book, let me first provide a critical analysis of the flow-based theories of globalization as distinguished above. First, all three perspectives are from a bird's-eye view, written from outside or above. Even Appadurai, who is sensitive to subjective interpretations of connectedness, perceives scapes as never touching down on the ground and as not locally produced. While we want to give an account of the growing connectedness, we must not retreat to a view of everywhere, yet a view from nowhere. In my conclusion, I will explicitly call for theorizing globalization and the environment from a concrete geographic location, and a committed and accountable position.

Second, globalization for theorists such as Appadurai, Castells, and Urry is about increasing the speed and circulation of things, people, money, and ideas. This implies an increasing openness of borders. As a result, the social is seen as constituted by mobilities and flows, rather than the social constituting the latter. With the social being a derivative of flows, it is presented as fluid and structurally amorphous. Castells explicitly says that there is no systemic dominance in this matrix of relationships.

Third, implicit in the concepts such as networks and flows is a certain level playing field, in which inequalities disappear and nodes in the network are seen as equal, or at least their inequality is hard to conceptualize within the network/flows framework. Difference itself is reduced to the dichotomy of being in the network or switched off, greatly reducing social complexities.

This is partially the result of conceptualizing flows as natural occurrences, as automatic mechanisms over which no actor has control, as it is nicely encapsulated in Castells's concept of the "power of flows." By claiming that after being built, networks act autonomously—that is, quite independently even of those actors who brought them into existence—Castells feels justified in avoiding the question of who benefits from the network's operation, just as he eschews the question of who can dam and divert the flows, and who is simply flooded and wiped out by them. Building on our collective volume *Global Ethnography*, (Burawoy et al. 2000), O'Riain and I put it this way:

For all their differences, each of these approaches disconnects the social from any particular place—seeing contemporary social relations as characteristically stretching across places. Such approaches tend to reify these networks, flows and other "mobilities" (Urry 2000) as themselves defining society. Although recognizing that networks can be exclusionary, these approaches provide little analysis of power relations within networks and therefore find it difficult to explain reproduction and change in networks. . . .

Furthermore, these approaches neglect the agency of actors and their "sense making" activities as forces in shaping the flows themselves. While the network is at least activated by and even defined by the connections among actors, the concept of flows posits a world of disembodied flows of information, signs, finance and other resources—it is the actor's connection to these flows that defines the actor, not how they activate connections as in the network metaphor. (Gille and O'Riain 2002, 274–275)

There is an additional problem with the consequences for the treatment of place. Castells (1997), Urry (2000), Appadurai (1990), and even Harvey (1990) define the new globalized social as constituted by mobilities and flows, and in this view of the world, localities lose not only control but also the ability to make independent sense of the processes that affect them. Localities are at the receiving "end" of flows; in themselves, they are merely static points. They derive their meaning and identity solely from the flows that pass through them or from being (or not being) a node in the network. It is assumed that since flows are of a global scale, no culture and no politics can survive at a local scale. As Castells (1989) argues, meaning evaporates from place.

Flows-based theories of globalization, in sum, tend to not only eschew but prevent a local and from-below perspective, and with their (varying degrees of) ignorance of the power and inequality cannot help but discredit ethnographic and politically committed studies of the processes associated with globalization (cf. Burawoy et al. 2000). When favoring a "global flows" analysis, however that may be defined, there is always a risk of overlooking power and inequality in favor of a fluid, phenomenological view of globalization. Let me now spell out these conceptual legacies in the context of environmental thinking in more detail, and recommend some amendments and additions to the flows-centered framework as put forward in this book.

## Implications for the Concept of Global Environmental Flows

What are the implications of this evaluation of the notion of flows for an attempt to conceptualize the relationship between globalization and the environment? First, I will revisit an earlier attempt to illuminate the potential pitfalls of the concept of environmental flows. Second, I will assess what it means to import this and *only this* particular set of globalization theories to environmental sociology. Finally, I will ask how useful the concept of environmental flows is in particular empirical cases.

Mol and Spaargaren (chapter 2, this volume) are not the first ones to apply the concept of flows to study the relationship between globalization and environmental change. Rosenau (1997) and Zartman (1997) both come from political science backgrounds, with their work focusing on international politics and policymaking. It is instructive to look at how and why both have proposed the metaphors of flows, rivers, streams, and waterways to capture the complexity of the human-nature interaction as well as the "interactions between international regimes and other political levels" (Sjöberg 1997, 3). Like Mol and Spaargaren, Rosenau uses these metaphors specifically in order to dynamize our understanding of environmental changes,

No matter how institutionalized rule systems may be, governance is not a constant in these turbulent and disaggregated times. It is, rather, in a continuous process of evolution that fluctuates between order and disorder as conditions change and emergent properties consolidate and solidify. To analyze environmental challenges by freezing them in time is to insure failure in comprehending their nature and vagaries, not to mention the potential for effective governance as nature's threats become ever more immediate. (1997, 8–29)

Using a naturalistic concept, such as that of flows, for both social and environmental processes has its dangers, though. It reinforces a cybernetic image not just of nature but of the world. In this image, society, as nature, is and should be ultimately self-regulating. Consider Zartman: "[Formalization] is a response to a problem triggered by an exogenous challenge or an endogenous breakdown in current attempts at self-regulation—a relatively sharp escalation in the feeling of need. This step represents an important threshold in building a regime" (1997, 59). The argument for global environmental governance—both as practice and an analytic concept—usually goes like this: environmental problems got out of hand, they increasingly cross borders, and therefore nation-states cannot deal with them, so they need to delegate certain issues to supranational levels, and it is also at such levels that the details of collaboration need to be worked out. Regulation should take the form of knowledge and policies that circulate the globe, sending commands one way and feedback the other way, culminating in what they and others call global governance. Rosenau acknowledges and welcomes the etymological relationship between the Greek roots of the words *governance* and *cybernetics*, and defines the former as "the process whereby an organization or society steers itself, and the dynamics of communication and control are central to that process" (1997, 24), equipped with systems of rule, patterns of interaction, and control mechanisms. Flows then are subject to control by global governance. They involve micro-macro processes "whereby values and behaviors at one level get converted into outcomes at more encompassing levels" (Rosenau 1997, 25).

I am discussing this earlier attempt to theorize global environmental governance to shed light on the risk of bringing together the concept of flows with global environmental change. When we apply the term flows, we must be clear about what is implied in that concept, along with any unintended meanings and undisclosed propensities. As Mol and Spaargaren (chapter 2, this volume) correctly note, the danger already in Urry's theory is that it smuggles in Odum's ecological systems theory. In addition, in relation to the concept of global environmental flows, there is also the danger of falling back on a Parsonian view of society in which even social problems, when viewed from sufficient social, spatial, and scalar distances, have a function for societal reproduction.

We must also consider what the concept of flows implies when applied to the study of globalization and the environment. In particular, flows should incorporate earlier concepts—such as the environmental division of labor, environmental inequality, and environmental actors—because they, by definition, prevent an agentless and politically neutral view of globalization. Despite many globalization theorists' claim of the above-mentioned multidirectionality of social, economic, and environmental linkages, the circulation of natural resources, risks, or waste still follows paths dependent on economic and political (power) inequalities. Furthermore, globalization does not simply increase the circulation of certain (or all) things and the interconnectedness through the ever-growing openness of borders. Neither is the mobility of all things environmental even and uninhibited by boundaries. To summarize: some things and some people enjoy or endure more mobility than others, some actors have more say in what risks flow by their homes than others; some borders are opening while others are becoming ever so impenetrable; and against Castells's argument that power emanates from flows rather than from people or social organizations, some of the latter still exercise considerable amounts of control not just in general but in particular, over flows of capital, materials, and people. We must therefore still ground flows in the power of places—that is, we have to complement the concept of flows with redefined notions of place and social agency.

To evaluate the empirical relevance of the theoretical framework of networks and flows, and to demonstrate the need for this grounding, let us descend from the sphere of abstraction to the realm of the concrete. Let us look at what things actually circulate that may be considered as constitutive of environmental flows.

## Materials

• Plants, including seeds
• Animals
• Pathogens (e.g., parasites, pests, bacteria, fungi)
• Goods
• Waste
• Pesticides and fertilizers (as commodities and as residues on goods)
• Pollution and emissions (air-, soil-, and waterborne, including greenhouse gases)

## Money

• Capital
• Loans
• Aid
• Virtual money (e.g., debt swaps)

## Knowledge systems

• Scientific results
• Standards of scientific research
• Technologies (e.g., productive facilities, monitoring systems, maps)
• Experts, consultants, and activists
• Environmental management systems (e.g., ISOs, Environmental Management Systems, audit systems, certificates, etc.)
• NGOs and civil society know-how
• Institutional and organizational forms (e.g., laws, policies, governance structures, and the EU's "acquis communautaire")

To an audience of environmentally oriented social scientists, it is not necessary to explicate each; let us instead ponder the nature of each of these flows. Which of these flows circulates on its own and/or unintendedly? Do these things flow independently of each other? Are there no boundaries, whether human-made or "natural," to these flows?

When seeking a reply to the first question, we immediately see what a huge mistake it is to treat global warming as the paradigmatic case of global environmental change. Only the three Ps—pollution, pathogens, and pesticides—meander around the globe relatively independently of human intention. Everything else is circulated by purposeful agents, who construct the channels for these fluids and flows, and even some of these are put in motion on purpose for specific economic purposes, such as waste dumping. This is not to imply that goods, money, and knowledge flow *only* in the "originally intended direction" (though Pickering would even question whether there is such a thing independent of material agency) but to insist that it is rather problematic to assume that all of these things are flows *in the same way*.

Before going further, I must clarify what actually constitutes an environmental flow. Is there only one of these things in a flow, such as pesticides? Or is it a bundle of different things circulating together that constitute a flow? For example, it could be argued that pesticides spread not only by nature (through wind and water) but also through global commodity chains. The pesticides used for grapes in Mexico make their way to the United States when the latter imports grapes. In this case, goods and pesticides go hand in hand. Pesticides also "spread" due to the flow of agricultural technologies and aid. If we take the first view—that flows are constituted by homogeneous things—we must insist that flows do exhibit some social patterns, though the degree and nature of this socialness varies. If we define flows in the second way, we immediately undermine the basic assumption of a flows-based view of the world—namely, that there is no or little determination, and no social patterning can be discerned. Flows do have a patterned directionality. The global South does not provide aid to the North to cut its greenhouse emissions, and the North does not import toxic waste for incineration from the South, just to give a couple of simplistic examples. I think our most difficult task resides exactly in researching and making intelligible the seeming multidirectionality, the seeming underdetermination, of globalization without abandoning questions of (and a commitment to) issues of power and social inequality.

Finally, we must insist that while global warming seems to be a universal phenomenon, and it does seem that certain of those three Ps have no known natural boundaries, social agents do manage not only to facilitate flows but also to raise obstacles to them. People in different parts of the world do reject the import of toxic waste or the establishment of a hazardous waste treatment facility in their neighborhoods. Others do not have the knowledge or power to do so. Some borders are opening, such as national frontiers to trade, while others are closing, such as borders to immigrants. Even within trade relations, there is a simultaneous opening and closing: some countries can freely export their agricultural products while disallowing the import of some other agricultural products from the very countries they export to. In sum, we must apply the flows concept in a way that does not prejudge the openness, directionality, and independence of global environmental flows.

Instead, I suggest we complement the flows framework with additional concepts that safeguard against the above-detailed risks.

## Alternative Views of Globalization

In searching for a more grounded and sociologically more nuanced view of the relationship between the environment and globalization, we need:

1. A view "from below," or from concrete, accountable locations
2. To avoid fetishizing the global
3. To avoid a priori favoring the global as the most important level of analysis and scale of action (this is what Tsing [2000] calls globalism)
4. To see globalization as a contested process

First of all, flows-based views of globalization need to be replaced with those that see it in more nuanced terms. Sassen's (2000) recent work is useful here: for her, rather than an all-encompassing world of fluidity, globalization implies a repatterning of fluidities and mobilities, on the one hand, and stoppages and fixities, on the other. In order to see these new patterns, we need multiple levels of analysis (more about this later).

Like Sassen (1995), McMichael (1996) is also committed to a view of globalization that still has agency in it—agency that is not only imputed to disembodied flows and scapes. While Sassen has mostly researched the role of states and municipal governments in this regard, McMichael puts an emphasis on supranational agents and powerful economic actors in replacing the development project with that of globalization. Rather than having the developing world "catch up," the globalization project is an international neoliberal agenda aimed at inserting regions or cities into global free trade networks as competitive suppliers for a particular niche of the world market, increasingly subordinating national economic policies to international financial regulation.

The issue of scales is an important one in most studies of globalization. Most argue that action shifts to supranational levels, which for some entails the withering away of the nation-state, and for others the emaciation of the local. To counter this view, Brenner (1999) contends that globalization is not simply about ascending a ladder of stacking hierarchical scales but rather about the jumbling and fluidity of scales. Sassen (1995) asserts that some state functions "ascend" while others "descend," and instead of placing the nation-state somewhere between the global and local levels, she sees the state as not only manifesting at different scales but also actively constructing them. First of all, nation-states and municipal governments actively (whether defensively or proactively) produce institutions that attract or repel certain globally circulating things, such as capital or people. Second, some governmental functions of the nation-state migrate to the local level—for·example, when local (municipally or regionally based) NGOs provide welfare services to those in need—while others—such as making monetary policy—migrate to the global level, as is the case with members of the WB and the IMF. Third, with the migration of such functions, the nature and the agency of the local and the global are radically redefined, and this fluidity requires that various actors make conscious decisions about what scale(s) they should pursue a certain issue at. Demanding action from agents at various scales, those scales themselves are reconstituted, resulting in what might be called a variable hierarchy. Tsing (2000) also argues for a constructionist view of scales in what she calls scale making. Note that while we retain the fluidity and relative indeterminacy that inspired the flows-based concepts of globalization, with scale making and the concept of variable hierarchy, we do not preclude capturing inequality and agency. Tsing's (2000) concept of a place-making project is the most explicit response to flows-type theories of globalization I know of to date, and I turn to this notion in the next section.

## Place-Making Projects: A New Agenda for Empirical Research

To combat the reified and mostly bird's-eye view analyses of globalization, many of which have fetishized not only the global but also the mobility and fluidity associated with globalization, some scholars called for a return to locality-based research. A few of them suggested looking at globalization through the eyes of the local, but a local that is dynamic, heterogeneous, not hermetically sealed from the outside, and whose boundaries are politically contested (Massey 1994; Gille and O'Riain 2002; Gupta and Ferguson 1997; Tsing 2000). They thus committed themselves to a research angle that avoids naturalizing, essentializing, or romanticizing localities and communities. Place-making projects are efforts to define and redefine the nature of a locality in the pursuit of concrete economic and political goals, and to select the proper geographic scale for action. Studying place-making projects ultimately implies the study of globalization as a contested process—contested at various geographic scales.

A sad example of place-making projects is Goldman's (2001) study of the WB's environmental projects. He describes how the WB flies in consultants to remote areas of Laos and Vietnam for a few days. Based on these consultants' "knowledge," the WB divides up the countries' territories into rice-cultivating and fishing zones in order to make way for dams or other "sustainable" projects, radically redrawing the existing ecological and agricultural boundaries while redefining the nature of livelihoods in the impacted places.

A historical illustration is provided by Anderson (2003), who analyzes the history of the concept of tropics, and argues that the climatic typology was not only motivated by certain colonial interests and racism but also materialized in specific social and ecological practices. Depending on whether the tropics were defined as habitable (to white settlers) or not, this led to different attitudes toward the natives, sometimes as disciplinable and salvageable, and at other times as lost due to the "laziness" that the climate fosters in them. It also invited different ecological projects (plantations versus an Eden of biodiversity), and thus transformed places and livelihoods in different ways. But such projects are usually contested. De Soto's (2000) ethnography documents a battle around the recultivation of a heavily polluted industrial region located in the middle of the former East Germany. Two visions competed here: a modernist one, supported by various EU funds, that would create a high- and supposedly clean-tech industrial park interspersed with green areas and lakes; and the vision supported by the Bauhaus/green group that would reach back to the local historical traditions of environmental renewal, but would also preserve the monuments of socialist industrialization.

Another case of contestation, this time demonstrating what earlier I referred to as scale making, comes from Hungary. A Hungarian village disenfranchised under state socialism used its newfound freedom after 1989 to invite what then seemed a profitable venture: a French MNC's proposal to build a toxic waste incinerator. Here, a lot of what may have appeared as an exclusively environmental siting controversy centered on the environmental and economic nature of the district, composed of the surrounding villages.[1] Proincinerator forces claimed that the facility would not only bring resources to rebuild the run-down infrastructure of the villages; also by way of the high technology and international connections, it would insert the district into the bloodstream of Europe. Greens and opposing villages, however, saw the EU and its French representative as only interested in turning them into wastelands at a huge profit enriching the West. They decided to pursue the case not only at the local and national level but also at the continental and global levels: they established connections with western greens and Europeanized their rhetoric. For the proincinerator party, Europe was a missionary, civilizing force; for the greens, it was primarily a criminal, colonizing one. Furthermore, both sides had rather different visions of what European should mean in the local context. Those against the incinerator wanted to build the localities' future on traditional economic activities, primarily farming. Yet proincinerator actors saw no future in those areas and claimed that the only salvation lay in foreign, high-tech capital infusion.

An underlying theme in this battle of spatial symbols is how a society decides what constitutes the boundary of a sovereign sphere of decision making. The village needing the incinerator to rejuvenate itself economically obviously thought that boundary should lie at the village borders; only those living in the village should have a legitimate say in the fate of the incinerator. Greens and the opposing villages, however, saw not the human-made, administrative limits but the "natural" ones; as long as pollution from the incinerator could spread to their houses, they had a right to oppose the facility. That place-making projects can be contested independently of and even despite formal ownership claims is powerfully demonstrated by Peluso (2003) in her study of Javanese villagers resisting colonial forest conservation projects. While the administration thought it had clearly drawn the formal boundaries of the conservation areas, in the legal paradigm of the villagers who were deprived of forest use due to the conservation, it was not landownership but tree ownership that created rights to use the forest.

> Whereas officials would refer to "being inside" or "outside the reserve," local people refer to places throughout the landscape more specifically by the names of ancestors who planted durian trees there, who had swiddened there, or who had been involved in some memorable event in those places. . . . They have their own zones, which do not actually concede the primacy of the government's classifications (and the intended limits on their activities). (Peluso 2003, 248)

The concept of reembedding as suggested by Mol and Spaargaren (chapter 2, this volume) is a good starting point to make sense of these cases, while the concept of place- and scale-making projects as formulated by Tsing has an added benefit. The flows originating in, touching down on, and transforming localities, and the nature of flows changing, is a social and material process much more permeated with power, history, and culture than the concept of reembedding indicates. There is still a danger with this concept of viewing places as rather static or passive. In contrast, with the notion of place and scale making, we are ready to redefine the concept of place itself. A useful point of departure in this regard is geographer Massey's (1994) "global sense of place." She proposes a concept of locality based on four key arguments: places are not static; places do not have the kind of boundaries that warrant a simple counterposition to the outside; the identity of a place is not homogeneous; and yet places are unique, and their specificity resides in the distinct mixture of local and wider social relations. In short, the locality—the site—is historically produced in interaction with a variety of external connections, and this process also produces distinctive patterns of inequality internal to the locality. This allows us to view places and localities not as the mechanical opposite of flows—as static, isolated, well bounded, and homogeneous—but rather as constituted by and constituting those flows. In this dynamic, specific and historically formed social relations play a significant role rather than merely global trends and forces.

There are several advantages to applying the idea of place-making projects to the study of globalization and the environment. First, it requires an empirical grounding and accountability, discrediting global and universal views from everywhere but nowhere in particular. Second, it demands that we ask questions about the agency of social actors, materiality, and space. Since flows imply a view of the social and the material world as *always already disembedded from place*, materiality, spatiality, and sociality always appear to be dependent on flows. While this may be the case sometimes, we need a theory that doesn't preclude their independence and agency by virtue of the applied conceptual framework.

## Conclusion: Environmental Problems as Rival Place-Making Projects

What defines a global environmental problem for flows-based theories is whether it has effects at the global level, and whether it appears as an "uprooted" and unintended nature that renders it hard to deal with from one concrete location. Not surprisingly, the ideal type of global environmental problem is global warming. Many scholars and activists— such as Agarwal and Narain (1991), Sachs (1999), Shiva (1999), Buttel and Taylor (1992), and Dove (2003)—have provided a mortal critique of the biases as well as political and economic consequences of the global environmental change discourse. Following them, I would argue that these are basically local problems created by easily identifiable (western/northern) social actors, who, using the problems they created as an excuse, now demand that all, even those not responsible, regulate their economies in ways that western/northern scientists and policy-makers see fit. A place-making-project view of the world would eliminate this bias. There, only environmental destruction by global actors would count as global environmental problems. According to Mato's (1997) definition, global actors are agents who regularly exert their effects at the global level.[2] Under such a definition, for example, the WB's dam-building projects would count as global problems, even though a dam's effects may only be local or regional, but greenhouse gases produced by western/northern corporations would not count. These problems should therefore receive at least the same amount of attention and resources that are now accrued to global warming.

Besides the definition of global environmental problems, the basic dynamics and also the solutions offered are different in place-making views of the world. In the flows-based perspective, and with sustainability as the principle, global environmental governance tends to become the solution to paradigmatic global environmental problems such as global climate change and global deforestation. What I would add is that with prioritizing the global level as the most important scale of action and level of analysis, sustainability tends to become the goal rather than livability (see Evans 2001). Livability, like sustainability, fuses social and ecological concerns, but it places the main emphasis on the livelihoods of concrete, place-based actors, especially those expected to comply with global environmental governance.[3] Sustainability is also a more abstract concept usually referring to maintaining an existing economic mode of survival, albeit with an ecological conscience. Livability does not prioritize the reproduction of existing economic modes of operation; instead, it calls for remaking concrete places (in Massey's sense) so as to render them livable for their residents, both environmentally and socially.

Furthermore, in global environmental governance the emphasis is usually placed on highly codified regulations and formalized policies, which tend to discredit and displace functioning informal, unwritten, communal, or tradition- or local-knowledge-based environmental protection measures (Maughan 1996). The solution, in return, is not global environmental governance but alternative place-making projects that depart from the interests and culture of those who demand environmental compliance. While in global environmental governance the involvement of local actors is usually an afterthought and occurs according to the terms of the policymakers, alternative place-making projects would not only look "participatory" (Rahnema 1992) but would constantly be infused with the perspectives, interests, and cultures of affected actors at various scales.

In this chapter, I aimed to demonstrate that the theory we choose to guide our research has tangible consequences not only for our findings but for the policy implications as well. While social environmental theory is in need of a conceptual retrofit to make sense of an increasingly global world, we must not abandon our interest in and commitment to empirically concrete, place-based, though not parochial, research and theorization. What is at stake is not merely the success of environmental policy but the social justice implied in it.

## Notes

1. The case is analyzed in more details in Gille (2000, 2001).

2. Mato (1997, 170–171) classifies local, national, transnational, and global agents based on the impact of their activity. Local agents are those individuals and organizations whose social practices are mainly concentrated in the same locality in which they are based, although from time to time they develop these practices beyond this locality and maintain relations with social agents from abroad. Depending on the level of analysis, this locality may be regarded as a small town or community, a system of towns or communities, a state or province, or a subnational region. National agents are those whose practices are regularly developed at the national level. Transnational agents are those whose practices are regularly developed across international borders. Global agents are a subclass of transnational agents whose practices are regularly developed not just transnationally but at the worldwide level.

3. In referring to actors and research as place based, I am following Massey's insightful distinction between place based and limited to place. The argument is that one may conduct research and act politically from a particular location without ignoring the "external" connections of that locality—that is, without the parochial fallacy that Harvey (1990) accuses such research and politics of committing.

## References

Agarwal, A., and S. Narain. 1991. *Global Warming in an Unequal World: A Case of Environmental Colonialism.* New Delhi: Centre for Science and Environment.

Albrow, M. 1995. *The Global Age: State and Society beyond Modernity.* Cambridge: Polity Press.

Anderson, W. 2003. The Natures of Culture: Environment and Race in the Colonial Tropics. In *Nature in the Global South: Environmental Projects in South and Southeast Asia,* ed. A. L. Tsing and P. Greenough, 29–46. Durham, NC: Duke University Press.

Appadurai, A. 1990. Disjuncture and Difference in the Global Cultural Economy. *Public Culture* 2, no. 2:1–24.

Brenner, N. 1999. Beyond State-Centrism? Space, Territoriality, and Geographical Scale in Globalization Studies. *Theory and Society* 28:39–78.

Burawoy M. et al. 2000. *Global Ethnography.* Berkeley: University of California Press.

Buttel, F. H., and P. J. Taylor. 1992. How Do We Know We Have Global Environmental Problems? Science and the Globalization of Environmental Discourse. *Geoforum* 23, no. 3:405–416.

Castells, M. 1989. Conclusion: The Reconstruction of Social Meaning in the Space of Flows. In *The Informational City: Information Technology, Economic Restructuring, and the Urban-Regional* Process, 348–353. Oxford: Basil Blackwell.

Castells, M. 1997. *The Information Age: Economy, Society, and Culture.* 3. vols. Oxford: Blackwell.

De Soto, H. G. 2000. Contested Landscapes: Reconstructing Environment and Memory in Postsocialist Saxony-Anhalt. In *Altering States: Ethnographies of Transition in Eastern Europe and the Former Soviet Union,* ed. D. Berdahl, M. Bunzl, and M. Lampland, 96–113. Ann Arbor: University of Michigan Press.

Dove, M. R. 2003. Forest Discourses in South and Southeast Asia: A Comparison of Global Discourses. In *Nature in the Global South: Environmental Projects in South and Southeast Asia,* ed. A. L. Tsing and P. Greenough, 103–123. Durham, NC: Duke University Press.

Evans, P., ed. 2001. *The Politics of Urban Livelihood and Sustainability.* Berkeley: University of California Press.

Gille, Z. 2000. Cognitive Cartography in a European Wasteland: Multinational Capital and Greens Vie for Village Allegiance. *Global Ethnography: Forces, Connections, and Imaginations in a Postmodern World,* ed. M. Burawoy et al., 240–267. Berkeley: University of California Press.

Gille, Z. 2001. Social and Spatial Inequalities in Hungarian Environmental Politics: A Historical Perspective. In *The Politics of Urban Livelihood and Sustainability,* ed. P. Evans, 132–161. Berkeley: University of California Press.

Gille, Z., and S. O'Riain. 2002. Global Ethnography. *Annual Review of Sociology* 28:271–295.

Goldman, M. 2001. Constructing an Environmental State: Eco-governmentality and Other Transnational Practices of a "Green" World Bank. *Social Problems* 48, no. 4:499–523.

Gupta, A., and J. Ferguson. 1997. Discipline and Practice: The Field as Site, Method, and Location in Anthropology. In *Anthropological Locations: Boundaries and Grounds of a Field Science,* ed. A. Gupta and J. Ferguson, 1–46. Berkeley: University of California Press.

Harvey, D. 1990. *The Condition of Postmodernity: An Inquiry into the Origins of Cultural Change.* Oxford: Blackwell.

Maughan, G. 1996. *Second Nature.* Haywards Heath, West Sussex: Cyrus Productions. Video.

Massey, D. 1994. *Space, Place, and Gender.* Minneapolis: University of Minnesota Press.

Mato, D. 1997. On Global and Local Agents and the Social Making of Transnational Identities and Related Agendas in "Latin" America. *Identities* 4, no. 2:167–212.

McMichael, P. 1996. Globalization: Myths and Realities. *Rural Sociology* 61, no. 1:25–55.

Peluso, N. Lee. 2003. Territorializing Local Struggles for Resource Control: A Look at Environmental Discourses and Politics in Indonesia. In *Nature in the Global South: Environmental Projects in South and Southeast Asia*, ed. A. L. Tsing and P. Greenough, 231–252. Durham, NC: Duke University Press.

Pickering, A. 1995. *The Mangle of Practice: Time, Agency, and Science.* Chicago: University of Chicago Press.

Rahnema, M. 1992. Participation. In *The Development Dictionary: A Guide to Knowledge as Power*, ed. W. Sachs, 116–131. London: Zed Books.

Rosenau, J. N. 1997. Global Environmental Governance: Delicate Balances, Subtle Nuances, and Multiple Challenges. In *International Governance on Environmental Issues*, ed. M. Rolén, H. Sjöberg, and U. Svedin, 19–56. Dordrecht, Netherlands: Kluwer Academic Publishers.

Sachs, W. 1999. *Planet Dialectics: Explorations in Environment and Development.* New York: Zed Books.

Sassen, S. 1995. The State and the Global City: Notes Towards a Conception of Place-Centered Governance. *Competition and Change* 1:31–50.

Sassen, S. 2000. Spatialities and Temporalities of the Global: Elements for a Theorization. *Public Culture* 12, no. 1:215–232.

Shiva, V. 1999. Ecological Balance in an Era of Globalization. In *Global Ethics and Environment*, ed. N. Law, 47–69. New York: Routledge.

Sjöberg, H. 1997. Introduction: The Challenge of Global Environmental Governance. In *International Governance on Environmental Issues*, ed. M. Rolén, H. Sjöberg, and U. Svedin, 7–18. Dordrecht, Netherlands: Kluwer Academic Publishers.

Tsing, A. 2000. The Global Situation. *Cultural Anthropology* 15, no. 3:327–360.

Urry, J. 2000. *Sociology beyond Societies: Mobilities for the Twenty-First Century.* New York: Routledge.

Zartman, I. W. 1997. Negotiation, Governance, and Regime Building. In *International Governance on Environmental Issues*, ed. M. Rolén, H. Sjöberg, and U. Svedin, 57–68. Dordrecht, Netherlands: Kluwer Academic Publishers.

# 6

# Globalization, Environmental Reform, and U.S. Hegemony

Frederick H. Buttel

Environmental sociology has made some quite dramatic changes over the past decade or so. Perhaps the single most important transformation of environmental sociology has been from its late 1970s' and 1980s' emphasis on the sociological explanation of environmental degradation (and on convincing sociology colleagues that the environmental crisis was a singular threat to humankind and that the explanation of environmental crisis was therefore a high priority) to its mid- to late 1990s' stress on environmental improvement, environmental governance, and environmental reform. One of the concomitants of the 1990s' transformation of environmental sociology was the rise of new theoretical perspectives—at least from an environmental-sociological point of view—that related to improvement and reform (for an overview, see Buttel 2003). The single most noteworthy theoretical development was the rapid rise of ecological modernization theory from the mid-1990s to roughly 2000. In addition, WST, which prior to the mid-1990s had occupied an obscure alcove within U.S. sociology, attracted considerable attention as a result of the application of this theory to the international diffusion of environmental protection. Frank, Hironaka, and Schofer published several high-visibility articles in the *American Sociological Review* and *Social Forces* (Frank 1997; Frank et al. 2000) on the global diffusion of environmental regulatory practices. Frank and colleagues (2000) advanced the thesis that there is an ongoing development of "world society," one of the components of which is a demonstrable, though largely invisible, progressive international diffusion and adoption of modern environmental protection practices, mainly as a result of the formation and development of international environmental organizations. In addition to the work of Frank and colleagues on the world-societal proliferation of environmental protection, whole new areas of research and inquiry (such as new instruments of environmental governance, international environmental regime formation and governance, and ecolabeling) were opened up in the environmental social sciences.

It is interesting to note, however, that this vibrant period of emphasis in the environmental social sciences on reform proved to be sufficiently short-lived so that, in sociology at least, by the time my review paper on the topic was published (Buttel 2003), this account of the evolution of environmental sociology was already somewhat out of date in two major respects. First, the lead perspective in the late 1990s' and early 2000s' growth of interest in environmental reform and improvement—that of ecological modernization—had recently come under aggressive criticism —at least in the United States—and as a result, for some the stature of ecological modernization began to noticeably decline. Second, just as the tide of criticisms of ecological modernization (York et al. 2003; York and Rosa 2003) was rising, the major figures from the ecological modernization school were already at work grappling with some new issues and problematics under the umbrella of environmental flows, the topic of the present book.

As noted in the epilogue to this volume, the environmental flows perspective addresses creatively some of the major intellectual challenges facing environmental sociology and the environmental social sciences. Two of these challenges—the conceptualization of the environment, and the posture toward globalization and the national state—will be stressed in this chapter. The bulk of my chapter will be devoted to laying out some considerations with respect to the contemporary role of the United States in the international power relations governing environmental politics. A political science–based analysis of the ("environmental obstructive") power as deployed by this hegemonic nation-state ought not to be neglected as the environmental social sciences community reads, grapples with, and begins to apply notions of environmental flows. From that notion of the United States, I go on to discuss and balance in some detail the (U.S.-based) criticism of ecological modernization theory.[1] The imperative for environmental flows researchers, then, is to resist the implication of some flows analyses that notions of social structure, nation-states, and modernity no longer have any relevance to understanding global socioeconomic and environmental changes.

## The Utility of an Environmental Flows Perspective

There are two especially useful contributions that the environmental flows perspective can make to environmental sociology and the environmental social sciences more generally. The first, which I will comment on at considerable length here, is that an environmental flows perspective is potentially a major step forward from the oversimplified views of the environment and ecology that have prevailed in the environmental social sciences. The second major potential contribution lies in introducing new insights into globalization processes.

Most of environmental sociology has yet to go beyond Odum-style ecosystem biology (which is now considered passé in ecology circles), and has been largely confined to one or another variant of the largely placeless additions-withdrawals (Schnaiberg 1980) dichotomy, which typically leads to an implicit stress on additions (i.e., pollution) and a globally driven view of the environment. The implicit story line of environmental sociology has been that what really matters with regard to the environment is that pollution processes occur in particular (largely urban-industrial) sites/places, from which pollutants undergo dispersion (sometimes a short distance, but more often than not globally, as in the case of greenhouse gases). The environmental social sciences conceive of the modern world essentially as a globe whose social structure and processes are driven by *transformative industrial systems*, albeit ones buttressed by a dynamic service sector (essentially the digital economy plus the consumer-retail sector) that leads to environmental degradation in the spheres of production and consumption. What environmental sociology has generally tended to ignore is the opposite imagery—that of raw materials being extracted from a range of geographic spaces, most of them peripheral, and undergoing concentration in (mostly urban-industrial) space as part of the combined, but distinct processes of production and consumption.[2] To be sure, there are theoretical pieces in the environmental social sciences that give due recognition to the "ecoregulatory" sphere of renewable resources (Dickens 1991), but in the main this remains a theoretical premise, and does not involve active research on the social relations along the commodity chains that connect resource peripheries and industrial-transformation spaces. Further, some scholars do consider the ecoregulatory and nonrenewable minerals sectors to be of importance (e.g., Frank et al. 2000), but they take them to be mere variants of industrial-transformation processes or just another arena within which there is an inexorable advance of environmental protection measures (a penetrating critique of which can be found in Boyd et al. 2001).

It is also worth noting that environmental sociologists and other social scientists have had a tendency to privilege problematics that are the foci of major environmental groups, out of the understandable tendency to be responsive to these groups' research needs, and as a result of the fact that environmental groups are the key actors in the social definition of the phenomena that come to be seen as major, pressing, or worrisome environmental problems. Long-distance, transboundary raw materials commodity chains tend not to receive much attention from these groups, and thus from most environmental social scientists, because the social and ecological costs of extraction are relatively invisible (for an exception that proves the rule, again see Ayres 2004). Equally important, the victims of extractive economies tend to be the southern subaltern or else rural people in the advanced countries. These groups are generally relatively powerless, and often they are so dependent on the perpetuation of extractive economies that they become active agents in support of unfettered extraction (McCarthy 2002). Regardless, extractive communities and people are generally less likely to protest than would be the neighbors of a metropolitan chemical factory or toxic waste dump in the United States or Europe. From a social sciences point of view, what is especially interesting about these long-distance and/or transboundary commodity chains is that the intrinsic links between extraction and industrial transformation, combined with their spatial and social distanciation, imply that there is a fragmentation of the mobilization capacity of groups that might otherwise want to contest the extraction-production-consumption juggernaut.

To be sure, there have been some significant works in the environmental social sciences on global raw materials flows (e.g., Bunker 1996;

Bunker and Ciccantell 1999; Podobnik 2002), the distinctive properties of the extractive materials sectors (Boyd et al. 2001), and the socioenvironmental significance of the distanciation of extraction, production, and consumption practices (Princen et al. 2002; for a brief overview, see Buttel and Field 2004). Perhaps, however, because so much of the research that takes raw materials commodity chains seriously has come from the world-systems perspective, which is not a widely embraced stance in the United States in either the environmental social sciences or the social sciences more generally, these crucial works have not stimulated much research in the field.[3] Nonetheless, the notion of environmental flows has great promise as a perspective for diversifying the conceptual approach of the environmental social sciences to environmental phenomena, and for expanding the range of environmental phenomena that are seen to be worthy of research and explanation. A flows perspective does not diminish the attention paid to urban- and industrial-driven additions but rather it potentially introduces a much more variegated view of local and global environments, and of the complex interrelations among extraction, transformation, transboundary flows, commodity chains, wastes, production, and consumption.

It should be noted as well that for approximately a decade there has been a sizable group of environmental social scientists whose concern about how the environment is conceptualized has little to do with what kind of ecological representation of biophysical reality is privileged. Many environmental social scientists feel strongly that *any realist conception* of the environment is flawed because realist views are unable to take into account the coproduction of the biophysical and the social, and the hybrid character of both. For many environmental social scientists, the critique of realism was first manifest in the environmental social constructionist literature and the debate that ensued (e.g., Yearley 1991; Hajer 1995; see the overview in Buttel et al. 2002). But the objection to realism in the environmental social sciences is far more broadly based than is revealed in the environmental social constructionism literature (see, for example, Blühdorn 2000; Goldman and Schurman 2000). It is useful to note in this regard that one of the first comprehensive presentations of Urry's ideas about flows was in Macnaghten and Urry's *Contested Natures* (1998), which many environmental social scientists have seen as a significant piece of work in the field. McNaughten and Urry's *Contested Natures* was most fundamentally an attack on realist (as well as idealist) perspectives on nature, and their concluding chapter (247–277) makes the case for why the ostensible intellectual bankruptcy of realism and idealism, along with the new realities of globalization, makes a flows perspective the logical direction for the social sciences to pursue.

Environmental flows is arguably a more direct response to the concerns of the critics of realism than it is to the shortcomings of the metropolitan-focused images from ecosystem biology. It is useful to bear in mind here that the intellectual origins of flows and network studies (i.e., the work of Urry and Castells) lie in debates over "world cities" (as well as about "regimes of accumulation").[4] Urry and Castells were at earlier points in their careers neo-Marxist urban sociologists who were very much engaged with the emerging literatures on world cities written by geographers and other urban studies scholars such as Chris Pickvance as well as urban planning theorists such as John Friedmann. This literature is highly metropolitan oriented (Luke 2003). The flows perspective is essentially a postmodern or post–political economy take on a shared empirical observation that there are basically two kinds of space that matter in the world. The first is that of "Global Cities," where capitalization implies that the reference is to a handful of major metropoles such as London, Frankfurt, Hong Kong, Beijing, Tokyo, New York, and so on. The second is that of "global cities," the hundreds of other urban places, ranging from large to modest size, whose dynamics are induced to a greater or lesser degree by the handful of powerful urban command points of production, finance, and economic and cultural authority. Luke, in his ecological critique of these views, notes that "the collective of global cities begins to constitute a 'world of near complete internationalized urbanization'" (2003, 13).[5] One group of geographers and urban studies scholars, including Peter Taylor and Saskia Sassen, has maintained that the predominance of this form of internationalized urbanization can best be understood from the perspective of global capital accumulation, the trend toward the financialization of the world economy, and so on. Urry, by contrast, locates this pattern in a globally disorganized capitalism that is continually diffusing, and within which there is no hegemonic power or, put somewhat more bluntly, no "structure" in the conventional sociological sense. Despite their differences, all of these scholars are increasingly more likely to extend this view of internationalized urbanization to interrogating the industrial metabolisms of urban life. But in so doing there is little recognition that flows, fluids, and networks involve nonmetropolitan as well as metropolitan spaces, and that there exist raw materials supply lines without which late capitalism would cease to function as we know it.

Mol and Spaargaren's notion of environmental flows needs to be understood as, in part, an implicit recognition of a more materialized view of flows than is apparent in Urry's and Castells's primary works. The promise of the environmental flows perspective is that it can deal simultaneously with concerns about the inability of the traditional environmental social sciences to transcend ecosystem biology, and the need to recognize hybridity. Thus, the reservations expressed above about Urry's work tending to privilege intermetropole flows and to downplay flows and fluids with nonmetropolitan origins or destinations should be seen as a cautionary note, and as encouragement that the material as well as the social components of flows should be kept in mind. The continuing challenge is to avoid the slippery slope of an entirely dematerialized, postmodern view in which environmental features are conceived of largely by analogy (Ray 2002).

The second major rationale for a flows perspective is the new leverage that it can allow in approaching globalization phenomena. As just noted, flows scholars have been steeped in a variety of literatures, particularly those on global urban hierarchies and the regulation/post-Fordism debates, that have played strong roles in shaping our understanding of globalization. Flows theorists make a strong and useful case that sociology grew up during a unique world historical epoch in which there was a strong tendency toward a concurrence of the nation-state, the national state, national culture, national economy, and national territory. Sociology thus took the "society" to be the self-evident unit of analysis, and tended to see departures from the sovereign, social-insurance-providing regulatory state based on a fixed territory and citizenship as being atypical or anomalous. Globalization was accordingly viewed from the vantage point of national states: diminished sovereignty, the ostensible imperative of states to forego state sovereignty in order to make possible needed international environmental agreements, and so on.

Flows scholars have offered new insights regarding how to think about globalization and its concomitants. Notions of networks, fluids, and scapes call attention to the fact that there is a considerable component of turn-of-the-century social and economic life that consists of intense flows of money, symbols, electronic impulses, goods, wastes, materials, technology, workers, and so on, in which national boundaries matter less and less. Also, the environmental flows perspective sheds new analytic light on international regimes by seeing their increased role in governance as an indicator of disorder rather than an indicator of the progressively more orderly character of geopolitical relationships.

### Some Imperatives for an Environmental Flows Research Program

While I recognize the importance of the environmental flows response to the challenges of the conceptualization of the environment and globalization in the environmental social sciences, I also want to set forth some notions about phenomena that environmental flows scholars need to bear in mind as they develop this research program. My tack here is to lay out three major imperatives for environmental flows research or, for that matter, social sciences research that aims at a macro understanding of contemporary environment-society relations.

Two of these imperatives have been noted in the preceding section. First, while there is a need to transcend the shortcomings of the traditional environmental-sociological conception of the environment, a lapse into postmodern paralysis or moving toward a view of the world in which a few dozen or few hundred metropolitan command posts comprise its essence is not a step forward for the environmental social sciences.

Second, there is an imperative for environmental flows researchers to come to grips in both theoretical and empirical terms with the role of the United States as a force underlying environmental destruction. There is a certain hesitation on the part of social scientists to comment openly or express strong views about the United States as an environmental agent. In particular, there tends to be a reluctance to come to terms with the often negative part the United States is playing in shaping the global environment and economy. There is an understandable fear that such views might be seen as mere anti-American ideology or Eurocentricity. Much of the current scholarship in the flows, fluids, and networks analytic tradition tends in particular to downplay the U.S. political-economic, geopolitical, and environmental roles.[6] I would argue that much of what appear to be structureless networks, flows, or fluids have a great deal to do with the distinctive role of the United States in global society after the turn of the century. The United States is, on the one hand, a hegemon but a declining one (see the elegant discussions of this in Arrighi 1994), and at the same time it is an increasingly powerful and aggressive superpower in what is, for all practical purposes, a unipolar world. The other major developed-country zones—Europe, Japan, and Oceania—are of some economic significance yet are not upwardly mobile hegemons and are inconsequential as military powers. The most likely rising hegemon, when viewed over a multiple-decade perspective, is China. China today, however, is still too poor, too backward, too resource challenged, and too weak militarily to be a hegemonic contender or threat, although some contend that the U.S. hegemonic rivalry with China was one of the main reasons for the scuttling of the Kyoto protocol by the United States. The current reality that strikes some as negating the concept of social structure is arguably a transitional period of global stratification. Such a circumstance does not herald the swan song of modernity but rather the fact that the parameters of global modernity are considerably different than those that prevailed during the heyday of the European social insurance state, the U.S. New Deal, and the cold war of the 1960s.

Third, and related to the second, is the imperative that notions of disorganized capitalism and deterritorialized information networks should not lead to a view that the world economic disorder is novel, or that this turbulence negates notions of social structure. I feel that one place to begin for a useful corrective to exaggerated views of disorganized, postmodern capitalism is Arrighi's (1994) underappreciated analysis of the four predominant systemic cycles of accumulation—associated with Genoese, Dutch, British, and U.S. hegemony—that have characterized the world economy during the time from late medieval Europe to the present. Space does not permit even a cursory exposition of Arrighi's multiple and complex contentions. What is most relevant about Arrighi's analysis, though, is the observation that one concomitant—and precipitant—of decline in all of these systemic cycles of accumulation is the shift from accumulation based on production expansion to accumulation based on financial expansion. Arrighi's view is that there are cyclic or periodic shifts in cycles of accumulation, and that the two most important components are global expansionism and financialization. In particular, Arrighi stresses the world historical tendency for hegemonic powers and/or capital to advocate strongly for the desirability of the self-adjusting global market, which in turn tends to lead to financialization, disorder, instability, competition from rising hegemons, and hegemonic decline (see also Krippner 2002).

At one level, Arrighi's portrayal of financialization in the slow erosion of U.S. hegemony has much in common with the notions of disorganized capitalism (Lash and Urry 1987) and international economic turbulence that appear in the flows and networks literature. Arrighi, particularly in his analysis of the ongoing decline of U.S. hegemony, often uses the same kind of terminology (disorder, turbulence) that Urry does. But Arrighi parts company in a profound way from networks and flows scholars with his insights into the cyclic character of the four world historical "systemic cycles of accumulation." He argues that financialization—the shift of accumulation in the direction of transboundary rentier relations made possible by global dominance over money capital—has been integral to the decline of all of the systemic cycles of accumulation. Thus, Arrighi maintains that financialization has some inherent contradictions (e.g., the tendency toward monetary crises as well as the tendency of the world hegemon to become a debtor nation). Arrighi's assertions represent a powerful challenge to notions that digital-Internet-capitalist disorder and the flows attendant to it are entirely novel, that this disorder is not understandable through structural analysis, and that turn-of-the-century disorder signals an irreversible end of global modernity. The imperative for environmental flows researchers, then, is to resist the implication of some flows analyses that notions of social structure and modernity no longer have any relevance to understanding global socioeconomic and environmental changes.

## Globalization, Environmental Governance, and the U.S. Engine of Environmental Destruction

The major remaining part of this chapter will focus on the argument and hypothesis that to understand the dynamics of global society today, one must have an understanding of sociopolitical tendencies in the United States, and how these are reflected in the activities of the U.S. state and U.S. capital (and also U.S. NGOs and social movements). First, though, it is useful to stress what for some is self-evident about the United States: the fact that the United States is a singular and enormous environmental force in the world today. Indeed, there is at some level a prevailing environmental social sciences critique of the role of the United States. This critique has generally—and quite correctly and understandably— tended to begin with data on the U.S. share of pollutants such as greenhouse gases along with the consumption of energy, materials, automobiles, and so on. The stylized facts of this assessment are that the United States accounts for about one-quarter of the world's fossil energy consumption and about the same share of its greenhouse gas emissions (for a useful analysis of these data see Podobnik 2002). These data are well established and largely clear in their implications: the United States is a powerful engine of environmental destruction. Equally or more dramatic are the data on the U.S. consumption of nonenergy materials. During the twentieth century, the quantity of nonenergy materials consumed in the United States annually grew from 161 million metric tons in 1900 to 2.8 billion metric tons in 1995 (Matos and Wagner 1998). The materials consumption in 1995 amounted to the equivalent of 10 metric tons per capita per year, or ten times the level of 1900 (so much for dematerialization!). Omitting crushed stone and construction sand and gravel, three-quarters of raw materials use consists of industrial minerals, primary or recycled metals, and nonrenewable organics (predominantly plastics), revealing the industrially driven character of materials consumption. The per capita consumption of most classes of nonenergy materials increased despite major technological advances in the efficiency of extraction, conversion, and manufacturing. Ninety percent of materials consumption (excluding energy) in the United States is accounted for by nonrenewable materials.[7] As the world's largest and most dominant economy, the United States has a great deal to do with the global environmental balance sheet.

The foregoing story about the United States as an engine of environmental destruction would probably not be disputed by many analysts. What is at issue, of course, is how we should think about this account in sociological terms. This general account was very much on the minds of the U.S. sociologists who pioneered in the development of environmental sociology. The first two decades of U.S. environmental sociology were dominated by the coexistence of treadmill-of-production and kindred neo-Marxist theories of the self-expansion of capital and capitalism, on the one hand, and theories that posited the power of the dominant social paradigm and HEP among the public and within the academy, on the other. Both theory groups were cognizant of the singular significance of the U.S. environmental destruction engine and endeavored to explain its origins.

For a variety of reasons, the notion of the United States as the most predominant agent of global environmental destruction slowly began to give way to other approaches to social understandings of the global environmental challenge during the 1990s. There was no single theory that emerged to deflect attention from the observation of the singular U.S. role in environmental destruction. These diverse set of theories, however, tended to have in common a focus on governance, typically within a global (or globalization) framework. In addition, these theories have tended to cast the U.S. environmental role in a relatively more benign light.

One important group of theories pertains to global environmental regimes and international environmental organizations. For example, regime theorists examine the formation of international regimes as a result of processes such as power, interest, or knowledge (Haas et al. 1993; Young 1994). While some see that the rise of international regimes derives from the power and sovereignty of national states and the state system, many analysts of environmental regimes postulate that in a globalization context, regime formation requires or leads to the diminution of state sovereignty. A particularly influential strand of literature on international environmental regimes stresses the role of "epistemic communities" (Haas 1992) of scientists, state officials, and NGO staff who have a shared culture, exchange ideas and data, and may be more devoted to a mission (e.g., environmental protection) than they are to the real or perceived interests of their country. These epistemic communities comprise one major mechanism of diffusion of sounder environmental practices. In a related fashion, world society theory argues that the proliferation of international environmental organizations promotes the elaboration of international standards of good practice. Accordingly, the establishment of international standards of good practice may over time lead to these new standards, both environmental and nonenvironmental, being diffused to "laggard countries" (Frank et al. 2000). Scholars such as Wapner (1996) have stressed the importance of "world civic politics," in which environmental activist groups focus their efforts at the level of global civil society rather than at the level of societal politics. Finally, ecological modernization theory, particularly Mol's (2001) internationally oriented version of it, emphasizes a variety of mechanisms according to which globalization can be expected to result in an international transmission of environmental policy instruments and sounder governance practices as well as environmentally sound technologies.

There are arguably two major reasons why the environmental role of the United States was seen as more benign after 1990 in comparison to the picture sketched in, say, Schnaiberg's (1980) *The Environment* a decade earlier. These reasons were that the United States accounts for a disproportionate share of the world's environmental groups, and second, that U.S. scientists and officials play especially prominent roles in environmental epistemic communities and international environmental organizations. It may also be that the bulk of the scholarly literature advocating international regimes as a corrective to more narrow nation-state interests has been published disproportionately by Americans or in the United States.

Until the Bush administration's cavalier and unabashed disregard for international laws, norms, and values, there had been a general presumption in much social sciences scholarship that the (or at least one) pivot of the global diffusion of sound practices was the United States. Our European colleagues and many of those from the South had doubts about many of the specifics of this, to be sure, but most accepted, even if grudgingly, that U.S. domination of international regimes and organizations served to render their operations and practices more rational, efficient, and legitimate. There is no better example of this than DeSombre's (2000) *Domestic Sources of International Environmental Policy*. In her view, the United States is a trendsetter in most areas of environmental policymaking. Her book is largely devoted to specifying the conditions under which U.S. regulatory policies on endangered species, air pollution, and fisheries conservation become adopted by other national states or within international regimes.

I would contend that this image of the United States and the role it plays in global society is an outmoded one, based on an image of the United States as it was in the 1960s and 1970s—a post–New Deal state at the apogee of its regulatory and fiscal capacity, and with the self-assurance of having dealt reasonably successfully with a civil rights crisis and having implemented a social insurance state that was within reach of measuring up to European standards. Indeed, by the 1970s the United States had come a long way in a short period of time.

Skowronek (1990), in his now-classic study of the development of the U.S. federal government, has noted that the rise of the natural resource management agencies and the regulatory apparatus that went along with them was one of the most critical changes in the "modernization" of the U.S. state. For Skowronek, as recently as the late nineteenth century the U.S. state was a government of "courts and parties," in which a conservative Congress strongly protected states rights, and blocked attempts to have a stronger federal role in the economy and society, while a conservative court system staunchly protected the prerogatives of property. At the time, there was little impetus or mechanism for collective interests or concerns to be reflected in national governmental policies, especially if doing so might involve significant public expenditure, the reduction of states rights, or federal intervention in the decision making of private capital.

Ultimately, however, many of the accumulating excesses of the highly decentralized governmental system in the United States created massive social and natural resource problems that could not be dealt with through the traditional governmental order of courts and parties. Farmers, among many other groups, agitated for protection from railroad, farm machinery, and other monopolies that had been permitted to develop to an extraordinary degree under the protection of a conservative property-protecting judiciary. Middle-class reformers clamored for federal laws that would protect the young and the working class from the problems of an unregulated workplace. WWII inadvertently put into place some institutions of a centrally coordinated and planned economy (Hooks 1991). Most significantly for the present purposes, there was a growing voice in support of the need for federal regulation of the activities of loggers, miners, and others who were seen to be despoilers of the country's natural bounty and patrimony (Hays 1959, 2000). The "nationalization" of environmental and resource laws in the United States during the twentieth century was an enormous achievement. Kraft notes that

Environmental policy was "nationalized" by adopting federal standards for the regulation of environmental pollutants, action-forcing provisions to compel the use of particular technologies by specified deadlines, and tough sanctions for noncompliance. Congress could no longer tolerate the cumbersome and ineffective pollution control procedures used by state and local governments (especially evident in water pollution control). Nor was it prepared to allow unreasonable competition among the states created by variable environmental standards. (2001, 87)

There can be little doubt that the environmental regulatory state in the United States has greatly contributed to environmental protection in the United States. Unfortunately, the U.S. environmental regulatory state is on its way to being (selectively) dismantled (Cohen 2004). Most of the landmark environmental laws in the United States were passed by the mid-1980s, and there has been virtually no major environmental legislation since 1990 (Kraft 2001, 87). U.S. environmental groups and activists have essentially been fighting rearguard battles—sometimes successfully, but often not—to protect the environmental legislation already on the books, and there has been little progress over the past decade (Dryzek et al. 2003). Further, there have been devastating setbacks in environmental policy since the advent of the Bush administration (Cohen 2004). For example, the USEPA has relaxed Clean Air Act enforcement to such a degree that state governments are now suing the USEPA for failing to enforce the act.[8] For nearly two decades, the U.S. government has frustrated the establishment of global environmental regimes that did not benefit U.S. capital.

My general argument here is twofold, and is partly unexceptional and perhaps partly not. The first, and unexceptional, portion of my assertion is that for two decades, and particularly over the last two years, the United States has been a highly negative influence on the development of the globalized version of the Polanyian (Polanyi 1957) vision—of an international regulatory counterweight to the tendency within capitalism toward the "fictitious" commodification of social relations and nature. Almost everyone in the environmental policy field is aware that the United States was heavily responsible for watering down the Kyoto Framework Convention on Climate Change and then obstructing its ratification (Dryzek et al. 2003). More generally, there is a growing recognition that the U.S. government has for quite some time been a key force for deregulation, neoliberalism, structural adjustment, and weakening of the state capacity in realms such as environmental regulation and social welfare provisions. It is also common knowledge that neoliberal America often provides moderately effective offshore veto power with respect to policy alternatives that are not in the interest of U.S. capital (Peck and Tickell 2002).

The perhaps more-exceptional part of my argument is that rather than the generally negative role of the United States being a passing phenomenon, I believe instead that the U.S. role will continue to be adverse for several reasons that I will discuss at some length. My basic claim is that the United States has a huge structural reservoir of affinity for right-wing politics, leading to the indefinite right-wing domination of Congress and the machinery of geopolitics.

This structural reservoir has some considerable relationship to the U.S. class structure (e.g., the high degree of inequality, which leads to a large presence of high-income and wealthy groups; or the fact that only 13 percent of the U.S. labor force is unionized). While the United States is often seen as the homeland of concentrated, globally footloose corporate capital, the country has a huge class of petty capitalists and high-income individuals who are often among the most aggressive parts of the

U.S. conservative movement (Burris and Salt 1990). Union workers—and workers in general—are so insecure because of footloose U.S. capital that they are generally not willing to take militant stances.

The reasons for the United States having a large reservoir of affinity for right-wing politics are by no means confined to class, however. The U.S. religious scene is dominated by conservative sects and religions—namely, evangelical Protestantism and Catholicism. Religion in general, and the conservative sects in particular, have a hold on the U.S. citizenry to a degree that is not common elsewhere across the Western world (for an insightful analysis of the antecedents of the power of the U.S. Christian Right, see Burris 2001). The United States is a sufficiently large country so that for many of its citizens, even understanding what goes on in the United States as a whole—let alone in the rest of the world—doesn't present itself as an obvious necessity. In contrast to Europe and most other countries, where highly ideological conservatives and extreme right-wing individuals and groups are largely out of the mainstream, in the United States there is an aggressiveness, pride, and self-assurance on the part of the right-wing such that it is clearly the dominant, or most activist, component of the Republican Party. The Republican Party, which as recently as thirty years ago tended to be dominated by moderate northeastern and midwestern Republicans, is now largely dominated by the right wing, particularly by the evangelical Christian Right. Interestingly, Bush is not actually part of the extreme right wing. Politically, Bush lies somewhere between traditional moderate Republicans and the right wing. He has, however, appointed many prominent right-wing intellectuals to his administration, sees the Far Right as the anchor of his base of support, and has taken on the right-wing position as far as defense and aggression in the Middle East are concerned. Most important, he is acutely aware of the ascendance of the U.S. right wing, especially in Congress, state legislatures, and private think tanks.

What, then, is the essence of the U.S. right-wing agenda? There are basically two components. The first is the rollback of the state by way of tax cuts. The second is the rollback of the social agenda—affirmative action, the extension of civil rights protections, the welfare state, and state intervention on behalf of environmental goals. Much of the social agenda is seen by the U.S. Right as being driven by other countries, particularly those in Europe, and as being furthered through "world government."

What to some is most fascinating and alarming about the nature of the contemporary Far Right is the degree to which overt antienvironmentalism is integral to its ideology and program (Austin 2002; McCright and Dunlap 2000). In large part, this is because environmentalism is associated with the so-called world government (Luke 1998), which has long been an anathema to the U.S. right wing, but which was not a consequential matter in U.S. politics until the right wing of the Republican Party became its dominant segment. As an example of how mainstream antienvironmental sentiments are in the Republican Party, consider the case of Republican Rep. Ray Allen in the Texas legislature who in 2003 introduced a bill, titled the "Animal Rights and Ecological Terrorism Act," through the legislature's Defense Affairs and State-Federal Relations Committee.[9] This bill would have essentially criminalized public protests by environmental and animal rights groups. It would have even criminalized taking pictures or videos of an animal or environmental facility. The bill ultimately died in committee during late May 2003. Nonetheless, the fact that such a bill could be even dreamed of and introduced by a relatively rank-and-file career politician in the Texas legislature says a great deal about the extent to which the Far Right is integral to the Republican Party, and about the influence of antienvironmental ideas within the contemporary Far Right.[10]

While the United States will remain a major homeland for environmental NGOs, environmentalism is declining as a social force in this country.[11] To wit, despite superbly efficacious communication strategies by the Bush administration that have led most citizens to believe otherwise, it is clear that Bush has been America's most antienvironmental president of the past fifty or so years—Reagan included. But there has been virtually no public backlash against Bush's antienvironmental policies (Brechin and Freeman 2004) beyond the 15 or so percent of the electorate—highly partisan Democrats—that is even more convinced that regime change ought to begin at home.

At a more ecological-structural level, the vastness of the U.S. territory is highly consequential in reinforcing the tendency toward indefinite domination by the Far Right's agenda. The United States, because it is a huge country, has an enormous internal frontier and exhibits many characteristics of a frontier economy. Of the country's three thousand five hundred or so counties, about one-tenth of them have a population density of fewer than seven persons per square mile—and as a result, they are formally classified by the Bureau of the Census as "frontier counties." As Princen (2002) notes, frontier spaces tend to be associated with frontier economies. A frontier economy is one in which many economic and resource extraction activities occur outside the surveillance of the state and citizens. A frontier economy makes it much easier to externalize the costs of production on to peripheral regions and marginal people. Much of the behavior of U.S. corporations is aimed at re-creating the conditions of the frontier economy.[12] Further, the spatial center of gravity of the U.S. Right lies in the regions (the West, the Southwest, and the South) where the frontier economy is most predominant (Walker 2003).

## U.S. Ecological Modernization Criticism

This understanding of contemporary U.S. hegemony as the engine of environmental destruction sheds light on some of the fierce U.S. debates and criticism around ecological modernization.

Ecological modernization, which as recently as 2000 seemed to have inexorable momentum as both a theoretical perspective and research program, has attracted a swarm of critics and detractors in recent years, especially in the United States. To be sure, ecological modernization had been scrutinized from virtually the outset of the publication of its major works in English, and in some instances even earlier (e.g., Hajer 1995; Murphy 1996). This early criticism came from many quarters: postmodernism (Blühdorn 1997), discourse analysts/constructivism (Fisher and Hajer 1999), and some neo-Marxists (Boland 1994). It was also quite fragmented: the various critics had a wide range of views about the shortcomings of ecological modernization and relatively little in common with one another. Nonetheless, since 2002 or so there has been a specific rising chorus of criticism of ecological modernization. This recent criticism is more shrill than the earlier versions. It also comes from somewhat new quarters—particularly from various U.S. neo-Marxists and treadmill-of-production theorists (most prominently, Schnaiberg et al. 2002) as well as from the grouping I call the "neohuman ecologists" (York et al. 2002, 2003; York and Rosa 2003; York 2003). Further, the new line of criticism is more empirically driven, essentially by way of challenging ecological modernization on the available evidence about whether there exist demonstrable ecological modernization–type improvements in the environmental control/protection track records of various nation-states and/or global environmental regimes.

This criticism has a strong coalitional character in two respects. First, the critique of ecological modernization involves a kind of coincidence of interest (in the Weberian sense) among a quite diverse set of scholars who nonetheless all share—also with ecological modernizationists— strong materialist, objectivist, and proenvironmental convictions. Second, while these critics come from different theoretical points of view, their concerns have converged on similar criticisms (cf. Carolan 2003; York and Rosa 2003). It is my observation that the bulk of this criticism comes from either the United States or scholars who emphasize the U.S. empirical case. I would even venture the hypothesis that the most recent and most shrill criticism of ecological modernization has its origins in the growing frustration of U.S. environmental sociologists and others in the environmental scholarly community with the state of environmental policy affairs in the United States. I am sympathetic with this perspective, as will become evident in the sections to follow. It must be stressed to an international audience that one should not underestimate the force behind or the significance of the antienvironmental tendencies that are now manifest in, and radiating out from, the United States. The consensus on this judgment is now so strong that relatively mainstream specialty journals in the field, such as *Society and Natural Resources* (which I coedit), have seen fit to publish refereed and richly detailed pieces on the antienvironmental character of the Bush administration and the U.S. radical Right more generally (Cohen 2004). The attack on ecological modernization is in some sense a phenomenon of U.S. environmental sociologists wishing to draw a line in the sand by denying that European trends toward more effective environmental governance observed by many ecological modernizationists are generalizable to other regions outside Europe or are of any world historical significance.

The recent criticism of ecological modernization tends to take on a more aggressively proenvironmentalist, and often a more apocalyptic, posture than did the earlier criticism. At one level—though arguably the least important one—ecological modernizationism can be seen to hypothesize, or to suggest that there is reason to believe, that there are (political modernization) processes currently under way that have the potential to provide "solutions to," or that will attenuate the worst trends of, environmental destruction. I observe that some environmental sociologists, particularly many Americans among them, find this line of thinking problematic on two counts. First, the ecological modernization claim is then considered to be incompatible with convincing other sociologists that the environment is a proper focus of sociological scholarship, since in the United States much of the case we have made to the sociological community for the importance of environmental sociology is that this field is essential because of the fact that we are headed toward inexorable environmental calamity. Second, as noted earlier, the ecological modernization account is felt to have little applicability in the U.S. context, particularly given the rapid growth of raw materials consumption in this country, and its obstructionist role in international environmental regulation and governance.

Although generally speaking the U.S. criticism of ecological modernization—and particularly the recent lines of criticism by the neohuman ecologists—has arguably been overdone, there is at least one useful point that has arisen. In the debate, there has emerged the potential opening up of a new research program on the "Jevons effect" or "Jevons paradox." The Jevons paradox refers to the work of William Stanley Jevons (1835–1882) titled *The Coal Question* (1865; for an extended discussion, see Clark and Foster 2001). Jevons, who was in all other respects an unexceptional scholar, noted in *The Coal Question* (1865) that growth in the efficiency of coal utilization in nineteenth-century Britain had led to growth in the aggregate level of coal consumption. Most simply put in twenty-first-century terminology, the notion of the Jevons effect is that ecological efficiency (e.g., more fuel-efficient autos, industrial-ecological innovations in industry, and dematerialization) will, all things being equal, contribute to more rapid economic growth and a greater aggregate consumption of raw materials than would otherwise be the case. The Jevons effect or paradox is potentially one of the most important new concepts in environmental sociology. The Jevons effect features prominently in the thought of a range of scholars, such as John Bellamy Foster and the neohuman ecologists, whose work otherwise has little in common. The notion of the Jevons effect is a line of argument that challenges prevailing formulations of ecological modernization. But the Jevons effect does not really have an anchor in any particular theory, even though the neohuman ecologists have made major attempts to claim that it is at root a human-ecological concept. I do not believe, however, that the Jevons effect is in any way an endogenous part of neo-Malthusian reasoning because the classic exemplar of this approach, Thomas Robert Malthus, never said anything implying that there was an intrinsic downside to efficiency, viewed either conventionally or in terms of ecological efficiency. The notion of the Jevons effect could just as well be grafted onto the theory of ecological modernization as an even stronger argument for the need for the autonomy of "the environment," as a persuasive case for a more aggressive pursuit of ecological modern-ization strategies such as strong ecological and consumption taxes, and as a warning that the embrace of ecological modernization is not a reason for complacency on account of the fact that solutions to environmental problems will be automatically forthcoming. The Jevons effect could also be a useful contention *within a global environmental flows perspective* for why there is an *unrelenting reality of disorder* in the contemporary flux of environmental flows. Such an assertion would add a structural dimension to global environmental flows analysis, and at the same time generate some linkages between flows analysis and the more mainstream environmental social sciences.

## Concluding Remarks

The environmental flows notion, combined with complexity theory and a commitment to a more interdisciplinary approach to conceptualizing the environment than has been common in the social sciences to date, has much potential for environmental social sciences analysis. In this chapter, I have aimed to outline the contributions that environmental flows can make while at the same time suggesting some potential pitfalls of a flows perspective. Much of the chapter has focused on the U.S. case, and the multiple respects in which one can account for its environmental destruction tendencies and anticipate that these are not idiosyncratic concomitants of recent presidential elections. My argument here is that any perspective that sees the U.S. case as being essentially epiphenomenal will not be a step forward in the environmental social sciences. In fact, there are good reasons to believe that the kind of unipolarity exhibited by the U.S. state over the past few years cannot be sustained, and that the world is likely to be increasingly multipolar, with Europe, Japan, China/East Asia, and Russia as major contenders for power in every sphere. Nonetheless, the United States seems likely to remain the world's most dominant nation for some time (Chase-Dunn et al. 2002), with considerable ability to obstruct international or global governance of environmental flows. And if my assessment in this chapter is correct, U.S. power is not likely to be used to reinvent its own government or that of other countries to play the role of innovative environmental states, is not likely to take much constructive leadership in international environmental affairs, is likely to obstruct international agreements, and is likely to take concrete steps to maintain the massive throughput of environmental flows that characterize our world today.

The role of Europe—the individual nation-states there, and particularly the EU—will be crucial in tempering U.S. power. A key imperative for the emerging environmental flows perspective is to be able to recognize the social and ecological bases of present-day global systems of power.

## Notes

1. The epilogue to this volume expands on the point that there are some major barriers to environmental flows views rising to prominence in the way that ecological modernization did in the mid- to late 1990s.

2. A popularized, but elegant elaboration of the view that industrial-country scholars and policymakers tend to ignore the specifics of the raw materials basis of production and consumption in the industrial world is Ayres (2004).

3. Another group of scholars that takes the spatial and extractive components of the environmental flows chains seriously is that of sociologists of natural resources and their social sciences colleagues. A good share of these scholars are members of the International Association for Society and Natural Resources,

which involves a sizable minority (about 40 percent) of scholars trained in sociology. Their work has tended not to have much cross-fertilization with the environmental scholars in the disciplinary social sciences associations. Thus, while much of this work has implications for a more comprehensive view of environmental flows, it has not been widely appropriated by environmental sociologists (Buttel and Field 2004) because of the historic distance between environmental sociology and the sociology of natural resources in the United States.

4. Urry's notion of "disorganized capitalism," which appears in virtually all of his works on flows (e.g., in McNaughten and Urry 1998, 266–270), is a critique of the notion of the neo-Marxist/regulationist tradition, particularly its conception of post-Fordism as the successor to the Fordist regime of accumulation (Lash and Urry 1987).

5. The internal quote is from Roger Keil, an environmental science and political science scholar from York University, Canada.

6. To be sure, the United States is widely recognized as having a disproportionate number of world cities, and cities that are important network nodes or have high connectivity scores. By the same token, Urry (2003, 129, 138), though acknowledging that the United States exhibits "many icons of power" and is "the most powerful and dominant of such societal empires currently strutting the world stage," goes on to stress that it has a "porosity of borders" and that the globe is better characterized as "an intractably disorganized world" than a U.S.-driven empire. Urry is referring here to Hardt and Negri (2000), and their argument that the concept of "empire" or "imperial sovereignty" has replaced that of nation-state sovereignty. Urry's reference to "an intractably disorganized world" is a quote from Gray (2001).

7. These data are based on a set of comprehensive studies by Matos and Wagner (1998) of the U.S. Geological Survey. It should be noted, though, that the U.S. share of global materials consumption decline slowly over the course of the twentieth century, and has declined during the last two decades of the twentieth century in tandem with the declining world economic hegemony of the United States. Smil (2003) offers an exceptionally comprehensive analysis of the global energy situation and includes useful data on the U.S. component of the global energy economy.

8. See <http://story.news.yahoo.com/news?tmpl=story&cid=578&ncid=578&e =19&u=/nm/20030604/ts_nm/environment_epa_lawsuit_dc>.

9. See <http://www.capitol.state.tx.us/tlo/78R/billtext/HB00433I.HTM>.

10. For some details on the national and subnational structure of the Far Right antienvironmental movement in the United States, see <http://www.wsn .org/history.html>.

11. See the conclusion, however, of the impressive comparative analysis of environmental movements by Dryzek and colleagues, in which they suggest "a resurgence of environmental activism in the ecological modernization laggards, the USA and UK" (2003, 191).

12. See Princen's (2002) fascinating discussion of "distancing and the quest for frontiers." Princen's theory is based on the notion that rational producers and resource decision-making entities can be expected to strive to externalize the costs of production, and that "business strategy and state policy creates a never ending search for frontiers, defined in political, economic, and ecological terms." The two main processes of creating a frontier economy—one that lacks jurisdictional authority over externalized costs, little social resistance to the externalization of costs, and free or inexpensive waste sinks—are shading (the obscuring of costs) and distancing (the spatial separation of production and consumption). For Princen, the U.S. political economy is the prototypical frontier economy (among the advanced countries).

## References

Arrighi, G. 1994. *The Long Twentieth Century*. London: Verso.

Austin, A. 2002. Advancing Accumulation and Managing Its Discontents: The U.S. Antienvironmental Countermovement. *Sociological Spectrum* 22:71–105.

Ayres, E. 2004. The Hidden Shame of the Global Industrial Economy. *Worldwatch* 17 (January/February): 20–28.

Blühdorn, I. 1997. A Theory of Post-Ecologist Politics. *Environmental Politics* 6:125–147.

Blühdorn, I. 2000. *Post-Ecologist Politics*. London: Routledge.

Boland, J. 1994. Ecological Modernization. *Capitalism-Nature-Socialism* 5:135–141.

Boyd, M., W. S. Prudham, and R. A. Schurman. 2001. Industrial Dynamics and the Problem of Nature. *Society and Natural Resources* 14:555–570.

Brechin, S. R., and D. A. Freeman. 2004. Public Support for the Environment and an Anti-Environmental President: Possible Explanations for the George W. Bush Anomaly. *Forum* 2:1–20. <http://www.bepress.com/cgi/viewcontent.cgi?article=1027&context= forum>.

Bunker, S. G. 1996. Raw Material and the Global Economy: Oversights and Distortions in Industrial Ecology. *Society and Natural Resources* 9:419–429.

Bunker, S. G., and P. Ciccantell. 1999. Economic Ascent and the Global Environment: World-Systems Theory and the New Historical Materialism. In *Ecology and the World-System*, ed. W. Goldfrank et al., 107–122. Westport, CT: Greenwood Press.

Burris, V. 2001. Small Business, Status Politics, and the Social Base of New Christian Right Activism. *Critical Sociology* 27:29–55.

Burris, V., and J. Salt. 1990. The Politics of Capitalist Class Segments: A Test of Corporate Liberalism Theory. *Social Problems* 37:601–619.

Buttel, F. H. 2003. Environmental Sociology and the Explanation of Environmental Reform. *Organization and Environment* 16 (September): 306–344.

Buttel, F. H., P. Dickens, R. E. Dunlap, and A. Gijswijt. 2002. Sociological Theory and the Environment: An Overview and Introduction. In *Sociological Theory and the Environment: Classical Foundations, Contemporary Insights*, ed. R. E. Dunlap, P. Dickens, F. H. Buttel, and A. Gijswijt, 3–32. Lanham, MD: Rowman and Littlefield.

Buttel, F. H., and D. R. Field. 2004. Environmental and Natural Resource Sociologies: Understanding and Synthesizing Fundamental Research Traditions. In *Society and Natural Resources: A Summary of Knowledge*, ed. M. J. Manfredo, J. J. Vaske, D. R. Field, P. J. Brown, and B. L. Bruyere. Jefferson City, MO: Modern Litho.

Carolan, M. S. 2003. Ecological Modernization Theory: What about Consumption? *Society and Natural Resources* 17:247–260.

Chase-Dunn, C., R. Giem, A. Jorgenson, T. Reifer, J. Rogers, and S. Lio. 2002. The Trajectory of the United States in the World-System: A Quantitative Reflection. Paper presented at the World Congress for Sociology, Brisbane, July.

Clark, B., and J. B. Foster. 2001. William Stanley Jevons and the Coal Question. *Organization and Environment* 14:93–98.

Cohen, M. 2004. A Midterm Appraisal of the Bush Administration's Environmental Record. *Society and Natural Resources* 17:1–21.

DeSombre, E. R. 2000. *Domestic Sources of International Environmental Policy: Industry, Environmentalists, and U.S. Power*. Cambridge: MIT Press.

Dickens, P. 1991. *Society and Nature; Towards a Green Social Theory*. New York: Harvester Wheatsleaf.

Dryzek, J. S., D. Downes, C. Hunold, and D. Schlosberg. 2003. *Green States and Social Movements*. Oxford: Oxford University Press.

Fisher, F., and M. Hajer, eds. 1999. *Living with Nature*. New York: Oxford University Press.

Frank, D. J. 1997. Nature, Science, and the Globalization of the Environment, 1870–1990. *Social Forces* 76:409–435.

Frank, D. J., A. Hironaka, and E. Schofer. 2000. The Nation-State and the Natural Environment over the Twentieth Century. *American Sociological Review* 65:96–116.

Goldman, M., and R. Schurman. 2000. Closing the "Great Divide": New Social Theory on Society and Nature. *Annual Review of Sociology* 26:563–584.

Gray, J. 2001. The Era of Globalization Is Over. *New Statesman*, September 24.

Haas, P. M. 1992. Introduction: International Epistemic Communities and International Policy Coordination. *International Organization* 46:1–37.

Haas, P. M., R. O. Keohane, and M. A. Levy, eds. 1993. *Institutions for the Earth*. Cambridge: MIT Press.

Hajer, M. 1995. *The Politics of Environmental Discourse*. London: Clarendon.

Hardt, A., and M. Negri. 2000. *Empire*. Cambridge: Harvard University Press.

Hays, S. P. 1959. *Conservation and the Gospel of Efficiency*. New York: Atheneum.

Hays, S. P. 2000. *A History of Environmental Politics since 1945*. Pittsburgh: University of Pittsburgh Press.

Hooks, G. 1991. *Forging the Military-Industrial Complex*. Urbana: University of Illinois Press.

Jevons, W. S. 1865. *The Coal Question: An Inquiry Concerning the Progress of the Nation, and the Probable Exhaustion of Our Coal-Mines*. London: Macmillan.

Kraft, M. E. 2001. *Environmental Policy and Politics*. 2nd ed. New York: Longman.

Krippner, G. 2002. What Is Financialization? Paper presented at the annual meeting of the Allied Social Science Association, San Diego, January 3–5.

Lash, S., and J. Urry. 1987. *The End of Organized Capitalism*. Madison: University of Wisconsin Press.

Luke, T. W. 1998. *A Rough Road out of Rio: The Right-Wing Reaction in the United States against Global Environmentalism*. Unpublished manuscript, Virginia Polytechnic Institute and State University.

Luke, T. W. 2003. "Global Cities" vs. "Global Cities": Rethinking Contemporary Urbanism as Public Ecology. *Studies in Political Economy* 70:11–33.

Matos, G., and L. Wagner. 1998. Consumption of Materials in the United States, 1900–1995. *Annual Review of Energy and Environment* 23:107–122.

McCarthy, J. 2002. First World Political Ecology: Lessons from the Wise Use Movement. *Environment and Planning A* 34:1281–1302.

McCright, A. M., and R. E. Dunlap. 2000. Challenging Global Warming as a Social Problem: An Analysis of the Conservative Countermovement's Counterclaims. *Social Problems* 47:499–522.

McNaughten, P., and J. Urry. 1998. *Contested Natures*. London: Sage.

Mol, A. P. J. 2001. *Globalization and Environmental Reform*. Cambridge: MIT Press.

Murphy, R. 1996. *Sociology and Nature*. Boulder, CO: Westview Press.

Peck, J., and A. Tickell. 2002. Neoliberalizing Space. *Antipode* 34:380–404.

Podobnik, B. 2002. Global Energy Inequalities: Exploring the Long-Term Implications. *Journal of World-Systems Research* 8:252–274.

Polanyi, K. 1957. *The Great Transformation*. Boston: Beacon Press.

Princen, T. 2002. Distancing: Consumption and the Severing of Feedback. In *Confronting Consumption*, ed. T. Princen, M. F. Maniates, and K. Conca, 103–131. Cambridge: MIT Press.

Princen, T., M. F. Maniates, and K. Conca. 2002. Confronting Consumption. In *Confronting Consumption*, ed. T. Princen, M. F. Maniates, and K. Conca, 1–20. Cambridge: MIT Press.

Ray, L. 2002. "Crossing Borders": Sociology, Globalization, and Immobility. *Sociological Research Online* 7, no. 3. <http://www.socresonline.org.uk/7/3/ray.html>.

Schnaiberg, A. 1980. *The Environment*. New York: Oxford University Press.

Schnaiberg, A., D. Pellow, and A. Weinberg. 2002. The Treadmill of Production and the Environmental State. In *The Environmental State under Pressure*, ed. A. P. J. Mol and F. H. Buttel, 15–32. London: Elsevier.

Skowronek, W. 1990. *Building a New American State*. New York: Cambridge University Press.

Smil, V. 2003. *Energy at the Crossroads*. Cambridge: MIT Press.

Urry, J. 2003. *Global Complexity*. Cambridge: Polity Press.

Walker, P. A. 2003. Reconsidering "Regional" Political Ecologies: Toward a Political Ecology of the Rural American West. *Progress in Human Geography* 27:7–24.

Wapner, P. K. 1996. *Environmental Activism and World Civic Politics*. Albany: State University of New York Press.

Yearley, S. 1991. *The Green Case*. London: Routledge.

York, R. 2003. Cross-National Variation in the Size of Passenger Car Fleets: A Study in Environmentally Significant Consumption. *Population and Environment* 25:119–140.

York, R., and E. A. Rosa. 2003. Key Challenges to Ecological Modernization: Institutional Efficacy, Case Study Evidence, Units of Analysis, and the Pace of Eco-Efficiency. *Organization and Environment* 16:273–288.

York, R., E. A. Rosa, and T. Dietz. 2002. Bridging Environmental Science with Environmental Policy: The Plasticity of Population, Affluence, and Technology. *Social Science Quarterly* 83:18–34.

York, R., E. A. Rosa, and T. Dietz. 2003. Footprints on the Earth: The Environmental Consequences of Modernity. *American Sociological Review* 68:279–300.

Young, O. R. 1994. *International Governance*. Ithaca, NY: Cornell University Press.

# II

**Empirical Perspectives**

# 7

# Governing Nature? On the Global Complexity of Biodiversity Conservation

C. S. A. (Kris) van Koppen

At first sight, biodiversity conservation is not primarily about flows. It rather seems an effort to keep valuable species and ecosystems where they are, and maintain the natural character of special places. As far as flows are concerned, they often appear as something biodiversity is to be protected from, as for instance in cases of the importation of exotic species, the influx of toxic or nutrifying substances, or the arrival of large numbers of tourists. On closer investigation, however, flows are much more central to biodiversity, even when we would limit our view to the physical dimensions of ecosystems. Flow attributes of biodiversity become apparent in the concept of ecological networks, say, which is gaining a prominent place in nature conservation policy and management.

An illustrative example of the role of networks in biodiversity conservation is the PEEN. The PEEN is a projected network of nature reserves, buffer zones, corridors, and stepping-stones. The concept of the PEEN, developed under the auspices of the UNEP, the IUCN, and the European Council, was adopted in 1995, and then elaborated in two consecutive five-year action plans. It includes the EU Natura 2000 network, but also encompasses nature areas in many of the Russian Federation states as well as countries such as Iceland, Cyprus, and Turkey (Council of Europe 1998), thus covering Europe in its broadest sense. In the proposal for the new action plan, the ecological premise of the network is charactized as follows:

The basic premise of the ecological network concept is straightforward: the fragmentation of habitats can be counteracted by creating buffer zones to protect the remaining natural areas; these core areas will be connected by stepping-stones and corridors which allow species to range freely over wide areas, either to colonise new areas or follow natural migration pathways. Ecological networks are crucial to allow biodiversity and ecosystems to adapt to present and future external pressures. Of particular relevance, in this respect, are the expected impacts of climate change throughout Europe. (ECNC et al. 2003, 3)

As this description exemplifies, current ecological views tend to be dynamic in time and space, and increasingly take account of the interaction of flows and places. Particular flows—involved in the migration of specific animals, and the dispersion of certain plants and micro-organisms—are considered vital in maintaining biodiversity under conditions of continuous change. These conditions of change are both induced by natural processes and, as in the case of climate change, by human action. The concept of ecological networks is introduced, among others, to further thematize and explore these dynamics.

Yet ecological networks have strong social and political connotations too. They are introduced in conservation policy to bundle varying management practices into one overarching concept, and to create a vantage point from which different national and regional policies can be mutually adapted and linked to international policies and organizations. Turning to these social dimensions of biodiversity, the PEEN is a fascinating case as well. The PEEN is developed within the framework of the Pan-European Biodiversity and Landscape Conservation Strategy, of which it is the cornerstone and first objective. The main initiator of this strategy was the Council of Europe, but its social network extends well beyond European states. Global actors play major roles, such as the UNEP (which together with the European Council holds the secretariat of the strategy), the IUCN, and the UN Economic Commission for Europe. A wide spectrum of other sorts of organizations contribute to the strategy (ECNC 2004b). Among these organizations, there are also regional and business actors. The recent Pan-European Strategy conference in Madrid, for instance, featured the *Brabant-European Partnership Manifesto* on the cooperation between the Pan-European Strategy initiative and the Dutch province of Brabant. The manifesto resulted from a previous workshop organized by the European Centre for Nature Conservation, the Dutch agricultural ministry, the Hungarian environmental ministry, the province of Brabant, and a major Dutch bank. The central aim of the manifesto was to underscore the importance of broader involvement in the biodiversity and landscape issues of small- and medium-size business as well as large businesses (ECNC 2004a). Behind this network of diverse organizations, both in character and scale, the EU obviously is an important "attractor." Doubtlessly, many of the participating non-EU countries welcome the PEEN as a step toward further European integration and, if possible, accession to the EU. The rather implicit but crucial influence of the EU is also apparent from the pivotal role of the EU-based European Centre for Nature Conservation in the management of the Pan-European Strategy.

The example of the PEEN does not stand alone. Many ecological networks are under development worldwide, often nationally based but also, increasingly, internationally based. Some of them, such as the PEEN, still mainly exist on paper; others are well established in terms of designation, legal protection, and management, as for instance the Dutch National Ecological Network and large parts of the EU Natura 2000 network. In some of the networks, physical flows between different core areas are vital, while in other networks the "nodes" are mainly linked by social and political relationships. UNESCO's (2002) World Network of Biosphere Reserves, for example is a worldwide network linking nature areas via education, science, and policy. Likewise, the global system of biodiversity hot spots, which is rapidly gaining prominence in biodiversity debates (see below), can be considered a network from the perspective of a common conservation ecology logic, but not so much in terms of physical exchange.

These varying examples may serve to illustrate how ecological networks and flows are tied up with social networks and flows that increasingly extend to the global level, often in complex and differentiated ways. If we take the word flow in a broad sense, encompassing both physical flows (e.g., of animal migration, nutrients, and energy) and social flows (e.g., data and expertise, money, and regulatory measures), then we might say that ecological and social networks together constitute the space of flows that is characteristic of today's efforts of biodiversity conservation (Castells 1996). This space of flows not only links together the particular places that are to be preserved for biodiversity conservation but deeply influences their character. Being part of Natura 2000, or a biodiversity hot spot, changes a nature reserve in multiple ways. It may increase its impact on national and international conservation agendas, but it can also alter the regulatory measures taken, the availability of funding, the priorities in species preservation, the layout of the reserve, the park management, and the involvement of businesses and NGOs. Relationships between the space of places (nature areas, buffer zones, and stepping-stones) and the space of flows (featuring social and eco-logical networks) are close and mutual. Biodiversity conservation, there-fore, can be characterized as a hybrid and often global scape, in a sense that is central to this volume (see chapter 1).

The aim of this chapter is to investigate this hybrid scape, with a focus on the debates and networks that characterize biodiversity conservation to date. In the first part, "Biodiversity in Debate," I introduce key issues in the current debates on biodiversity, starting with the main strands of thinking—the "cases"—and then elaborating these strands in terms of their implications for the assessment of the physical and social aspects of biodiversity. In the second part, "Biodiversity Configurations," I make an effort to link these conceptual strands to the social and physical net-works that are actually involved in biodiversity conservation. Four con-figurations are distinguished within the biodiversity scape: one building on the "classical" nature conservation approach, which is bound up with national government decision making; and three more recent, diverging configurations, labeled local development, global ecology, and product chains. The chapter will conclude with an evaluation of the perspectives presented.

## Biodiversity in Debate

Biodiversity, we might say, is nature conservation globalized. When bio-diversity made its full appearance on the global stage at the 1992 UNCED in Rio de Janeiro, a new page was turned in the development of global nature management. The CBD, accepted at the conference and now including more than 180 parties, is the most authoritative global document on nature conservation to date.

According to the CBD, biodiversity is defined as variety on different levels: species variety—that is, variety between different species; variety within a species—that is, variety between individuals and populations of one species; and variety between communities and ecosystems. In its most comprehensive meaning, then, biodiversity emerges as a term that encompasses individual diversity, species diversity, landscape variety, and ecosystem diversity. Moreover, the biodiversity concept is closely linked to the ecosystem concept because, on the one hand, the functioning of ecosystems is dependent on the biodiversity they harbor and, on the other hand, ecosystems themselves constitute an important level of biodiversity (Millennium Assessment 2003). In line with the concept's comprehensiveness, the CBD attributes a wide range of values to biodiversity, referring to the "intrinsic value of biological diversity and . . . the ecological, genetic, social, economic, scientific, educational, cultural, recreational and aesthetic values of biological diversity and its components" (Secretariat of the Convention on Biological Diversity 2005, 3). In other words, in its broadest sense biodiversity encompasses all of the nature that conservationists are concerned about. Biodiversity conservation is often used as synonymous with nature conservation.

The broad definition of the biodiversity concept and its values, however, is usually founded on the much narrower base of a molecular approach to genetics, as it is characteristic of modern biology and biotechnology. In the words of Dobson: "It could be argued that individual genes (sequences of DNA on chromosomes that code for a specific function) are the fundamental currency of biological diversity. After all, species are ultimately defined by differences in their genes. Moreover, all species require a diversity of genes spread among the population if they are to retain the ability to adapt to changing environments" (1995, 10). Biodiversity, in this narrower, science-based meaning, is rooted in the evolutionary genetics of modern conservation biology, as propagated by Wilson (e.g., 1992; Wilson and Peter 1988) and Soulé (e.g., 1986; Soulé and Wilcox 1980), among others. To many conservationists, this implies a certain "modernization" of the nature concept that is central to conservation. The homeostatic, tableaulike view of nature is substituted with a nonequilibrium view that allows for dynamic, unpredictable changes in time. In addition, classical motivations of nature conservation based on the aesthetic and emotional appreciation of wildlife and wilderness are dismissed or modified in favor of the preservation of genetic diversity per se through ecology-based resource management (Grumbine 1995; Harrop 1999).

Both the codification of biodiversity in the CBD and the promise of a modern, science-based approach to nature conservation have contributed to the more prominent position of biodiversity within national and international environmental policy frameworks. In the Netherlands, for instance, government officials welcomed biodiversity as a "hard" and "modern" policy notion in comparison to the "soft" concept of nature (Rientjes 1999). For the first time in Dutch environmental policy, the Fourth National Environmental Policy Plan of 2001 explicitly addressed the issue of nature conservation under the title of biodiversity management. It positioned biodiversity as one of the core environmental problems to be coped with (Ministerie VROM 2001). As the Dutch example may illustrate, translating the issue of nature conservation into biodiversity management has made it easier to situate biodiversity among the other environmental flows that are central to environmental policy, such as carbon dioxide, CFKs, waste flows, pesticides, fossil fuels, and minerals. Similar to these abiotic environmental flows, it is assumed that biodiversity can be scientifically assessed in a sufficiently reliable and unequivocal way. Yet the situation is more complex than that, as I will demonstrate below.

## The Case for Global Life Support

In line with the science-based interpretation of biodiversity as an environmental resource, policy argumentations with respect to biodiversity conservation tend to concentrate on a scientifically strict, resource-oriented approach (e.g., Gaston 1996; Bengtsson et al. 1997; Swanson 1997). Representatives of this approach maintain that there is an urgent need for global action, and only hard scientific arguments based on issues of survival and economy will be effective in generating such action. Such assertions point to the importance of biodiversity for plant breeding, pharmaceuticals, and safeguarding the regulatory functions of the biosphere. For the purposes of this chapter, I will summarize these functions as global *life support*. Often, this emphasis on global life-support contentions goes together with a top-down global approach to biodiversity management. Swanson (1997, xiii), for instance, presents the following key protocols for his framework of global biodiversity management:

• The creation of a common scientific framework for the analysis of the global facets of the biodiversity problem
• The elision of all concern ancillary to the global problem, i.e., the segregation of all other parts of the problem that do not absolutely necessitate international action for their resolution
• The integration of all of the ancestral conservation movements concerned with diversity into this single framework

Succinctly, this strategy is characterized by Vane-Wright as an effort "to place biologically determined priorities within an appropriate sociopolitical framework" (1996, 333).

This is not to say that this biodiversity management approach disregards the interests of local people—in most cases, from the South—involved in conservation. Generally, the role of local stakeholders is considered in at least two respects. First, nature management ought to be geared toward local access to natural resources as far as it is not harmful to the aim of conservation. Biodiversity management, in principle, departs from the ideal type of wilderness in the sense that it values species diversity rather than the "pristine" or "wild" state of nature. Several biodiversity studies acknowledge that human cultivation, though often a threat to biodiversity, in particular situations can also add to it (UNEP 1995; Furze et al. 1996). Second, financial compensation ought to be awarded to the local population for the resource losses suffered and the conservation services rendered by them. For authors such as Swanson (1997) and Gadgil (1996), mechanisms for financial compensation are the key to biodiversity preservation. Nevertheless, within this perspective of biodiversity policy, local involvement is limited to "functional participation" (Pimbert and Pretty 1997). Local people are consulted, practically involved, and compensated at the time, and to the extent that they are functional to the biodiversity strategy. The aims and motives of this strategy are predetermined in other forums, in particular the forum of conservation biology, which bases its priorities on the "calculus of biodiversity" (Vane-Wright 1996).

But the case for a biodiversity policy, based on global life support, is vulnerable to criticism. As the protagonists of biodiversity conservation are ready to observe and deplore, a practical weakness is that to date no effective financial mechanism exists for compensating for land use restrictions and biodiversity conservation services. The one-time financial compensations that are sometimes rewarded for in situ research or bioprospecting are no adequate base for the long-term engagement of locals in biodiversity management (Swanson 1997; Pimbert and Pretty 1997, 309). An argumentative weakness lies in the deficiency of global life-support claims for most of the nature conservation projects that are considered to contribute to biodiversity conservation. The rare species that are central in nature conservation projects do not match very well with the species that are considered most useful for pharmaceutical purposes or plant breeding. Most of the endangered species that are prominent in worldwide conservation efforts, such as large predators, primates, elephants, and rhinoceroses, have hardly any significance for agricultural breeding programs or medicine development. Interestingly, some of the advocates of biodiversity conservation therefore criticize nature conservationists' focus on preserving species with an emotional and aesthetic appeal, and plead for the protection of species for their genetic or regulative functionality in the ecosystem (Grumbine 1995; Harrop 1999).[1] Perhaps in the longer term, such criticisms will provoke a shift in nature management. In current nature conservation practices, though, "bread-and-medicine" arguments play only a minor role (Hargrove 1989).

Among the life-support arguments provided, resilience appears to be the strongest candidate. The resilience of ecosystems refers to their ability to maintain their vital regulation functions under conditions of environmental change. The resilience notion echoes an old and familiar theme within the nature conservation movement: natural diversity is crucial for the long-term stability of the biosphere. Like the diversity-stability hypothesis some twenty years ago, the concept of resilience provides a scientific and economic argument for the conservation of what nature conservationists find valuable for aesthetic and moral reasons too (see Hannigan 1995). But just as it was the case with the diversity-stability hypothesis (Goodman 1975), from a natural sciences point of view the links between biological diversity and resilience are clouded with uncertainties. A review of the *Global Biodiversity Assessment* (UNEP 1995), still the most comprehensive research document on biodiversity world-wide, reveals few empirical findings on the relation between diversity and resilience. Resilience is not listed in the document's glossary, nor is it in the index.[2] While it is plausible that there is a general relation between functional diversity and ecosystem resilience, there are few data to support concrete prescriptions on the management of species and ecosystem diversity. The argument of resilience, while providing a general rationale for precaution with regard to biodiversity degradation, hardly produces concrete and specific guidelines for biodiversity management.

Many biodiversity researchers openly acknowledge the scientific uncertainties surrounding the ecosystem functions of biodiversity (e.g., UNEP 1995, 284, 293, 297; Kunin and Lawton 1996, 297; Perrings et al. 1995; McCan 2000). In policy proposals and accounts for a broader audience, however, much more evidence and certainty is suggested than is tenable from a biological science point of view. The resource arguments for biodiversity conservation then frequently turn into a pseudo-scientific wrap to cover other motives and interests. Some of these contentions are easy prey for antienvironmentalist debunkers such as Stott (1999).

### The Case for the Moral Rights of Nature

Still, not only antienvironmentalists dismiss the case of life-support arguments. Prominent conservationist authors such as Terborgh (1999) also put forward the notion of intrinsic values—that is, the moral rights of species existence as the principle reason for biodiversity conservation. A focus on resource values, according to Terborgh, will eventually lead to the destruction of biodiversity, as forests are "worth more dead than alive." The concept of moral rights, however, is no less controversial with regard to biodiversity conservation. While it is highly plausible that we can attribute moral values to nonhuman beings, it is disputable whether we can attach an absolute intrinsic value to nature, let alone to an abstract and scientifically constructed item such as species diversity. Several authors have asserted that the concept of intrinsic values should therefore not be taken in an absolute moral sense but rather in the broader sense of noninstrumental (or nonuse) values, including moral, aesthetic, and other cultural values (e.g., Hargrove 1989; Krebs 1996;

van Koppen 2000).[3] As many studies have pointed out (e.g., Ghimire and Pimbert 1997; Neumann 1998; Dupuis and Vandergeest 1996), the cultural values that have motivated the efforts of so-called classical nature conservation projects were usually of northern origin, with a strong cultural-aesthetic undertone. Therefore, they can be characterized as a "northern aesthetic." Whether such cultural values are of global or only local interest is principally a matter of international debate and consent.

## The Case for Local Values

While both the global life-support and moral rights cases emphasize top-down intervention for the preservation of biodiversity, there is an influential strand in biodiversity debates advocating the importance of local values and bottom-up management. Authors such as Shiva (Shiva et al. 1992), Von Weizsäcker (1993), and Guha (1997) criticize the biotechnological, authoritarian, and northern-biased view that they allege dominates the biodiversity debates. Without dismissing the whole case for biodiversity conservation, these authors defend an approach that gives full recognition to the different local contexts and cultural views of biodiversity conservation, and puts a high value on equity and socioeconomic development in the South. Their criticism is in line with the participatory approach to nature conservation that has emerged in the last few decades (e.g., Ghimire and Pimbert 1997). Advocates of participatory biodiversity management, which can be found both outside and within international nature conservation organizations, aim to engage local stakeholders in ways that go beyond functional participation, and fully acknowledge the importance of local values of biodiversity (see Furze et al. 1996; Wilshusen et al. 2002). As only a few of these proponents would fully dismiss global arguments and values, their aim instead is to integrate global and local values in biodiversity management. The title of a recent review of biodiversity assessment by Vermeulen and Koziell (2002), *Integrating Global and Local Values*, is characteristic of such an approach. As Vermeulen and Koziell state:

Different people can be expected not only to have very different understandings of what biodiversity means, but also to prioritise the various facets of diversity differently, and to make different judgements on the trade-offs between biodiversity and nonbiodiversity values. The values that people attach to biodiversity will affect the ways in which biodiversity is assessed, and in turn the land use and natural resources management decisions that are based on these assessments. Management of biodiversity, then, is just as much a battleground as management of any other aspect of biological resources. (2002, 15–16)

Proponents of the previous cases tend to be skeptical of such a bottom-up, participatory approach, as they expect that combining local development and nature conservation will have adverse consequences for the latter. Among other things, they fear that locals may lack the competencies or motivation to protect nature, and that development projects, when they are successful, may increase migration to the area and so indirectly increase the pressure on nature (cf. Wilshusen et al. 2002).

## Implications for Biodiversity Management and Assessment

Taking stock of these cases for biodiversity conservation, it is apparent that the concept of biodiversity is prominently visible in international policy, but strategies for biodiversity management are clouded with complexity. None of the positions in the debates, as described above, can claim superiority, and none can be dismissed. In other words, the biodiversity scape is characterized by ambivalent, or rather polyvalent, debates. Use and nonuse values, local and global values, can be called on to promote and direct biodiversity management. Table 7.1 presents an illustrative scheme of the major biodiversity values involved in these debates. In the general literature, most of these values are often listed as motives for biodiversity conservation (e.g., Kunin and Lawton 1996). But in biodiversity management and assessment, simply adding up the different motives will frequently not do; designating, managing,

**Table 7.1**
Biodiversity values

|  | Use values (instrumental) | Nonuse values (intrinsic) |
| --- | --- | --- |
| General interests (universal and global values) | Biosphere resilience Genetic information Global regulation functions | Moral rights of existence World heritage |
| Local interests (locally specific values) | Local regulation functions Local resource use | Locally acknowledged cultural values |

and monitoring nature areas and networks requires choosing value priorities.

One important way in which value priorities become manifest is the selection of the species that are the primary focus of conservation efforts. Because it aptly demonstrates the entanglement of the social and physical aspects of biodiversity conservation, I will elaborate on the assessment of species. As was mentioned earlier, biodiversity components are usually categorized in three ways: intraspecies genetic diversity, species diversity, and ecosystem diversity. Present-day biodiversity assessments, however, are most often directed at the level of species. A vast range of methods exist for assessing species diversity. Most of them involve the assessment of a selected set of species in terms of occurrence and population density or number (Gaines et al. 1999). The selection of species provides an indication of which conceptualization of biodiversity is implicitly or explicitly underlying biodiversity management and assessment.

In the biodiversity monitoring literature (e.g., Noss 1990; Gaines et al. 1999; Dale and Beyeler 2001), roughly four main categories of species are distinguished for biodiversity assessment:

• Ecological indicators—species that signal the effects of perturbations on many other species with similar requirements
• Keystones—species on which the diversity of a large part of a community depends because of the special role they play in the ecosystem (e.g., in modifying the habitat for other species, or facilitating vital energy or substance flows)
• Umbrellas—species with large area requirements, encompassing the habitat requirements of many other species (umbrellas are therefore another type of indicator)
• Special interest species—including popular, charismatic species and species that are vulnerable due to their rarity

Comparing these categories to table 7.1 leads to the following observations. Two of the categories—ecological indicators and umbrellas—do not directly represent biodiversity values. These categories are meaningful as pointers toward a broader set of species, and thus their value ultimately depends on the value of this broader set. The category of keystone species appears to be particularly relevant to regulation functions, including resilience. The special interest species are mainly related to nonuse cultural values; in classical conservation efforts, such special interest species often were central.

It should also be observed that the categorization still clearly reflects a classical conservationist approach. Keeping the biodiversity debate in mind, two other categories should be added:

• Genetically informative species—for agricultural or medical purposes
• Species for direct local, national, or international use—corresponding to the production functions of nature

## Social Causes and Consequences

The biodiversity debates, as they were described above, do not only pertain to the values and species that are central to biodiversity; they also relate to different views on the wider social context of biodiversity management. To demonstrate this, I will elaborate on two aspects: the social causes of biodiversity degradation (or as they are called in the environmental literature, the social drivers) and the indirect social consequences of biodiversity conservation (indirect meaning apart from the biodiversity values preserved). The social drivers of nature degradation have always been an important theme in nature conservation. Often, they were found in local practices such as farming and hunting. The values preserved were typically situated at the national and international levels. Increasing political control of the area, as an indirect consequence, in many cases constituted an additional yet crucial motive for the establishment of nature reserves.

Under the influence of the participatory trends in conservation, however, the local costs and benefits as well as the (inter)national drivers of degradation have received more attention in research and practice. Generally speaking, advocates of the participatory approach will stress the merits of the existing traditions of local resource management, and will tend to interpret unsustainable changes in these traditions as a result of supralocal economic and political forces, such as the arrival of foreign ecotourist companies, the selling off of local resources by nonlocal elites, or the suppression of ethnic minorities by national regimes.

With respect to the consequences of biodiversity management, the participatory approach emphasizes the criteria of sustainable use—that is, continuing local access to biodiversity resources—and a fair and equitable distribution of costs and benefits. It is good to observe that "costs and benefits" has a wider connotation than the "fair and equitable sharing of benefits" as referred to in the CBD objective, where it specifically concerns the benefits of genetic resource use. Costs and benefits may include, for instance, the costs of resource access restrictions and the benefits of ecotourism. Advocates of the participatory approach tend to be cautious of disempowering the local residents as a result of increased control by national agencies or even military pressure. The IUCN (2000) *Draft Test Guide* lists a wide range of indicators that reflect these concerns, focusing on several aspects of human well-being such as mortality and morbidity rates, fertility, food sufficiency, income (e.g., from tourism services), education, participation, and gender and ethnic equity.

The social context factors are schematically represented in table 7.2. The issue of exactly who should be involved in the actual assessment of

**Table 7.2**
Social Aspects of Biodiversity Conservation

|  | Social drivers | (Indirect) social consequences |
| --- | --- | --- |
| National or global level | • Nonlocal exploitation (e.g., corporate logging)<br>• (Inter)national political and economic pressure<br>• (Inter)national intervention in local culture | • Science and education<br>• Public health<br>• Economic benefits of ecotourism<br>• Political control (usually enlarged by conservation projects) |
| Local level | • Local exploitation (often increased by market integration)<br>• Local population growth (including migration to or from the area)<br>• Local ignorance and attitude | • Local access to resources (usually decreased by conservation projects)<br>• Other local costs and benefits (infrastructure, jobs in ecotourism, and conservation)<br>• Political power shifts (within a community and vis-à-vis the state) |

biodiversity is also subject to debate. Over the last twenty years, several forms of participatory monitoring have been applied in a wide range of projects. Several reasons are put forward for including local (nonscientist) stakeholders in biodiversity monitoring such as increasing monitoring capacity, enhancing local acceptance, bringing in local knowledge and values in biodiversity management, and contributing to local empowerment (Lawrence 2002). From a science-based perspective, participatory monitoring might be interesting for reasons of capacity and acceptance, but only if the participants were sufficiently instructed to keep to the standards set by conservation biologists.

Interestingly, the involvement of lay investigators in nature monitoring is a widespread practice in western countries. For instance, in the Netherlands volunteers play a major role in biodiversity investigation networks (Vogel 2002).

## Biodiversity Configurations

While the previous section presented some of the key issues in biodiversity debates, this one aims to link elements of the biodiversity discourse to the networks that put them into practice in order to further explore the structure of the biodiversity scape. As mentioned in the chapter's introduction, the biodiversity scape is characterized by particular combinations or—as I will call them—configurations of discourses and networks. Four configurations are distinguished: classical conservation, local participation, global ecology, and product chains.

### Classical Conservation

Traditionally, conservation organizations and national governments have been the main actors in conservation networks. Focusing on developing countries as the main arena of global conservation efforts today, we can distinguish domestic governments as the main executive actor, and foreign governments as well as global conservation organizations as the main donors. The prominent global conservation organizations are the IUCN—an influential global organization for nature conservation with some eight hundred governmental and nongovernmental members—the nongovernmental WWF, and the government-based UNEP and

UNESCO. These bodies were the main nature organizations contributing to the preparation of the CBD, and now cooperate in worldwide evaluations such as the *Global Biodiversity Assessment* (UNEP 1995) and the *Living Planet Report* (WWF 2000). Many nationally based environmental and nature conservation organizations cooperate in this global network.

The classical perspective on nature conservation is characterized by a focus on national or state frameworks (national parks and reserves, national monitoring centers, and national lists of species to be monitored). Special interest species—including national flagship species such as the eagle in the United States, the panda in China, and the koala in Australia—are prominent in monitoring. National heritage values ("nature monuments") are among the central motives here. In this perspective, globalization is primarily a matter of adapting national and international lists of endangered species and ecosystems, and garnering international support for the conservation efforts of developing countries.

Notwithstanding the recent changes in global nature policy and management—stimulated by the rise of the biodiversity concept—this classical configuration is still present in many of today's biodiversity policies and practices. As an illustration, box 7.1 gives the example of the core set of biodiversity indicators elaborated under the direction of the SBSTTA of the CBD. The SBSTTA core set is probably the most important global effort to outline the assessment of biodiversity to date. It still reflects the classical perspective in many ways, yet it points to other configurations of the biodiversity scape as well.

### Local Participation

One of these other configurations is that of local participation. As was discussed before, the significance of combining biodiversity conservation and local socioeconomic development is increasingly acknowledged, including by international conservation organizations. To some extent, these organizations also engage in networks of integrated conservation and development projects. The networks that propagate a local development perspective to assessments, however, are more diverse and

**Box 7.1**
SBSTTA core set of biodiversity indicators

The SBSTTA of the CBD has been elaborating biodiversity indicators for several years and proposed a core set of indicators in a memorandum for its fifth meeting in Montreal (SBSTTA 1999). This set is meant to assist parties and other governments in designing or improving their national monitoring programs. The aim of the indicators, as stated by the SBSTTA, is to serve as a tool for the adequate management of biodiversity at the local and national levels, and for regional and global overviews of the status and trends of biodiversity components. They may also have a wider role in increasing public awareness. The context of the SBSTTA core set is the CBD process. The indicator set should contribute to all three objectives of the convention: biodiversity conservation, sustainable use, and equitable benefits. The core set is based on the "ecosystem approach," a conceptual framework that goes well beyond biology as it not only refers to the conservation of an ecosystem's structure and functioning but also includes principles such as decentralizing the management to the lowest possible level, the involvement of all relevant sectors of society and scientific disciplines, and consideration of scientific as well as indigenous and local knowledge and practices. Probably, this core set will be an important point of reference for all monitoring programs with strong ties to the CBD process (e.g., for Costa Rica, Camacho-Sandoval and Duque 2001).

On the ecosystem level, the core set centers on the use of overlay maps, based on vegetation inventories, remote sensing data, and so on, to quantify nature areas and show trends in fragmentation and conversion. On the species level, it includes indicators for species richness, the abundance and distribution of a "selected core set of species," and quantifying the number of threatened endemic species. The memorandum does not list concrete species, but comments that species selection is to be based on country-specific conditions, and can include keystone species, flagship species, and species of scientific interest as well as economically useful species. It does not explicitly mention culturally valued species, but in principle the core set leaves room for a wide range of species, reflecting different biodiversity values. On the genetic level, the core set focuses on crop and land race diversity.

In addition to these indicators for ecosystems, species, and races, the core set encompasses several indicators for pressures (in a broad sense, including drivers) such as population density adjacent to key habitats, harvesting and other uses of biodiversity (in terms of domestic and local production and consumption), infrastructure, and pollution, among others. Although they are categorized as pressure indicators, many of them are also relevant to sustainable use. Also, a few "response indicators" are given, quantifying the measures for biodiversity conservation (mainly in terms of the percentage of area protected). According to the memorandum, many of these indicators should be taken from national statistics. No indicators are specified for the fair and equitable distribution of benefits. It is the intention of the SBSTTA to elaborate on response indicators for sustainable use and equitable benefits over a longer time period, in a second track.

loosely knit, and also comprise NGOs and governmental departments involved in development (for cross-sections of such networks, see Lawrence 2002; Vermeulen and Koziell 2002).

The local development perspective typically focuses on local and regional projects. Many of these projects have been, continue to be, carried out worldwide. Well-known examples of such projects are the CAMPFIRE programs in Zimbabwe (McIvor 1997) and the Joint Forest

**Box 7.2**
A field-based biodiversity monitoring system in the Philippines

From 1996 to 1998, Filipino and Danish professionals from different backgrounds (biology and the social sciences) developed a field-based monitoring system with the objective of improving the information available for decision makers in protected areas through the regular collection of data on natural resources and their utilization (Danielsen et al. 2000). The system is meant to help local communities improve the management of resource use, and was designed to build on and strengthen existing community-based monitoring. It was developed on the basis of fieldwork in three natural parks, bearing in mind the developing countries' monitoring context, where the large size of the protected areas, high numbers of species, incomplete taxonomic knowledge, and limited economic resources make it necessary to keep monitoring systems simple and cost-effective.

The main indicators of the monitoring system are the abundance of designated species, size of vegetation-type areas, and intensity of local resource uses. These data are recorded on a regular basis by park staff members during routine patrols by using a photo documentation method and by means of transect walks. Both direct sightings and indirect signs (e.g., tree stumps for logging) are used. In addition, focus groups with community representatives are used to discuss harvest volumes and the number of people engaged in biodiversity-impacting activities. The species selected were thought to provide useful proxy information about the specific biodiversity of three national parks. Species, of which the abundance clearly depended on human use (hunting) or habitat were preferred; species that were difficult to identify were discarded.

The system, which has proved to be feasible, was almost in full operation by 1999. Yet, maintaining the system is no easy task. The focus group discussions, for instance, are time-consuming, and demand new management skills from park staff members who are often accustomed to a "fine and fences" approach. Better institutional support is needed to keep the system in good shape (Danielsen et al. 2000).

Management projects in India (Poffenberger and McGean 1996). The aim of such projects is to combine socioeconomic development and biodiversity conservation, both for reasons of effective nature management and development itself. A major policy principle is the decentralization of decision making. Typically, such projects try to balance local values—such as local resource use and cultural values—against global values of biodiversity. These characteristics are reflected in the biodiversity assessment: the indicators applied usually comprise both locally and (inter)nationally important species as well as parameters of socioeconomic development. In some cases, local residents are actively involved in monitoring. For examples, see boxes 7.2 and 7.4.

The role of organizations such as the IUCN and the WWF regarding local development approaches is ambivalent. Some offices and individuals take a clear stand in favor of participation, but often the stance is dependent on the specific situation. This ambiguity is also present in the SBSTTA core set of biodiversity indicators (box 7.1). The approach of the SBSTTA emphasizes the key role of societal choices, and stresses decentralization and stakeholder involvement, but the current set of indicators still very much reflects a classical perspective (SBSTTA 1999; Vermeulen and Koziell 2002).

**Global Ecology**

Quite in contrast to the local participation configuration, there are also conservationist networks that promote a top-down, expert-based approach. In this view, as discussed earlier, global life-support arguments and ecological science are central. The networks that propagate this global ecology approach often have an international scope and are strongly influenced by conservation biology. It is worth noting that conservation biology is not just a subdiscipline of ecology but rather a network of biological scientists with a strong normative orientation to nature (cf. Galusky 2000). Conservation biologists played an important role in the conceptual development of biodiversity that preceded the CBD (Suplie 1995; van Koppen 2002). The hot spot approach propagated by CI, an important NGO in global nature conservation, is characteristic of this configuration of global ecology (see box 7.3).

**Box 7.3**
Biodiversity hot spots for conservation priorities

The hot spot approach is detailed in an influential article written by Norman Myers, Russell Mittermeier, Christina Mittermeier, Gustavo da Fonseca, and Jennifer Kent. Most of the authors are linked to CI (Myers et al. 2000). Similar approaches are found in "Toward a Blueprint for Conservation in Africa" (Brooks et al. 2001), and to some extent, in "Systematic Conservation Planning" (Margules and Pressey 2000) and "Balancing the Earth's Accounts" (James et al. 1999).

Hot spots are identified in order to support most species at the least cost. They are defined as "areas featuring exceptional concentrations of endemic species and experiencing exceptional loss of habitat" (Myers et al. 2000, 853). The focus is on endemic species because they are considered to be "the most prominent and readily recognizable form of biodiversity" (853). Hot spot boundaries are determined on the basis of "biological commonalities" (within a hot spot, there is a certain degree of biogeographic homogeneousness). The data are collected on the basis of literature and expert estimations. Vascular plants and four categories of animals (birds, mammals, reptiles, and amphibians) are included. To qualify, a hot spot should have lost 70 percent of its primary vegetation. Together, the twenty-five hot spots feature several habitat types, but tropical forests are predominant (fifteen hot spots), while sixteen hot spots are in the tropics, which largely means developing countries. In sum, the twenty-five hot spots contain the sole remaining habitats of 44 percent of Earth's plant species and 35 percent of its vertebrate species. Since the origins of the hot spot strategy, some $400 million has been invested in this approach by the MacArthur Foundation, the W. Alton Jones Foundation, CI, the WWF, and other NGOs. Myers and colleagues argue that more biodiversity conservation funding should be concentrated in this "silver bullet" strategy, thereby safeguarding the hot spots with an investment of about $500 million annually.

CI's efforts find support among companies such as SC Johnson, a multinational manufacturer of consumer products for home cleaning and storage, insect control, and personal care. In its public report of 2004, *Earning Your Goodwill*, the company states:

Through an important contribution to Conservation International and its Conservation Carbon project, SC Johnson is the first global consumer packaged goods manufacturer to support the restoration of up to 45 acres (18 HA) of degraded forests in the Choco-Manabi corridor of Ecuador to offset our 2004 Public Report. In cooperation with the locally based Jatun Sacha Foundation, this environmental offset will support ongoing conservation efforts in one of the world's most critically threatened "hotspots" of biodiversity by planting more than 15 native tree species.... By partnering with CI and the Jatun Sacha Foundation, we are acting upon

**Box 7.3**
(continued)

> our longstanding commitment to preserve finite world resources for future generations.
> (SC Johnson 2004, 41)
>
> The hot spot approach has met with approval, but also criticism. In a letter to *Nature*, G. M. Mace, together with sixteen colleagues, criticizes the article by Myers and colleagues for duplicating conservation efforts and not taking into account recent advances in systematic priority setting. Maze and colleagues also point out that the scale level of the hot spot approach is too coarse, and that by focusing only on biodiversity patterns, the approach fails to address the evolutionary processes that maintain biodiversity. Notwithstanding this criticism, however, the letter states, "We strongly support initiatives to produce clear, efficient and practical goals for conservation to guide biodiversity planners and decision-makers in governments, agencies, conventions and non-governmental organizations" (Mace et al. 2000, 393). Another criticism in conservation circles is that the focus on hot spots suggests that biodiversity is only important when it occurs at high levels (Abbott et al. 2002).

CI is actively engaged in raising private money to jump-start hot spot conservation efforts. While the local development perspective partially works around the national government level by emphasizing decentralization, the global ecology perspective, as it is defined here, distances itself from national states and governments in stressing its global standpoint. It was not without reason that CI, in its efforts in favor of the hot spot approach, was criticized by Jeff McNeely (of the IUCN), who said that CI needed "to reach out to governments whose nations include the hotspots, so as to introduce more reality into planning" (Dalton 2000, 926).

**Product Chains**

Quite recently, a new category of actors emerged in biodiversity conservation. The networks of these actors are built around companies—mainly large TNCs—and their product chains, within the context of corporate governance. An important driving force of this emergence is the desire of companies to retain their "license to operate" and strengthen their supply chain. As it is phrased in *Business and*

*Biodiversity,* a recent report of Earthwatch, the IUCN, and the WBCSD: "Companies require sustainable supply chains. As biological resources feature in all production processes, the sustainable use of these resources is a key feature of every company's supply chain. By not adequately addressing this issue, a company entails the risk of not being able to sustain demand. In addition, a company's reputation may be damaged" (Abbott et al. 2002, 17). Well-known manifestations of a product chain approach to biodiversity conservation are the FSC and the MSC ecolabels. The first provides a standard for sustainable wood production, while the second supplies a mechanism to safeguard the sustainability of fisheries. Both have enacted a scheme for certification; products that are certified are allowed to carry an ecolabel. In this way, the councils seek "to harness consumer purchasing power to generate change and promote environmentally responsible stewardship" (MSC 2002; see also MSC Executive 2002; FSC 2002; chapter 9, this volume).

The product chain configuration not only brings in companies and consumers as new actors in biodiversity conservation but also explicitly links biodiversity conservation to production and consumption. Biodiversity assessment, within the product chain approach, is still in a pioneering stage. Assessment methods are under development that, similar to environmental LCA, enable estimates of the biodiversity impact of a product over its entire life cycle. A Dutch example is the IBIS system, developed by a consultancy with funding from the Dutch environmental ministry (De Lange 2000). In choosing the criteria for ecolabeling products for biodiversity conservation, different perspectives are possible, in accordance with the other configurations distinguished here. In the example of FSC labeling (see box 7.4), both national (state) and local requirements were incorporated.

An indicative overview of the different configurations is presented in table 7.3.

### Evaluatory Conclusions

As many have observed, environmental policy arrangements increasingly depart from the national state level, both to lower, regional, or local levels, and to higher, international, or global levels. This tendency is

**Box 7.4**
FSC certification of Hoopa tribal forest, United States

This case concerns the FSC certification auditing of forest management by the Hoopa tribe in California. In 1991, the Hoopa tribe gained self-governance rights over the local commercial forests. The FSC certification was approved for an area of 35,600 hectare in 1999, with SmartWood as the certifier. The audit provided a comprehensive assessment of the biodiversity. The audit team consisted of U.S. nationals, including two people with ecological training and one Native American forester. No new empirical inventories of biodiversity were carried out, but the assessment was based on the available extensive records of past forest management. The assessment of the "ecological issues" was based on the past and present landscape structure (including the age and species composition of different stands), the status of threatened and endangered species as defined in state legislation (three bird species), and a recent survey of rare or vulnerable species. This survey linked state and local biodiversity values by giving special attention to fish species, which are traditionally important to the Hoopa people.

According to Vermeulen and Koziell (2002), from which the case is borrowed, this certification case provides a good example of how to sidestep biodiversity per se and instead concentrate on the outputs of ecosystems that are of interest to key stakeholder groups (in this case, on the one hand, the California State authorities, and on the other hand, the specific needs of the local people). Of the four cases of FSC certification audits, described by Vermeulen and Koziell, some do investigate local values or link to local socioeconomic issues, and others do not.

clearly visible in the configurations of biodiversity management that have developed out of the classical, nationally based one. The local development configuration diverges from the national level by concentrating on local or regional arrangements, while many of the organizational networks promoting this perspective operate on a global level. The global ecology configuration transcends the national level by an effectively global approach to biodiversity assessment. Global priority setting, as in the hot spot approach, may lead to measures on the local and regional levels that are not bound to national borders or regulatory frameworks. The product chain configuration cuts through national borders together with the global product flows that are its substrate.

Like the classical conservancy configuration, the new configurations have a specific range of legitimacy and adequacy as well as specific

Table 7.3
Four configurations of biodiversity management

|  | Classical conservation | Local development | Global ecology | Product chains |
|---|---|---|---|---|
| Aims | Establishment of a national conservation framework | Integrating biodiversity management and development | Effectively safeguarding global biodiversity | Minimize or compensate product chain impacts |
| Social networks | (Inter)national conservation organizations and national governments | (Inter)national and local NGOs for conservation and development, and governments | International conservation organizations, conservation biologists, and sponsors | Transnational companies, conservation organizations, and consumers |
| Typical areas | National parks | Cultivated and seminatural landscapes | Biodiversity hot spots | Related to products |
| Typical values | Heritage value and northern aesthetics | Local as well as national and global values | Absolute moral value and global life support | May differ (related to other configurations) |
| Typical species | National special interest species, including national flagship species | Local special interest species and locally used species | Species for genetic diversity, keystone species, and species diversity per se | May differ (related to other configurations) |
| Social drivers | Local drivers | Nonlocal drivers | Pragmatic | Related to product chain |
| (Indirect) social consequences | National welfare and national control | Local welfare and local control | Pragmatic | People, planet, and profits |
| Actors involved in monitoring | Experts and amateurs | Experts and local residents | Experts | May differ (related to other configurations) |

**Table 7.3**
(continued)

|  | Classical conservation | Local development | Global ecology | Product chains |
|---|---|---|---|---|
| Policy context | Governmental decision making on national level (decisionist) | Decentralization of decision making to local levels (participatory) | Expert decision-making on global level (technocratic) | Corporate governance or earning goodwill (market) |
| Globalization | National to international heritage | Integrating local and global values | Global ecological priorities | Global production and consumption chains |
| Examples | Nationally based biodiversity conservation | Integrated conservation and development projects | Hot spot approach | Ecolabeling |

limitations. The merits of the *local development configuration* are revealed in many case studies. Local participation can contribute to both conservation effectiveness and social development and justice, and in doing so, it helps solve the actual and potential conflicts between nature conservationists and local populations worldwide. But even when the integration of conservation and social development is feasible, this configuration has fundamental limitations. The political decision making needed to facilitate and mandate participatory approaches is usually situated at a national or even international level. And reasonably so, since the interests and stakeholders involved in conservation issues are often not limited to the local level. Higher-level decision making is needed to represent these interests and determine the legitimate room for local initiatives. Usually, the national level is regarded as the adequate policy level to represent the common interest. The actual policymaking authority is still largely situated in the nation-state. But as observed earlier, this situation is shifting. National borders are quite often irrelevant to conservation issues, not only in a perspective of global ecology, but also from the angle of local development. International regulatory frameworks and cross-border nature conservation projects are more and more important in biodiversity management, resulting in new challenges to national policymaking.

Global ecological priority setting—a key characteristic of the *global ecology configuration*—will most probably become a factor of increasing significance in determining biodiversity policy. Science-based approaches have the appeal of rationality and objectivity. Yet the global application of scientific methods of assessment and prioritization is dependent on two conditions: first, there should be political consensus on the normative premises of scientific reasoning, and second, there should be consensus among peer scientists on the validity of scientific reasoning itself. Both conditions are hardly fulfilled in most instances of biodiversity management—and this poses a serious limitation to the configuration. Different groups of conservation scientists propagate different values of biodiversity, and the relationship of biodiversity with global life-support functions and ecosystem resilience is still clouded with uncertainty. The emergence of the *product chain configuration* introduces still another dynamic in the biodiversity scape. This configuration's legitimacy and adequacy is rooted in the dramatic growth of MNCs, which seek to earn public trust—their "license to produce," as it has been called—by demonstrating responsibility for the planet. Nevertheless, the product chain configuration is limited in that it does not encompass typical biodiversity values or measures. When actual conservation programs and projects are concerned, it is dependent on other perspectives: national conservation, local development, global ecology, or combinations of them.

Configurations are not mutually exclusive and indeed can intertwine. The example of FSC certification (box 7.4) shows how state, local, and production chain perspectives go together. And SC Johnson's sponsoring of CI has elements of the configurations of product chain, global ecology, and local development. The reason for this chapter's effort to map these different configurations is not to provide different baskets in which the phenomena of international biodiversity conservation can be separated. It is rather to show how, within the complex global biodiversity scape, different discourses and networks coincide and interfere with each other.

At this point, I would like to state that assuming such complexity does not render the political structuring of the biodiversity scape impossible or obsolete. Political structuring, in my view, is not to be found in some master configuration but rather in building active checks and balances, and adequate interfaces, within and between the configurations. This is not the place to deal with this matter in more detail, but let me give just one example. As was demonstrated, ecological expertise on global ecosystem functions exerts more and more influence on conservation worldwide. Many of the ecological statements on global life support, however, lack an adequate underpinning. Taken together, this necessitates a more elaborate and better communicated scientific scrutiny of biodiversity claims. Therefore, the option of an international scientific body for biodiversity assessment, comparable to the IPCC and possibly in line with the SBSTTA of the CBD, would deserve serious consideration.

### Hybrid Systems, Hybrid Arrangements

The exploration of the biodiversity scape presented here highlights some of the theoretical points made in chapter 1 (this volume). In the case of biodiversity conservation, the flows perspective shows the need for environmental sociology to think in terms of hybrid systems—that is, systems with jointly physical and social aspects. Ecological networks are good examples of such hybrid systems. Explaining an ecological network—how nature areas in the network are designated, how they are thought to link, which species are assessed, and so on—is not just a natural sciences issue, nor primarily an issue of social discourse. It can only be understood properly by taking the social and the physical together. The global network of biodiversity hot spots, for instance, is a set of areas that are framed for their high rate of biodiversity, *and* a core topic in a particular conservation ecology discourse, *and* a political device of a specific social network of conservationists and sponsors. Only by integrating these dimensions can we better understand what sort of biodiversity is considered hot, and what such an identification means for the ways a place is inserted into the global flows of money, rule, and expertise. A similar argument can be made for the other configurations.

The analysis presented here may also shed some light on another theoretical point of this book: hybrid arrangements. In line with the assertion of the opening chapter, my chapter shows that new configurations have emerged in the last decades, invoking new networks with new rules and resources for biodiversity conservation. Traditionally, nature conservation has been a domain where the role of the state is paramount. Even when working from an international perspective, nature conservation organizations used to closely cooperate with states in order to achieve their aims. As a consequence, state control over areas was often augmented by conservation projects. Even to date, as was mentioned in the CI example, organizations cannot feasibly operate without arrangements with national states. Yet the situation has started to change over the last decade, and nature conservation organizations show more and more interest in cooperating with other civil society actors as well as business organizations (see, for instance, McNeely 1999). As I noted earlier, the range of potential hybrid arrangements is wide since different configurations can and sometimes have to be combined. For the integration of biodiversity conservation and socioeconomic development, hybrid arrangements that combine the local development and product chain configurations seem to be of particular interest.

## Notes

The author thanks Gert Spaargaren for his helpful suggestions on an earlier version of this chapter, and Jan Breitling for his assistance with a paper that was the start of it.

1. In this vein, Harrop even attacks the flagship of nature conservation, the giant panda: "An animal whose idiosyncratic and unnecessarily obscure diet is one of its worst enemies. . . . Logic, without emotion, might demand that we allow this animal to slip into oblivion as a species" (1999, 685).

2. The *Global Biodiversity Assessment* discusses the issue of resilience in chapter 5 (and in chapter 12, it recaps the ecological findings from an economic angle). It presents general considerations on the relation between diversity and ecosystem functions together with a modest number of empirical studies. The main conclusion is that uncertainty prevails; in many cases, species matter in a fashion that can be demonstrated, and in other cases species have been lost without demonstrable change to the ecosystem functioning (UNEP 1995, 324). Interestingly, however, the authors reverse the argument:

We cannot safely assume that a "weedy world" (that is, a world with a small number of ubiquitous species, K.) will support the human enterprise as effectively or for as long as one rich in organisms. . . . And even if ecologists show that "weedy" species are all we need to supply basic services to humanity, they cannot show that the ethical and aesthetic arguments for maximizing the preservation of biodiversity are incorrect. They lie outside the realm of science, but contain some of the most powerful reasons for saving our only known living companions in the universe. (UNEP 1995, 284–285)

3. The Millennium Assessment (2003) takes an interesting position in this debate: it distinguishes cultural services as well as intrinsic values. Cultural services include the aesthetic, spiritual, religious, and moral values of nature. Intrinsic values are seen as completely independent of human appreciation. Thus, since they cannot be evaluated in any way, it means that de facto intrinsic values are placed outside the domain of ecosystem assessment.

## References

Abbott, C., C. André de la Porte, R. Barrington, N. Bertrand, C. Carey, A. Fry, A. Prag, and F. Vorhies. 2002. *Business and Biodiversity: The Handbook for Corporate Action.* Geneva: WBCSD.

Bengtsson, J., H. Jones, and H. Setälä. 1997. The Value of Biodiversity. *Trends in Ecology and Evolution* 12, no. 9:334–336.

Brooks, T., A. Balmford, N. Burgess, J. Fjeldså, L. A. Hansen, J. Moore, C. Rahbek, and P. Williams. 2001. Toward a Blueprint for Conservation in Africa. *Bioscience* 51, no. 8:613–624.

Camacho-Sandoval, J., and H. Duque. 2001. Indicators for Biodiversity Assessment in Costa Rica. *Agriculture, Ecosystems, and Environment* 87:141–150.

Castells, M. 1996. *The Rise of the Network Society.* Vol. 1 of *The Information Age: Economy, Society, and Culture.* Oxford: Blackwell.

Council of Europe. 1998. *Report concerning the Map on Nature Conservation Sites Designated in Application of International Instruments at Pan-European Level.* Strasbourg: Council of Europe.

Dale, V. H., and S. C. Beyeler, 2001. Challenges in the Development and Use of Ecological Indicators. *Ecological Indicators* 1:3–10.

Dalton, R. 2000. Ecologists Back Blueprint to Save Biodiversity Hotspots. *Nature* 406:926.

Danielsen, F., D. S. Balete, M. K. Poulsen, M. Enghoff, C. M. Nozawa, and A. E. Jensen. 2000. A Simple System for Monitoring Biodiversity in Protected Areas of a Developing Country. *Biodiversity and Conservation* 9:1671–1705.

De Lange, V. P. A. 2000. Reducering ecologische voetafdruk via productenbeleid. *ROM Magazine* 12:6–9.

Dobson, A. P. 1995. *Conservation and Biodiversity.* New York: Scientific American Library.

Dupuis, E. M., and P. Vandergeest, eds. 1996. *Creating the Countryside: The Politics of Rural and Environmental Discourse*. Philadelphia: Temple University Press.

ECNC. 2004a. *Brabant-European Partnership Manifesto*. Geneva: Council of Europe.

ECNC. 2004b. The Strategy Guide. <http://www.strategyguide.org/>.

ECNC, IUCN, and Council of Europe. 2003. *Follow-up of the Kiev Biodiversity Resolution: Pan-European Ecological Network Action Plan Proposal*. Geneva: Council of Europe.

FSC. 2002. *FSC Social Strategy: Building and Implementing a Social Agenda*. Bonn: FSC International Center.

Furze, B., T. De Lacy, and J. Birckhead. 1996. *Culture, Conservation, and Biodiversity: The Social Dimensions of Linking Local-Level Development and Conservation through Protected Areas*. Chichester, UK: Wiley.

Gadgil, M. 1996. Managing Biodiversity. In *Biodiversity: A Biology of Numbers and Difference*, ed. K. J. Gaston, 345–365. Oxford: Blackwell Science.

Gaines, W. L., R. J. Harrod, and J. F. Lehmkuhl. 1999. *Monitoring Biodiversity: Quantification and Interpretation*. General technical report PNW–GTR–443. Portland, OR: U.S. Forest Service.

Galuksky, W. J. 2000. The Promise of Conservation Biology. *Organization and Environment* 13, no. 2:226–232.

Gaston, K. J., ed. 1996. *Biodiversity: A Biology of Numbers and Difference*. Oxford: Blackwell.

Ghimire, K. B., and M. P. Pimbert, eds. 1997. *Social Change and Conservation: Environmental Politics and Impacts of National Parks and Protected Areas*. London: Earthscan.

Goodman, D. 1975. The Theory of Diversity-Stability Relationships in Ecology. *Quarterly Review of Biology* 50, no. 3:237–266.

Grumbine, R. E. 1995. Using Biodiversity as a Justification for Nature Protection in the U.S. *Journal of Social Relations* 21, no. 1:35–59.

Guha, R. 1997. The Authoritarian Biologist and the Arrogance of Anti-Humanism: Wildlife Conservation in the Third World. *Ecologist* 27:14–19.

Hannigan, J. A. 1995. *Environmental Sociology: A Social Constructionist Perspective*. London: Routledge.

Hargrove, E. C. 1989. *Foundations of Environmental Ethics*. Englewood Cliffs, NJ: Prentice Hall.

Harrop, S. R. 1999. Conservation Regulation: A Backward Step for Biodiversity? *Biodiversity and Conservation* 8:679–707.

IUCN. 2000. *An Approach to Assessing Biological Diversity with Particular Reference to the Convention on Biological Diversity (CBD): Draft Test Guide*. Gland, Switzerland: IUCN.

James, A. N., K. J. Gaston, and A. Balmford. 1999. Balancing the Earth's Accounts. *Nature* 401:323–324.

Krebs, A. 1996. "Ich würde gern mitunter aus dem Hause tretend ein paar Bäume sehen:" Philosophische Überlegungen zum Eigenwert der Natur. In *Naturschutz—Ethik—Ökonomie*, ed. H. G. Nützinger, 31–48. Marbury, Ger.: Metropolis.

Kunin, W. E., and J. H. Lawton. 1996. Does Biodiversity Matter? Evaluating the Case for Conserving Species. In *Biodiversity: A Biology of Numbers and Difference*, ed. K. J. Gaston, 283–308. Oxford: Blackwell.

Lawrence, A. 2002. *Participatory Assessment, Monitoring, and Evaluation of Biodiversity: Summary of the ETFRN Internet Discussion, 7–25 January 2002.* Oxford: Environmental Change Institute.

Mace, G. M., A. Balmford, L. Boitani, et al. 2000. It's Time to Work Together and Stop Duplicating Conservation Efforts. *Nature* 405:393–393.

Margules, C. R., and R. L. Pressey. 2000. Systematic Conservation Planning. *Nature* 405:243–253.

McCan, K. S. 2000. The Diversity-Stability Debate. *Nature* 405:228–233.

McIvor, C. 1997. Management of Wildlife, Tourism, and Local Communities. In *Social Change and Conservation: Environmental Politics and Impacts of National Parks and Protected Areas*, ed. K. B. Ghimire and M. P. Pimbert, 239–269. London: Earthscan.

McNeely, J. A. 1999. *Mobilizing Broader Support for Asia's Biodiversity: How Civil Society Can Contribute to Protected Area Management.* Manilay, Philippines: Asian Development Bank.

Millennium Assessment. 2003. *Ecosystems and Human Well-being: A Framework for Assessment.* Washington, DC: Island Press.

Ministerie VROM. 2001. *Een wereld en een wil: Werken aan duurzaamheid. Nationaal Milieubeleidsplan 4.* The Hague: Ministerie VROM.

MSC. 2002. About MSC. <http://www.msc.org>.

MSC Executive. 2002. MSC Principles and Criteria for Sustainable Fishing. <http://www.msc.org>.

Myers, N., R. Mittermeier, C. Mittermeier, G. da Fonseca, and J. Kent. 2000. Biodiversity Hot Spots for Conservation Priorities. *Nature* 403:853–858.

Neumann, R. P. 1998. *Imposing Wilderness: Struggles over Livelihood and Nature Preservation in Africa.* Berkeley: University of California Press.

Noss, R. F. 1990. Indicators for Monitoring Biodiversity: A Hierarchical Approach. *Conservation Biology* 4:355–364.

Perrings, C., and B. W. Walkez, eds. 1995. *Biodiversity Loss: Economic and Ecological Issues.* Cambridge: Cambridge University Press.

Pimbert, M. P., and J. N. Pretty. 1997. Parks, People, and Professionals: Putting "Participation" in Protected Areas Management. In *Social Change and*

*Conservation: Environmental Politics and Impacts of National Parks and Protected Areas*, ed. K. B. Ghimire and M. P. Pimbert, 297–330. London: Earthscan.

Poffenberger, M., and B. McGean, eds. 1996. *Village Voices, Forest Choices: Joint Forest Management in India*. New Delhi: Oxford University Press.

Rientjes, S. 1999. Biodiversiteit: De introductie van een nieuw begrip in beleid en onderzoek. *Beleid en Maatschappij* 26, no. 4:252–261.

SBSTTA. 1999. Development of Indicators of Biological Diversity. Note presented by the executive secretary at the fifth SBSTTA meeting, Montreal.

SC Johnson. 2004. *Earning Your Goodwill*. Public report. Racine, WI: SC Johnson.

Secretariat of the Convention on Biological Diversity. 2005. Convention on Biological Diversity, 5 June 1992. In *Handbook of the Convention on Biological Diversity Including Its Cartagena Protocol on Biosafety*. Montreal: Secretariat of the Convention on Biological Diversity.

Shiva, V., P. Anderson, H. Schucking, and A. Gray. 1992. *Biodiversity: Social and Ecological Perspectives*. London: Zed Books.

Soulé, M., ed. 1986. *Conservation Biology: The Science of Scarcity and Diversity*. Sunderland, MA: Sinauer Associates.

Soulé, M., and B. Wilcox, eds. 1980. *Conservation Biology: An Evolutionary-Ecological Perspective*. Sunderland, MA: Sinauer Associates.

Stott, P. 1999. *Tropical Rainforests: A Political Ecology of Hegemonic Myth Making*. London: Institute for Economic Affairs.

Suplie, J. 1995. *"Streit auf Noahs Arche": Zur Genese der Biodiversitäts-Konvention*. Berlin: Wissenschaft Zentrum Berlin.

Swanson, T. 1997. *Global Action for Biodiversity*. London: Earthscan.

Terborgh, J. W. 1999. *Requiem for Nature*. Washington, DC: Island Press.

UNEP. 1995. *Global Biodiversity Assessment*. Cambridge: Cambridge University Press.

UNESCO. 2002. *Biosphere Reserves: Special Places for People and Nature*. Paris: UNESCO.

Vane-Wright, R. I. 1996. Identifying Priorities for the Conservation of Biodiversity: Systematic Biological Criteria within a Socio-political Framework. In *Biodiversity: A Biology of Numbers and Difference*, ed. K. J. Gaston, 309–344. Oxford: Blackwell.

van Koppen, C. S. A. 2000. Resource, Arcadia, Lifeworld: Nature Concepts in Environmental Sociology. *Sociologia Ruralis* 40, no. 3:300–318.

van Koppen, C. S. A. 2002. Echte natuur: Een sociaaltheoretisch onderzoek naar natuurwaardering en natuurbescherming in de moderne samenleving. PhD diss., Wageningen University.

Vermeulen, S., and I. Koziell. 2002. *Integrating Global and Local Values: A Review of Biodiversity Assessment*. London: IIED.

Vogel R. L. 2002. *Inventarisatie van het aanbod van de verspreidingsgegevens van flora en fauna in Nederland* (Inventory of data supply on distribution of flora and fauna in the Netherlands). Nijmegen, The Netherlands: Vereniging Onderzoek Flora en Fauna.

Von Weizsäcker, C. 1993. Competing Notions of Biodiversity. In *Global Ecology: A New Arena of Political Conflict*, ed. W. Sachs, 117–131. London: Zed Books.

Wilshusen, P. R., S. R. Brechin, C. L. Fortwangler, and P. C. West. 2002. Reinventing a Square Wheel: Critique of a Resurgent "Protection Paradigm" in International Biodiversity Conservation. *Society and Natural Resources* 15:17–40.

Wilson, E. O. 1992. *The Diversity of Life*. London: Allen Lane.

Wilson, E. O., and F. M. Peter, eds. 1988. *Biodiversity*. Washington, DC: National Academic Press.

WWF. 2000. *Living Planet Report 2000*. Gland, Switzerland: World Wide Fund for Nature.

# 8

# Governing Climate Risk: A Study of International Rivers

Itay Fischhendler

Much consideration has been given in recent decades to the neo-Malthusian premise that conflicts over increasingly scarce transboundary natural resources can be expected as a result of population and economic growth (e.g., Homer-Dixon 1991; Gleick 1993). Thus, it was assumed that if sovereign nations do not find a framework for the cooperative management of scarce natural resources, the degradation of these resources and even armed confrontations are likely to result (Waterbury 2002, 9). As part of the need to regulate environmental flows, particular attention was paid in these debates to the field of water resource management. This special interest can be explained by the fact that approximately 263 river basins in the world, covering 45.3 percent of Earth's total land surface, are shared by two or more countries (Wolf et al. 1999).

In view of this situation, and with competition for water resources becoming ever more strained, it is vitally important that nation-states cooperate over shared water basins (WWAP 2003). Such cooperation is essential for optimizing the use of water resources to achieve either Pareto or social optimal results, and to prevent the escalation of disputes that originate from unilateral action (Just and Netanyahu 1998; Bennett et al. 1998).

Regimes are conceived of as devices for promoting cooperative behavior to influence the behavior of states, firms, or individuals, often by establishing principles, norms, and rules as well as decision-making procedures (Krasner 1983; Young and Levy 1999). They permit governments to attain objectives that would otherwise be unattainable (Keohane 1984, 97). International agreements signed between states are a major element of regimes, and they often provide the mechanisms for regulating the use of common natural resources (Young and Levy 1999; Susskind 1994). In the sphere of water resources, the role of these mechanisms is to regulate the quality and quantity of water between riparians sharing international rivers (Benvenisti 1996), frequently by setting the amount of water the upstream riparian delivers downstream (Wolf 1998). The last millennium has witnessed more than one thousand international treaties signed (FAO 1978), three hundred of which were agreed to in the last century, in an attempt to regulate water use among international basins (Wolf 1991). These include cases of treaties signed and performed successfully for decades between hostile countries, such as the 1960 Indus Treaty between India and Pakistan, and the 1967 Mekong Treaty between Cambodia, Laos, Thailand, and Vietnam.

Along with the many treaties signed between states, numerous global institutions and programs have also become involved in the effort to govern transboundary water flows. These include, for example, the WWAP, the UNEP, the WB, the GWP, and the WWV. The most prominent attempt to set a new water order that transcends the nation-state is perhaps the UN convention on the Law of Non-Navigational Uses of International Watercourses, adopted by the UN General Assembly on May 21, 1997. As a result, uniform guiding principles for the use of transboundary water were set regardless of political boundaries. The EU tread in the UN's footsteps as the EU negotiated a new framework directive that establishes some uniform principles of integrated management in international river basins.

Alongside these global attempts to overcome the seeming failure of the nation-state to govern water flows, many local initiatives to establish water self-governance arrangements are also advanced today. These have been argued to be more socially as well as economically beneficial than the efforts at either the nation-state or global level. Hence, these attempts suggest that the answer to Hardin's (1968) tragedy of the commons can be found in local practices (e.g., Ostrom 1990; Korten 1996) such as water drainage associations as well as water and sanitation associations. The success of these local and community-based agreements for addressing collective (water management) problems indicates the relevance of different forms of "network management" as they are developed at the local or regional level. A case in point is the management of the Rhine basin pollution (Dieperink 1995). Here, there was cooperation among many local actors—often across political boundaries—to put pressure on the Rhine states to solve the problem of deteriorating water quality.

In the process of building a regime for shared water resources, riparians must also consider variations in water availability. These changes can result from meteorologic drought (climate fluctuations) or socioeconomic drought (human actions) (Hoyt 1942; Wilhite and Glantz 1985). Since demand and supply swings may hinder the riparians' ability to supply the amount specified by the treaties, it is essential that mechanisms are built into them to accommodate changes in circumstances (Benvenisti 1996, 2002; Koremnos et al. 2001; Gleick 1993), such as seasonal fluctuations (Wolf 1998; Tarlock 1994; Benvenisti 2002). The Bonn Ministerial Declaration (2001) on freshwater provides an example of the need to institutionally accommodate climate changes. It states, "Decision-making mechanisms under uncertainty should ensure flexibility to respond to both rapid onset disasters and long-term changes to water resources."

This chapter seeks to understand how nation-states address these unpredictable events of water availability and flow while negotiating water treaties. It particularly asks whether states, while negotiating a new regime, adopt the available mechanisms to address events of climate uncertainty. It also aims to examine whether and how the regimes evolve during crisis events in order to deal with climate risk, especially given new local and regional water organizations. It is hypothesized that nations most often exclude or leave aside many of the possible risk management mechanisms not because of a lack of awareness of climate fluctuation but because many of these mechanisms change the power balance within and between states, and undermine the longevity of the regulatory regime set to regulate the resource. Thus, this chapter tries to identify the cooperative mechanisms available to address regional climate risk, while accommodating the need of the nation-state to maintain its hegemony over transnational institutions and secure a long-standing water regime. Special attention is given to the role of new local and regional initiatives in overcoming the apparent failure of the nation-state to deal with climate risk. By analyzing how hydrologic uncertainty is governed and evolves over time, we gain a better understanding as to what types of hybrid arrangements are required to accommodate both the needs of the physical environment and the state.

The first part of this chapter focuses on the negotiation process of three water treaties and seeks to identify the underlying reasons behind the actual inclusion—or exclusion/neglect—of such mechanisms. The most important mechanisms in this respect will be all kinds of drought mitigation measures. Second, I examine the ramifications of not adopting comprehensive mitigation measures by reviewing how the treaties performed their intended tasks and actually evolved during drought conditions. Particular attention is given to the effects that crisis conditions (droughts) and emerging new political constellations have on the evolution of the regulatory regimes designed to accommodate climate risks. Finally, I draw conclusions by comparing and contrasting three case studies in water flow management. The first case concerns the current drought along the lower Rio Grande and the 1944 treaty between Mexico and the United States; the second case is the 1961–1964 drought along the Great Lakes and the 1909 treaty between Canada and the United States; and the third is the 1997–1999 severe water shortage in the Jordan Basin and the 1994 peace treaty between Israel and Jordan that adjusted the international waters in the Jordan Basin.

## A Review of Available Mechanisms and Arrangements for Dealing with Climate Change Uncertainties

Several relevant mechanisms for addressing climate uncertainty can be identified. First, a treaty may specify that the upper riparian delivers to the lower riparians a minimal amount of water. An agreement with wide margins of water flow can help ensure that the treaty requirements are met, even during crises. Downstream riparians, however, may not agree to receive a minimal amount of water when the upper riparian—under normal conditions—is able to deliver. Thus, riparians can use an escape-clause mechanism to cover only exceptional situations. This mechanism allows countries suffering from drought to deliver less water than they would under normal conditions. In that way, countries can respond to unpredicted shock situations while preserving the treaty itself (Koremenos et al. 2001). This escape clause often specifies the absolute quantity in volumetric terms that the upstream riparian has to deliver in times of a drought. Nevertheless, since downstream riparians often oppose the use of such a mechanism, as it implies that they will receive less water in times of drought, it is often accompanied by a so-called deficit mechanism. This allows the upstream riparians to reduce their water flow, while compelling them to return the water a few years later, when the drought ends. Another type of escape clause enables the signatories to revoke the treaty if deemed necessary and then renegotiate it in order to redivide the resources. Several years' advance notice is necessary before taking this measure (Elias 1974), which implies that in a crisis situation, the signatory countries still have to deliver the required water. A less implicit escape clause enables the adoption of a periodic review process. This allows the different sides to evaluate the treaty performance, and especially the water allocation, every few years, thereby updating it in line with current hydrologic conditions and political developments as well as new scientific knowledge (Susskind 1994). Such a mechanism was adopted in 1972 by Canada and the United States when they signed the Great Lakes Water Quality Agreement.[1]

Another way to enhance treaty flexibility is to allocate water according to percentage and time of flow. This mechanism is commonly used among Berbers in the High Atlas Mountains and the Bedouin in Israel's Negev Desert (Wolf 1998). Yet this type of mechanism, which spreads the risk of drought among parties, puts downstream users at particular risk if changes occur upstream. Such is the case on the Ganges River, where nowadays Bangladesh experiences decreasing flow due to greater upstream use by India (Wolf 1997).

The establishment of joint institutions to manage the shared water and optimize its use in times of crisis, such as drought, is also an option (Feitelson and Haddad 1999; Najjar 2001). These institutions may be granted wide scope and a basinwide jurisdiction that includes management elements such as the right of initiating joint projects like desalinization plants or storage reservoirs aimed at increasing the available water supply. They may even include a conflict resolution mechanism that allows these joint institutions to change the water allocation between states as a response to drought (Feitelson and Haddad 1999). These institutions are often supported by external bodies that provide financial and technical help, mostly during the implementation phase of the treaty. One example of going beyond the process of merely negoti- ating the allocation of water flows and seeking third-party involvement for joint development is the recent Nile Basin Initiative and the role of the WB (2003), which has come to play a major part in coordinating donor involvement and establishing a consultative group to raise finances for such cooperative projects.

These joint institutions will have greater flexibility to mitigate crisis situations if they are given control over the different parts of the hydro- logic cycle, including the allocation of surface water and groundwater, and the regulation of water quantities (Feitelson 2000). This combined management grants parties greater operational leeway by advancing spatial and temporal trade-offs between the different components of the hydrologic cycle and between water quality and quantity, especially during climate change (Mariño 2001). A balancing mechanism is thus established in which difficulties in the delivery of water in one place can be offset by water deliveries at another place, where the water is abun- dant. Furthermore, in the event of climate change altering the water flow, it may be easier for the joint bodies to determine how to redivide the resource if the treaty specifies an order of preference for the uses of shared water (Goldeman 1990).

The next section explores whether states, while negotiating a new regime, adopt the available mechanisms to address events of climate uncertainty. It also examines how regimes evolve during crisis events in order to assess their ability to address climate risk. Here, I focus on the negotiation process of three treaties, and look at how these treaties func- tioned and evolved during drought events.

**Governing Water Flows between National Borders: Three Case Studies**

Three cases were examined in this study. They were selected because they reflect social and biophysical arrangements that are in need of revision due to changes in the political, economic, and/or environmental back- ground conditions; decisions made in the past to exclude or leave aside some of the possible mechanisms for dealing with climate uncertainties must now be revised. These cases provide an opportunity to identify how new hybrid arrangements were developed to cope with the changed circumstances and accommodate unpredictable environmental flows. Moreover, the three cases represent conditions of power asymmetry between the parties involved. It will be demonstrated how these power asymmetries affect both the decisions to (not) consider risk-handling mechanisms and the way the regulatory regimes have (not) been able to resolve the problems at hand. Identifying how asymmetrical power relations affected the evolution of regimes can provide new insights into the role of equality and power in relation to the governance of environmental flows.

In each case study, I first delineate the climate-uncertainty mechanisms that were included in or excluded from the agreement. Second, the underlying reasons for the inclusion or exclusion of drought mitigation measures are examined. The ramifications of not adopting comprehensive mitigation measures are assessed by reviewing how the treaties performed and evolved during drought conditions. Special attention is paid here to the roles of NAFTA and the subsequent trade liberalization agreements as well as their impacts on the governance of climate risks.

## The Lower Rio Grande Basin

### The 1944 Treaty and Its Climate-Uncertainty Mechanisms: A Review
Already at the beginning of the twentieth century the United States and Mexico were trying to divide their transboundary water along their two major international basins: the Rio Grande and the Colorado (Timm 1941; Hundley 1966) (figure 8.1). In 1944, a treaty was achieved to divide these waters.[3] The 1944 Treaty stipulated that on the Rio Grande, Mexico must deliver to the United States one-third of the flow reaching the main channel of the river, subject to the America's right to an average of at least 350,000 acre-feet per year (article 4, 1944 Treaty). In case of an "extraordinary drought," the treaty includes an escape clause that enables Mexico to deliver less than this minimum amount in a five-year cycle, but requires it to make up the deficit over the subsequent five years (article 4, paragraph B[d], 1944 Treaty). Furthermore, the treaty provides an order of preference for the uses of shared water between the two sides that can ease the process of determining an equitable

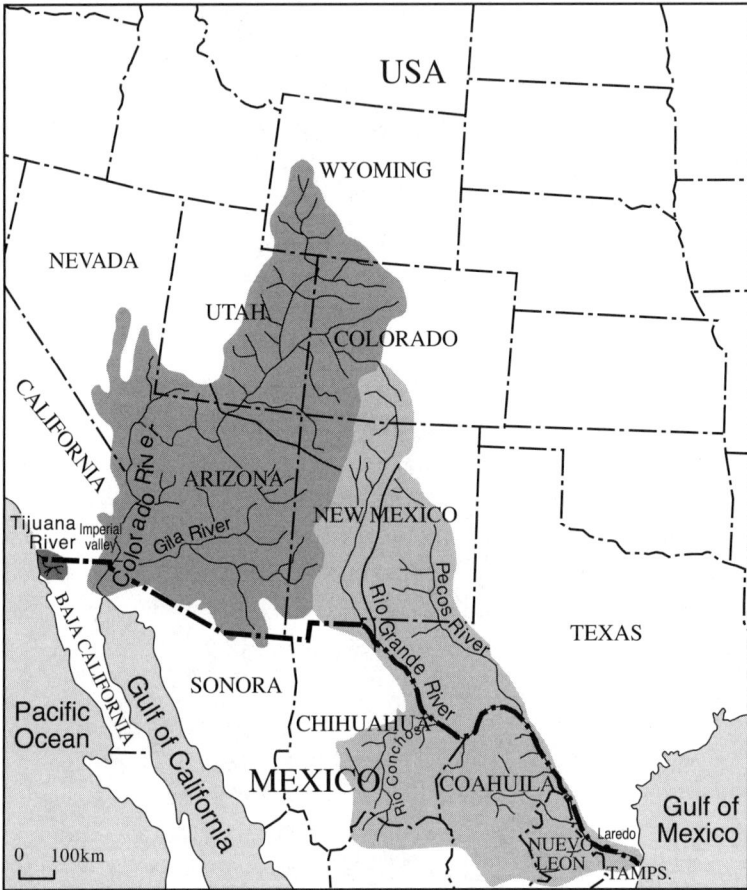

**Figure 8.1**
The transboundary basins between the United States and Mexico

utilization in the event of climate-related flow alteration (Goldeman 1990). The treaty was supplemented with a minute mechanism that allows for the establishment of new joint actions around a particular issue, on the condition of approval from the two governments and their presidents (Herrera and Friedkin 1967). The parties to the treaty also agreed on the construction of two international dams to mitigate seasonal variability in the water flow and make possible the generation of hydroelectricity along the Rio Grande (part 2, articles 5 and 7, 1944

Treaty). To administer the treaty, a permanent institution, the IBWC, or CILA, was established. The IBWC was comprised of a Mexican and a U.S. section. This body's authority was restricted to only the boundary surface waters, however. To understand the rationale for the mechanisms included and excluded in the 1944 Treaty, the next section identifies some of the riparians' underlying assumptions and interests at the time the treaty was negotiated.

## The Underlying Reasons for (Not) including Risk-Regulating Mechanisms

When the treaty was negotiated, the Mexican National Irrigation Commission estimated that the six tributaries would provide an average annual flow of 1,153,000 acre-feet of water, thus leaving Mexico on the Rio Grande with 803,000 acre-feet of water a year (Alba 1945). As the major focus for development at that time was the Mexicali Valley along the lower Colorado River (Hundley 1966, 80), the Mexicans predicted a low development rate along the lower Rio Grande Basin and especially along the Delicias River (Alba 1945).[2] Consequently, it was estimated that the water allocated to the lower Rio Grande Basin should be enough to cover any future projects, including the water delivered to the United States (Alba 1945). As a result of prioritizing the Colorado Basin over the Rio Grande Basin, Mexico had an interest in having a treaty that was broad in jurisdiction and scope. This, it was thought, would later facilitate the advancement of a trade-off in which Mexico would deliver more water to the United States on the Rio Grande in exchange for more water on the Colorado, as in fact happened (Northcutt 1946; Gomez 1945).

The Mexicans were aware of the temporal and spatial fluctuations in water availability that might occur during droughts. Hence, they insisted that the treaty contain a drought stipulation enabling Mexico to deliver its water to the United States not on an annual basis but a five-year cycle, which could be extended to ten years if necessary (Gomez 1945). This stipulation was based on the assumption that no more than a few consecutive years of drought were to be expected. A second five-year cycle would be sufficient to enable Mexico to pay the debt accumulated in the first five years (Gomez 1945). Some irrigation managers along the Rio

Bravo were concerned with the lack of equity in this drought stipulation, as during droughts it allowed the United States to halt the delivery of Colorado water while not granting the same flexibility to Mexico with respect to the Rio Grande (Alba 1945). Still, the Mexican federal government argued for the mechanism's efficiency, which on the Rio Grande provided Mexico with a flexible delivery schedule—in contrast to the rigid monthly schedule the United States was obligated to on the Colorado (Alba 1945).

Mexico was looking for a comprehensive treaty in scale and scope, but within the United States there was fear that the IBWC would become a supranational organization that could advance transbasin trade-offs and have basinwide authority. This fear, expressed most vociferously by the states of California and Nevada as well as the Bureau of Reclamation (which was afraid of the IBWC taking control of its water infrastructure), finally restricted the IBWC's authority to surface flow across the boundary line, excluding the transbasin water-balancing mechanism (U.S. Senate 1945, 1683; Glaeser 1947), and subordinated it to the domestic laws of the individual states (U.S. Senate 1945, 124). The result was a treaty that covered only limited aspects of the international waters problems (Mumme 1982, 91) and a water commission that was limited in power, which as is shown below, hampered its ability to meet the challenge of climate uncertainty.

### Regime Function and Evolution during Droughts

By 2002, the Rio Grande had experienced ten consecutive years of drought. The average annual rainfall until the year 2000 in the basin was 20 percent less than normal (RJ Brandes Company 2000) and the flow of the lower Rio Grande tributaries was decreased by 66 percent. The drought conditions have also been accompanied by rapid agricultural and urban development in the Mexican border state of Chihuahua, which contributes most of the water delivered to the United States. This increase in agricultural development is reflected in the land irrigated around the Delicias River, which by 1990 had exceeded the development rate predicted at the time the 1944 Treaty was negotiated by 50 percent.[4] This means that some 421 million cubic meters of water were consumed beyond the predictions—an amount that could have served as a counter-weight to the Mexican annual water deficit.[5]

As a result of the unpredicted change in conditions, in 1977 Mexico had already invoked the extraordinary drought stipulation, as it was about to complete a five-year cycle of water deliveries to the United States and was not able to meet its commitment. Yet, continued drought and ongoing development along the basin meant that by 2000, Mexico had accumulated a water deficit of 1.4 million acre-feet (IBWC 2002).

The nondelivery of water has caused the twenty-eight Texas irrigation districts, which are entirely dependent on this water transfer, an estimated $1 billion in losses (Taylor 2002a) and a loss of four thousand jobs just in the year 2002 (Texas Comptroller 2002). The U.S. farmers' losses, and frustration, pushed the farmers to pressure U.S. policy-makers to seek an immediate solution to the crisis. Mexico, in turn, employed the Minute mechanism incorporated into the 1944 Treaty: it delivered to the United States its 50 percent share of the water originating from undesignated inflows to the Rio Grande and later provided more water through the transfer of ownership from the two international reservoirs along the Rio Grande (IBWC 2002). Between October 1999 and September 2000, three hundred thousand acre-feet of water were delivered through these means (IBWC 2002). This use of the Minute mechanism also resulted in another Minute (Minute 307), which obliged Mexico to deliver six hundred thousand acre-feet of water by September 30, 2001 (IBWC 2002) and raised the need to develop new drought mechanisms for future crises (Minute 307). Still, only about half of the water assigned by Minute 307 was transferred to the United States (IBWC 2002).

The Mexican government, aware of the difficulty it would have in paying its deficit, suggested amending the existing drought escape clause through a new Minute, with an escape clause that would allow Mexico to stop delivering water to the United States altogether in times of drought. This solution was advanced on the basis of reciprocity since the United States has such a mechanism for the Colorado (Székely 2001; Luévano 2001). The United States, however, has refused to accept this solution, which was supported by twenty-two NGOs that proposed updating, rather than renegotiating, the treaty to develop a drought management plan (Binational Declaration 2001). It has been suggested that this plan could include reservoir management, agricultural conservation, and stakeholders' participation.

An alternative suggested by the state of Chihuahua is to renegotiate the existing treaty. So far, the Mexican federal government has refused to pursue such a course, as the treaty pertains to both basins—that is, a renegotiation process over the Rio Grande may affect the Colorado water deliveries to Mexico (Luévano 2001). Mexico agreed to emergency water deliveries in return for NADB aid money to improve Mexico's irrigation system along the Rio Grande (Pierson 2002).[6] The United States may be hoping that the Mexican president can use the financial linkage ($40 million in aid) to overcome opposition to debt repayment by the Mexican farmers who are also suffering from the drought (Gregor 2002). As a result, in June 2002, Minute 308 was signed, securing the emergency water delivery of ninety thousand acre-feet of water, and on July 3, 2003, minute 309 was signed. This latter Minute made provision for about one-third of the water saved, as a result of an improvement of the irrigation system. This improvement was financed by NADB money being used to account for the Mexican water debt.

Despite all these solutions, however, the Mexican water deficit for October 2002 stood at 1.5 million acre-feet (Texas Comptroller 2002). Moreover, no bilateral emergency plan exists yet to optimize the use of resources in times of drought, and there is a fear that this conflict may escalate if the United States takes the retaliatory step of withholding water along the Colorado (Taylor 2002b; Texas Commission on Environmental Quality 2002).

## The Main Dynamics Illustrated by this Case Study
The U.S. fear of strong transnational institutions restricted the scope and jurisdiction of the regime, and left the regime vulnerable to future changes in environmental flows. Yet the high level of border integration and the nature of the treaty as a package deal allowed the treaty to evolve during the drought on the Rio Grande. Much of the regime evolution at this time can be attributed to the new NAFTA regional institutions and the local partnerships that seemed to play a major role in circumventing

**Table 8.1**
Recent mechanisms evolved during the crisis on the Rio Grande Basin

| Mechanism | Aim | Year initiated | Players involved | Initiators |
|---|---|---|---|---|
| Drought escape clause | Allow Mexico to accumulate a water deficit | 1992 | IBWC, CILA, U.S. irrigation districts | Mexican irrigation districts |
| Meetings between two presidents | Resolve conflicts | 2001 2002 2003 | Two presidents, U.S. State Department, Mexican Foreign Affairs Ministry | U.S. irrigation districts |
| Minute 234 | Reinforce the use of the drought escape clause | 1969 | NADB, IBWC, CILA; | IBWC, CILA |
| Minute 307 | Develop new drought mechanisms; deliver 600,000 acre-feet | 2001 | NGOs, Mexican | |
| Minute 308 | | 2002 | | |
| Minute 309 | $40 million in aid money Deliver 90,000 acre-feet | 2003 | National Water Authority, Mexican Foreign Affairs Ministry, U.S. State Department | |

the nation-state sovereignty barrier that would have otherwise hindered the flexibility of the treaty.

## The Great Lakes

### The 1909 Treaty and Its Climate-Uncertainty Mechanisms: A Review
In 1909, after three years of negotiations, the United States and Canada signed a treaty that set the guiding principles for governing their shared boundary waters (figure 8.2), including ways to determine the priority of interests for the use of the waters (article 8, 1909 Treaty). This treaty includes an escape clause to enable its unilateral revocation within twelve months' notice (article 14, 1909 Treaty). A binational organization, the IJC, was established, and granted the judicial, investigative, and administrative powers to implement the treaty.

**Figure 8.2**
U.S.-Canada transboundary watersheds

The IJC's judicial power allowed the commission to issue orders in response to applications for the use, obstruction, and/or diversion of the boundary waters, if such use affects the natural water level of flows on the other side (articles 3 and 4, 1909 Treaty).[7] In addition, the IJC could make binding decisions on matters of dispute referred to the commission by the two signatory governments (article 10, 1909 Treaty). But neither commission approval nor specific agreement between the parties was required for the ordinary use of waters for domestic and sanitary purposes (article 3.2, 1909 Treaty), and the IJC's judicial authority was restricted mainly to boundary waters (article 2, 1909 Treaty).

The IJC's administrative authority was restricted to the measurement and apportionment of the two-transboundary rivers, the St. Mary and the Milk (article 6, 1909 Treaty). Article 6 laid down principles for dividing these waters and gave the commission a role in applying these principles. It specified that the water of the two rivers was to be apportioned equally between the two countries, but more than half could be taken from one river and less than half from the other, by either country. The investigative power authorized the commission, when called on by the two governments, to investigate matters of difference (article 9, 1909 Treaty). This was made possible through a Reference mechanism, included by mutual consent, that specified the questions and restrictions to be investigated by the commission. Yet this mechanism did not have an arbitral status, nor was it legally binding. Boards of control could be appointed by the commission to report on compliance with orders, while study or advisory boards could be established to assist in executing References (Chacko 1932).

### The Underlying Reasons for Including and Excluding Mechanisms

Canada, which feared the United States as a powerful neighbor, advanced a comprehensive treaty that established a strong and permanent basinwide authority with equal power for both sides (Gibbons 1953; Commons Debate 1909). This was to provide equal footing for Canada, thereby legally restraining the U.S. government from transbasin diversions, which Canada feared would have a deleterious effect on the levels of the Great Lakes, especially during drought conditions (Third Report 1907, 178). Canada also hoped that it would give the federal government control over provincially owned resources, such as nonboundary rivers and lakes (Cohen 1976).

Yet because the U.S. government was influenced by the Harmon Doctrine and concerned about restrictions over the Chicago Diversion, it rejected the establishment of a joint body that might impinge on its sovereignty and limit its capacity to divert more water from the Great Lakes in the future (U.S. Congress 1907).[8] Consequently, it insisted on restricting the IJC authority to boundary waters, which has resulted in the IJC having no jurisdiction over tributary diversions (Bloomfield and Fitzgerald 1958; Bourne 1974), including Lake Michigan and the Chicago Diversion (Dreisziger 1974). In addition, the United States restricted the commission's findings and recommendations to the governments by making them advisory only, which mitigated governmental fears of ceding sovereignty to a quasi-independent third party (Duda and LaRoche 1997).

The Canadian acknowledgment of limits to the spatial jurisdiction of the IJC was set in return for the formulation of a treaty that included guiding principles for the entire border—not just along the Great Lakes, as the United States had wished—and an arbitration provision, despite U.S. fear of a judicial tribunal (U.S. State Department 1958; Carroll 1988). But while the U.S. government feared a supranational body, this arbitration mechanism was conditioned on mutual consent by both sides, and the approval of permit applications for boundary diversions had to pass through the two governments first. This left ambiguity as to whether the IJC could or could not independently intervene to stop a diversion project that had not gone through the appropriate application procedures (Great Lakes Governors Task Force 1985, 16). Another issue that was left unresolved concerned the ways in which transboundary waters would be divided in the future. Except for Niagara Falls and the St. Milk and Mary rivers, the treaty did not regulate the appropriation of the water but simply set guiding principles for governing its use. Since Canada was seeking a comprehensive arrangement to deal with problems that yet had to develop, however, the option of settling the appropriation issue for most of the boundary line was impossible.

## Regime Function and Evolution during Droughts

The Great Lakes experienced severe drought between 1961 and 1964 (Changnon and Harper 1994). The result of this below-average precipitation was a drop in the Great Lakes to unprecedented levels between 1963 and 1965 (Cohen 1988). The drought, along with the high-intensity use of the Great Lakes (International Great Lakes Level Board 1973), led to reductions of 19 to 26 percent in the hydroelectric utilities on the Niagara and St. Lawrence rivers, a reduction of cargo load, and crop-yield reductions (Cohen 1988).

As a response to this drought, both governments agreed to use the Reference mechanism and establish boards to investigate further regulation on the Great Lakes (Changnon and Harper 1994). The IJC appointed a new panel of experts—the International Great Lakes Levels Board—to conduct the investigation. The board recommended a set of measures, including the need to investigate consumptive use and water diversions in the entire basin (IJC 1976). As a result, another reference was issued in 1977 that in practice expanded the IJC's scope and geographic jurisdiction to investigate these issues at the scale of the entire basin and not just along the boundary lines, as the 1909 Treaty had designated (IJC 1981, 1985).

The investigation acknowledged the need to legally and intuitively adapt to the changed hydrologic and consumptive use conditions, and thus recommended a bilateral "data committee" and task force (separate from the commission) to monitor basinwide diversions and consumption. It also recommended that despite the incapacity of the 1909 Treaty to provide an adequate response to the current conditions, both governments should refrain from amending or renegotiating the treaty, as this could make national positions too rigid and also make it more difficult to find practical solutions to the problems at hand. Instead, it proposed supplementing the treaty with clarifications and guidelines for further action (IJC 1985). Consequently, the 1909 Treaty was supplemented with other international mechanisms, mostly at the state/province level, to expand the Great Lakes regime's jurisdiction. Some of these mechanisms are summarized in table 8.2.

### The Main Dynamics Illustrated by This Case Study
Canada's attempt to use flexibility provisions as a vehicle for changing the power balance within its borders, and between itself and the United States, resulted in a deadlock in negotiations. The impasse was resolved only when a compromise was reached. The compromise included restricting the joint body to boundary waters, restricting the commission's findings and recommendations to an advisory nature only, and an arbitration mechanism conditioned for mutual consent. This, during a drought, forced the authorities to supplement the 1909 Treaty with other international mechanisms, mostly at the state/province level, in order to accommodate future risks. It seems that these local initiatives are better equipped to address the unique needs of the borderland communities.

### The Jordan Basin

### The Peace Treaty and Its Climate-Uncertainty Mechanisms: A Review
In October 1994, Israel and Jordan concluded a peace treaty, which included an annex addressing both water and the environment. A joint water committee was established to implement the agreement pertaining to the shared water along the whole border, including the water of the Yarmouk and Jordan rivers and Arava groundwater (figure 8.3). The treaty specified that Israel has to deliver twenty million cubic meters from Lake Kinneret (the Sea of Galilee) to Jordan in the summer period and ten million cubic meters in the winter time (annex 2, article 2a and 2d). In addition, Jordan was entitled to store, during the winter period, a

**Table 8.2**
Recent mechanisms evolved during the crisis on the Great Lakes Basin

| Mechanism | Aim | Year initiated | Players involved | Initiators |
|---|---|---|---|---|
| Reference | Establish boards to investigate regulation on the Great Lakes | 1964 | IJC, states, provinces, local players | IJC, IJC |
| | Expand the IJC's scope and jurisdiction | 1977 | | |
| | Establish transboundary watershed boards, and integrate quality and quantity issues | 1977 | | |
| Great Lakes water quality agreement, its 1978 amendment, and its 1986 protocol | Adopt an ecosystem approach | 1972 | Federal governments, IJC | Great Lakes states, provinces, federal governments |
| The Council of the Great Lakes governors, and the Great Lakes charter and annex | Adopt basinwide management | 1985 | Great Lakes states, provinces | States, provinces |
| BEC | Implement the Great Lakes water quality agreement Direct communication channels between federal governments | 1995 | Federal governments, Ontario and Great Lakes states | Federal governments |

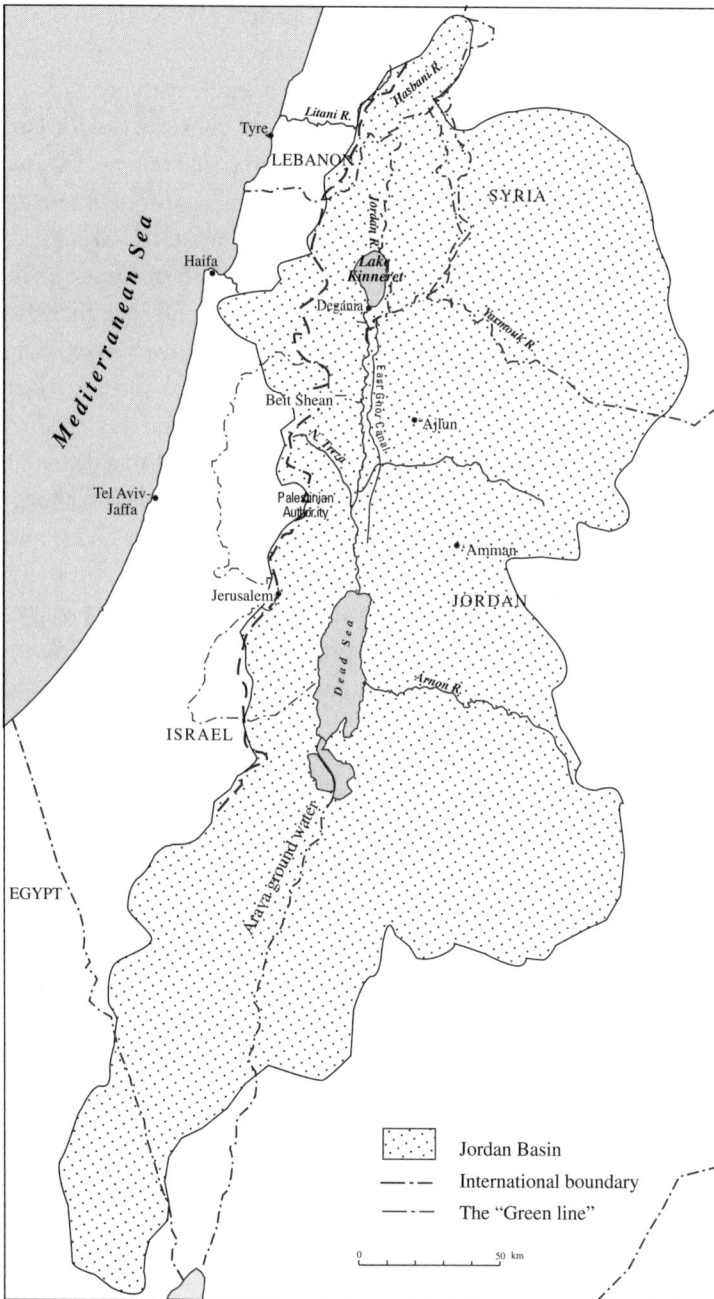

**Figure 8.3**
The Jordan Basin

minimum average of twenty million cubic meters of floods in Lake Kinneret, and both countries agreed to cooperate in finding sources for the supply to Jordan of an additional fifty million cubic meters a year of potable-standard water. In return for these waters delivered to Jordan, Israel would annually receive twenty-five million cubic meters of water from the Yarmouk and was permitted to pump an additional twenty million cubic meters from that river in the winter (annex 2, article 1). Also, Israel would continue to use the wells in the Arava, despite their location on the Jordanian side of the border (article 4), and even increase their yields by ten million cubic meters per annum above the existing level. Israel was entitled to maintain its current uses of Jordan River waters south of Lake Kinneret as well. Conversely, Jordan was entitled to an annual quantity equivalent to that of Israel, provided that Jordan's use did not adversely affect Israeli water needs. The treaty also set forth the principle of mutual assistance to alleviate water shortages and the principle that the parties should refrain from harming each other's water resources (article 6). The treaty also advanced several projects that would enhance the water supply, primarily to Jordan, including the building of a new dam beyond the Adasiya diversion to the King Abdallah Canal.

## The Underlying Reasons for Including and Excluding Mechanisms

As Israel had a larger storage capacity in Lake Kinneret, and an urgent need to receive good-quality water in the Arava that would be beyond the reach of the Israeli National Water Carrier, it advanced an agreement based on a trade-off. Under this trade-off, Jordan provided Israel with groundwater from the Arava in the south in return for Israeli water from Lake Kinneret in the north (Haddadin 2001, 395). Furthermore, Israel agreed to allow Jordan to use Lake Kinneret as a joint storage facility since Israel regarded its use of the Yarmouk water in the winter as equivalent to the water deposited by Jordan in Lake Kinneret during the summer (Haddadin 2001).

Israel was afraid that exhausting negotiations with the Jordanians on the water deliveries from Lake Kinneret might delay the peace process between Israel and Jordan, and endanger the trade-off between the Arava groundwater to Lake Kinneret water (Rosenthal 2002). This, together with the belief that Lake Kinneret's storage capacity provides flexibility to cope with drought situations, motivated Israel to make concessions on Lake Kinneret, including refraining from a binding escape clause and a periodic review of the treaty. Instead, Israel favored a "gentlemen's agreement" in which both sides would share water deficiencies during a crisis and disputes would be resolved amicably though negotiations (Rosenthal 2002; Wolf 2001). Israel in particular favored such an arrangement since in the past it had lost its cause to Egypt in the Taba arbitration (Haddadin 2001, 389) and was afraid of any international tribunal that might impinge on its sovereignty (Rosenthal 2002).

The difficulties during the negotiation phase—especially because the Palestinians were excluded from the negotiations, and because the water balance and accounting technique on the Jordan Basin was controversial—left several issues unresolved (Shamir 2002; Reisner 2003). Among them was the joint committee's scope of authority, the source of the annual additional fifty million cubic meters, how the Dead Sea tributaries were to be divided, how much each side would receive of the Jordan River's water south of Lake Kinneret, and whether Jordan would have the right to unilaterally proceed with the project to dam the Yarmouk. Israel wished to shift the water resources debate from the Jordan Basin to other water resources, to be developed jointly (Beaumont 1997). It seems that some of the ambiguities in the language describing the source of the extra fifty million cubic meters served this purpose. This ambiguous language suited the Jordanian leaders as well since the lack of specificity allowed them to go back to their constituents claiming victory (Reisner 2003), as they did after the treaty was signed.

## Regime Function and Evolution during Droughts
For over three decades, Israel has been in a water crisis situation (Israel Water Commission 2002) as a result of recurrent drought events (Amiran 1995), rapid development, and most significantly, decades of continuous overextraction of water (Israel State Comptroller 1990; Israel Water Commission 2002). Jordan, not unlike Israel, also has been under continuous water crisis management (Haddadin 2001, 499; Beaumont 2002) due to a large population increase (Haddadin 2000) accompanied by deteriorating infrastructure and recurrent droughts.

Consequently, already in 1997, as the water stress in both countries increased, Jordan demanded that Israel provide it with the additional fifty million cubic meters of water stipulated in the treaty annex (Haddadin 2001, 419). Since the annex did not specify by whom, how, and when the water had to be delivered, however, a controversy around these issues arose (Haddadin 2001, 419–427; Cohen 1997). The tension was resolved when Israel, as a gesture of good faith, agreed to provide Jordan with an extra twenty-five to thirty million cubic meters of water from Lake Kinneret over the next three years, pending the construction of a desalinization plant (Izraeli 2002). An exchange of letters between both sides constituted the new agreement (Haddadin 2001, 426).

In the same year, while the Jordanians wished to increase their water storage in Lake Kinneret and build a diversion weir on the Yarmouk, the Israelis tried to amend the water annex. Israel felt that the restriction on the Israeli use of Yarmouk waters jeopardized Israeli interests in the Beit Shean area, and that the use of Lake Kinneret as a joint storage facility had to be offset by Israeli water diversions north of Lake Kinneret (Haddadin 2001, 437). The Jordanians objected. In the end, Israel agreed to increase the Jordanian storage in Lake Kinneret to sixty million cubic meters and approve the Jordanian's diversion structure on the Yarmouk.

The following winter (1998–1999) was among the driest on record, with Lake Kinneret levels very low already at the beginning of the year (Mekorot Water Company 1999). As the 1997 agreement implied that Israel had to provide Jordan with fifty-five million cubic meters from this water source, which would reduce the lake's water levels to a dangerous point, Israel notified the Jordanians of its intention to reduce the water it planned to deliver that year by 60 percent (Ben-Meir 2002; Sobelman 1999). The basis for such a reduction, Israel claimed, was the deficit Jordan had accumulated in delivering Yarmouk water to Israel—water that Israel interpreted as being in return for that provided to Jordan during the summer from Lake Kinneret (Izraeli 2002).

Yet Jordan, which received low-quality water from Israel, perceived such a unilateral water reduction as conflicting with the principles of mutual assistance and no significant harm, as contained in the treaty. Jordan thus interpreted any reduction in the water deliveries from Israel as a violation of the treaty (Sobelman 1999). Furthermore, the fact that water policy decision makers in the two countries were not the people who had negotiated the treaty further contributed to the lack of willingness to resolve the conflict amicably by sharing deficiencies as agreed on in the 1994 annex (Wolf 2001).

Israel, in the face of the strong Jordanian protest, found itself in a complicated situation. On the one hand, it was afraid that the impending conflict might reflect on both countries' relations since the water agreement is part of the Israeli/Jordanian peace treaty. But on the other hand, Israel was afraid to set a precedent by which Jordan would receive Israeli water from Lake Kinneret in the summer without responding with an equal amount from the Yarmouk in winter (Izraeli 2002). This quandary in fact softened both sides' position, and a compromise was reached (Ben-Meir 2002) in which the water delivered to Jordan was reduced by just a few million cubic meters to cover only the water deficit Jordan had accumulated (Izraeli 2002; Mekorot Water Company 2002). Nevertheless, to deliver the water, Israel had to lower the redline of Lake Kinneret by yet another meter (Ben-Meir 2002), which further increased the likelihood of salinization of the lake.

In 2000, when the three years of the 1997 agreement expired and the desalinization plant was not yet built, the question emerged of whether Israel should continue to provide the additional twenty-five to thirty million cubic meters. Again, the Israeli fear that any reduction in the water delivered to Jordan might affect the peace agreement motivated the water commissioner to continue to make the deliveries, hoping that in the future the financial means to build the joint desalinization plant would be found (Ben-Meir 2002).

It seems that despite these solutions, which provided a partial remedy to the various controversies during the water shortage, it remains unclear how the treaty will function while the basin's upper riparians—Syria and Lebanon, which are not partners to this agreement—increase their water use (Kliot and Shmueli 1998). There is also uncertainty over how the treaty will function given Jordan's plans to further dam the Yarmouk and the treaty's lack of clarity pertaining to such an action.

### The Main Dynamics Illustrated by the Case Study

The peace talks between Israel and Jordan provided a window of opportunity to regulate their transboundary environmental flows. Yet as Israel was concerned about any new regional arrangement that might

**Table 8.3**
Recent mechanisms evolved during the crisis on the Jordan Basin

|  | Aim | Year initiated | Players involved | Initiators |
|---|---|---|---|---|
| Exchange of letters | Deliver Jordan additional 25–30 mcm from Lake Kinneret | 1997 | Both foreign ministers, Jordanian Ministry of Water and Irrigation, Israel Water Commission | Jordanian Ministry of Water and Irrigation |
|  | Increase storage in Lake Kinneret | 1998 |  |  |
|  | Approve diversion structure on the Yarmouk | 1998 |  |  |
| Unofficial negotiations | Update water deliveries to Jordan Build the desalinization plant | 1998 | Israel Water Commission, both foreign ministers | Israel Water Commission |

undermine the existing power balance between the states, many of the hydrologic considerations were sidestepped. During a crisis, both sides found it difficult to address changes in the governance of the water flows, especially given the low level of economic and political integration between the two states. As a result, only weak and temporary arrangements were established to address the immediate and future environmental risks.

## Discussion

Although these three case studies were negotiated under different circumstances, they share many similarities—in fact, all three treaties excluded and included essentially the same mechanisms (tables 8.4 and 8.5). This suggests that some of the barriers to adopting risk-handling mechanisms are relatively universal in character, instead of being connected in specific ways to the interests and practices of (nation-)states. This section tries to identify the main driving forces behind the exclusion of these mechanisms. It primarily focuses on the discrepancies between demands stemming from the physical characteristics of (the scapes of) flows, on the one hand, and the political and institutional demands of nation-states, on the other. Finally, it examines how this

**Table 8.4**
Mechanisms excluded, their infringement on sovereignty, and their threat to treaty longevity

| Mechanism | U.S.-Mexico | U.S.-Canada | Israel-Jordan | Infringement on sovereignty/ change in power balance | Threat to treaties longevity |
|---|---|---|---|---|---|
| Formal binding conflict resolution mechanism | – | – | – | + | |
| Basinwide management | – | – | – | + | |
| Escape clauses | + | – | – | | + |
| Water deliveries based on percentage of flow | – | – | – | + | + |
| Balancing mechanism | – | – | – | + | |

*Note*: + = occurring; – = not occurring.

**Table 8.5**
Mechanisms included, their infringement on sovereignty, and their threat to treaty longevity

| Mechanism | U.S.-Mexico | U.S.-Canada | Israel-Jordan | Infringement on sovereignty | Threat to treaties longevity |
|---|---|---|---|---|---|
| Joint body (with limited scope and jurisdiction) | | | | – | – |
| Nonbinding reference/minute mechanism | + | + | + | – | – |
| Ambiguity in treaty language | + | + | + | – | – |
| Joint infrastructure projects | + | – | + | – | – |

*Note*: + = occurring; – = not occurring.

alleged conflict between nature and politics was settled by adopting hybrid arrangements to govern uncertainty.

## The Nature-Politics Interface

Given the potential risk of climate fluctuation, treaties must include flexibility provisions to spread the risk equitably between the different coriparians. It is often the professional community that advocates the adoption of mechanisms to address climate risk. This was clear in the contemporary Israeli/Jordanian case, where the hydrologic community called for flexibility provisions in the treaty's language, including an explicit periodic review process. Yet these mechanisms not only provide protection against unpredictable flows but also have a profound effect on the power balance between and within states, especially under a decentralized system. This is particularly the case when a joint body is created with broad scope and geographic jurisdiction. Granting an international body such authority is perceived, predominantly by the powerful riparian, to provide the other riparians equal power in decisions concerning domestic and international water, thus impinging on the former's hegemony.

Not surprisingly, it is the weak riparian that often proposes this mechanism since it can provide the weak riparian better protection against negative externalities while enhancing its power in situations where the international body commands a central place in the network of relationships. Indeed, it has already been observed that actors seeking to improve their power position may promote reforms in the size of governing units (Casella and Frey 1992), municipal boundaries (Razin and Hazan 2001), and even the (geographic) jurisdiction of transboundary water commissions (Blatter and Ingram 2000). This was the case regarding Canada and Mexico in relation to the United States: each aspired to a treaty and institutions that were more comprehensive in scale and scope than preferred by the United States, essentially to improve their own power positions. But the United States discarded this mechanism, as it would have given Canada and Mexico equal footing in water-related issues along both the northern and southern U.S. borders. This was also the case with respect to Jordan, which had an interest in including an arbitration and multiyear deficit mechanism—something that was opposed by Israel. These experiences suggest that autonomous joint governance mechanisms are not likely to be adopted under unbalanced power relations.

Also, the domestic initiation of a supranational institution is perceived to change the power balance within states, thus impinging on the federalist system. This is the case when shared management is agreed on, and the new joint authority advances spatial and temporal trade-offs between the different components of the hydrologic cycle. In the U.S.-Mexico case, the United States refused to adopt such a mechanism as it had the ability to sacrifice the interests of one state in one part of the country in order to secure the benefits to another state elsewhere, thereby impinging on the federalist system. In the U.S.-Canada case, Ontario was expected to oppose any treaty sufficiently wide in scale and scope that it would apply to the Georgian Bay and its surrounding streams, as such an agreement would provide the new transnational body with authority over domestic issues (Fischhendler 2004).

Uncertainty mechanisms not only affect political power and autonomy but also the longevity of the pending treaties. Transboundary natural resources are often regulated for a long period of time in order for the nation-state to secure the large capital investments needed for joint infrastructure and preventing the defection of either side from the regime due to a change in the background conditions. As a result, politicians consider it essential that treaties be secured for lengthy periods, especially when they include several issues negotiated concurrently. Mechanisms that threaten the continuity of treaties are therefore excluded. This was the case in terms of the nonadoption of a periodic review process and a system for water deliveries based on flow percentages in the Israeli/ Jordanian example. A treaty update ran the risk of both sides being unable to agree on water reallocation, particularly if the political background conditions have substantially changed. These mechanisms were further perceived to exacerbate the ability to market the treaties to politicians. The Israeli case illustrates how the water experts were aware that marketing a treaty with "ifs" and "buts" was not feasible because the politicians would reject it. Instead, a treaty focusing on flow percentages and based on deliveries of a fixed amount of water was advanced (Shamir 2002). This tendency to allocate water based on a fixed amount also allowed Israel to maintain its water management independence, which was important since Israel was afraid that flow percentages would allow Jordan to interfere in this area (Reisner 2003). Thus, it seems that escape clauses, although hydrologically sound, have the potential to both impinge on sovereignty and threaten the longevity of treaties (table 8.4). These preliminary findings necessitate further study of the channels of communication between the professionals, who calculate the hydrologic details of a given treaty, and the politicians, who market the agreement as a whole.

The decision to exclude climate-uncertainty mechanisms or compromise on less stringent mechanisms is sustained by the tendency of the politicians to choose optimistic water-availability scenarios based on average values rather than extreme or peak hydrologic values. When policymakers predict high water availability and low vulnerability of the resource, the uncertainty for the implications of excluding these mechanisms decreases, and in turn, the expected benefits of adopting these measures are reduced. This was the case when Israel assumed that Lake Kinneret's storage capacity provided sufficient flexibility to enable the delivery of twenty-five to thirty million cubic meters of water to Jordan during the summer, especially in light of its belief that the additional fifty million cubic meters would not come from this source. It was also clearly the case when Mexico predicted low development rates, high water availability, and the short duration of droughts on the Rio Grande, reinforcing its decision not to adopt a more stringent escape clause. Finally, I identified processes of negotiating all boundary waters together, in order to be able to establish linkages and trade-offs across borders. This linkage strategy, intended to enhance cooperation, actually generated a fear that any attempt to discuss one part of the treaty would reflect on its other parts. The result is that the mechanisms of escape clauses and periodic review processes have been deliberately left out of international treaties aimed at safeguarding the interests of all signatory parties. This was the case with respect to Israel, which was afraid that adopting stringent escape clauses and a periodic review process on Lake Kinneret would be countered by a Jordanian insistence on the same mechanisms in relation to the Arava, where it was crucial for Israel to receive water at any time (Rosenthal 2002). Thus, Israel refrained from insisting on these mechanisms. Table 8.4 summarizes the mechanisms excluded from the treaties, and the perceived threat of each to national sovereignty and treaty continuity.

**Bridging Nature and Politics: Hybrid Arrangements to Govern Risk**
Despite the widespread exclusion of several mechanisms, some other arrangements are frequently considered. Arrangements that have the capacity to circumvent the alleged conflict between political and natural resources and interests are included in the process (table 8.5). One such mechanism is the adoption of a joint regime that includes only the basin boundary water. Rather than creating a joint body with broad scope and geographic jurisdiction, a spatial compromise is adopted. This compromise, by maintaining the existing power balance between and within the states and protecting the basin's critical areas against externalities, resolves the deadlock in treaty negotiations. This spatial strategy may be especially relevant when the environmental benefits of inclusion are low, while the political and transaction costs of inclusion are high. Such may be the case when a transboundary regime is delineated under a decentralized system where new joint regional institutions are expected to fail since they threaten existing institutions at the local/national level (Ingram 1973). Yet as discussed below, both the IBWC and the IJC find it difficult today to address upstream diversions, as they were designed to govern boundary issues and have little discretion to initiate basinwide drought proceedings.

Another mechanism included in treaties is arbitration. It is only possible to adopt this mechanism under a unanimous decision-making process. This occurred when the United States supported the Canadian wish to add a reference mechanism and expand the IJC's scope to include permit approval. These steps were conditioned on mutual consent and an application procedure that had to pass through both governments first. This was also the case when Israel agreed that Jordan could further dam the Yarmouk, on the condition of a joint consultation. It also appears that when the mechanisms are not legally binding, the parties are more willing to accept them and to adjust to new conditions as they emerge. Examples include the case of the United States supporting a nonbinding arbitration mechanism in the 1909 Treaty, when the riparians agreed to voluntarily adopt the Great Lakes charter, and the case of Jordan agreeing to incorporate an informal gentlemen's agreement in its pact with Israel. These experiences highlight the role of "soft laws" in formalizing flexible agreements, as suggested by Abbott and Snidal (1998). They stress, too, how inexplicit mechanisms reduce the adjustment costs since they enable modifying the treaty's terms of conditions without paying the full cost of negotiations.[9] The effectiveness of this mitigation measure in the water sector has received support from Dieperink (2000), who draws our attention to the 1987 Rhine Action Program, adopted by the International Rhine Commission. This program, which was not legally binding (except in a political sense), was almost fully implemented; contrast this to many other initiatives to improve the state of the Rhine environment that were legally binding—and failed (Dieperink 2000).

It seems that when the different sides cannot agree on many of the issues negotiated, they adopt vague and ambiguous standards instead of clear guidelines for dividing up their shared water. This was the case with Israel and Jordan as well. By leaving many issues unresolved, the two sides prevented major delays in signing their peace agreement, and later were able to show flexibility regarding the scope of the joint commission and the annual schedule of water deliveries (Izraeli 2002). Finally, in both the U.S.-Mexico and Israeli-Jordanian cases, the parties sought to increase their capacity to address uncertainty through joint infrastructure development aimed at providing more available storage water during droughts. It is this technological strategy that further stressed the need for treaties to be binding for long periods of time, as the defection of either side from the regime could jeopardize the large capital investments needed for joint infrastructure. Thus, adopting expensive technical solutions further contributed to the exclusion of risk-handling mechanisms that run counter to the continuity of the regime. Table 8.5 summarizes the mechanisms included in the treaties, and their perceived threat to sovereignty and treaty continuity. Given the fact that many of the mechanisms identified in the introduction were excluded in the treaties studied, the next section reviews how these treaties function in practice.

## The Treaties' Functions and Evolution

Drought followed the ratification of all three treaties, triggering the need to adjust the agreements to the new hydrologic conditions. In all three cases, the option of renegotiating the existing treaties was excluded since they were based on package deals. The nature of the treaties as package deals left an institutional and legal footprint in which one treaty and one institution were both established for all the boundary waters. This raises the risk that any attempt to discuss one part of the treaty would reflect on its other parts, thereby hampering the possibility of updating the agreements based on the new conditions.

These package-deal treaties, combined with a belief that under today's conditions a better treaty will not be achieved, stops riparians from amending or renegotiating the existing agreements. This hesitation exists despite the fairly widespread recognition of the treaties' limited capacity to accommodate climate-uncertainty conditions. Yet an agreement was not possible unless the (package-deal) linkage was made. Thus, the question for further study is not whether or not to adopt a linkage but rather how to reduce the cost of the linkages.

Instead of renegotiation, riparians seek to use many of the mechanisms incorporated in the treaties to deal with crisis situations. Some examples of the mechanisms used include the Reference and the Minute, as in the U.S-Mexico and U.S.-Canada cases. Since their establishment, the IBWC (2002) and the IJC (2001) have authorized 127 minutes and 44 references, respectively. On some occasions, however, employing these mechanisms raises questions about the legitimacy of their use. For example, Canada and the United States liberally used the Reference mechanism in their treaty to expand the IJC's spatial jurisdiction to include the entire basin, although the treaty was designed as a boundary treaty (Bourne 1974). This was also the case with the NADB money allocated to resolve the dispute along the Rio Grande, which resulted in a controversy over the legitimacy of such a mechanism (Taylor 2002c).

In other cases, even mechanisms that were built into treaties proved impotent in crisis situations. In the Israel and Jordan situation, the joint desalinization plant was not established, and the gentleman's agreement concluded in 1994 proved ineffective as the water officials who negotiated the treaty were replaced.[10] As a result, Israel lowered Lake Kinneret levels to provide Jordan with an annual fifty-five million cubic meters of water (Ben-Meir 2002). In the case of the Great Lakes, the IJC's judicial power to make binding decisions on matters of dispute has never been exercised, as the political cost of using the mechanisms was expected to be high (Council of the Great Lakes Governors 1985). Another example concerns the escape clause for an extraordinary drought event on the Rio Grande. This clause was not only found to be inadequate for the Mexicans during a prolonged drought but also resulted in a controversy between Mexico and the Texan agricultural sector because the treaty was left vague, without defining the threshold for extraordinary drought conditions (Kelly 2001b).

Yet this vagueness, which often leads to controversy around the interpretation of the treaties, may also broaden the treaties' ability to accommodate climate change and, as was mentioned, speed up the ratification process.

As a result of treaties' limited capacity to deal with conditions of uncertainty, this study illustrates how a controversy can develop when one side finds it difficult to meet its obligations. A controversy of this nature runs the risk of turning a water matter into a major political conflict. Such is the case with the United States and Mexico, where the failure of the latter to meet its treaty requirements resulted in the intervention of both countries' presidents to prevent the matter from escalating into a conflict that would involve nonwater issues as well.[11] It was also the case of fifty million cubic meters with Israel and Jordan: the 1997 and 1998 controversies around the additional and the drought-related water crisis were resolved only when high-level politicians got involved.

Nevertheless, these conflicts trigger amendments to the treaties, thereby introducing new mechanisms aimed at resolving future disagreements. One such example is the Great Lakes Charter, Commission and Water Quality Agreement, supplementing the 1909 Treaty, triggered by a drought event. Another is the Israeli-Jordanian exchange of letters of understanding aimed at resolving the controversy over the additional fifty million cubic meters. The Canadian-U.S. case, meanwhile, demonstrates that these mechanisms are often voluntary and their evolution

slow. Thus, they do not provide a real-time solution to a crisis. It is interesting to note that it was the more powerful riparian that took on the
burden of the drought. This was the case with respect to Israel and the
United States. Despite Jordan and Mexico not meeting their treaty conditions, Israel and the United States, respectively, sought solutions to
avoid the collapse of the regimes.

When economic, political, and environmental networks are established
across shared basins, the parties are more willing to adapt the treaties to
new background conditions in times of crisis, regardless of the lack of
formal mechanisms to address climate uncertainty in the treaties' language. This was the case with regard to the United States and Mexico
as well as the United States and Canada, whose treaties, due to the high
level of border integration, evolved much further than that of the Israel-
Jordan one, where the disagreement over the treaty language was a
source of conflict. This is especially the case today given the creation of
the recent NAFTA institutions, as was noted with regard to the U.S.-
Mexico case.[12] These institutions are likely to play an increasing role in
providing alternative communication channels—alternatives to the
IJC and the IBWC—as they facilitate direct negotiations between
governments and especially between local entities. It is likely that this
will act as a counterbalancing force for the autonomy of the nation-state,
hence requiring a reconsideration of the adequacy of the nation-state-
bound mechanisms for addressing risk. This implies that the ability of
the treaty to address uncertainty should be analyzed not just according
to the treaty language but also as part of regional economic, cultural,
and political networks established during the treaty implementation
phase. This, in turn, raises the need to understand how to integrate environmental issues with other political and economic flows in order to
overcome the treaties' lack of formal flexibility to address climate risks.
One possible option stressed by this study is to design treaties based on
linkages across areas and issues. In all three case studies, it turns out that
during times of drought both sides sought to supplement the treaties with
Minutes, References, and exchange of letters, rather than to renegotiate
the treaties. The costs of renegotiation were exacerbated in those cases
where treaties were based on linkages. Bernauer (2002) has already
observed that the use of linkages is especially common under

nonintegrating settings, where compensation seems to be a prerequisite for cooperation.

Finally, the U.S.-Mexico and U.S.-Canada cases demonstrate how many of the new initiatives for incorporating a consideration of risk into regulatory regimes occur at the local level where there is a strong civil society. In the latter case, this has resulted in many partnerships between the Great Lakes provinces and states. In the former case, several borderland NGOs now endorse the need to supplement the treaty of 1944 with a new drought management plan.

## Conclusion

Putting the nation-state at the center of analysis explains why many of the so-called obvious mechanisms to enhance a treaty's flexibility to cope with climate uncertainty are deliberately omitted. This is because their inclusion could disrupt the balance of power between and within nations, and also threaten the prolonged existence of the regime. These dynamics characterize all three cases. Nation-states rejected a periodic review process and procedures for water deliveries based on flow percentages because, during a crisis situation, these mechanisms might undermine the longevity of regimes that were often established decades earlier. Also, nation-states were hesitant to create a joint body with wide jurisdiction and scope, especially one that included a formal arbitration mechanism. Such a mechanism was excluded from the three treaties since it would have changed the power balance within and between the states.

Since many of the risk-handling mechanisms identified above benefit some states (often the less powerful ones, either in terms of power balance or location in the basin) at the expense of other states, it is unlikely that these mechanisms will be included in treaty texts and language. This is particularly so under the current conditions, in which there is no strong international water law that can set a global blueprint for how risks should be shared fairly and equitably between states. It is not surprising, then, that despite the need to adopt mechanisms to address events of climate uncertainty, many treaties lack such language (Tarlock 1994; Goldeman 1990) and flexible allocation methods remain in the minority (UNEP 2002). Still, although some risk mechanisms were excluded from treaties, other alternative risk mechanisms were adopted instead. To understand their nature and performance there is a need to transcend the centric nation-state analysis, and incorporate both changes in the background environment conditions and new players in the local and global arenas.

It was often unforeseen drought, transcending political boundaries, that provided the incentive for players to build some flexibility into water allocation treaties and policies in order to address hydrologic fluctuation and develop forms of adaptive management. Otherwise, the ability to maintain the treaty might have been hampered in situations of changing conditions, thereby giving rise to a possible conflict. Among these arrangements are restricting the jurisdiction of the cooperative regime to include only the basin boundary water rather than seeking a basinwide regime and adopting technological solutions to increase the water availability. Examples include the desalinization plant in the Israeli-Jordanian case, the reservoirs built along the Rio Grande, and the irrigation improvements currently being adopted to mitigate the drought along the Rio Grande. Finally, the different parties adopted vague and ambiguous standards instead of clear guidelines for dividing up their shared water.

In addition, the aspirations of new players and regional institutions led to the addition of some flexibility in treaties. NAFTA and the NADB, for example, have been influential in the evolution of treaties since 1994. In the U.S.-Mexico case, they facilitated many of the recent Minutes aimed at addressing the current hydrologic crises. In contrast, in the U.S.-Canada case, it was the proliferation of local entities that made the existing agreements evolve beyond the treaty language; it was the several partnerships between the Great Lakes provinces and states that supplemented the 1909 Treaty with the Great Lakes charter and annex.

Even if there are no formal local or regional arrangements to foster flexibility, when economic and political transboundary networks are established, treaties still evolve. In the Israeli-Jordanian case, diplomacy between the two countries was the driving force behind supplementing the water agreement with a mechanism for redistributing the risk among the players. The political network effect was reinforced by the linkage between water and the peace process.

Another factor not explored in this study is the role of the private sector in providing more adaptive management during crisis events. As Feitelson (2003) has already suggested, if this strategy of adaptive management is adopted for transboundary aquifers, the different parties sharing the aquifer will have to cooperate during droughts in order to get the best possible deal from the franchisee. Indeed, the U.S. Congress and the IBWC (2004) just recently decided to explore the option of a public-private service provider for the treatment of wastewater that originates in Tijuana, Mexico, and pollutes the city of San Diego. It is assumed that incorporating a public entity will depoliticize the process and ensure more reliable wastewater treatment than if it is up to the Mexican federal government to treat the wastewater (Schlesinger 2004).

It is therefore crucial to develop hybrid arrangements between governmental and nongovernmental local actors and institutions. These arrangements would allow flexibility provisions to be included in environmental treaties, so that the necessary adaptations in regime management would be possible without changing the power balance and without necessitating a renegotiation of the treaty. It also implies that the ability of the treaty to address uncertainty should be analyzed not just according to the treaty language but also as part of networks between the states and other actors established during the treaty implementation phase. In other words, many of the hybrid risk arrangements can be understood only by looking beyond the nation-state.

The need to reconsider the (in)adequacy of many of the conventional risk-handling mechanisms is further emphasized as new forms of water governance emerge today. In many places, authority is transferred vertically to regional entities, while authority over other issues—e.g., nonwater issues—is decentralized to the lower tiers of governance. This has in some places transformed the state from a sovereign subject into a strategic actor that coordinates between the regional and local tiers. Consequently, a hierarchy of nested institutions is often established, with different institutions at various levels (local, national, and regional) having control over different aspects of the water cycle. Many of the EU water directives and the NAFTA environmental institutions and programs are examples of this fragmentation of water politics. Their increased power has changed the traditional role of nation-states in the water sector. How this new power order might challenge the traditional role of the state and even encourage flexibility in cooperative arrangements is glimpsed in the EU's role in strengthening the Rhine Commission and the Rhine Chemical Convention (Huisman et al. 2000). Another example is the role of the OECD in issuing recommendations concerning the management of transboundary resources (UNEP 2002, 5).

In conclusion, with respect to the theme of the governance of environmental flows, this study stresses the political cost of some of the traditional (climate) risk-handling mechanisms, and calls for inventing mechanisms that are both politically feasible and hydrologically effective. By seeking to establish hybrid arrangements between different actors at different levels, regimes can be made more flexible and thereby more suited to address (climate) uncertainties that in the near future undoubtedly will become important challenges for the transnational management of water flows.

## Notes

1. This agreement, which was signed in 1972, and updated in 1978 and 1987, was aimed at incorporating water-quality standards to the Great Lakes. Yet this was done within the existing 1909 treaty framework (see Becker 1996).

2. This river accounts for about 57 percent of the Mexican irrigated water used along the Rio Grande (Kelly 2001a).

3. For the full text of this treaty, see <http://ibwc.state.gov/new/whatsnew.htm>.

4. In 1990, irrigated farmland amounted to 96,355 hectares (Kelly 2001a), compared to the 63,371 hectares predicted when the 1944 Treaty was negotiated (Alba 1945).

5. This is based on the estimate that the 96,355 hectares of irrigated land in 1990–1991 used 1,261 million cubic meters of water (Kelly 2001a); thus, it can be extrapolated that a 50 percent use above expected levels resulted in the consumption of an additional 421 million cubic meters of water.

6. The NADB was established as part of NAFTA. Its aim is to help border communities build modern water and environmental infrastructure in order to provide safe drinking water, treat wastewater, and dispose of solid wastes (Killgore and Eaton 1995).

7. Boundary waters are defined as "the waters from main shore to main shore of the lakes and rivers and connecting waterways, or the portions thereof, along which the international boundary between the United States and the Dominion of Canada passes, including all bays, arms and inlets thereof, but not including

tributary waters, and waterways, or waters flowing from such lakes, rivers and waterways, or the waters flowing across the boundary" (preliminary article, 1909 Treaty).

8. The Harmon Doctrine, as first stated in 1895 by the U.S. attorney general in relation to the Mexican claims on the upper Rio Grande, argues for the absolute jurisdiction of a nation over the water resources within its own territory. The Chicago Diversion, initiated by the city of Chicago, already began diverting Lake Michigan water at the end of the nineteenth century (Naujoks 1946; Injerd 1993).

9. The adjustment costs are the direct costs of implementing changes in the contract such as the cost of bargaining over terms, or the indirect costs in the form of adjustments that are not implemented (for more details, see Wernerfelt 2004).

10. It seems that the reason why the desalinization plant was never built was the lack of willingness on the parts of both Israel and Jordan to invest the money required, along with the decision of Germany and Japan not to financially support the project.

11. One meeting took place on March 16, 2001, and resulted in the signing of Minute 307 (Kelly 2001b; Border 2001); another meeting, in March 2002 at the Poverty Conference in Monterey, did not yield any results.

12. These include the NACEC, the BECC, and the NADB (see Killgore and Eaton 1995).

## References

Abbott, K., and D. Snidal. 1998. Why States Act Through Formal Organizations. *Journal of Conflict Resolution* 42, no. 1:3–32.

Alba, A. O. 1945. *Statement of Adolfo Orive Alba, Mexican National Irrigation Commission, at the Roundtable Discussions of the Water Treaty in the Mexican Senate Offices.* July 31. Translated by the U.S section of the IBWC.

Amiran, D. 1995. *Rainfall and Water Policy in Israel.* Jerusalem: Jerusalem Institute for Israel Studies.

Beaumont, P. 1997. Dividing the Waters of the River Jordan: An Analysis of the 1994 Israel-Jordan Peace Treaty. *International Journal of Water Resources Development* 13, no. 3:415–424.

Beaumont, P. 2002. Water Policies for the Middle East in the 21st Century: The New Economic Realities. *International Journal of Water Resources Development* 18, no. 2:315–334.

Becker, M. L. 1996. Implementing a Binominal Ecosystem Management Strategy in the Great Lakes Basin: Will the Remedial Action Policy Process Succeed in Restoring the Area of Concern. PhD diss., Duke University.

Ben-Meir, M. 2002. Personal interview with Meir Ben-Meir, Israeli water commissioner (1996–2000), Tel Aviv, October 31.

Bennett, L. L., S. E. Ragland, and P. Yolles. 1998. Facilitating International Agreements through an Interconnected Game Approach: The Case of River Basins. In *Conflict and Cooperation on Transboundary Water Resources*, ed. R. Just and S. Netanyahu, 61–85. Boston: Kluwer Academic Publishers.

Benvenisti, E. 1996. Collective Action in the Utilization of Shared Freshwater: The Challenges of International Water Resources Law. *American Journal of International Law* 90:384–415.

Benvenisti, E. 2002. *Sharing Transboundary Resources: International Law and Optimal Resource Use*. Cambridge: Cambridge University Press.

Bernauer, T. 2002. Explaining Success and Failure in International River Management. *Aquatic Sciences* 64, no. 1:1–19.

Binational Declaration. 2001. *The Rio Conchos and the Lower Rio Bravo/Rio Grande*. Austin: Texas Center for Policy Studies.

Blatter, J., and H. Ingram. 2000. States, Markets, and Beyond: Governance of Transboundary Water Resources. *Natural Resources Journal* 40, no. 2:439–471.

Bloomfield, L. M., and F. G. Fitzgerald. 1958. *Boundary Water Problems of Canada and the United States*. Toronto: Carswell Company.

Bonn Ministerial Declaration. 2001. Ministerial Declaration, the Bonn Keys, and Bonn Recommendations for Action. Paper presented at the International Conference on Freshwater, Bonn, December 3–7.

Border: Joint Effort to Solve a Natural Resource Crisis May Help Bring U.S., Mexico Closer. 2001. *Los Angeles Times*, May 29.

Bourne, C. B. 1974. Canada and the Law of International Drainage Basins. In *Canadian Perspective on International Law and Organization*, ed. R. Macdonald, C. L. Morris, and D. M. Johnston, 469–499. Toronto: University of Toronto Press.

Carroll, J. 1988. *Environmental Diplomacy: An Examination and a Prospective of Canadian-U.S. Transboundary Environmental Relations*. Ann Arbor: University of Michigan Press.

Casella, A., and B. Frey. 1992. Federalism and Clubs: Towards an Economic Theory of Overlapping Political Jurisdictions. *Europe Economic Review* 36:639–644.

Chacko, C. J. 1932. *The International Joint Commission*. New York: AMS Press.

Changnon, S., and M. Harper. 1994. History of the Chicago Diversion. In *The Lake Michigan Diversion at Chicago and Urban Drought*, ed. S. A. Changnon, 16–38. Ann Arbor: University Cooperation for Atmospheric Research.

Cohen, A. 1997. Israel Will Desalinate an Annual 50 mcm of Water from the Kinneret Springs and the Gilboa [in Hebrew]. *Haaretz*, May 25, p3a.

Cohen, M. 1976. Canada and the United States: Dispute Settlement and the International Joint Commission—Can This Experience be applied to the Law of the Sea Issues? *Case Western Reserve Journal of International Law* 8, no. 46:69–76.

Cohen, S. 1988. Great Lakes Levels and Climate Change Impacts, Responses, and Future. In *Social Responses to Regional Climatic Change Forecasting by Analogy*, ed. M. Glantz. Boulder, CO: Westview Press.

Commons Debate. 1909. Vol. 42, first session, May 14, 6639.

Dieperink, C. 1995. Between Salt and Salomon. In *Managing Environmental Disputes: Network Management as an Alternative*, ed. P. Glasbergen, 119–136. Boston: Kluwer Academic Publishers.

Dieperink, C. 2000. From Open Sewer to Salmon Run: Lessons from the Rhine Water Quality Regime. *Water International* 25, no. 3:347–355.

Dreisziger, N. A. F. 1974. The International Joint Commission of the United States and Canada, 1895–1920: A Study in Canadian-American Relations. PhD diss., University of Toronto.

Duda, A., and D. LaRoche. 1997. Sustainable Development of International Waters and Their Basins: Implementing the GEF Operational Strategy. *International Journal of Water Resources Development* 13, no. 3:383–401.

Elias, T. O. 1974. *The Modern Law of Treaties*. Dobbs Ferry, NY: Oceania Publications.

FAO. 1978. *Systematic Index of International Water Resources Treaties, Declaration, Acts, and Cases by Basin*. Vol. 2. Legislative study 15. Rome: FAO.

Feitelson, E. 2000. The Upcoming Challenge: Transboundary Management of the Hydraulic Cycle. *Water, Air, and Soil Pollution* 123:533–549.

Feitelson, E. 2003. When and How Would Shared Aquifers Be Managed? *Water International* 28, no. 2:145–153.

Feitelson, E., and M. Haddad. 1999. *Identification of Joint Management Structures for Shared Aquifers: A Comparative Palestinian-Israeli Effort*. WB technical paper 415. Washington, DC: World Bank.

Fischhendler, I. 2004. Spatial Adjustments as a Mechanism for Resolving River Basin Conflicts. PhD diss., Hebrew University of Jerusalem.

Gibbons, A. 1953. Sir George Gibbons and the Boundary Treaty of 1909. *Canadian Historical Review* 34:124–137.

Glaeser, M. 1947. The Mexican Water Treaty, Part II. *Journal of Land and Public Utility Economics* 22:354.

Gleick, P. 1993. Water and Conflict, Freshwater Resources, and International Security. *International Security* 18, no. 1:79–112.

Goldeman, G. 1990. Adapting to Climate Change: A Study of International Rivers and Their Legal Arrangements. *Ecology Law Review* 17:741–802.

Gomez, M. R. 1945. *Statement of the Ministry of Foreign Affairs, Mexican Secretary of Agriculture and Development*. City of Mexico, April 21. Translated by the U.S. section of the IBWC.

Great Lakes Governors Task Force. 1985. *Water Diversion and Great Lakes Institutions*. Chicago: Council of the Great Lakes Governors.

Gregor, A. 2002. Farmers in the Valley Told to Be Patient. *Express-News Rio Grande Bureau*, July 18.

Haddadin, M. 2000. Water Issues in the Hashemite Jordan. *Arab Studies Quarterly* 22, no. 2:63–77.

Haddadin, M. 2001. *Diplomacy on the Jordan: International Conflict and Negotiated Resolution*. Boston: Kluwer Academic Publishers.

Hardin, G. 1968. The Tragedy of the Commons. *Science* 162:1243–1248.

Herrera, D., and J. F. Friedkin. 1967. The International Boundary and Water Commission, United States and Mexico. Paper presented at the International Conference on Water and Peace, Washington, DC, May 23–31.

Homer-Dixon, T. F. 1991. *Environmental Change and Acute Conflict: A Research Agenda*. New York: Social Science Research Council.

Hoyt, W. G. 1942. Droughts. In *Hydrology*, ed. O. E. Meinzer, 579. New York: Dower Publications.

Huisman, P., J. de Jong, and K. Wieriks. 2000. Transboundary Cooperation in Shared River Basins: Experiences from the Rhine, Meuse, and North Sea. *Water Policy* 2:83–97.

Hundley, N., Jr. 1966. *Dividing the Waters*. Berkeley: University of California Press.

IBWC. 2002. *Deliveries of Waters Allotted to the United States under Article 4 of the United States–Mexico Water Treaty*. Report of the United States Section of the International Boundary and Water Commission.

IBWC. 2004. Minute 311: Recommendations for Secondary Treatment in Mexico of the Sewage Emanating from the Tijuana River Area in Baja California, Mexico.

IJC. 1976. *Future Regulation of the Great Lakes*. Ottawa: IJC.

IJC. 1981. *Great Lakes Diversions and Consumptive Uses: Report to the International Joint Commission*. Ottawa: IJC.

IJC. 1985. *Great Lakes Diversions and Consumptive Uses: A Report to the Governments of the U.S. and Canada under the 1977 Reference*. Ottawa: IJC.

IJC. 2000a. *Protection of the Waters of the Great Lakes: Final Report to the Governments of Canada and the U.S.* Ottawa: IJC.

IJC. 2000b. *Transboundary Watersheds: First Report to the Governments of Canada and the United States under the Reference of November 19, 1998 with Respect to International Watershed Boards*. Ottawa: IJC.

IJC, 2001. *A Docket History of the International Joint Commission*. Draft paper. Ottawa: IJC.

Ingram, H. 1973. The Political Economy of Regional Water Institutions. *American Journal of Agricultural Economics* 55, no. 11:10–18.

Injerd, D. 1993. Lake Michigan Water Diversion: A Case Study. *Buffalo Environmental Law Journal* 1:307–315.

International Great Lakes Level Board. 1973. *Regulations of Great Lakes Water Levels.* Report to the IJC. Ottawa: IJC.

Israel State Comptroller. 1990. *Report of the Management of Water Markets in Israel* [in Hebrew]. Jerusalem: Comptroller General's Office.

Israel Water Commission. 2002. *Report on the Water Status in Israel* [in Hebrew]. Israeli Parliament, June. Jerusalem.

Izraeli, M. 2002. Personal interview with Moshe Izraeli, a special consultant to the Israel Water Commission, Tel Aviv, November 3.

Just, R., and S. Netanyahu. 1998. International Water Resource Conflicts: Experience and Potential. In *Conflict and Cooperation on Transboundary Water Resources,* ed. R. Just and S. Netanyahu, 1–27. Boston: Kluwer Academic Publishers.

Kelly, M. 2001a. Report on the Rio Conchos Basin: Preliminary Overview. Texas Center for Policy Studies. <http://www.Texascenter.org/borderwater/rioconchos.html>.

Kelly, M. 2001b. *Water Management in the Binational Texas/Mexico Rio Grande/Rio Bravo Basin.* Austin: Texas Center for Policy Studies.

Keohane, R. O. 1984. *After Hegemony: Cooperation and Discord in the World Political Economy.* Princeton, NJ: Princeton University Press.

Killgore, M. W., and D. J. Eaton. 1995. *NAFTA Handbook for Water Resource Managers and Engineers.* U.S.-Mexico Policy Studies Program and American Society of Civil Engineers. University of Texas at Austin.

Kliot, N., and D. Shmueli. 1998. Real and Ideal Institutional Framework for Managing the Common Arab-Israeli Water Resources. *Water International* 23, no. 4:216–226.

Koremenos, B., C. Lipson, and D. Snidal. 2001. The Rational Design of International Institutions. *International Organization* 55, no. 4:761–799.

Korten, F. 1996. *Building National Capacity to Develop Water Users' Associations Experience from the Philippines.* WB staff working paper 528. Washington, DC: World Bank.

Krasner, S. D. 1983. Structural Causes and Regime Consequences: Regimes as Intervening Variables. In *International Regimes,* ed. S. D. Krasner, 1–21. Ithaca, NY: Cornell University Press.

Luévano, J. 2001. Personal interview with Jesús Luévano, secretary of IBWC, Mexican section, city of Juárez, Chihuahua, July 7.

Mariño, M. A. 2001. Conjunctive Management of Surface Water and Groundwater. In *Regional Management of Water Resources,* ed. A. H. Schumann, M. C. Acreman, R. Davis, M. A. Mariño, D. Rosbjerg, and X. Jun, 165–173. Wallingford, UK: IAHS Publications.

Mekorot Water Company. 1999. *Water Supply Report for the Year 1999 and Water Supply Estimation for the Year 2000* [in Hebrew]. Tel Aviv.

Mekorot Water Company. 2002. *Annual Data for the Years 1994–2001 concerning the Water Deliveries to Jordan* [in Hebrew]. Tel Aviv.

Mumme, S. 1982. The United States–Mexico Groundwater Dispute: Domestic Influence on Foreign Policy. PhD diss., University of Arizona.

Najjar, I. 2001. Crisis Management. In *Management of Shared Groundwater Resources: The Israeli-Palestinian Case with an International Perspective*, ed. E. Feitelson and H. Marwan, 429–445. Ottawa: International Development Research Center.

Naujoks, H. 1946. The Chicago Water Diversion Controversy. *Marquette Law Review* 30, no. 3:150–176.

Northcutt, E. 1946. *Light on the Mexican Water Treaty from the Ratification Proceedings in Mexico: A Report to the Colorado River Water Users' Association.* Washington, DC: U.S. Government Printing Office.

Ostrom, E. 1990. *Governing the Commons: The Evolution of Institutions for Collective Action.* Cambridge: Cambridge University Press.

Pierson, E. 2002. Water Expert Says Mexico Holding out for Conservation Money. *Brownsville Herald,* June 27.

Razin, E., and A. Hazan. 2001. Redrawing Israel's Local Government Map: Political Decisions, Court Ruling, or Popular Determination. *Political Geography* 20:513–533.

Reisner, D. 2003. Personal interview with Daniel Reisner, a member of the Israeli negotiation team for the peace agreement, Tel Aviv, January 14.

RJ Brandes Company. 2000. *Preliminary Analysis of Mexico Rio Grande Water Deficit under the 1944 Treaty.* RJ Brandes Company, Austin.

Rosenthal, E. 2002. Personal interview with Eliyahu Rosenthal, a member of the Israeli negotiation team for the peace agreement, Jerusalem, October 28.

Schlesinger, D. 2004. Personal interview with Dave Schlesinger, director of the Operation Bajaagua Project, San Diego, July 2.

Shamir, U. 2002. Personal interview with Uri Shamir, a member of the Israeli negotiation team for the peace agreement, Haifa, November 1.

Sobelman, D. 1999. Jordan: We Will Insist on the Implementation of the Water Agreements [in Hebrew]. *Harretz,* March 16, 7a.

Susskind, L. E. 1994. *Environmental Diplomacy: Negotiating More Effective Global Agreements.* New York: Oxford University Press.

Székely, A. 2001. Telephone conversation with Alberto Székely, special adviser to the Mexican president, August 8.

Tarlock, D. 1994. Global Climate Change and the Law of the Great Lakes Diversions. In *The Lake Michigan Diversion at Chicago and Urban Drought: Past, Present, and Future Regional Impacts and Repossesses to Global Climate Change,* ed. S. A. Changnon, 91–113. Boulder, CO: University Cooperation for Atmospheric Research.

Taylor, S. 2002b. Officials Seek to Keep Water from Reaching Mexico. *Monitor*, November 5.

Taylor, S. 2002c. Ag Commissioner Disappointed with NADBank Funding Decisions. *Brownsville Herald*, December 14.

Texas Commission on Environmental Quality. 2002. Legal Status of the 1944 Utilization of Waters Treaty between the United States of America and Mexico. <http://tceq.state.tx.us/. . .a/mexico-treaty_position.html>.

Texas Comptroller. 2002. Letter from Carole Keeton Rylander, the Texas Comptroller, to Texas Senator Eduardo Lucio, October 1.

Third Report of the Canadian Section. 1907. Report of the Canadian section of the International Waterway Commission for 1906. In *Sessional Paper* 19.

Timm, C. 1941. *The International Boundary Commission: United States and Mexico.* Austin: University of Texas Press.

UNEP. 2002. *Atlas of International Freshwater Agreements.* New York: UNEP.

U.S. Congress. 1907. Diversions of Water from the Great Lakes. U.S. *Congressional Record.* 59th Cong., January 31, 2027–2044.

U.S. Senate. 1945. Committee on Foreign Relations. *Water Treaty with Mexico.* 79th Cong., 1st sess.

U.S. State Department. 1958. *Legal Aspects of the Use of Systems of International Waters.* 85th Cong., 2nd sess., doc. 118.

Waterbury, J. 2002. *The Nile Basin: National Determinants of Collective Action.* New Haven, CT: Yale University Press.

WB. 2003. Nile Basin Initiative. <http://www.worldbank.org/afr/nilebasin/faq.htm>.

Wernerfelt, B. 2004. Governance of Adjustment. Paper presented at a workshop on institution design, University of California, Berkeley, January 29.

Wilhite, D. A., and M. H. Glantz. 1985. Understanding the Drought Phenomena: The Role of Definition. *Water International* 10:111–120.

Wolf, A. 1991. From Rights to Needs: Water Allocation in International Treaties. In *Management of Shared Groundwater Resources: The Israeli-Palestinian Case with an International Perspective*, ed. E. Feitelson and H. Marwan, 133–151. Ottawa: International Development Research Center.

Wolf, A. 1997. International Water Conflict Resolution Lesson Learned from Cooperative Analysis. *International Journal of Water Resources Development* 13, no. 3:333–365.

Wolf, A. 1998. Indigenous Approaches to Water Conflict Resolution and Implications for International Waters. Paper presented at the Water and Food Security in the Middle East Conference, Nicosia, Cyprus, April 20–23.

Wolf, A. 2001. E-mail correspondence with Aaron Wolf, Oregon State University, April 16.

Wolf, A., T. Natharius, A. Jeffery, J. J. Danielson, B. S. Ward, and J. K. Pender. 1999. International River Basins of the World. *International Journal of Water Resources Development* 15, no. 4:387–427.

WWAP. 2003. Water for People, Water for Life. UN World Water Development Report. 2003. *Water of People, Water for Life*. UN: World Water Assessment Programme. <http://www.unesco.org/water/wwap>.

Young, O. R., and M. A. Levy. 1999. The Effectiveness of International Environmental Regimes. In *The Effectiveness of International Environmental Regimes*, ed. O. R. Young, 1–32. Cambridge: MIT Press.

# 9

# Environmental Governance of Global Food Flows: The Case of Labeling Strategies

Peter Oosterveer

Every day, consumers find more labeled food products in the super-markets. Some labels claim special health characteristics of the food item, and others refer to special production circumstances such as being produced in an animal-friendly or organic way. In addition, the so-called fair-trade label indicates that special attention has been paid to the interests of the food producers. Labels are increasingly used to govern sustainable food production and consumption in a situation of global food trade.

Most food labels are issued and/or certified by state agencies. Private labels, based on third-party certification, claiming attention to the social and environmental consequences of food production are relatively new, but their number has grown rapidly over the last ten years. According to some commentators, the increasing numbers of private labels confuse the customer, are not based on any real improved practice of food production, and only represent a form of "corporate greenwashing." Why are these independently certified labels emerging so strongly, and do they indeed create a new way of regulating the negative social and environmental consequences of globalizing food production and consumption?

In this chapter, I argue that neither the existing national government-based forms of regulation nor the global WTO-based types of policies are sufficient to effectively govern the environmental and social consequences of the global food trade. Private labels, for various reasons, might prove to be an alternative. Building on Castells's analysis of the global network society, I will construct an understanding of global food governance through labeling, and exemplify that with the cases of the fair-trade label for coffee and the MSC label for fish.

## Food Production and Consumption in the Global Network Society

The production and consumption of food has become a global phenomenon. Food today is increasingly traded at the international level and
the range of food products sold in supermarkets from foreign countries
is constantly growing. Worldwide, the quantity of food exported
increased fourfold between 1961 and 1999, from 190 million to 774
million tons. By 2000, more than one out of ten food products was
exported, representing a total value of US$256 billion (Millstone and
Lang 2003, 60). The process of globalization, however, not only refers
to the growth of the international trade in food and food products but
also fundamentally changes the organization of the production, trade,
and consumption of food. So, for example, the increased demand in
Western societies for fresh tropical fruits and vegetables necessitates a
reduction of the time between production and consumption as well as
strong coordination within the food-supply chain. More and more, this
coordination is in the hands of a decreasing number of large retailers,
who source their products from all over the world.

This process of globalization in food production and consumption is
part of a much larger trend of globalization. In his analysis of the
network society, Castells interpreted globalization as a process where the
space of flows is increasingly replacing the space of places, as mentioned
in earlier chapters. In the twenty-first century, social practices are less
organized on the basis of face-to-face interactions, and more on
exchanges and interactions without geographic contiguity. Modern information and communication technology creates the conditions under
which social practices in different geographic locations can be linked
more closely. If the functional unity between social practices at distant
locations gains some permanence, it becomes possible to observe the
space of flows. For example, the state can no longer be considered a
nation-state where power over a national territory and its inhabitants is
clearly located in the hands of a sovereign national government. The state
in the age of globalization is a network state, made out of a complex
web of power sharing and negotiated decision making between international, multinational, national, regional, local, political, and nongovernmental institutions and private actors (Castells 2000).

The space of flows changes not only the spatial dimension of social life but its time dimension as well. Time and space are no longer closely bound together. While, during most of human existence, biological time was the prime organizing rhythm, this changed to clock time in the industrial age and today we live in the age of timeless time (Castells 1996). In timeless time, time is becoming self-maintaining, random, and incursive, breaking down rhythmicity. New information and communication technologies are used in a relentless effort to annihilate time.

Due to this process of globalization, the organization of food production and consumption takes on different characteristics (figure 9.1). Although a direct link between production and consumption (the self-provision of food) has long since disappeared, until recently most food was produced and consumed within the same time-space frame. Food production and consumption were closely connected to concrete geographic locations and particular times or seasons. For example, in Europe fresh strawberries belonged to early summer and fresh apples to autumn. This specific time-space frame is dissolving, however, as the specific places and times of food production are increasingly becoming irrelevant for the specific places and times of food consumption. The physical distance between the place of production and the place of consumption no longer plays a role. Western food processors and retailers especially are sourcing their food products globally. The global sourcing of food has become possible because of increased communication, the decreased costs and time of transportation, and improved technologies in maintaining the quality of food products. For instance, fresh tropical fruits

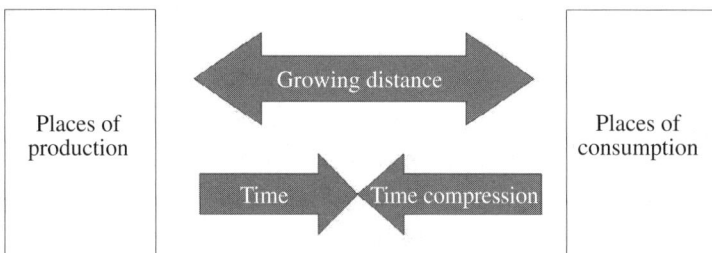

**Figure 9.1**
Globalization of food production and consumption

are available daily in supermarkets in Western Europe and the United States, and they come from all over the world; avocados come from Thailand one day and from the Ivory Coast the next, while the average consumer does not notice any difference.

The agricultural calendar is less and less of a guide for consumers' choice of food in Western countries. Food producers are trying to prolong the production season of certain food products and retailers source products from all over the world. Consumers expect to find most food products all year round on the supermarket shelves. The availability of fresh green beans might serve as an illustration of this development. While in the past these beans could be consumed in the Netherlands only during the summertime, today they can be bought all year long. During summer, green beans are produced locally, in spring and autumn they are imported from Spain, and in winter they are flown in from Africa. So the availability of fresh green beans in the supermarket is no longer an indication of the summer season. The synchronization of time between different actors involved in food production and consumption in the form of just-in-time production is becoming a prerequisite for global agri-food networks. In other words, food production and consumption is becoming disembedded from its specific physical and social practices of the past. A space of flows in connection with timeless time is being created in the global world of food. This process changes the organization of agri-food networks, and influences the lives of both producers and consumers (Beardsworth and Keil 1997).

Living in a world dominated by the space of flows and timeless time forces people to orient their life according to global processes devoid of specific place or time characteristics. Yet people themselves do still live in concrete places and perceive their space as concrete place-based entities relevant for identity formation. This place-based identity tends to get contradicted by the categories of space and time produced in global network structures. Castells observes a "contrasting logic between timelessness, structured by the space of flows, and multiple, subordinated temporalities, associated with the space of places" (1996, 468). Because the dominant trend in contemporary society is toward networked ahistorical spaces of flows, which impose their logic over segmented spaces of place, the meanings and dynamics of these spaces of place get altered.

Although the outcome of the interactions between the space of flows and the space of places (between simultaneous globalization and localization) is not predetermined, the local level cannot avoid the dynamics of the space of flows. Human action at a certain place may have pervasive influences on the daily lives of people at large distances.[1] This results in a segmentation of our society between the space of places with its time discipline and socially determined sequencing, and the space of flows with its global networks and timeless time. According to Castells, this space of flows is the driving force behind the material structuring and restructuring of this segmented society.

The interactions between the space of flows and the space of places are especially relevant for food production and consumption. Although the space of flows is becoming increasingly dominant, food still has material aspects in both its production and consumption (Fine 1998; Goodman 1999). Financial networks may be considered "footloose," but most agri-food networks cannot yet be completely disembedded from place and time (cf. figure 9.2). Despite their global scape, these networks still encompass the material production of food at specific locations. Food consumption may be less directly linked to place; nevertheless, it remains embedded in specific and localized social practices. Thus, the

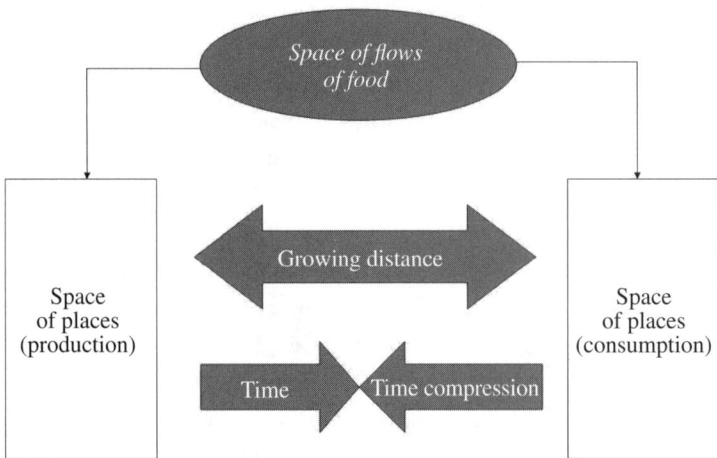

**Figure 9.2**
Flows and places in globalized food production and consumption

space of places cannot be neglected despite the process of the globalization of food production and consumption.

The tension between the global flows of food and the space of places of food production and consumption becomes visible when farmers in less developed countries are confronted with global food safety norms. Otsuki and colleagues (2001) make clear that, for example, the harmonization of standards for aflatoxins in dried fruits and nuts within the EU can have devastating consequences for farmers in Africa. The harmonized regulation of aflatoxins facilitates trade within the EU, but because African farmers cannot comply with these standards, they will loose their market share while farmers in other countries will increase theirs. The localized character of food consumption in the context of globalized food networks is exemplified in the efforts of global fast-food chains to adapt their menus to local taste. Therefore, only McDonald's customers in the Netherlands can buy a McKroket, a special fast-food version of the typically Dutch *kroket* (croquette).

Another clear case of the existence of the space of flows of food is the introduction and spread of GM food. The distances in place between planting and consuming GM crops may be large, as GM food may be globally traded in the space of flows and eaten by consumers all over the world. At the same time, the distance in time between producing and consuming GM food and their eventual harmful environmental or health effects may be too large to repair the damage. GM technology also blurs the clear distinction between—and thus hybridizes—nature and culture (or technology), and confuses the distinctive roles of science and non-science in decision making. Hence, the governance of GM food takes place in the context of basic uncertainty, due to the absence of scientific evidence about the long-term effect of the use of GMOs, the difficulties in balancing economic against environmental and safety arguments, and the potential future positive contributions for the environment and the economy of this technology. In this context, the governance of GM food is confronted with the challenge of how to combine the space of flows that would require global product-based standards for the safety of GM food products, and the space of places where producers and consumers are concerned about the potential negative impacts.

The different dynamics within the space of places in relation to those in the space of flows have to be taken into account when the governance of the environmental and social consequences of food production and consumption is concerned. To organize food governance in the network society, we need to analyze in detail how global flows of food interact with place-based food production and consumption.

### Governance in the Network Society

The rise of the network society has far-reaching consequences for governance arrangements that traditionally were dominated by nation-states. Economic networks are transcending these traditional political structures more frequently and in more encompassing ways than before. In order to countervail the erosion of nation-state powers, states are transferring selected powers to supranational agencies and institutions, such as the EU and the WTO. Arrangements within these new supranational regimes are directly linked to the space of flows of the network society. Governance in the space of flows needs to be global and abstract, devoid of specific characteristics of place and time in order to facilitate global trade ("free trade") and remove national barriers to international commerce.

Since 1995, when agriculture was included in the GATT/WTO, the governance of global food trade has been coordinated within the WTO. In general, WTO regulations are based on economic considerations, but in the case of food, safety issues are included as well. Global food safety regulations are built on the example of existing national regulations and standards. These national food safety standards are negotiated within the Codex Alimentarius Commission, and translated and reworked into global food safety standards based on generally accepted scientific evidence.[2] This food safety regulation is a form of governance in the space of flows because it is based on abstract principles—that is, not related to specific considerations of place and time. The global food safety standards agreements define criteria for the presence of specific substances in food products, but they do not define criteria for food production methods. Governing global food trade is thus acceptable for the WTO only if it covers characteristics of the product itself (product related). International food trade governance on the basis of local production circumstances is not allowed when these circumstances do not lead to changes in the products themselves. Countries are therefore not allowed to distinguish between food produced *with* special care for social and environmental consequences and food produced *without* those concerns. Using the terminology applied within the WTO, this means that governing international trade on the basis of nonproduct-related production and process methods is not allowed.[3] Members of the WTO elaborated the TBT and the SPS Agreements to formalize these principles regarding food.

The TBT Agreement was already adopted in 1979 within GATT (the WTO's predecessor) to ensure that product standards and technical regulations do not create unnecessary barriers to trade. The TBT Agreement covers agricultural and industrial products, and contains rules with regard to technical regulations. Countries are allowed to develop their own standards if they inform other countries about these standards when considerable trade effects are expected or when the standards are new. The TBT Agreement particularly encourages the use of internationally accepted standards and regulations, like those of the ISO. If countries use different standards, the agreement stimulates the application of two basic principles. The principle of equivalence encourages countries to accept each other's standards when these standards may seem different but are the same in content: substantially equivalent. The second principle is based on mutual recognition, stimulating countries to accept the results of each other's assessment procedures and to avoid double testing.

The SPS Agreement, developed as part of the Agreement of Agriculture within the WTO in 1995, distinguishes between the justified use of sanitary and phytosanitary measures and the unjustified use for protectionism. The SPS Agreement aims to protect animal and plant life as well as human health, and allows countries to impose standards and conditions for the importation of food. These standards and conditions should be harmonized as far as possible using the guidelines and recommendations of the following standard-setting organizations: the FAO/WHO Codex Alimentarius Commission, the OIE, and the IPPC. Countries are entitled to impose stricter standards under the conditions that they are nondiscriminatory and supported by scientific evidence. Several aspects of the SPS Agreement are not fully clear, but so far the agreement has been interpreted rather restrictively to facilitate global free trade as much as possible (Charnovitz 2002a).[4]

While the WTO regulations are aimed at facilitating global food trade, NGOs and other critics express concerns about the social and environmental consequences of trade liberalization, such as the declining world fish stocks, the poverty of coffee producers in developing countries, and the results of introducing GMOs in agriculture. According to several scientists and environmentalists, these consequences can only be diminished by reducing the scale of food production and consumption (e.g., Princen 1997; O'Hara and Stagl 2001; Halweil 2002). They conclude that the necessary checks and balances for the sustainable use of resources can be organized only via some form of "de-globalization" through the creation of local and regional food supply chains. Princen is most outspoken in concluding that "market expansion and factor mobility increase distance on many dimensions rendering ecologically informed and ethically responsible decisions impossible" (1997, 251). He rejects the globalization of food production and consumption because it "inherently destroys the basis for sustainable food production (and) sustainable production requires effective feedback from all decisions in a production chain. When distance approaches zero in, say, a household or a self-sufficient community, that feedback is likely to exist. But as distance increases, feedback diminishes and the need for accountability and governance increases, possibly exponentially" (250).

De-globalizing food production and consumption to solve the tension between the globalization of food chains and its social and environmental consequences has three important weaknesses, however. The first weakness relates to feasibility. The larger part of today's food production and consumption is organized globally and the tendency is more toward increasing rather than decreasing globalization in agri-food chains. Therefore, a comprehensive relocalization of global agri-food chains does not seem feasible in the short term. Second, de-globalization is problematic in that it denies a large group of farmers in developing countries the opportunity to produce for Western markets in an effort to raise their income. Finally, and more fundamentally, it is not evident that small-scale production is necessarily socially and environmentally superior to global food production in all respects. Face-to-face inter-action between producers and consumers is not the only possible way to organize the necessary feedback mechanisms for sustainable food pro-duction.[5] When de-globalization is questioned as the only feasible answer to the negative localized social and environmental consequences of the globalized food trade, a search for new forms of governance becomes pressing. What form of governance can deal with the tensions between the global and local levels in such a way that it fits into and corresponds with the dynamics of the network society? Until now, several attempts have been made to govern the international food trade while taking spe-cific localized social and environmental consequences into account.

### Governance in the Space of Flows versus Regulation in the Space of Places

For governance arrangements to be applicable at the global level while simultaneously reducing the social and environmental consequences at the local level, they need to combine dynamics in the space of flows with dynamics in the space of places. Recent attempts to develop this kind of governance arrangements can in general be regrouped in two categories.

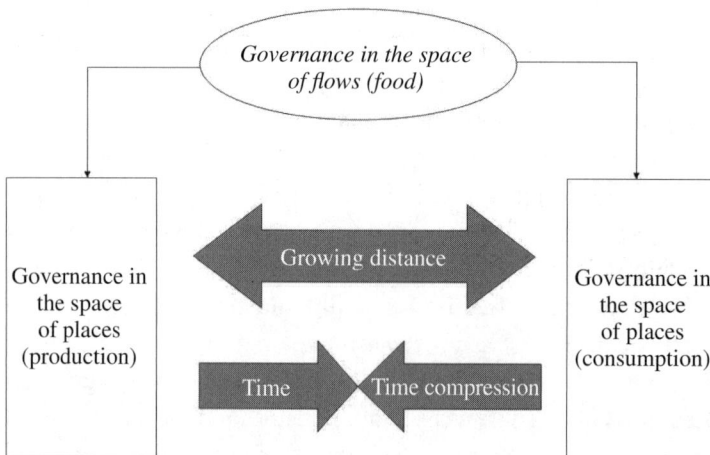

**Figure 9.3**
Governance and globalized food production and consumption

The first category consists of attempts to strengthen global governance, building primarily on the powers and the example of national states. The second category includes ways to engage nonstate actors in governance arrangements. Both categories will be discussed briefly.

Enhanced global governance may take different forms, such as an enlarged WTO or a strengthened and reformed UN structure. A specific form of strengthened global governance put forward to solve the tension between global arrangements and local consequences is the combination of trade politics at the global level with global environmental and social politics (Shaw 2000). This would result in building institutions for global governance to replace sovereign national states in some respects, like the IWC (see below). This approach starts with the recognition that some environmental problems go beyond the capacities of national states and thus need effective supranational institutions. These institutions should comprise a persistent and connected set of rules and practices prescribing behavioral roles, constraining activities, and shaping expectations (Haas et al. 1993). Global governance in such forms combine governance in the space of places with governance in the space of flows under the responsibility of a global nation-state-like structure. These solutions are attractive as they build on the familiar example of the nation-state. But they are not completely satisfactory because a global governance system currently lacks clear ways to establish democratic legitimacy, and risks leading to large-scale and inflexible bureaucracies. Other actors than nation-state-like structures in international politics may focus on single issues, and would thus be much more flexible, faster, efficient, and powerful than a global governance system (Kleinwächter 2003).

Other attempts to build more responsive global governance arrangements start with the observation that under the current conditions of globalization, nation-states are embedded in broader frameworks of governance and politics. These broader frameworks consist of multiple layers, from the local to the global, and multiple actors, from private firms to nongovernmental interest groups (Mol 2001). A more flexible and innovative governance arrangement would build on nonstate actors, such as private firms and NGOs, in the regulation of food production and consumption. Examples are certification programs such as the HACCP and the ISO. Such nonstate initiatives involve new forms of governance, which are more flexible and better integrated in networks that stretch from the global to the local. Moreover, they can cover specific social and environmental concerns in the space of places by establishing direct relationships between producers and consumers. In order to be able to reach beyond the level of isolated improvements, however, such governance arrangements in the space of places need to be supplemented by consistent and systematic governance in the space of flows. The most promising solution therefore seems to combine governance in the space of flows with governance in the space of places involving both state and nonstate actors. The main challenge is not to choose between the global or the local as the single most important level of governance, or between state or nonstate actors, but instead to identify ways in which both levels and different social actors can be combined. Globalized food production and consumption cannot be governed by global government-like institutions such as the WTO alone because they run the risk of developing governance in the space of flows without sufficient regard for the specific consequences in the space of places. Private governance arrangements could offer an alternative, provided they are backed up by the effective and consistent governance of agri-food chains in the space of flows. The answer should be found in a combination of governance in the space of flows with governance in the places of production as well as consumption. Two interesting efforts to create this hybrid governance regime, fair-trade coffee and the MSC, will be discussed in the next sections.

### Fair-trade Coffee, Including the Environmental and Social Consequences of Global Trade

Around 125 million people in over fifty developing countries grow coffee, mainly in peasant households on farms of less than ten hectares. Coffee has been traded internationally for centuries and is part of global chains, linking producers in countries like Brazil, Colombia, and (recently) Vietnam with consumers in Europe, the United States, and Japan.

Until the 1980s, national states played a vital role in promoting the production of coffee through credit-based input schemes, extension services, national systems of quality control and pan-territorial pricing. International trade was dominated by a small number of large trading companies based in the United States and Europe. Simple quality conventions combining price with certain crude physical crop properties formed the major mechanism linking suppliers with these international traders. With the involvement of producer-country's governments, the global regulation of the international coffee trade was formally established through the ICA (1962–1989).

The character of this global arrangement started to change by 1990, when the producer cartel had collapsed and government support to coffee producers in developing countries was considerably reduced due to the implementation of structural adjustment programs. Until now, no successful innovative forms of government-based global coffee trade regulation, replacing the ICA, have been identified and implemented, despite several attempts. The institutional framework of the international coffee market is moving away from a formal and relatively stable system in which the producers participate toward a system that is more informal, inherently unstable, and buyer dominated (Ponte 2001). International coffee trade has changed into a complex and dynamic global flow, in which private contracts between producers, traders, roasters, and retailers dominate, displaying a great diversity of producer-trader networks, and in combination with a growing differentiation of consumer tastes, making the simple matrix linking crop quality and price disappear. Complex standards are proliferating because the degree of differentiation in coffee blends and prices has grown significantly over the last few years.[6] Contemporary quality standards for coffee are more voluntary and less mandatory; they pay more attention to production and processing methods and less to objectively verifiable product attributes (Ponte 2002).

The disappearance of global governance arrangements as well as the simple quality-price matrix reinforced the already existing asymmetrical distribution of power in the coffee chain. Farmers in the producing countries saw their position weaken while three global residues of power (importers, roasters, and retailers) strengthened their position (Fitter and Kaplinsky 2001). The coffee price for farmers showed a declining trend, becoming quite dramatic over the last ten years and resulting in the lowest world market coffee price in real terms for one hundred years. In the early 1990s, coffee-producing countries earned around US$10–12 billion, while the value of coffee sold by retailers was about US$30 billion. In 2002, the value of retail sales exceeded US$70 billion, but coffee-producing countries only received US$5.5 billion (Osorio 2002).

In the past, coffee farming had little environmental impact, but recent efforts to increase productivity have led to an increase in pollution and a loss of biodiversity. Latin America especially has witnessed a shift from traditional shade-grown production to "sun" coffee or "monoculture shade" coffee (UNCTAD and IISD 2003). This intensification of coffee production resulted in the increased use of pesticides, fungicides, and fertilizers, and a reduction of biodiversity, especially with regard to the number of different bird species. Biodiversity is a sensitive issue because coffee is often grown in areas of high biodiversity importance and high vulnerability (UNCTAD and IISD 2003). The introduction of monoculture coffee systems also meant aggravating soil erosion and deforestation.

Thus, the development of the international coffee trade into a complex and dynamic global flow had several negative social and environmental consequences locally while simultaneously making governance at the places of production more difficult. Forced by limited financial resources and pressure from the IMF to refrain from interference with trade, national states in developing countries were increasingly unable to play an active role in the organization and regulation of the international coffee trade. These negative consequences of the globalizing coffee chain form the driving forces behind the creation of fair-trade labeled coffee. The first fair-trade coffee was produced in Guatemala and exported to the Netherlands in 1973, and thirty years later, nearly 200 coffee cooperatives representing 675,000 farmers, more than 70 traders, and around 350 coffee companies are involved. In 2000, 64,100 tons of fair-trade coffee (around 1 percent of the global coffee production) was sold with a retail value of US$393 million, mainly in Europe. North American fair-trade coffee sales amounted to only 10,400 tons in 2000, for a retail value of US$64.4 million, but this market is growing rapidly (Ponte 2002).

The standards for fair-trade coffee are defined by the FLO (2003) international, and they include social, economic, and environmental criteria. The fair-trade coffee label strives at the establishment of a system of international coffee trade based on fair conditions for farmers and workers in disadvantaged parts of the third world. Organized farmers in developing countries are guaranteed a minimum price for their coffee, independent of the world market price, and direct and long-term relationships are built between the producer organization and the importer, providing a basis for financial, technical, and organizational support.[7] Roasters and retailers buying coffee from small farmers' organizations, which are registered with FLO, also have to fulfill specific requirements before this coffee can be labeled as fair trade and sold in conventional shops or through alternative trade channels. The consumer price for fair-trade coffee is higher in comparison with conventional coffee to cover the additional social and environmental costs (see <http://www.maxhavelaar.nl>). Although initially the fair-trade label was based on social and economic criteria alone, more recently environmental considerations have been included as well. A substantial part of fair-trade coffee (36 percent of the total in 2000) is simultaneously organically labeled and the fair-trade standards now include environmental criteria, like integrated crop management and specific guarantees for shade-grown production (Blowfield 1999; Abbott et al. 1999).[8]

The fair-trade label is voluntary, and was developed independently of national and international government regulations. Although the European Commission expressed its sympathy for these initiatives, it can only support fair trade through financing promotion campaigns because the EUs obligations within the WTO do not allow other kinds of assistance. Therefore, fair trade has remained a private labeling initiative operating within the major global distribution circuits and has not established a separate supply channel as was attempted before—for example, in the Netherlands by selling solidarity coffee through the *Wereldwinkels* (solidarity shops). So on the one hand, fair-trade coffee remains part of the global flow of coffee including existing trade arrangements, while on the other hand, it builds new social relationships between the coffee producers and consumers beyond the economic relationship of buyer and seller. The strategy underlying these new relationships is to give coffee a specific meaning for the consumers (around ecology, solidarity, fairness, etc.) (Renard 1999).

Regarding consumption, fair-trade coffee builds on domestic and civic norms, values, and mentalities around global responsibility. The label was developed following consumer concerns around the negative effects of the coffee trade for farmers' incomes in developing countries and the harmful consequences of modern coffee production techniques for the environment. Consumers, buying fair-trade coffee, are provided with "personal relationships with farmers (through images, publicity, educational materials), trust and security in socially-responsible value claims and the elusive feel good factor" (Raynolds 2002, 415). The specific characteristics of this "personal relationship" are emphasized because NGOs, seen as acting in the interests of the farmers in developing countries, are controlling the fair-trade label, and not private companies. In this way, otherwise-similar products in impersonal markets are differentiated, encouraging consumers to take these differences into account in their purchasing decisions.[9]

Social practices regarding coffee production are also changing because market transactions, although still guided by commercial norms and practices, are now clearly influenced by more progressive arrangements as well. On the one hand, quality standards are inflexibly and rigorously monitored, and delivery schedules and purchasing contracts are based on existing industrial norms. But on the other hand, fair-trade prices are based on the notion of a fair return, covering the production costs in addition to a social premium for development purposes. Social and cultural objectives are thus included in global trade together with the existing economic objectives. The FLO requirement that coffee producers are collectively organized enforces traditional civic norms, values, and conventions. In addition, coffee producers' organizations are provided with technical expertise and market information via the fair-trade networks, supporting these groups in strengthening their position in conventional markets too. A stronger position in the conventional coffee market is particularly important because although producer groups may be fair-trade certified, this does not guarantee coffee sales under fair-trade conditions since consumer demand remains insufficient. For example, in

Central America on average, only 15 to 20 percent of the coffee production from registered cooperatives is sold under fair-trade conditions and the remaining 80 to 85 percent still has to be sold under conventional trading conditions (Roozen and van der Hoff 2001).[10]

In brief, the case of fair-trade coffee shows the reality of a governance arrangement that establishes meaningful links between the places of production and consumption without necessarily dissolving global flows. Labeling coffee on the basis of social and environmental criteria by an NGO is a way to organize particular coffee production practices and link this to the coffee consumer without disregarding the governance in the space of flows. This approach offers an interesting innovative arrangement that combines contributions from civil actors, private firms, and official and multilateral institutions in bringing economic, social, and environmental considerations into the regulation of global trade. Another positive aspect of this approach is the active involvement of producers (and to a lesser extent, consumers) in translating general criteria for sustainable management to a specific local context. A weakness concerns the costs involved, which may create a problem for food producers in developing countries. Calling in private agencies for the certification process requires substantial funds, and even when NGOs take this responsibility, the process demands a large investment of time.

The most important weak point of the fair-trade label, however, is its limited direct effect. Today, fair-trade coffee only accounts for 1 percent of the global coffee trade. Therefore, to increase the impact of global "fair coffee" trade, future governance options are being discussed by several social, political, and economic actors. These different considerations and governance options can be summarized under three viewpoints, using the theoretical framework presented above.

First, fair-trade coffee is considered just an additional niche market in a highly differentiating consumer market. This would not result in a growth of governance in the space of places but would instead limit governance arrangements to the conventional coffee network itself, to governance in the space of flows, as is shown in figure 9.4, in which the boldness of the arrow indicates the intensity of the relationship. Within this approach, the involvement of global governance remains quite

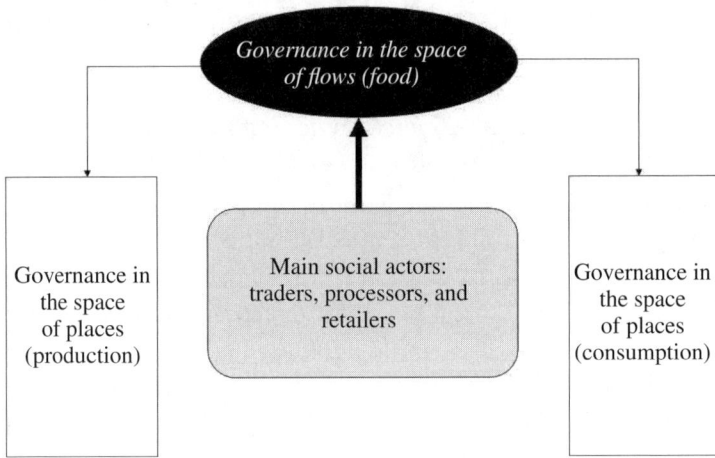

**Figure 9.4**
Governance of coffee trade organized through the market

limited, while regulation with regard to social and environmental interests remains restricted to private market actors.

The second viewpoint perceives fair-trade coffee as fundamentally different from other niche markets because it is based on the values of solidarity, ecology, and fairness linking southern producers with northern consumers—contrary to conventional relationships dominated by market exchanges. According to this view, fair-trade coffee partly escapes the market logic, but continues to function within the conventional coffee networks to a certain extent. It tries to find difficult compromises between ethical principles and the market (Renard 1999; Whatmore and Thorne 1997; Raynolds 2002). This view is illustrated in figure 9.5, where the environmental and social interests at the place-bound spaces of consumption and production are dominating the governance arrangements, while governance in the space of flows remains subordinated to these interests. This standpoint has the advantage of creating an alternative network between the coffee producers and consumers, but the disadvantage of remaining limited to a minuscule part of the global coffee market. The central actors in this view on the future governance of fair-trade coffee remain the fair-trade NGOs.

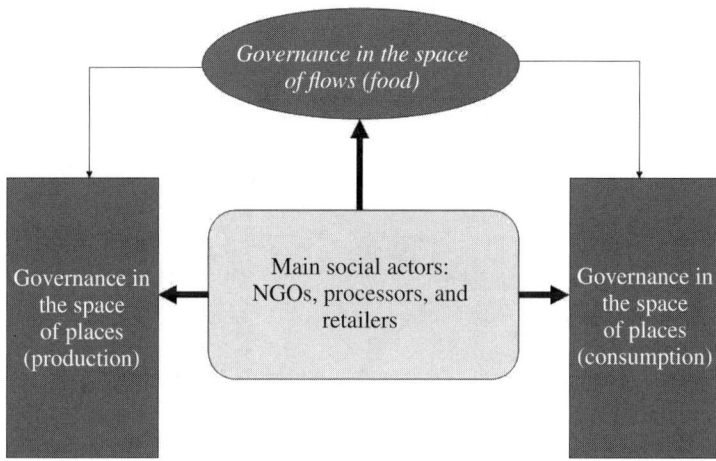

**Figure 9.5**
Governance of global coffee trade organized mainly through civil society actors

The third option sees fair trade as a model for the reorganization of the international coffee market as a whole—an objective that can be achieved in two different ways. Including fair-trade principles in the WTO regulations to achieve lasting and global social and environmental improvements is the first alternative. Only a global commodity institution managing the market can really solve the social and environmental problems (Oxfam 2002b).[11] Whether such a global government-like agreement would dispose of the necessary flexibility to maintain the global flow of coffee while facilitating social and environmental governance at the local level remains a disputed question. A second alternative, which is shown in figure 9.6, brings environmental and social interests into the governance of the space of flows through the direct involvement of private actors in collaboration with state actors. In this way, existing economic networks are combined with civil society and governmental networks to create complex linkages between products and prices, on the one hand, and information, communication, and participation, on the other. These combined efforts of national governments, multilateral institutions such as the WTO and the UNCTAD, private firms, and NGOs would initiate a dynamic process of governance.

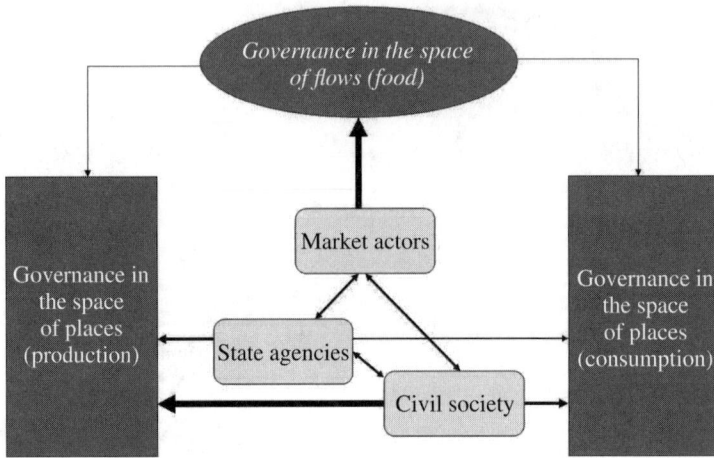

**Figure 9.6**
Governance of global coffee trade combining civil society, state, and market actors

Through this arrangement, consumers are provided in integrated ways with reliable information about the production circumstances through-out the coffee network. Concretely, this would require the labeling of all coffee that is traded globally to provide consumers with tools to influ-ence the way their coffee is produced. In combination with government regulation in the space of places, both of production and consumption, this governance approach could encompass a much larger part of the global coffee trade.

According to some observers, this way of combining governance in the space of flows with governance in the space of places offers the most promising possibility to integrate environmental and social interests more fully in the global coffee trade. This would happen not through formal laws and certain limited private activities but through collabora-tion between the different actors concerned.

### The MSC: Global Environmental Regulation

Fish has become, in relative terms, the food product that is most traded globally. Today, 40 percent of the world's fish production—worth over

US$52 billion—enters international trade (Dommen 1999). In 1993, developing countries provided some 50 percent of this international trade, earning US$11 billion (Stone 2002).[12] Parallel to a substantial growth in the global marine fish production from 20 million tons in 1950 to over 120 million tons in 1997, there is a general consensus that fish stocks are declining because of overfishing and that improved fisheries' management to conserve marine biodiversity is essential.[13] As fish trade is globalized, and fish stocks and fishing boats move easily across national borders, sustainable fisheries' management needs to be global too.[14] Global fish governance needs to combine these environmental considerations with social and economic interests, because fish is the primary source of proteins for 950 million people and offers employment to 400 million people (Garcia and Willmann 1999).

The environmental problems caused by overfishing can be divided between the depletion of fish stocks, the reduction of biodiversity, and the destruction of habitats. Some 70 percent of the world's commercial fisheries are now considered fully or overexploited and only 4 percent are underexploited. Such overfishing reduces the existing fish stocks, which will inevitably result in lower catches. The levels of bycatch (non-target fish catch) have also skyrocketed (to some twenty-nine million tons worldwide), contributing to a loss of biodiversity as well. Pollution through processing activities at sea, and habitat degradation through trawling and the use of prohibited fishing methods (e.g., dynamite) add to the effects of overfishing, to be aggravated by activities such as public and industrial waste discharge, tourism, and offshore oil and gas exploitation. The destruction of coastal zones, wetlands, and mangrove areas by the growing aquacultural activities is impairing the role of these areas as natural spawning grounds and nurseries for the replenishment of marine stocks (Garcia et al. 1999).

The lower catches and revenues caused by overfishing particularly weaken the position of the ten million small-scale fisheries, which fish for subsistence as well as local markets in developing countries. As the competition from often foreign-based commercial fishing vessels is increasing, the number of conflicts between these small-scale (artisanal) fisheries and industrial fishing companies is growing. These large fishing companies seem to bear little responsibility for the sustainability of local fish stocks because they move easily from one fishing area to another. Their behavior may result in the destruction of the artisanal fisheries and thus undermine the food security of coastal populations.

These combined trends result in increasing pressure on the available resources and a demand for regulatory arrangements to safeguard the fishing resources for the future. Governing fisheries, however, is complicated because fish is an open-access resource. "Fishing grounds are unrestricted 'commons' areas, and the ownership of a fish is not allocated until the moment of capture" (Stone 2002, 290). This particular characteristic of fisheries is the reason why their governance has remained limited for a long time. Until the establishment of the two-hundred-mile exclusive economic zones in 1977, oceans formed a common resource where everyone had equal fishing rights. Yet even after the creation of these exclusive economic zones, the problems of overfishing and conflicts over access to certain fish stocks remained. Multilateral governance arrangements seem indispensable. FAO-sponsored international commissions were created, charged with managing specific species (for example, the IWC [International Whaling Commission]) or a specific area (Peterson 1993). Global fish governance started with the UN Convention on the Law of the Sea (1982), but until today this convention is implemented to a limited extent only. The 1992 UNCED underlined the need to create effective fisheries' and coastal areas' management regimes, and the voluntary FAO Code of Conduct for Responsible Fisheries (1995) and the UN Fish Stocks Agreement (1995) formulated new guidelines to protect existing fish stocks.[15] Despite these initiatives, though, their effects remain modest. Some governments do not seem very committed, while others lack the capacity to put these guidelines into practice. In addition, the participation from NGOs and other stakeholders is insufficient (Peterson 1993). Fisheries' issues have remained relatively low on governments' agendas and have attracted little public attention beyond from those directly involved. Fish has therefore become a globally traded food flow without a systematic global governance arrangement. Nevertheless, because this global flow is unsustainable, as is nearly unanimously agreed on, a new way of global governance of fish production and trade is needed.

Some analysts consider the reduction of fishery subsidies as the best solution to the problems of overfishing. During the Johannesburg 2002 UNCED, fishery subsidies and nontariff barriers were identified as the main factors leading to the depletion of fish stocks. "Subsidies to fishing encourage inefficient producers to remain in the market and this results in depletion of fisheries" (Gowdy and Walton 2003, 7). Equally, the WTO pleaded for the reduction of fisheries' subsidies to spread economic and environmental benefits among its members during its 2001 meeting in Doha.[16] According to this seemingly dominant discourse, the sustainability of fisheries would increase if the subsidies by national governments were ended and the access to fishing resources were arranged through private instead of public ownership. Using the theoretical model for global governance presented in the beginning of this chapter, this view would leave governing fishing practices and the global fish trade to the market and the market actors involved (see figure 9.7).

Several governments, in particular the Japanese, oppose this thesis by claiming that inadequate fisheries management is a more important factor leading to overfishing than subsidies. In addition, not all subsidies have similar consequences. Some subsidies are beneficial for both fish

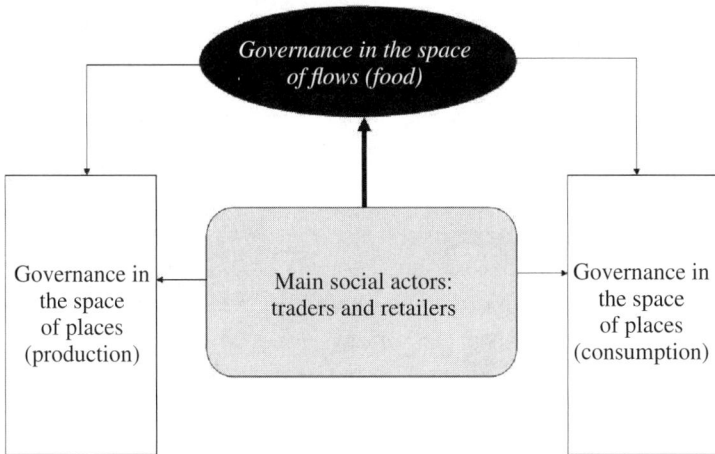

**Figure 9.7**
Governance of fish production and consumption limited to the global market

stocks and the livelihoods of fishing communities, and should thus be distinguished from trade-distorting subsidies (Dommen 1999). Reducing the fishery subsidies in the absence of a consistent global and local governance arrangement will only strengthen the uncontrolled global fluid character of the international fish trade, and will not reduce the negative localized social and environmental consequences.

The recent establishment of the MSC is an interesting new initiative to improve fisheries management by more directly linking fish production with the fish trade. In 1997, the multinational company Unilever and the environmental NGO WWF took the initiative to establish the MSC, based on the assumption that all actors involved in catching fish in a specific area have a common interest in guaranteeing the future of this fishery by developing a common and coherent sustainable management plan. The WWF viewed improving the sustainability of fisheries with the use of a specific fish label as an interesting opportunity for sustainable development, which would also reinforce other already existing certification schemes.[17] Unilever realized that the future of its commercial fishing activities would be jeopardized if the threat from overfishing was not reversed. Initiated by these two global, private actors, the MSC has since 1999 evolved into an independent, global nonprofit organization responsible for the labeling of sustainable fisheries using its own MSC label.[18] The objective of the MSC is to bring environmental, commercial, and social interests together in sustainable fisheries. Although the organization acknowledges that initially a transition to a more responsible and sustainable fisheries' exploitation will lead to reduced catches, ultimately a sustainable management plan will result in a growth of the fish stocks and thus better yields. The MSC initiative tries to achieve this transition by harnessing "consumer purchasing power to generate change and promote environmentally responsible stewardship of the world's most important renewable food source" (⟨http://www.msc.org⟩). In order to reward environmentally responsible fishery management and fishing practices, a product label is developed on the basis of general standards for sustainable fisheries. Until May 2003, seven fisheries have received the MSC label—three in the United Kingdom, and the other four in the United States, New Zealand, Australia, and Scotland. Seven others—located in the United States (two), Mexico, Chile, Canada, Norway, and the United Kingdom (on islands located in the southern Atlantic)—are currently undergoing the certification process. Finally, another group of thirty fisheries remains in different phases of the certification procedure.

Certifying a specific fish stock may be complicated because of the many different interpretations of sustainable fisheries that have to be combined, as is clearly shown in the example of the New Zealand Hoki (see box 9.1).

MSC-labeled fisheries have to apply certain management arrangements on the basis of three general MSC principles:

• A fishery must conduct itself in a manner that does not lead to over-fishing or the depletion of the exploited fish population

**Box 9.1**
An example of the complications involved in MSC labeling: the Hoki case

The New Zealand Hoki is labeled by the MSC as a sustainable fishery, and Unilever is selling the product as fish fingers (Iglo). From 2005 onward, Unilever intends to sell only MSC-labeled fish, but this intention can only be implemented if enough certified fish are available (Deere 1999). As the New Zealand Hoki represents a major fish stock, its labeling is important. Granting the MSC label to the Hoki fishery has been heavily criticized by the New Zealand Royal Forest and Bird Protection Society. The society's main objection concerns the killing of seals and albatross by the Hoki fishery. Interestingly enough, although invited to do so, this NGO refused to participate in the certification process itself and now criticizes the result. The MSC replied to this criticism that the labeling was conditional and that several corrective actions have to be taken by the fishery to retain its certification. In addition, the MSC claims that without the certification process, many of the issues brought up by the New Zealand Royal Forest and Bird Protection Society would still be unresolved. The MSC thus argues that the label is not developed to confirm that a fishery is already sustainably managed but that it is engaged in taking a series of corrective actions toward sustainability that otherwise would not have been taken (Seaweb 2001).[1]

*Note:* 1. See also Greenpeace Germany's (2000) statement about the MSC that no fisheries should be certified that also catch endangered species, such as is the case with the New Zealand Hoki. Greenpeace states that the MSC criteria are much too weak to really contribute to sustainable fisheries.

• A fishing operation should allow for the maintenance of the structure, productivity, function, and diversity of the ecosystem on which the fishery is dependent

• A fishery is subject to an effective management system that respects local, national, and international laws and standards, and incorporates institutional and operational frameworks that require the use of the resource to be responsible and sustainable

Guided by a certifying agent and accredited by the MSC, these general principles are translated into a concrete and detailed management plan for a specific fishery, and in this plan all actors concerned agree on the amount, way, and timing of catching fish as well as the implementation of certain accompanying measures to protect the fish stock. All stakeholders have to participate in the process to achieve trust in the label. So, for example, certifying agents have agreed to actively contact environmental NGOs and request their participation in the process. The MSC considers support from these NGOs vital "if our program is to offer industry the credibility they expect" (2002, 1).[19] Governments do not have a special position in the certification process, and are considered a participant at the same level as the fisheries and the retailers.

The MSC label is an environmental one, and does not include additional social or economic criteria because the organization considers that labeling in developing countries would become too complicated. The inclusion of criteria that demand higher social and economic performances than required by the national legislation would put these sustainable fisheries in an even more unfavorable economic position vis-à-vis conventional fisheries. Even without such criteria, MSC labeling is already very complicated in developing countries. The available information about the fish stocks and fishing practices in these countries is often insufficient to develop a sustainable management plan. Moreover, the lack of local certification capacity obliges these countries to hire expensive foreign certifying agencies. As such, although the MSC label could be an incentive to implement environmental improvements for developing countries too, these countries can fulfill the conditions only with great difficulty.[20]

The MSC label enables consumers to buy fish caught with care for the environment, which is guaranteed by an independent private organization. The MSC is preparing public information campaigns to inform consumers about the environmental impact of labeled fish products, and to encourage retailers to sell fish products from sustainably managed and MSC-labeled fisheries. Since the market for MSC-labeled fish remains largely restricted to exclusive restaurants and shops, and has not yet entered the mass markets for fish, communication to the general public remains rather limited. Entering mass markets for fish consumption and using mass media would require the availability of larger quantities of certified fish, and thus the certification of more fisheries.

To conclude, the MSC label can be considered an interesting attempt to combine local environmental protection with the global fish trade. This private initiative brings together different social actors in an effort to reduce the negative environmental consequences of uncontrolled globalized fish production and consumption. The MSC label offers an alternative to the dominant discourse of global institutions like the WTO by developing a form of governance that actively engages all actors concerned in the production of fish. Interestingly, the formal role of national states and governmental institutions remains limited in the MSC-labeling procedure, as they are regarded as one among many other stakeholders in the process. This choice underlines the private character of the MSC label, despite the legal obligations national states have to protect fish stocks within their exclusive economic zones and cooperate with other governments in the management of shared fish stocks on the high seas (Deere 1999). In reality, though, governments often need to provide the necessary scientific data as the basis for management plans and in some cases even finance the MSC certification process itself. The MSC label can be viewed as an interesting attempt to develop environmental governance within the local space of production (the fishery) in combination with governance in the global space of fish flows. The MSC label has an explicit focus on reducing the environmental risks involved in catching fish without ignoring the importance of providing food for a global food market. The producers are actively involved in translating the general criteria of the label to practices fitting in a particular local context, thereby reinforcing the identity of a particular place. Currently, consumer involvement in the MSC label remains limited because the production of sustainable fish needs to grow first before it is worth approaching consumers on a broader scale. Figure 9.8 shows these particular characteristics of the MSC label.

Some commentators criticize the MSC label for its lack of attention to social concerns and its limited effectiveness in improving the environmental conditions of fisheries in general. If a label for sustainable fisheries could combine social considerations with the existing environmental ones, this might result in more active support from consumers. This alternative should, in addition, attempt to include the more sustainable fisheries as well as the less sustainable, though improving, ones. Building on the example of the MSC label, a more inclusive governance arrangement could be developed. Such a fair-trade fish label, as suggested by the Pacific Coast Federation of Fishermen's Associations (Grader et al. 2003), would incorporate social and economic criteria next to the existing environmental ones. This inclusion of the fair-trade coffee label experiences into the MSC label is depicted in figure 9.9. Although this model for governing the global fish trade follows a similar approach to the fair-trade coffee label, it needs to pay comparatively more attention to governance in the place of production because of the diversity in fishing circumstances and practices, and the obligation to include all actors concerned.

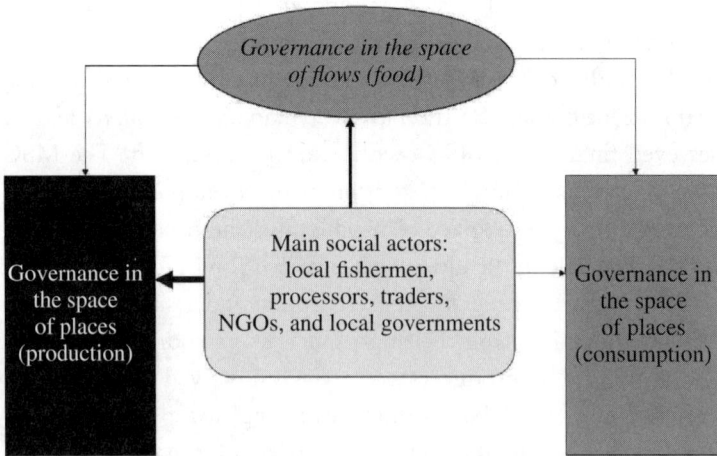

**Figure 9.8**
Governance of global fish production and consumption using the MSC label

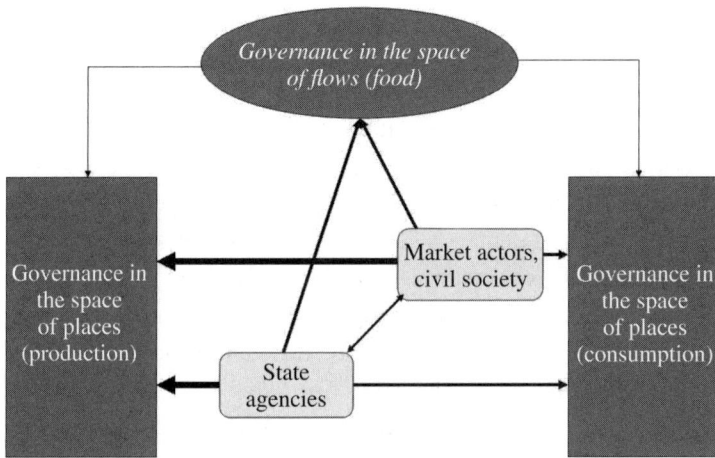

**Figure 9.9**
Governance of globalized food production and consumption

## Conclusion

The intention of this chapter was to answer the question, To what extent and in what specific ways can food labels represent new ways of governing the negative social and environmental consequences of the globalizing food production and consumption? Building on Castells's analysis of globalization in general, and on the tension he observes between the characteristics of global flows, on the one hand, and localized identities of places, on the other, a conceptual model for the governance of food was developed. With the help of this theoretical model, the governance arrangements of fair-trade labeled coffee and MSC-labeled fish were analyzed. These examples have shown that food labels can include care for the social and environmental effects of global food chains in their arrangement, in particular because they establish a new and comprehensive form of communication between the food producer and the food consumer.[21] As such, food labels provide an alternative to the dominant trend of governing global food production and consumption through market mechanisms only. Food labels deal with the place-bounded social and environmental effects of the global flows of food without entering into a form of de-globalization. They create an innovative arrangement that fits into global modernity.[22]

The standard nation-state-based regulation of food is giving way to new governance arrangements, blurring conventional distinctions between state and nonstate, and between local, national, and international levels of governance. Food labels represent one example of a hybrid governance arrangement for food, involving nonstate actors such as NGOs and private companies, and combining local and global levels in an intricate way. Food demands such a particular form of governance because of its organic character, which is particularly visible in its production and consumption stages. Labeling as a hybrid governance arrangement facilitates the combination of different concerns and different levels of governance. At the same time, this instrument complicates governance because responsibilities are not always clearly divided, nor is its relationship with existing nation-state-based regulations. Furthermore, a combination of governing food flows with the specific governance of localized food production and consumption can also be achieved through other means than labeling, such as the creation of fully controlled food supply chains or globally prescribed and officially enforced production guidelines. Comparing different alternatives in terms of their effectiveness and the probability of being implemented on a larger scale is part of the future research agenda. So is the question of the extent to which private governance arrangements, such as labels, can be applied in combination with forms of public governance and what this would mean for global governance arrangements that are in place today, such as the WTO and the Codex Alimentarius Commission.

## Notes

1. See, for example, the consequences of BSE in Western Europe for the sale of soybeans in Brazil (Oosterveer 2002).

2. The Codex Alimentarius Commission was founded in 1962 by the FAO and the WHO with the objectives of protecting human health and promoting fair practices in food trade on the basis of scientifically sound standards. The standards developed by the Codex Alimentarius Commission became very important because these standards are promoted within the WTO–SPS Agreement (FAO/WHO 1999; Hooker 1999; Motarjemi et al. 2001).

3. On the tuna dispute between Mexico and the United States, see Appleton (1999).

4. See, for example, the dispute between the United States and the EU about the use of growth hormones in beef production (Charnovitz 2002b; Cameron 1999).

5. For experiences in Africa, see, for example, Scoones and Toulmin (1999).

6. Ponte (2002) distinguishes seven environmental and socioeconomic standards, both voluntary (NGO based) and private (enterprise initiatives). UNCTAD and IISD (2003) identify two additional private ecolabels for coffee.

7. Max Havelaar guarantees the following minimum prices for coffee: 126 dollar cents per pound (456 grams) for arabica and 112 dollar cents per pound for rubusta (Roozen and van der Hoff 2001, 142, 145). Since 1988, more than €26 million has been transferred to coffee farmers above world market prices from sales in the Netherlands alone (143).

8. FLO (2003) has developed generic fair-trade standards, containing specifications on social development, economic development, environmental development, and labor conditions. Most consumers assume that ethically produced goods have a positive human and ecological impact (Blowfield 1999).

9. Consumers buy fair-trade products for reasons of health, environment, and animal welfare, and to support people in developing countries (Browne 2000, 79).

10. For instance, the La Central cooperative in Honduras is exporting 9.2 tons of coffee, but only 7 percent is fair trade because the market demand is limited (interview with Tatiana Lara, consultant at La Central).

11. See, for example, the sustainable commodity initiative launched by UNCTAD and IISD (2003) to improve the social, environmental, and economic sustainability of commodity production and trade by developing global multi-stakeholder strategies on a sector-by-sector basis. The identification of strategies for the coffee sector belongs to the first phase of this initiative.

12. Or nearly twice the earnings of the second major crop, which is coffee.

13. "In an hour, one factory ship could haul in as much cod (around a hundred tons) as a typical boat of the sixteenth century could land in a season" (MSC 2002).

14. The registration of fishing vessels under the jurisdiction of certain countries (certain flags) that do not or cannot comply with international environmental regulations is an example of this globalization process (Garcia and Willmann 1999).

15. The centerpiece in the voluntary FAO Code of Conduct for Responsible Fisheries is the creation of exclusive use rights combined with political institutions and economic instruments to protect the resource base (Garcia et al. 1999).

16. Estimates by the FAO calculate an economic waste due to these subsidies of US$54 billion (Stone 2002, 293).

17. The WWF (1999) has identified specific operational principles to integrate trade, development, and environmental policies (WWF, 1999) and translated for

example in the Forest Stewardship Council (FSC), a label developed for sustainably produced timber.

18. Other labels in fisheries are "mark of origin," "dolphin safe," "organic seafood," "marine aquarium council," and ISO (Deere 1999).

19. The participation of the WWF is used by the MSC as an argument against the criticism that standards are too low or that the certificate is given too easily.

20. Therefore, the WWF is elaborating a methodology for community-based fisheries certification (see ⟨http://www.wwf.org⟩) to counter these criticisms. Community-based fisheries certification maximizes the use of local knowledge and is based on a partnership with the local fishing communities. (See, for example, the report from a workshop by the WWF Endangered Seas Campaign [2000].)

21. Labeling can never cover all food products, however, and therefore national and global legal regulatory regimes are necessary as well, and even the labeling itself needs globally coordinated (national) legislation. Wessells (1998) defends the thesis that ecolabeling will necessarily be translated into governmental regulation because when labels become popular, they need guarantees to prevent deception, and only governments can really provide these guarantees.

22. Although I stress the innovative and creative aspects of food-labeling schemes, I am well aware of the fact that certification and labeling schemes are disputed, and subject to controversies and political debate. A case in point is the competition that arises regarding various schemes, some of which are sponsored by industries, and others by NGOs (Micheletti 2003; Consumers International 2004).

## References

Abbott, J., S. Roberts, and N. Robins. 1999. *Who Benefits?* London: International Institute for Environment and Development.

Appleton, A. E. 1999. Environmental Labeling Schemes: WTO Law and Developing Countries Implications. In *Trade, Environment, and the Millenium*, ed. G. P. Sampson and W. B. Chambers, 195–222. Tokyo: United Nations University Press.

Beardsworth, A., and T. Keil. 1997. *Sociology on the Menu: An Invitation to the Study of Food and Society.* London: Routledge.

Blowfield, M. 1999. Ethical Trade: A Review of Developments and Issues. *Third World Quarterly* 20, no. 4:753–770.

Browne, A. W., P. J. C. Harris, A. H. Hofny-Collins, N. Pasiecznih, and R. R. Wallace. 2000. Organic Production and Ethical Trade: Definition, Practice, and Links. *Food Policy* 25:69–89.

Cameron, J. 1999. The Precautionary Principle. In *Trade, Environment, and the Millennium*, ed. G. P. Sampson and W. B. Chambers, 239–270. Tokyo: United Nations University Press.

Castells, M. 1996. *The Rise of the Network Society.* Vol. 1 of *The Information Age: Economy, Society, and Culture.* Oxford: Blackwell.

Castells, M. 2000. Materials for an Exploratory Theory of the Network Society. *British Journal of Sociology* 51, no. 1:5–24.

Charnovitz, S. 2002a. Solving the Production and Processing Methods (PPMs) Puzzle. In *The Earthscan Reader on International Trade and Sustainable Development.* ed. K. P. Gallagher and J. Werksman, 227–262. London: Earthscan.

Charnovitz, S. 2002b. The Supervision of Health and Biodiversity Regulation by World Trade Rules. In *The Earthscan Reader on International Trade and Sustainable Development,* ed. K. P. Gallagher and J. Werksman, 263–287. London: Earthscan.

Consumers International. 2004. *Green Food Claims: An International Survey of Self-Declared Green Claims on Selected Food Products.* London: Consumers International.

Deere, C. 1999. *Eco-labeling and Sustainable Fisheries.* Cambridge: IUCN.

Dommen, C. 1999. *Fish for Thought: Fisheries, International Trade, and Sustainable Development; Initial Issues for Consideration by a Multistakeholder Policy Dialogue.* Natural Resources, International Trade, and Sustainable Development series 1. Geneva: ICSTD.

FAO/WHO. 1999. *Understanding the Codex Alimentarius.* Rome: FAO/WHO.

Fine, B. 1998. *The Political Economy of Diet, Health, and Food Policy.* London: Routledge.

Fitter, R., and R. Kaplinsky. 2001. Who Gains from Product Rents as the Coffee Market Becomes More Differentiated? A Value-Chain Analysis. *IDS Bulletin* 32, no. 3:69–82.

FLO. 2003. *Fair-trade Standards for Coffee.* January. Bonn: FLO International.

Garcia, S. M., and R. Willmann. 1999. *Status and Issues in Marine Capture Fisheries: A Global Perspective.* Rome: FAO Fisheries Department.

Garcia, S. M., K. Cochrane, G. von Santen, and F. Christy. 1999. Towards Sustainable Fisheries: A Strategy for FAO and the World Bank. *Ocean and Coastal Management* 42:369–398.

Goodman, D. 1999. Agro-Food Studies in the "Age of Ecology": Nature, Corporeality, Bio-Politics. *Sociologia Ruralis* 39, no. 1:17–38.

Gowdy, J. M., and M. L. Walton. 2003. Consumer Sovereignty, Economic Efficiency, and the Trade Liberalisation Debate. *International Journal of Global Environmental Issues* 3, no. 1:1–13

Grader, Z., P. Parravano, G. Spain, and N. Benjamin et al. 2003. Going beyond Fish Eco-labeling: Is It Time for Fair Trade Certification Too? *Fishermen's News of March 2003.* ⟨http://www.pcffa.org/fn-mar03.htm⟩.

Greenpeace Germany. 2000. *Das MSC-Siegel ist derzeit kein glaubwürdiges "Ökosiegel" für Fischprodukte* [The MSC Label Is Not a Trustworthy Label for Fish]. ⟨http://archiv.greenpeace.de/GP_DOK_3P/HINTERGR/C10HI100.HTM⟩.

Haas, P. M., R. O. Keohane, and M. A. Levy. 1993. *Institutions for the Earth: Sources of Effective International Environmental Protection.* Cambridge: MIT Press.

Halweil, B. 2002. *Home Grown: A Case for Local Food in a Global Market.* Worldwatch paper 163. Washington, DC: Worldwatch Institute.

Hooker, N. H. 1999. Food Safety Regulation and Trade in Food Products. *Food Policy* 25:653–668.

Kleinwächter, W. 2003. Global Governance in the Information Age. *Development* 46, no. 1:17–25.

Mennell, S. 1996. *All Manners of Food: Eating and Taste in England and France from the Middle Ages to the Present.* 2nd ed. Urbana-Champagne: University of Illinois Press.

Micheletti, M. 2003. *Political Virtue and Shopping: Individuals, Consumerism, and Collective Action.* New York: Palgrave.

Millstone, E., and T. Lang. 2003. *The Atlas of Food: Who Eats What, Where, and Why.* London: Earthscan Publications.

Mol, A. P. J. 2001. *Globalization and Environmental Reform: The Ecological Modernization of the Global Economy.* Cambridge: MIT Press.

Motarjemi, Y., M. van Schothorst, and F. Käferstein. 2001. Future Challenges in Global Harmonization of Food Safety Legislation. *Food Control* 12, no. 6:339–346.

MSC. 2002. *Fish 4 Thought: The MSC Quarterly Newsletter* 2 (January).

O'Hara, S. U., and S. Stagl. 2001. Global Food Markets and Their Local Alternatives: A Socio-Ecological Economic Perspective. *Population and Environment* 22, no. 6:533–554.

Oosterveer, P. 2002. Reinventing Risk Politics: Reflexive Modernity and the European BSE Crisis. *Journal of Environmental Policy and Planning* 4:215–229.

Osorio, N. 2002. The Global Coffee Crisis: A Threat to Sustainable Development. Paper presented at the World Summit on Sustainable Development, Johannesburg.

Otsuki, T., J. S. Wilson, and M. Sewadeh. 2001. Saving Two in a Billion: Quantifying the Trade Effect of European Food Safety Standards on African Exports. *Food Policy* 26:495–514.

Oxfam. 2002a. *Mugged: Poverty in Your Coffee Cup.* Oxford: Oxfam.

Oxfam. 2002b. *Rigged Rules and Double Standards: Trade, Globalisation, and the Fight against Poverty.* Oxford: Oxfam International.

Peterson, M. J. 1993. International Fisheries Management. In *Institutions for the Earth: Sources of Effective International Environmental Protection*, ed. P. M. Haas, R. O. Heohane, and M. A. Levy, 249–305. Cambridge: MIT Press.

Ponte, S. 2001. *Coffee Markets in East Africa: Local Responses to Global Challenges or Global Responses to Local Challenges?* Working paper 01.5. Copenhagen: Centre for Development Research.

Ponte, S. 2002. *Standards, Trade, and Equity: Lessons from the Specialty Coffee Industry.* Working paper 02.13. Copenhagen: Centre for Development Research.

Princen, T. 1997. The Shading and Distancing of Commerce: When Internationalization Is Not Enough. *Ecological Economics* 20:235–253.

Raynolds, L. T. 2002. Consumer/Producer Links in Fair Trade Coffee Networks. *Sociologia Ruralis* 42, no. 4:404–424.

Renard, M.-C. 1999. The Interstices of Globalization: The Example of Fair Coffee. *Sociologia Ruralis* 39, no. 4:484–500.

Roozen, N., and F. van der Hoff. 2001. *Fair Trade: Het verhaal achter Max Havelaar-koffie, Oké-bananen en Kuyichi-jeans* [The Story behind Max Havelaar Coffee, Oké Bananas, and Kuyichi Jeans]. Amsterdam: Van Gennep.

Scoones, I., and C. Toulmin. 1999. *Policies for Soil Fertility Management in Africa.* Edinburgh: International Institute for Environment and Development.

Seaweb. 2001. Controversy Surrounds Fishery Certification. Seaweb Ocean update. June. ⟨http://www.seaweb.org⟩.

Shaw, M. 2000. *Theory of the Global State: Globality as an Unfinished Revolution.* Cambridge: Cambridge University Press.

Stone, C. D. 2002. Too Many Fishing Boats, Too Few Fish: Can Trade Laws Trim Subsidies and Restore the Balance in Global Fisheries? In *The Earthscan Reader on International Trade and Sustainable Development,* ed. K. P. Gallagher and J. Werksman, 288–323. London: Earthscan.

UNCTAD and IISD. 2003. Sustainability in the Coffee Sector: Exploring Opportunities for International Cooperation; A. Background Document for Brainstorming Mechanisms for Sustainability in the Coffee Sector. February 13. ⟨http://www.iisd.org/pdf/2003/sci_coffee_background.pdf⟩.

Wessells, C. R. 1998. Barriers to International Trade in Fisheries. Paper presented at the first FAO e-mail Fish Trade and Food Security conference, October–November.

Whatmore, S., and L. Thorne. 1997. Nourishing Networks: Alternative Geographies of Food. In *Globalizing Food: Agrarian Questions and Global Restructuring,* ed. D. Goodman and M. J. Watts, 287–304. London: Routledge.

WWF. 1999. *Towards Sustainable Trade: For People and the Environment.* Gland, UK: WWF.

WWF Endangered Seas Campaign and WWF Australia. 2000. Community Fisheries Workshop Report: Using the MSC in Traditional, Community-Based Fisheries and Identifying Candidate Fisheries in the South Pacific. Paper presented at the Community Fisheries Workshop, Sydney, July 4–5.

# 10

# Greening Transnational Buildings: Between Global Flows and Local Places

Luciana Melchert Saguas Presas and Arthur P. J. Mol

In this era of globalization, transnational spaces are being created within urban settings, providing a link between the "local" and the "global." Urban office buildings of multinational companies are typical examples of such spaces, where global flows and networks meet local actors and institutions. There is an increasing emphasis and attempt in different metropolitan cities to improve the environmental performance of these— and many other—building types throughout their different phases of life: construction, operation, and demolition. Energy use, water consumption, building materials, waste handling, transportation issues, and labor conditions related to indoor air quality and green parks are but a few of the environmental themes that regularly emerge in debates on public and private initiatives to green transnational buildings. The dominant perspective on environmental reform in such spaces, and thus also on the environmental improvement of corporate offices, is that local and place-bound environmental politics and discourses are mainly responsible for the articulation of environmental interests and their incorporation into business practices. That is, local, place-bound environmental politics have to "tame" the dynamics of (global) economic actors and institutions to get any environmental improvement done in the place. In the tradition of ecological modernization studies, this chapter deviates from that presumption. By analyzing how environmental governance is implemented in transnational urban spaces, it illustrates that the dynamics of urban environmental restructuring have become much more complex and advanced.

In understanding the social processes and dynamics of various projects and attempts to improve the environmental performance of office stocks of multinational companies, one can no longer concentrate only on the local "environmental state"—that is, on the local authorities and utilities, and their environmental programs and policies. Nor can failures in achieving water efficiencies, applying environmentally friendly building materials, or utilizing passive and renewable energy be understood by focusing simply on the policies, economics, and cultures of multinational companies. It is at the intersection of the global and the local, of the space of flows and the space of places (Castells 1996), of the practices developed by multinational companies and global institutions, on the one hand, and those developed by the local infrastructures, authorities, and interest articulations, on the other, that environmental performance and improvements of such transnational spaces are to be analyzed and understood.

In developing and applying this interpretative framework on environmental reform in transnational urban spaces, this chapter explores how new hybrid arrangements of environmental management are emerging at the office stocks of multinational companies in different metropolitan cities. In effect, we are less concerned with quantifying the actual improvements in the buildings' environmental performance, but rather with developing a conceptual understanding of the mechanisms and dynamics instigating their environmental restructuring. What do the arrangements regulating and restructuring the environmental dimensions of urban office stock look like? How are traditional entities and actors of state and market "enmeshed" and "hybridized" in practices of environmental reform and in an arena where the local meets the global? After developing an initial conceptual model that moves beyond the simple dichotomies of state versus markets and global versus local, we then elaborate on a qualitative investigation into twelve case studies of the interception between corporate environmental strategies (of ING, Andersen, ABN AMRO, and IBM) and urban environmental policies (of Amsterdam, São Paulo, and Beijing) to understand how the dynamics of urban environmental governance is changing. After reporting on these empirical cases, we further develop the model to conclude on the state of the affairs of urban environmental reforms and the inadequacy of conceptualizing them as just place-bound political processes.

## Conceptualizing Environmental Reform in Transnational Urban Spaces

Cities have traditionally been analyzed as contiguous urban spaces undergoing their own dynamics and problems. During the past two decades or so, various urban theorists have started to forcefully include globalization dynamics in studying the city, claiming that it is now necessary to include a wider societal space to understand the urban complexity. In acknowledging the crucial role of globalization in transforming urban space, three main lines of thought have emerged: namely, the postmodern city (Harvey 1989), the global city (Friedmann 1986; Sassen 2001, 1994), and the informational city (Castells 1996). The three slightly differ in interpreting the global-local interplay of actors. Friedmann and Sassen emphasize the functionality of global capitalism and global networks "from above," portraying the global as a vehicle for carrying dynamic flows and economic forces, while the local remains the place of assimilation of such forces, in which the state becomes nearly irrelevant. In contrast, Harvey and Castells give more emphasis to local responses that emerge in global cities. They define the local as a "political space" enabling and prompting social movements of reaction and resistance.[1]

Taking this argument further, Castells developed his theory of the two spaces of social action, transforming the city at large. According to it, in the information age the urban is no longer delimited to the physical contiguity of a local place as it was in the past. Rather, urban centers are constructed through two spaces: the space of flows and the space of places. The former concerns the dense exchanges of networks of capital, information, technology, images, and so on, stemming from the global, which have become the "expression of processes dominating our economic, political, and symbolic life." The latter regards the urban experience as a local experience, with people living within the physical contiguity of place, with their historical diversities, identities, and forms of societal interaction (Castells 1996).

Castells's theory of the space of flows and the space of places has been discussed in more or less similar ways in terms of "glocalization," usually involving a more cultural view (cf. Robertson 1991, 1992). Recently, the work of urban sociologist Michael Peter Smith (2001) brought this perspective one step further by distinguishing "transnationalisms from below" that are now developing parallel to those from above. Observing local social constructions that emerge in response to globalization, Smith examines how such constructions may be connected across localities also producing transnational social spaces. He thereby suggests that the city should be understood as a crossroads of local, national, and transnational social relations: nodes of numerous connections—from above and from below—sustained either by socioeconomic opportunities or by means of advanced communication and travel. These numerous connections, which form what Smith terms "transnational urbanism," have disrupted the traditional association of urban spaces with straightforward local spaces, redefining the dynamics of urban governance.

In an effort to explore the implications of these new dynamics for the sphere of urban environmental management and planning, we developed a conceptual model to illustrate how the environmental reform of office buildings of multinational companies in urban metropolises is a result of an interface of practices developed between two spaces. The first space can be referred to as the global space of social action, the space of flows—that is, the practices of multinational companies and transnational institutions promoting environmental innovations in office buildings in different cities. In this chapter, we label this space of social action as the "global management of environmental flows," as it is global institutions, networks, and actors that constitute the social infrastructure for managing environmental flows. The environmental dynamics in the space of flows involve questions such as: How are corporate decisions made regarding the premises of multinational companies in different cities? Which innovative environmental techniques are promoted and put into use by multinationals? How are (environmental) management or technological approaches transferred between local branches of multinationals? At which managerial level are initiatives taken (the local or the global)? And how are environmental technologies financed? The other is the local space of social action, the space of places which this chapter labels as the "local management of environmental flows." Here the local practices, institutions, and networks involving city governments, utility providers, planning authorities, and other place-bounded actors enable and push for a more rational use of environmental flows. What environmental criteria are articulated and on which governmental level? Which institutional actors enforce them, and with what kind of stringency? What local strategy toward multinationals is developed, and what policy style is prevailing? What local (physical and social) environmental conditions codetermine actions in the space of places?

The essence of these two dynamics encountering each other in transnational buildings in metropolitan cities is portrayed in figure 10.1, which illustrates the greening of urban office buildings as a possible result of hybrid arrangements of environmental governance—that is, being dependent on two such spaces of environmental management. To the extent that both local and global management practices "meet" in the urban space, questions of how both groups of actors and institutions are interacting and interfering around environmental reforms in different urban nodes emerge. How does the space of flows and its regimes meet the space of places? How, if anything, do the specific environmental policies of multinational companies fit within the local circumstances and dynamics, and how does the space of places facilitate or hinder the implementation of the environmental regime of the space of flows? And what are the consequences? Do we see environmental homogenization in multinational office stocks in terms of environmental management practices? Do we see similar flow-place hybrids of environmental reform

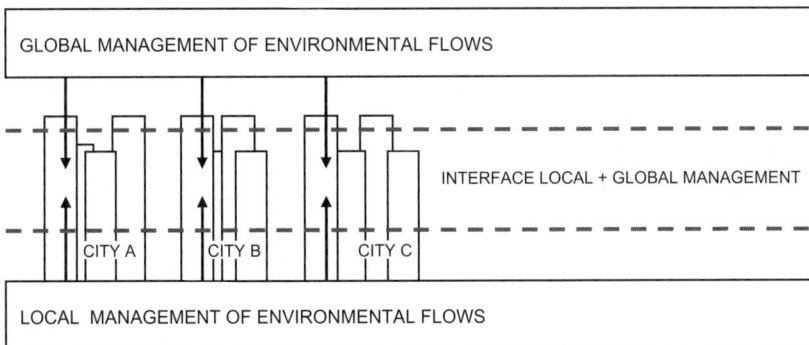

**Figure 10.1**
Conceptual model

emerging in different global cities? Do company characteristics make a difference? By applying this conceptual model, the chapter demonstrates how the interplay of the local and global management of environmental flows is transforming the traditional notion of urban environmental management as being the result of place-bound politics and policies.

## Environmental Restructuring of Multinational Office Buildings

To shed light on these questions and illustrate the usefulness of the conceptual model as put forward, this section analyzes twelve case studies of local-global interception in the environmental reform of transnational buildings. The empirical material is organized around four major global companies: ING, Andersen, ABN AMRO, and IBM. The environmental management activities and reforms resulting, or not, in the offices of these companies are assessed in three local places—namely, in Amsterdam, São Paulo, and Beijing. Deliberately, the companies were selected from different sectors (banks, consulting, and information technology), and the metropolises varied in region, state-market relations, and level of development. The empirical research into the environmental aspects of the premises of these multinationals focused on energy, water, and waste issues at the operational phase of the buildings.[2] The environmental aspects and management of design, construction materials, and demolition strategies are beyond the scope of this chapter.

## ING Group in Amsterdam, São Paulo, and Beijing

ING Group is a multinational financial institution of Dutch origin, operating in sixty-five countries in the field of banking, insurance, and asset management. ING's commitment to sustainable building dates back to the late 1970s with the construction of the NMB (now ING) headquarters in Amsterdam. The greening of this building was an initiative exclusively of the bank, which was "downgraded" by the municipality of Amsterdam. The bank's aim of producing an energy-sufficient structure, for instance, was not accepted by the energy company at that time (a public company), fearing competition if this was to be done on a large scale.[3] The building therefore uses 20 percent of its total energy consumption from main grid sources.

While this building has remained a landmark of environmental architecture ever since (Vale and Vale 1991), the company only defined its (local) environmental policy in 1995. This policy addressed issues such as waste processes and energy use (ING 2000a, 2000b). In terms of energy issues, ING's policies were originally triggered by an initiative of the Dutch Ministry of Economic Affairs (the main authority in the Netherlands dealing with topics of energy), requiring commercial facilities to reduce their energy consumption by 25 percent over a ten-year period, starting in 1996.[4] At ING, this led to the introduction of a behavioral campaign (ING's Energy Awareness Campaign) and the installation of advanced energy monitoring systems (ING's Energy Monitoring Program). The latter, developed in conjunction with Novem, claims to also facilitate meter readings and therefore the ability to charge private companies for their energy use.[5]

In view of these guidelines, most of the bank's current achievements in terms of sustainable building are related to energy consumption, although the company's environmental report also demonstrates a slight reduction in water consumption on the premises, and a heightened concern regarding commuting energy and related expenses (ING 2000b). The construction of the NMB headquarters in the 1970s strictly according to environmental and health criteria was exceptional, and the approach has not been replicated. The recent construction of the ING Group headquarters in Amsterdam South, for instance, has followed a different path to achieve environmental efficiency, favoring mostly energy-related issues. In the Netherlands, governmental as well as corporate programs tend to target energy use in buildings much more than water-related issues.

Also in 1995, ING endorsed the International Code of Conduct Charter, the most widely recognized voluntary agreement, known for its generic codes of environmental conduct. According to ING's head of public affairs, this step took place mostly to increase the bank's international credibility and thereby facilitate its access to international markets.[6] Finally, in 1999, the bank introduced a global environmental management framework (cf. ING 2000b) aimed at standardizing world-wide the environmental aspects of the group's properties, particularly around energy use and waste streams, among other things.

When looking at ING's offices in São Paulo and Beijing, however, it is clear that such an aim is not (yet) in place. According to the local managers, environmental criteria were not given explicit consideration during the decision-making phase of the selection of the premises in both cities.[7] In addition, no environmental criteria are applied to the daily running of the offices, except for basic commonsense environmental management activities, which are being carried out according to local initiatives—that is, voluntarily. In both cities, neither the company's Energy Awareness Campaign nor its Energy Monitoring Program are being implemented. The only significant environmental innovation is the implementation and use of a water-recycling system in the Beijing office, a standard launched by the Beijing Water Management Bureau. In São Paulo, ING's office does not display any environmental innovation. This is also attributable to the fact that the local environmental policy network only has incipient programs targeting office buildings, with rather limited effects. Currently, both in São Paulo and Beijing, environmental concerns at ING are being discussed, decided on, and financed by the local company management, leading to a mismatch between, on the one hand, ING's global environmental policy and ambitions, and on the other, the local environmental decisions and performance.

In this sense, the environmental restructuring of ING's office buildings in the three cities is showing more local diversity than global homogenization of environmental practices or strategies. In Amsterdam, the interface between the global and local management of environmental flows is mutually constructive. Both spaces of social action are geared toward synergistic effects, in which the local launches constraining policies and incentives (e.g., energy standards, subsidies, etc.), and the global, based on these, responds with environmental management strategies (e.g., the Energy Awareness Campaign and the Energy Monitoring Program). In São Paulo, the picture that emerges is quite the opposite. There, the management of environmental flows conducted by local and global actors is mutually discouraging, as neither seems to prompt environmental change. Only basic environmental management activities are being carried out, contradicting the advanced environmental statements of the company's global environmental report. Urban environmental policies are in their infancy, providing little incentives and norms for stringent environmental conduct. The environmental management situation at ING São Paulo is what some authors have termed "stuck in the mud" (e.g., Zarsky 1999). Finally, in Beijing, the environmental restructuring of ING's office is dependent on local policy agencies and infrastructures, is exclusively geared toward a decrease in water consumption, and is inconsistent with the company's global environmental policy. The environmental restructuring process at ING's office in Beijing has been unilaterally constructed, defined, implemented, and enforced by the locality.

We can conclude from the Amsterdam situation that environmental reforms can also be triggered and started at the level of the space of flows, with a global company strategy and referring to agreements such as the International Code of Conduct Charter. In other words, environmental performance at ING Amsterdam is not only related to the local actors and institutions but also to global company strategies. Yet the expectation that these space of flows environmental policies would be implemented in similar ways at other metropolitan nodes where ING is involved has not been fulfilled. One might conclude that the environmental management activities of ING in the other cities are driven primarily by local actors and policies, resulting ultimately in weaker environmental innovation and performance.

### Andersen in Amsterdam, São Paulo, and Beijing

Arthur Andersen, an international accountancy company established in 1913 with headquarters in Chicago and offices in eighty-five countries, was taken over by various other accountancy firms after being involved in the Enron financial scandal in 2002. Prior to its dissolution, however, as the Andersen premises in Amsterdam, São Paulo, and Beijing indicate, this company was not involved in the global management of environmental flows. The quite advanced environmental innovations introduced in the former Andersen building in Amsterdam South were primarily triggered by local developers and building companies, not by Andersen.[8] Being a pilot project for green construction, the Andersen building also received support from the Dutch government, through a facilitated construction permit, subsidies, and energy advise. Andersen, conversely, did not have specific environmental ambitions regarding its building nor environmental management in general, and seemed to occupy such a green building almost by accident. In Amsterdam, local Andersen managers report that they conducted basic commonsense environmental management activities voluntarily—that is, good housekeeping. No written commitments or policies were ever available, making this case study an example of greening unilaterally constructed by the locality.[9] Such an absence of corporate environmental management at Andersen is justified as the company considered itself a multinational "partnership" rather than a multinational company. As such, all units worldwide were fairly autonomous, including in terms of decisions on environmental management issues.

Against this background, it will not come as a surprise that Andersen's offices in São Paulo and Beijing were also rather poor in terms of environmental management. In both cities, local facility managers claimed that the company only pursued basic environmental management practices, mostly regarding the cleaning of air-conditioning systems and waste recycling. These decisions were made locally and financed with local budgets.[10] As a tenant, Andersen did not have any involvement in the design phase of both offices, and for that reason claimed it was not liable for the selection of certain energy and water-intensive technologies (although in São Paulo, the building went through a large refurbishment, during which Andersen did not ask for or introduce any specific environmental innovation). As in the case of ING, the only environmental innovation was the system of water recycling in Beijing. Although this system has now become standard, and is applied—and strictly enforced—by Beijing's Water-Management Bureau, the China World Trade Center tower where Andersen was located was one of the first in China to make use of it.

The interfaces of Andersen in the three cities, however, leave little doubt that the environmental performance and management of the company's offices are, irrespective of the location, dependent on the local management of environmental flows, either from policy or economic networks, or both. In Amsterdam, the management of environmental flows materializes as local policy and the infrastructure networks are strong, and as such the building that Andersen maintained in this city represented a breakthrough in terms of environmental standards. In Beijing, the local networks are rather strong in terms of water management (following water scarcity in Beijing), so the building Andersen occupied in this city had a particular system of water management. Both in Amsterdam and Beijing, the main company strategy of environmental change was dependent on the unilaterally constructed, defined, implemented, and enforced environmental management frameworks as put forward by local agents and institutions. Finally, in São Paulo, the near absence of strong local environmental policies and advocates resulted in nothing more than standard environmental management activities in the Andersen building such as waste recycling, not unlike the case of ING in the same city.

By evaluating the Andersen case in terms of our conceptual model, we are able to specify in more detail the crucial role played by local authorities in the environmental reform strategies of office buildings. The environmental strategies that local authorities deploy reach the company and its local facility managers either directly, or via the (representative experts of) local infrastructure networks involved in the provisioning of water, energy, or waste services, or via both. As the Amsterdam case clearly shows, local actors might use environmental strategies to set local benchmark standards or to attract transnational actors to their local nodes—for example, by stimulating and subsidizing green projects. In this sense, local actors may also lay out a kind of "green carpet" for companies that would prefer—now or in the near future—certain nodes in the global network that are characterized by high levels of environmental performance. In view of this, the local green office stock of a global company can be either the result of incidental or ad hoc local environmental policies, or it might prove to be the result of a global company strategy aiming to pick a green-equipped node in the global network of cities. The Andersen case indicates that the green building this company occupied in Amsterdam must be seen as the result of incidental or ad hoc policies.

## ABN AMRO in Amsterdam, São Paulo, and Beijing

After the merger of two banks, ABN and AMRO, in 1991, ABN AMRO Holding turned into the main financial services institution in the Netherlands and one of the largest in the world serving retail, wholesale, and private and asset management clients. It now has offices in seventy-six countries, with over one hundred thousand professional staff (ABN AMRO Bank, 2000a). In 1992, ABN AMRO endorsed the Charter of the International Chamber of Commerce. In 1995, ABN AMRO (2000b) formulated and approved an environmental policy, eventually leading to the implementation of its first environmental management system, concerning both in-house environmental management (such as waste management, transportation, energy, and environmentally and people-friendly offices), and sustainable financial products and services. In 1997, following the energy performance standard and the long-term agreement introduced by the Dutch Ministry of Economic Affairs, the bank launched an energy project for its Dutch premises consisting of three components: the installation of advanced energy monitoring (counting pulses of energy every fifteen minutes to detect and correct abnormalities), the introduction of energy management (through intelligent devices to make sure that lights are off when a human presence is not detected), and the reduction of energy use (by investing in technological substitution). An important component regarding the energy project is the fact that the bank has a fund of €2 million to be spent annually in the Netherlands, for investments that have a payback period of five years—an exception to the bank's policy of investing in two-year amortizing projects.[11]

So far, the ABN AMRO (2000c) global headquarters in Amsterdam is the greatest achievement of the energy project—a pilot project that introduced numerous environmental innovations, while going beyond the prescriptions set forth by the national and local governments. In addition to energy monitoring and management, ABN AMRO has also advanced technologies for acclimatization, including climate facades and climate ceilings. The municipality of Amsterdam, in turn, also contributed significantly to the greening of the building by establishing covenants or methods of cooperation that resulted in the decrease of single-car use by commuting employees, as the building only offered a limited number of parking spaces (this was done through Amsterdam's transportation authority, which compromised to improve the public transportation system). On the other hand, however, neither the bank nor the municipality of Amsterdam concerned itself with water consumption. In this sense, ABN AMRO (2000c) is not pursuing the same ambitions it has for energy when it comes to water use, alleging that water is not yet an environmental priority in the Netherlands.

The bank's environmental report states that in-house environmental management, unlike the energy project, is applicable on a global basis (ABN AMRO 2000b). At the moment, though, when analyzing the local premises of ABN AMRO in São Paulo and Beijing, such harmonized and homogeneous policy is not yet in place. In São Paulo, the local manager reports that the procedures during the acquisition and renovation of the properties of Banco Real in 1998 concerned mostly decorative elements, and did not focus on the above-mentioned in-house environmental policies as such.[12] In the running of these properties, only basic—and voluntary—environmental management activities are fulfilled, such as the cleaning of air-conditioning systems and basic waste recycling. No specifications are issued from the global corporate headquarters. Since local networks of environmental policy also do not have specific prescriptions that would prompt environmental innovations in office buildings in São Paulo, the building that ABN AMRO maintains in the city is fairly limited in this regard. In Beijing, ABN AMRO rents a small office space, which was selected in view of its location as well as standards of architecture and building services, without any explicit regard for environmental criteria. Standard or mainstream environmental management only is taking place here, as the local managers argue that the branch is too small and the budget too limited to compensate for any long-term investment.[13] The environmental innovation that does exist relates to the water-recycling system, introduced following the prescriptions of Beijing's Water Management Bureau, and an energy-saving system (including a smart-lighting system) introduced by the building managers. Decisions regarding the in-house environmental strategies of ABN AMRO in both cities are (at the moment) made locally, by local managers, although budgets are approved by the headquarters in Amsterdam. The greening of ABN AMRO's offices in Beijing and São Paulo is thus strongly dependent on local policy and economic networks. In addition, since the energy project in use in the Netherlands does not apply at the global level, there is a major discrepancy between energy projects inside and outside the Netherlands: The investment payback period is set at two years for the foreign branches and at five years in the Netherlands, decreasing the scope of possibilities of investing in technologies that might be costly in the short term.

As can be noted, the environmental restructuring of ABN AMRO's offices in the three cities shares several points in common with the greening of ING's offices. The environmental policies applied to each company's housing strategies were developed at the local level in the Netherlands, resulting from an active interplay between and mutual reinforcement of local/national urban policies and company strategies. While each company displayed a deliberate intention to generalize (part of) these local experiences into a companywide environmental strategy for the space of flows, this proactive stance did not automatically result in worldwide successes. When local actors at other nodes of the global network of cities are not willing or able to unfold a green carpet, the result is only a selective or partial strategy of environmental reform at these urban nodes.

### IBM in Amsterdam, São Paulo, and Beijing

IBM, the U.S. information technology multinational, currently employs around 310,000 people in one hundred countries and has a worldwide market share of 30 to 40 percent. Among the four companies analyzed in this chapter, IBM has the longest-standing environmental policy, including strategies introduced back in the 1970s. This is probably due to the fact that IBM also has computer production facilities, thereby compelling it, in comparison to the three service sector companies above, to develop and implement environmental regimes. In this sense, its global environmental policy is also more solid in terms of its scope and enforcement procedures, again as compared to those of the three other companies, and also applicable to the running of its offices. IBM's main rule is to follow the most restrictive standard, either the local one or the one set by the company, regarding the design and operation of its premises (such as concerning issues related to indoor environmental quality, fire safety, energy/water use, and so on).[14] Another rule is that all its premises worldwide need to reduce their consumption of water and energy annually by 1 and 4 percent, respectively (to achieve cost reductions), as well as carry out periodic environmental audits.

In the Netherlands, IBM is currently finishing the construction of an environmentally friendly building designed by an internationally renowned environmental architect, and most of this building's environmental features follow at least Dutch prescriptions. As in the case of ING and ABN AMRO, IBM has also installed an advanced energy-monitoring system in its Netherlands premises, claiming to have done so to facilitate the reading of energy meters in view of the liberalization of energy markets. To achieve the targets of energy and water reduction, IBM Netherlands makes use of behavioral campaigns, downsizes server areas, and substitutes obsolete technologies. In Amsterdam, the most restrictive rules are those set forth by the local/national authorities, such as an energy performance standard, a long-term agreement on energy, indoor disease management prescriptions (such as for Legionnaires' disease), and so forth. In this sense, the greening of IBM's new headquarters as well as its operations throughout the Netherlands is being considerably influenced by local policies. The environmental performance of IBM's premises worldwide is annually inspected by its Real Estate and Site Operations Department located in the United States.

Both in São Paulo and Beijing, rather similar environmental standards, though achieved through different strategies, are being applied in the IBM facilities. In São Paulo, environmental strategies included a study of energy and water saving initiated in 1996, to update the technologies used in the 1970s' building (originally constructed by IBM), leading to the retrofitting of lighting systems, the installation of water-efficient sanitary devices, and occupancy densification, among other improvements (Infra 2001). Decisions were made locally, but were eventually supervised by the U.S.-based Real Estate and Operations Department. The local facility management also included an environmental management system to control the indoor environment, waste management, and water quality. Local facility managers report that the global environmental policy does not impose energy- and water-efficiency standards as such, but that the building is annually inspected for the reductions of 1 and 4 percent mentioned above. As local environmental policies in São Paulo do not have a significant influence on the environmental performance of office buildings, all the environmental management innovations (such as the substitution of the above-mentioned technologies) are being introduced by the company. In Beijing, IBM's strategies to comply with the global environmental policy included the application of an environmental site assessment for the selection of the office building, through which the indoor environment as well as the management of energy and water are assessed to ensure that both meet IBM standards. The environmental management system consists of, among other things, waste management (through separation), water saving (through behavioral campaigns), and energy saving (through behavioral campaigns as well as saving strategies, like avoiding redundant use). The building is also checked annually for the reduction of energy and water consumption by IBM Japan, which is in turn inspected by the U.S. IBM.

In view of these findings, the environmental restructuring of IBM's offices in the three cities illustrates a specific local-global hybridization process. This is particularly the case with the buildings in Amsterdam and Beijing, as greening processes are constructed, implemented, and enforced by both the global company and the local agencies. Because the company environmental policy must follow the most restrictive rule, in Amsterdam urban environmental policies surpass to some extent the company's environmental strategy, thus becoming the dominant factor in the greening. In Beijing, the company environmental strategies surpass the local policies in terms of stringency and advancement, except perhaps for water saving. In São Paulo, the environmental restructuring of IBM's offices is exclusively dependent on the company's strategies, as urban environmental policies are only in their infancy. In this case, the greening is a process mainly put into practice and reinforced by the global.

IBM as a proactive and global actor can be regarded as a front-runner in developing and advancing environmental policies in the space of flows. This not only implies that corporate environmental strategies at the worldwide level are reconciled with global standards for sustainable housing strategies; it also implies that companies are learning how to deal with the interaction between the space of flows and the space of places. In the IBM case, this results in the company guideline to always follow the strictest regimes in place, whether they originate from local-level actors, institutions and dynamics, or company strategies. Therefore, to be a proactive company at the global level requires making corporate environmental policies work at all nodes in the world network society, regardless of the lack of incentives or synergies from local-level actors and dynamics.

### A Global Matrix of Urban Environmental Change

After interpreting the local-global interface of environmental manage-ment for different case studies, we now move beyond the sphere of empirical factors and attempt to construe the findings of this chapter in a more general and theoretical way. When exploring environmental change in office buildings, this study leaves little doubt that we are dealing with two different realms of management practices: the local urban perspective, comprising the realm of environmental *policies* mainly; and the global corporate perspective, comprising primarily the realm of environmental *management.*

In general, local environmental policies are elaborated with the ulti-mate aim of influencing the behavior of both local and global actors. Also in general, the degree of institutionalization of environmental cri-teria in local practices is positively correlated with the degree of impor-tance attached to the environment by a society at large—that is, the weight and political priority given to environmental protection in the local culture surrounding the nodes of the global network society. The environmental restructuring of office buildings is then primarily motivated to ensure the sustainability of the local environment and infra-structure. The dominant environmental discourse in this local realm is therefore one of optimizing the use of environmental flows, such as the physical streams of energy and water, and minimizing the deterioration of environmental stocks. And the dominant means to influence the behavior of stakeholders span from policies (e.g., standards), incentives (e.g., subsidies), and "monetarization" (e.g., an increase in energy prices or the introduction of ecotaxes), to forms of cooperation or negotiated agreements (e.g., covenants). It is self-evident that in different societies, environmental interests have different priority. Where other priorities dominate or monopolize the political agenda—such as poverty, economic problems, and so on—the environment (and its protective policies) is severely neglected, limiting the local urban influence in greening office stocks.

The global realm of corporate management has as its dominant perspective maximizing profits and business continuity. Environmental strategies are only viable if they do not (structurally) jeopardize these dominant goals. By the same token, environmental protection also goes hand in hand with the long-term survival of a company, so that the underlying discourse of corporate environmental management is one of limiting environmental impacts under conditions of continuity and profit maximization. For companies, the greening of their offices is sometimes welcomed as an opportunity to improve productivity and increase revenues, such as by reducing the running costs of their premises (e.g., through energy, water, and waste-treatment bills). In addition, it can be used as an opportunity for a company to perform as a (socially and environmentally) responsible organization, and as such attract clients, satisfy customers, and neutralize critics. The main corporate strategies developed to realize the goals of resource savings in corporate offices are based on or fit nicely within management principles—e.g., environmental management systems, environmental audits, environmental site assessments, energy-saving projects, environmental monitoring, environmental reporting, and so forth. These strategies may also include corporate standards (e.g., reducing energy consumption annually, following the most restrictive rule, and so on), which may in turn also push technological substitution.

As can be seen, both realms—global, corporate environmental management and local, urban environmental policies—do not in principle conflict. Yet a major contradiction in corporate environmental management concerns the increase in capital expenditure in the short term due to the investments involved, which sometimes goes against the profit component of the management discourse. Therefore, it seems correct to conclude (also from our cases) that the institutionalization of environmental care in corporations (a major theme in the ecological modernization literature) has to be *activated* or encouraged to a certain extent by urban policies and politics or by a specific branch of proactive cor-

porate strategies, such as those discussed above. Local policies and practices do play a role in overcoming the exclusive dominance of profit maximization and economic business continuity strategies—for example,
when making the primary steps to trigger environmental change in a
specific location. This explains why in cities with a well-developed local
environmental management structure—say, Amsterdam—companies are
more inclined to pursue environmental change. In addition to local policies, we also see that global network-based environmental institutions
and regulators (such as the International Code of Conduct or the WTO)
may "directly" trigger actors at the global level as well.

Finally, and transcending the dichotomy of local environmental policies and global environmental management, two other mechanisms
should be noted with regard to the greening of office buildings in major
cities: transnational urban environmental policies and local corporate
environmental management. Local urban environmental policies get
increasingly transnationalized via various mechanisms, to land in similar
ways in various cities. Local Agenda 21 initiatives, the Sustainable Cities
Program, renewable energy targets strongly triggered by such agreements
as the Kyoto protocol, best-practice and benchmark standards in energy
efficiency, and the international transfer of building codes are all policies
that started originally with policymakers at the local or national level,
but managed to become part of a global political space of environmental policymaking. Local policies, strategies, activities, and practices
become part of a global flow of environmental reform via international
conferences, international information systems such as journals or the
Internet, as well as global meetings such as those in Rio de Janeiro
(1992), Johannesburg (2002), and numerous ones in between, but also
via international economic and civil society interactions and exchanges.
And as such, they feed into and land in other localities. It should therefore not surprise us to find similar initiatives by local policymakers and
utility sectors in different metropolitan cities.

At the same time, the corporate environmental management of multinationals has a tendency to "localize." Local branches of multinational
firms develop their own initiatives in dealing with the environmental
dimensions of office buildings, and the central headquarters of multinational companies provide them room for this maneuvering, though to a

different extent for different firms on different environmental issues. Andersen illustrates a typical example of a multinational firm that leaves larger degrees of freedom to local offices in designing environmental care systems and developing a corporate environmental strategy, making the final result of environmental performance in the office buildings more dependent on the local urban environmental policies and local corporate management than on the transnational environmental management of Andersen as a global firm. Within the local IBM branches, the degree of freedom to develop local corporate environmental management is more limited, but it is still there. In this case, localizing environmental practices also takes on a specific meaning—namely, adapting company environmental performance to local-level standards only when they are stricter compared to the overall company strategies. Another illustration of local corporate environmental management is that of Andersen, which introduced a water-recirculation system originally launched by a Japanese engineering firm in the building it occupied in Beijing. Here, it became a standard later on for other buildings in that city, but in other cases it might subsequently internationalize via the transnational corporate structures. Other local economic actors (e.g., developers, architects, construction products manufacturers, etc.) also articulate and implement greening strategies in local office buildings.

As shown above, most dynamics can be accurately analyzed with the help of our conceptual model (see figure 10.1). Yet the last two mechanisms especially bring into focus new dynamics, which should also be addressed. It is not so much that the original model is incorrect but rather that reality turns out to be more complex. The greening of transnational buildings is not just dependent on and influenced by global corporate flows of environmental management and local spaces of environmental policy, politics, and utilities. The space of flows and the space of places also carry hybrid combinations of (local and global) political and economic dynamics working simultaneously. In other words, transnational urban policies and politics and local corporate environmental management also play a role in the current shaping of urban environmental governance, which depends strongly on the local environmental capacity and profile of the city, the structure and corporate image the firm is striving for, and the kinds of environmental issues that are prioritized in the space of places. Local, state-bound policies and politics and global corporate-bound management strategies are mixed, enmeshed, and reconfigured in new, hybrid categories and strategies for the governance of (in our example, quite local) environmental flows in urban office buildings. It is against this horizon that a sociology of environmental flows can be developed, and its further articulation and conceptualization is necessary to better understand new arrangements of environmental reform in global modernity.

## Epilogue: A Research Agenda for the Environmental Sociology of Flows

Our case study on local energy and water flows in relation to urban office buildings has been illustrative of how a sociology of environmental flows perspective sheds light on processes of greening office stocks in transnational spaces. But the focus on the governance of rather local water and energy flows also brought limitations and specificities. A more comprehensive sociology of environmental flows analysis would have to go beyond these local environmental flows related to the use phase of individual office buildings. Environmental flows related to the design, construction, decoration, and demolition of buildings (but also city centers), and the various networks and scapes governing the environmental flows and profile of office buildings through these phases, would provide us with a more inclusive analysis of the greening of office stocks in transnational urban spaces. Such an analysis will be global in nature, as architects, construction companies, and decoration products and companies will not likely remain restricted to an individual office building in one particular metropolis. But such a widening would also include a conceptual change in two directions.

First, such a focus would complement the sociology of environmental flows perspective with an environmental sociology of flows. That is, we would analyze from an environmental perspective the flows of, among other things, management concepts, capital investments, organizational schemes, branding, benchmarking, personnel mobility, and ideas that structure the greening of office buildings in transnational spaces. In the reported cases, we incidentally came across such dynamics (e.g., with respect to management concepts or international architects), without exploring them in full detail.

Second, such a more encompassing analysis might also blur the rather strict distinction we used in our case study between the environmental flows themselves and the networks and scapes governing them. Moving from the environmental flows of energy and water in one office building to transnational sociomaterial building systems or hybrids might then enhance our understanding of processes of greening office stock in transnational spaces.

These two innovations offer a challenge to the sociology of flows— that is, if one wants to apply the sociology of flows fully to an understanding of contemporary urban environmental analyses. While promising, it remains to be seen what such analyses would bring us in terms of new insights, a deeper understanding, or more relevant, realistic, and feasible environmental governance perspectives.

## Notes

1. Harvey and Castells, though sharing many concepts, diverge with respect to the power such movements may exert. For Harvey, economic globalization is triggering disorganized social actions, unable to develop a coordinated, transnational political force capable of facing the drawbacks of a globalizing modernity—a dead-end. Castells, conversely, deems that localisms are indeed a viable form of resisting the global capitalist hegemony.

2. For a detailed report on these cases, see Presas (2005).

3. An energy-sufficient structure, in this case, is an office building with an energy consumption that is totally independent from energy provision by public utilities. The building may even be able to supply energy to the grid.

4. Another strategy deployed by the ministry on that occasion was an energy performance standard, to be included in the Dutch building code (MINEZ 1999).

5. Novem is the Dutch agency for energy and environment (cf. ING 2000b; Novem 1991).

6. Interview with Pieter M. Kroon, head of public affairs, ING Group.

7. Interviews with Sergio de Biasi, chief operating officer at ING–Barings Brazil; Marceline Cozim, premises manager at ING–Barings Brazil; and Paul Lin, ING Real Estate, Beijing office representative.

8. In 2002, after its involvement in the Enron financial scandal, Andersen was taken over by Deloitte Touche Tohmatsu in the Netherlands, and the former Andersen building is now occupied by TBWA, a communication company.

9. Communication from Mario Vink, head of facility management, Andersen Netherlands.

10. Communication from Vicky Wu, former employee of Arthur Andersen real estate operations in Beijing; interview with Carlos Monea, head of facility management, Andersen Brazil.

11. Interview with Andre J. de Miranda, health and safety department, ABN AMRO holding.

12. Interview with Alessandra Campiglia, associate director, ABN AMRO Brazil. In 1998, ABN-AMRO consolidated its presence in Brazil with the acquisition of Banco Real, a Brazilian bank present in the country for more than eighty years, thus becoming the owner of all its assets and properties.

13. Interviews with Candice Pelger, assistant vice president, ABN AMRO Beijing; Patricia Lamberts, risk management department, ABN AMRO Beijing.

14. Interviews with Roger Cleophas, real estate and site operations department, IBM Netherlands; Marcela Rosemberg, facility management department, IBM Brazil; Jessica Li, human resources, IBM China.

## References

ABN AMRO Bank. 2000a. *Annual Report*. Amsterdam: ABN AMRO Press Relations Department.

ABN AMRO Bank. 2000b. *Environment Report, 1998–2000*. Amsterdam: ABN AMRO Bank.

ABN AMRO Bank. 2000c. *Portrait of a Building*. Amsterdam: ABN AMRO Corporate Communications.

ABN AMRO Bank. 2001. *Annual Report 2001, ABN AMRO Holding N.V.* Amsterdam: ABN AMRO Bank. AMRO Holding N.V.

Castells, M. 1996. *The Rise of the Network Society*. Vol 1 of *The Information Age: Economy, Society, and Culture*. Oxford: Blackwell.

Friedmann, J. 1986. The World City Hypothesis. *Development and Change* 17:69–83.

Harvey, D. 1989. *The Condition of Postmodernity*. Oxford: Blackwell.

IBM. 1999. Environmental Report. <http://www.ibm.com>.

Infra. 2001. IBM Tutóia. *Infra Retrofit* (June).

ING Group. 2000a. *Annual Report: Ten Years of Growth and Innovation*. Amsterdam: ING Group.

ING Group. 2000b. *ING in Society 2000*. Amsterdam: ING Group.

MINEZ (Ministry of Economic Affairs, the Netherlands). 1999. *Action Programme: Energy Conservation, 1999–2002*. The Hague: MINEZ.

Novem (Netherlands Energy and Environmental Agency). 1991. *Hoofdkantoor NMB: Postbankgroep*. Utrecht: Novem.

Presas, L. M. S. 2005. *Transnational Buildings in Local Environments*. Hampshire, UK: Ashgate.

Robertson, R. 1991. Social Theory, Cultural Relativity, and the Problem of Globality. In *Culture, Globalization, and the World-System*, ed. A. King, 69–90. London: Macmillan.

Robertson, R. 1992. *Globalization: Social Theory and Global Culture*. London: Sage.

Sassen, S. 1994. *Cities in a World Economy*. Thousand Oaks, CA: Pine Forge Press.

Sassen, S. 2001. *The Global City: New York, London, Tokyo*. 2nd ed. Princeton, NJ: Princeton University Press.

Smith, M. P. 2001. *Transnational Urbanism: Locating Globalization*. Oxford: Blackwell.

Vale, B., and R. Vale. 1991. *Green Architecture: Design for a Sustainable Future*. London: Thames and Hudson.

Zarsky, L. 1999. Havens, Halos, and Spaghetti: Untangling the Evidence about Foreign Direct Investment and the Environment. Paper presented at the OECD Foreign Direct Investment and the Environment, the Hague.

# 11

## Environment, Mobility, and the Acceleration of Time: A Sociological Analysis of Transport Flows in Modern Life

Mette Jensen

A paradox emerges as two contemporary trends clash: on the one hand, the environmental impacts of transport and the resulting quest for durable solutions, and on the other hand, the ever-increasing need for mobility among populations and in society. That paradox forms the background of this chapter on mobility in modern everyday life. What is the meaning of mobility to modern people, what are the rationales underlying their practice and approach toward mobility, and how do they view problems caused by mobility? The chapter focuses on time and the acceleration of time—phenomena that appear to be central to understanding mobility in modern life; the contradictions and paradoxes for modern individuals created by the increasing need for mobility versus a general concern about the environment; and sociological perspectives on "the good life" that may form a starting point for changes in the acceleration of time, mobility, and consequently, the environmental impacts. Finally, the chapter discusses why and how mobility is a pivotal part of, and should be understood as, flows in a network society.

### (Auto)mobility as a Hybrid System

I have already indicated that mobilities, as both metaphor and as process, are at the heart of social life and thus should be central to sociological analysis. (Urry 2000b, 49)

Late modern society creates an infinity of possibilities, and compels modern individuals to make a number of choices throughout their lives (Giddens 1991).[1] Apart from the strong desire among modern individuals for mobility, mobility is also a structuring element for both individuals and society. Mobility offers *some* possibilities, while simultaneously limiting and structuring *others*. Moreover, in many cases, it is impossible to evade mobility since it has grown to be a prerequisite to our participation in virtually all activities of modern society. It thus erects a number of structures that cannot be dispensed with, or only at considerable sacrifices.

According to Castells, the increasing problems with mobility are related to the transformation of the "old" modern society to the network society, which is constructed around flows of capital, flows of information, flows of technology, flows of organizational interaction, and flows of images, sounds, and symbols. These are processes dominating the economic, political, and symbolic life (Castells 1998, 412). And to these flows one should add the flow of mobility, as Urry (2000a, 2004) has argued so convincingly. Mobility is both a flow like the rest, but also a flow per se because it is, in the nature of the case, constantly "on the move." Hence, it is a flow in a double sense and can as such be considered the ultimate flow in the network society. This is exactly what the sociology of flows teaches us to understand. It is via the analysis of transport networks and mobility flows, and the way these are intertwining with human practices and the outcome of individual mobility choices, that we can understand modern society.

But mobility is not only a flow; it is also a system of (auto)mobility. Urry describes how, in this system, the car-driver is a hybrid between human activities and cars, roads, and so on: "The term 'automobility' captures a double sense, both of the humanist self as in the notion of autobiography, and of objects or machines that possess a capacity for movement, as in automatic and automaton" (2004, 26). It is not the car as such that is important, then, "but the system of these fluid interconnections" (Urry 2004, 26), these hybrids. If we are to understand the environmental dimensions of cars, we have to study automobility as a hybrid system, in which the material and environmental features of cars are inextricably bound up with and pulled into the social and institutional constituents of mobility. The car and the driver, the car-driver, can be considered a node in a network of (auto)mobility that is both moving and changing constantly, and in this sense the system of automobility should be understood in terms of flows in a networked society. The system of automobility is per se a nexus between the concrete car-driver and the network (society). A critical feature of the system (of automobility) is that it is constantly on the move, and this means that it is invariably changing as well, and in this sense an analysis of it will always be an assessment of the past. Thus, the future for (auto)mobility can never be predicted. But this is certainly not an obstacle to discussing the system and the problems it creates—which is in fact the intention of this chapter. The hybrid system of (auto)mobility with its systemic—and therefore not external or unintentional—environmental effects, forms a framework for our analysis of (auto)mobility in everyday life.

Increasing numbers of people transport themselves over ever-larger distances with growing speed, reducing the time spent per distance unit.[2] At the same time, these flows of passengers through motorized transportation networks—such as the car, railway, and air transport systems—are strongly related to environmental impacts. Local air emissions, noise levels, the deterioration of spatial quality, and car wrecks are as much a part of flows as global climate change and the consumption of non-renewable energy resources. No one seems to be able to control these increasing flows of mobility, nor reduce the social and environmental consequences of our collective choices. Urry (2003, 14) seems to be correct in suggesting that environmental and other negative effects can no longer be conceived of as unintended consequences, but rather as systemic features. Modern individuals are constrained to be mobile if they want to participate in activities in society, yet all the same, they continue to insist on freedom of choice. Our late modern society will not tolerate any restraints on this choice since it is identified with freedom, and freedom cannot be challenged without causing violent reactions. Our demand for mobility, the option of choosing an ever-greater mobility, is in contrast with our ability to cope with the environmental impacts of more traveling across ever-longer distances.[3] Mobility is just another choice we are faced with, and which we will choose, even if we know that it involves considerable risks; but the consequences are that our uncertainty vis-à-vis the future is pronounced (Beck 1992).

How are we to understand individuals living and transporting in flows of increasing mobility, well aware of the inherent environmental risks that come along with that? What is the meaning of mobility to modern people, and how have mobility flows not only become an integral part of their lives but also structure their daily activities? Such questions need further investigation before any questions of governance and the control of mobility flows for the sake of environmental quality can be addressed.

## Methodology of the Study

In exploring these questions, I carried out an empirical study in Copenhagen, Denmark, with qualitative and quantitative interviews. The qualitative part consisted of in-depth interviews with twenty individuals, lasting between 90 and 150 minutes, and the quantitative part was a questionnaire survey covering five hundred individuals. In the social sciences, mobility is a fairly new and unexplored topic, so an explorative qualitative approach and methodology is appropriate to shed light on the field. The qualitative interviews provided the basis for the questionnaire items to be formulated, thus ensuring coherency between both parts of the study. The findings of the quantitative study—for areas that lent themselves to comparison—were in agreement with and supported the analysis of the qualitative interviews (Jensen 2001, 304–305).

The interviewees all resided in Vanløse (a Copenhagen neighborhood) and were between sixteen and fifty-five years old. The male to female respondent ratio was about equal, with an appropriate age dispersion, and the survey included people pursuing different educational careers, living in houses of their own or apartments, and finally, using different means of transport. This chapter will draw especially on the analysis of the qualitative interviews since these are most useful to explain and understand the meaning of mobility to modern people, and thus of the (auto)mobility system.

A study dealing with the mobility of modern urban dwellers has to include—apart from mobility itself—their outlooks on other life aspects that influence their mobility. In this case, different issues turned out to be of importance for the respondents: the issue of time as a scarcity, and attached to this, the pressure of working and family life, but also questions about making a career, living a modern life, and so on, all emerged as significant to mobility. Let me start with the discussion of time.

## Time and Modern Everyday Life

I confront the issue of time directly and seek to shadow that a reconfigured sociology has to place time at its very centre. (Urry 2000b, 105)

Modern individuals are both under the influence of time and actively pushing forward the development that continually increases time pressure. Distances, both physical and virtual, are becoming ever shorter, in that they can be covered in less and less time. Increased mobility does not just mean that speed continues to increase but also that distances are reduced—not literally but in the sense that they can be negotiated more swiftly, and therefore appear to be shorter. This development builds up an increasing time pressure, both in society as such and individually, and is perceived concretely as an element of an ever-increasing day-to-day time pressure.

Time is thus structuring the everyday life of modern individuals. It could be argued that time (today) is one of the most significant and most restraining elements in the structure of modern everyday life (Hochschild 1997), and that there is a nexus between the floating (or flowing) of goods, people, information, and capital, and the compression of time (Bauman 2000). Although time and the compression of time cannot explain everything, they can very often contribute (sometimes greatly) to shedding light on a problem.[4] When it comes to comprehending how the current system of transport and mobility functions and is reproduced, the concept of time is a sine qua non.

Time, it turns out, is a dominant factor whenever we discuss and try to understand the driving forces of modern society and the meaning of the time-mobility nexus, both to society as such and the individual. In Rosa's (2003) "Social Acceleration: Ethical and Political Consequences of a De-Synchronized High-Speed Society," the pervading discussion coincides in every significant respect with the analysis of the concept of time in my study. Rosa offers a theoretical overview of the processes in modern societies, in which—as a central aspect—he incorporates a temporal dimension into the understanding of modern developments. He points out how, across the entire modernization process, time has been a crucial factor, and how sociologists (and thus sociology as such) have largely failed to look into this. Rosa argues that the acceleration of time has undergone a transformation. While its importance was initially in line with other dimensions or areas of late modern societies, today it has become paramount to every attempt to comprehend development. Consequently, Rosa (2003, 4) labels Western societies as accelerated societies, in which acceleration penetrates every nook and cranny of societal development. Three societal acceleration categories can be specified: technological acceleration, the acceleration of social change, and the acceleration of the "pace of life."[5] This accelerated development is intertwined with the acceleration of flows in modern society and forms a constitutive element in a globalized world. Only by integrating the time dimension in the analysis of mobility flows and networks is it possible to comprehend the dramatic changes taking place. To put it in terms of the sociology of flows, understanding timescapes is essential for analyzing the hybrid (auto)mobility system.

Time was also a critical factor for the respondents and the subject of frequent deliberations. Considerable resources went into planning time and launching a similar number of attempts to use it to better effect. The interviews indicated that to modern people, time is a central entity that is hard to handle, and that time pressure and modern individuals are linked together. Generally speaking, all the respondents were pressed for time. Being busy does not necessarily imply that you are also in a hurry, but in practical terms the two often go together. When you are *too* busy, then you are pressed for time. One could say that when time is a scarcity, it tends to build up pressure. The sense of being pressed for time is unpleasant and potentially stressful, and when time pressure becomes characteristic of people's everyday lives, it has a tendency to seep into all corners of their existence. With the respondents, this gave rise to many deliberations on time as a good in short supply.

One of them, Mathilde, told me about her husband's and her own long working hours: "He runs his own IT business, and if I do forty-five hours a week, he will do somewhere between seventy and eighty hours a week during peak periods. Obviously, that also means we need to have two cars."

Mathilde was quite keen on her work, and liked to talk about the excitement and challenges of it. All the same, she also regretted that both she and her husband were working this much:

*Mathilde*: I find we're too busy. We're enormously fed up with it. Every so often, we do feel that life is hell.

*Interviewer*: You do?

*Mathilde*: What I mean is that I think time is a scarcity factor, and actually, I'm getting enormously fed up because I cannot ever call my soul my own. And then I feel a bit like, "Gosh, we just don't seem to have much time left for thinking exciting thoughts or for doing anything alternative," because we seem to get on a mental train in the morning, and then it rushes off and you can't even find the time to touch the ground in passing.

*Interviewer*: Who is actually setting the agenda?

*Mathilde*: We do it ourselves. After all, we are free to get off. That's the weird thing about it—that schizophrenic attitude, like it's immensely stimulating to have a demanding job and be held in esteem and make a lot of money and feel you're using your brain—for this is quite a turbulent line of business we're in, you know. That's part of the game, and you're part of a team that's stimulating, too. And on the other hand, you feel like, "Oh man, this makes me sick. It's already Monday morning! Now the train starts off again." So it's some kind of schizophrenia, like every other week you'll come home and say, "Wow, want to hear about the exciting meeting we had?" And every other week it's like I almost have to pull myself up by the little hairs on the back of my neck to persuade myself to get started again.

Mathilde herself felt pressured by the strain of her everyday life, which was sometimes on the verge of being intolerable. But then, it was also immensely stimulating and a challenge she would hate to be without. There were two sides to Mathilde's daily time pressure. One was about the long hours she worked, compounded by the time spent on transport, which meant that she had few hours left to spend with her family. The other side of her time pressure was about the work intensity at the company she worked for. Here, the number of tasks and resulting short deadlines meant that she constantly had to rush with her actual working tasks: "Well, really I feel like I'm always in a hurry—I'm always busy, sometimes I can't even find the time to go to the toilet at work because I'm constantly on the run."

Given that she cannot even find time for a toilet break during work hours, she also may not have the time to take a leisurely lunch break, or put in a coffee break or two and relax a little. The stress arising from the intensified pace of work can be difficult to put aside when you are finally home from work, and several respondents explained how their family life and leisure were also impacted by a host of different activities and considerable time pressure. My study indicates that modern living per se is characterized by a vast diversity of activities both at work and during leisure, and under substantial time pressure.

### Time and Change

We have all experienced time and know what time is, but all the same, our experiences of time can vary greatly—not just between individuals but also from culture to culture, and from, well, time to time. Though we all know what time is, time is an elusive phenomenon. Time (and space) involves all relations in the world, yet is also an apt illustration of the fact that "precisely the very most familiar and obvious is often what we find the most difficult to comprehend in theoretical terms" (Klausen 1997, 149). Furthermore, time has to imply change, if we are to talk about "time passing." If nothing happens, time stands still (Klausen 1997, 150). Change, then, is a key element of time, without which we cannot grasp it.

When things are changing over time without people taking particular note as to when precisely it happens, it is due to the fact that most changes happen across a temporal space and not at any specific time. Temporal processes and points are closely interlocked, and can only be understood as such. One could say that points combine into processes, yet that these processes are more than just points. Many changes will evolve almost imperceptibly over time. When changes do not happen at defined points in time but across temporal processes or spaces, it tells us something about how we understand and constantly construct time.

If we view time as a social construction, it is obvious that any perception of time will necessarily depend on time and space, or the society of which it is a part. People's perception of time has changed across history. In our late modern society, things happen instantaneously and simultaneously; in a sense, the present is thus extended or expanded. The last traces of meaning from the past dissolve, and the future is in a way included into the present (Nowotny 1996). The old days when we could get our bearings to the future from the past are definitely behind us. The present timescape differs from the one of simple modernity.

## Time for Reflection

Instantaneousness and simultaneity are outcomes of increasing speed and time pressure, which altogether mean that the time left for reflection is reduced. In his book *All That Is Solid Melts Into Air*, Berman cites Octavio Paz for lamenting that "modernity is cut off from the past and continually hurtling forward at such a dizzy pace that it cannot take root, that it merely survives from one day to the next: it is unable to return to its beginnings and thus recover its powers of renewal" (1997, 35). According to Berman, a marked feature of modern society is a breakneck speed that leaves no time for the reflection needed if one is to understand and relate to one's own present. The significance of the past dwindles when social and societal changes happen as fast as they do nowadays. If we lose temporal and spatial continuity, our conception of changes will become fragmented and disintegrated. Or as Paz puts it, we are left "unable to return to [our] beginnings and thus recover [our] powers of renewal." If we do not have a vision of change, we also renounce contributing to it, since the *vision* of a change will be part of the social context, and hence influence the development or at least the societal discourse—which in turn also helps influence the development. It therefore can be difficult to visualize change. Still, it is important that we make the attempt, because such visions can form the starting point of a discussion on, say, a sustainable community—even if there is not necessarily the prospect of having it realized now, or for that matter, ever.

## Ambition and Mobility in Modern Everyday Life

Goethe's perspective and visions can help us see how the fullest and deepest critique of modernity may come from those who most ardently embrace its adventure and romance. But if Faust is a critique, it is also a challenge—to our world even more than to Goethe's own—to imagine and to create new modes of modernity, in which man will not exist for the sake of development, but development for the sake of man. (Berman 1997, 86)

Berman (1997) uses Goethe's *Faust* to illustrate modern people's restlessness and unrelenting aspiration—the aspiration that will enable people to accomplish ever more and greater results, thereby creating constant change. The deal in Faust's pact with Mephistopheles is that he—Mephistopheles—will assist Faust in obtaining wealth, power, and influence under one distinct condition: that Faust will forever continue pursuing his ambition. The moment Faust ceases to aspire, he will perish. At the end of the story, when Faust wishes to capture the beauty of the moment and speaks the famous words, "Verweile doch, du bist so schön" [("Stay, thou art so sweet")], he is lost and heading for his ruin. The fates he trampled on his way—Gretchen, Philemon, Baucis, and others—were obstacles in the way of development and thus fell as its necessary victims. Modern societal development does not allow itself to be stopped by anyone or anything but proceeds undauntedly at an ever-hotter pace—since Goethe's day and until now. *Faust* mirrors precisely the pace, restlessness, and ambition that have emerged as pivotal in the analysis of modern individuals and modern systems.

The respondents were all modern individuals, in the sense that they lived an active, busy life with a number of obligations. Above all, their obligations were related to their jobs, to which they were all committed, but also to family and leisure. They were, had been, and would be faced with some choices that would influence their lives. They felt that keeping pace could be a problem, yet found it difficult to think of any viable or immediate alternatives. Although they all wished for a slower pace and more time for reflection, they did not envisage that it would be possible to halt the development or reduce the pace. To some extent, they were all under a time pressure, which may have sprang from their working lives, but tended to permeate their entire existence.

The interviewed urban dwellers are "carriers" of tendencies in time. They are subject to a great time pressure, and their mobility is diverse and complex; it is both physical/corporeal and virtual. The busy individuals are constantly on the move, their communication is a constant flow via e-mails, mobile phones, television, and so on—all part of the system of mobility that per se is flowing or moving, and thus they are all actors in the network society. Mobility is part of a busyness that forms a marked feature of modern everyday life. Although the busy individuals are carriers of tendencies in time, of timescapes, I do not claim that these tendencies are the only ones present in current societal development. As indicated by Beckmann (2000), the reverse side of mobility could be said to be immobility, Beckmann claims that "mobilisation *needs* immobilisation" (2000, 2; emphasis added). I would contend instead that this is a case of mobility generating immobility, yet that they are not two sides of the same coin, in that mobility and immobility cannot be understood as parallel entities evolving in tandem. It is important to distinguish between the driving forces of development and the consequences of this same development. If we return to the Faust character, he can be perceived as a symbol of the driving forces of modernity, while Gretchen, Philemon, and Baucis became its victims. The same is true of mobility. Together with the increasing pace, it propels development, and immobility is a consequence of that development. Moreover, mobility itself—moving more and more often, and faster and faster—has grown to be a part of the aspiration of modern individuals, and simultaneously is creating the flows in modern life. We can thus observe how the mobility of the individual is linked to, constructs, and restructures the flows in modern networked society.

### Ever-Faster Transport

By way of exemplification, I would like to use the evolution of the means of transport to concretize the problem of accelerating pace. Over the last century, there has been a significant increase in the speed of modern transport. This holds across the board, from rail-borne transport by train and tram, to road transport by car, bike, bus, delivery vans, and trucks, to airborne transport by plane. In the early days of the modern means of transport, in the late 1800s, 15 miles an hour was considered a breakneck speed for trains and cars. Today, modern trains go ten times faster, with the result that not only do we arrive ten times more quickly but our perception of the journey itself has changed. From a modern high-speed train, it is no longer possible to glimpse sights of the passing landscape, which is reduced to horizontal lines, rushing past in changing formations outside the tinted and soundproof train windows. Indeed, this can be seen as an example par excellence of flowing modernity. Modern cars can travel at the same tremendous speed, and although the traveling speed via a car in and around a city has not gone up (it has occasionally even gone down in recent years), high speeds are a mainstay of motoring in a modern society. Even bicycles are considerably faster today than before; cycle computers record time and velocity for the cyclist, and often a state-of-the art bicycle design signals speed. Since the first airplanes, which traveled at 20 miles an hour in 1903, to the fastest planes of our day, at more than 2,000 miles an hour, their speed has increased more than a hundredfold. The fastest modern planes break through the sound barrier and move at a speed beyond human comprehension. The speed of the means of transport is the alpha and omega of late modern society, and greatly contributes to stepping up the general pace of life and thus the increasing pace of flows in society.

Virilio explains how and why speed continues to accelerate. In relation to war and the technological development within the war industry, Virilio (1994) describes how fast weapons are invariably overruled by still faster weapons, and how infrastructure and the means of transport are developed to reduce distance and increase speed in times of war. In times of peace, infrastructure and the means of transport remain, and they set a number of conditions for transport in civil society. Whenever a new infrastructure system and new modes of transport emerge, they will necessarily cause society to change. They both upset our material concepts and social relations, hence transforming the social space as such (Virilio 1994, 17). As a result of this process, Virilio claims, transport speed, and the speed of every new technology, will constantly increase in modern society—and thereby the speed of flows, dependent on technology, will grow as well.

The development seen with cars and motoring showcases and also is itself an integral part of the overall picture. Many think of the car as a necessity to make their day work or to "hold it all together" (Shove 2003, 412). It cuts the time spent on transport, while also enabling people's ever-longer transport—both in time and distance—on a daily basis (Hjorthol 1998; Berge 1997). This makes the car a time-saver and consumer at the same time, thus contributing to an increased time pressure.

## Work and Ambition

Today, we can also use the Faust character to comprehend why, in a modern society, it is not possible to partly jump on the bandwagon. You either have to be "in"—to aspire—with all your heart or stay out altogether. Similar to Faust, there is no such thing as a middle course for the modern individual: either you are a full-time, career-minded worker or the labor market will not really consider you. As Sennett's (1998) notes, you have to be flexible and hang on to the best of your capability if you want to secure your position among the "fortunate ones" with a job. Being flexible means being at your employer's or your workplace's disposal whenever they need you. The work/leisure divide tends to get blurred, often causing work to spill into one's leisure hours. Deadlines have to be met, so other concerns have to come second. If "the train" rushes on at an ever-increasing speed, it can be hard or impossible for an individual to make it slow down. Sennett relates how today's individuals are forced to keep moving in order to avoid being marginalized: "Immense social and economic forces shape the insistence on departure: the disordering of institutions, the system of flexible production—material realities themselves setting out to sea" (1998, 87).

The job has become a decisive factor in the lives of modern individuals—not just as a source of sustaining oneself materially but also as a prerequisite to building one's own identity and to be an active participant in modern society. In the frantic life resulting from modern aspiration, the need for breathing space between the many activities of the day is inevitable. One could also argue that modern people need a restraint on the speed of flows, but then immediately the question arises of whether this is at all possible. I will return to this later in the discussion of the good life.

### Hypermobility: Mobile Phone in the Car

In previous work (Jensen 1997a, 1997b), I outlined how many people conceive of the car as such as a breathing space between commitments related to work—respectively, family and leisure activities. In my study, interviewees were offered a much-needed break from the hustle and bustle of everyday life. For a while, they did not need to relate to the multitude of diverse demands made from many sides. The car in my study was fitted with comfortable seats and a nice audio system, so participants could get in after a demanding day at work, lie back in their seat, listen to some good music, reflect on themselves or just clear their minds, and forget about time and place (Jensen 1997a, 87). And this is how one interviewee responded:

*Interviewer*: What kind of place is the car to you? What will you do inside your car?

*Anne*: I'll prepare mentally, for what kind of day this is, what kind of meetings I'll be attending, or what I have to manage over the day. It's like when I get into my car, then my, so to speak, work schedule starts.

*Interviewer*: Is it a major thing for you, having those twenty minutes?

*Anne*: Yes, it is.

Although the interviews of the earlier study (Jensen 1997) were done in 1995, meaning that just four years have passed between both studies, I could already observe a shift in how people were using their time spent on the road in the more recent study (Jensen 2001). In 1995, cell phones were far less widespread than just four years later, in 1999.[6] Urry demonstrates how the large and increasing number of cell phones contributes to spreading the habit of talking on them while in transit: "Current developments such as the huge popularity of mobile telephones . . . suggest that many people want to engage in communication simultaneously with locomotion. Soon e-mail will be found in the car or train, electronic memos will be sent, and mobile banking and electronic shopping will be commonplace" (2000a, 8). The phenomenon can also be seen as a development in which cell phones end up constituting a line of communication from the user to just anyone, anywhere, and anytime, and thus forming a network where flows invariably connect (different) places. No place—certainly not the car—is sacrosanct to cell phone, which practically wedge themselves in, demanding attention constantly and everywhere.

Several respondents in my recent study described how they would use time in the car for specific tasks, primarily by talking on the cell phone. This could be a message telling a family member that you would be late from work, a piece of information you forgot to pass on to a colleague, a message to a child on their way to a music lesson, or a chat with a mother who you don't see enough of on a current basis. For instance, when asked what she would do while driving, one respondent replied: "I have to say that I sometimes talk on the mobile. As it happens, it's unbelievable how often things cross my mind while I'm driving, something I need to remember. And then it's like sometimes, while being stuck in a traffic jam on the Langebro [a bridge], I can actually put in delivering a few messages to someone. So I'll talk on the mobile."

Thanks to the cell phone, modern individuals do not have to merely transport themselves while driving. With the cell phone, in transit one can also fix a number of things that could otherwise seem difficult. One can practically be twice as active if *both* driving *and* talking on the cell phone. One can do two things at a time. The old saying, "Everything in due order," no longer applies. By talking on the cell phone while driving, we fill out the free space that time spent in the car could have offered, and thus believe that our everyday efficiency is boosted. We are mobile in more than one way, and are constantly part of, contribute to, and constitute the network society from which there is no escape.

Du Gay (Du Gay et al. 1997) characterizes "the Sony Walkman" as follows: "It is virtually an extension of the skin. It is fitted, moulded, like so much else in modern consumer culture, to the body itself. . . . It is designed for movement—for mobility, for people who are always out and about, for travelling light. It is part of the required equipment of the modern "nomad." . . . [I]t is testimony to the high value which the culture of late modernity places on mobility" (cited in Urry 2000a, 49). If anything, this profile of a Sony Walkman is even more to the point for the cell phone. It enables constant locomotion, being independent of time and space, and fits your body. As with the car, the cell phone can only be understood as part of a hybrid system of mobile communication, making any separation between social life and the material system meaningless. The car–cell phone combination opens up to a hypermobility that makes time and space merge. Together, they can fill all the gaps in our everyday lives with activity, leaving us with a sense of being extremely efficient. And by being as efficient as possible, we may have the impression that we can save some time along the line. But the reverse side of the coin is that a further condensation of time takes place, which in turn increases the time pressure. My study showed that the car–cell phone combination has become a common feature of modern life.

The interviews also showed that mobility will underpin and promote the continuous aspiration of modern individuals. Part of a harassed and stressful everyday life means that we have to be constantly on the move. Modern individuals, given their present pace, cannot downshift, much less come to a complete standstill. There is a certain inertia between the emotional and physical pace of modern everyday life, a phenomenon of which mobility in turn is a part, and which it intensifies.

## The Contradictions and Paradoxes of Environment and Mobility

This [book] will not resolve the contradictions that pervade modern life, but it should help us to understand them, so that we can be clear and honest in facing and sorting out and working through the forces that make us what we are. (Berman 1997, 14)

In today's society, the act of traveling/transporting oneself has assumed such an array of different modes that we can no longer talk about modernity without mentioning mobility, and vice versa. By impacting on a number of resources, social and individual, mobility gives rise to a host of problems, among which the environmental ones are significant. This issue of mobility and the environment engaged the respondents when it was touched on during the interviews, but when it came to praxis, the respondents found it difficult to act according to their understanding of the problem. This paradox was something that the respondents lived with, apparently without too many problems. Here, I will attempt to explain the background to this.

Like many other factors that give rise to environmental problems, attitudes toward transport in general and motoring in particular are replete with paradoxes. As in other studies (Læssøe 1999; Halkier 1999) of modern individuals' attitudes to environmental matters, my study has demonstrated an apparent contradiction in terms between the respondents' views on environmental problems and their actual practices. Altogether, this paradox between actions and attitudes is not unusual among modern individuals.

Precisely this polarity lies at the heart of Berman's (1997, 14) book on the roots of modernity, since being modern inherently means being modern *and* antimodern at one and the same time. Being modern means living a life full of paradoxes and contradictions, since we covet cherished objects and moments while everything is changing or even disintegrating, and while constantly wishing for and aspiring to the opportunities offered by such change (13).

On a concrete level, Berman's account of the modern—as an environment that promises to fulfill our every wish while also threatening to destroy everything we are and have—can inform a phenomenon, as I found in relation to my respondents: they want everything, and they do not want to make any sacrifices. They want to *both* maintain all the opportunities of a modern society—and hence not just the possibility but the guarantee of constant change—*and* have a clean, safe, and stable environment—an environment they can count on to still be clean, safe, and stable once their children and grandchildren have grown up. In my view, Berman's general (abstract) description of the modern tells us something about the (concrete) contradictions or paradoxes I found among my respondents.

For one of my respondents, there is no doubt that cars are an environmental hazard:

Basically, my opinion is that cars are no good for the environment. There's no doubt—since you can smell that. You can just go to the Rådhuspladsen [the town hall square], then you can hardly breathe. Studies have been made showing that cab drivers in Copenhagen have a sevenfold higher cancer risk than everyone else. And it is believed that it's because they sit there, in all those car exhausts that they pull in through their air-conditioning systems every single day. So I could never ever say that the car is good for the environment, and it never will be.

Later during the interview, when answering a question as to how not having a car would affect her everyday life, the respondent answered:

That would be horrible! I would feel it to be absolutely horrible. The times when my car is at the garage, we try to get things organized, so I can drive with my husband up to town somewhere or other and be set down, and then I have to continue with a cab from there. And I'll tell you straight out how that runs: If I don't have my car, and it's at the garage, then I'll go by cab, without any restraints, until I have my car back from the garage. Imagining taking the bus, that's completely . . . I can't even begin to visualize that, because I wouldn't have a clue as to how to fit everything in.

Berman (1997, 35) describes the modern individual's constant quest for events, entertainment, knowledge, and sensitivity, combined with a wish for being rooted in a stable and coherent private and social life, part of which could be a stable and clean environment, and the paradoxes arising from the implicit contradictions of wanting to have both. This depiction makes good sense when we try to understand how the respondents come to terms with *both* wanting and being fully part of a modern life with all that it takes, *and* wanting a clean and safe environment. The nexus between the two parts is both present and absent in their everyday life and their (modern) life as such.

To understand and explain these phenomena, it is far more interesting to think of them as a clash between different universes or givens, rather than an expression of contradictions. The ways people go about handling the conditions of their everyday life can be described by the daily activities they take part in. Here, their "unnoticed activities" play a key role (Bech-Jørgensen 1994). Unnoticed activities can be understood as everything we do without paying attention, but could explain well enough if someone drew our attention to them. In this regard, they differ from concepts of unconscious activities. Unnoticed activities will reestablish the givens that in a fundamental way, form the conditions of everyday life (Bech-Jørgensen 1994, 7). The givens of everyday life should not be understood as a single connected "body" of givens shared by all. On the contrary, these givens come in countless variations. We thus could talk about a clash between people's concrete everyday universe—including its unnoticed activities (e.g., people's unreflected relationship to their cars and their own car use)—and other aspects of everyday life, concerning their understanding and awareness of the societal discourse on collective car use, motoring, and the associated environmental problems.

On a daily basis, we live with those contradictions as discrete givens. When these different givens clash, however, they set off a continuous development that will gradually impinge on our everyday practices and in turn be influenced by the (modern) contexts around our everyday lives. This could hold some potential for change, and this would require more slowness, both in the lives of individuals and in society as such. The problem here would be that such a slower pace would collide with the ever-increasing speed that is part of modernity (Virilio 1994), and would therefore have trouble gaining ground in precisely a modern society. On the other hand, this field of tension, between slowness and speed, still holds a potential for change.

A way to discuss this potential for change is by exploring the concept of the good life. The good life has been discussed and analyzed since the days of the ancient Greeks, and has of course changed from time to time. In modern times, the good life can be a phenomenon of great complexity, but some characteristics can be presented.

## The Good Life

Based on the book *Det gode liv* [*The Good Life*] (Pahuus 1998), in order to deserve the label of a good life, a person's life has to include two key elements. The first is the core element in the good life, and concerns friendship and love, the possibility of life and spontaneity. The other, of a more general order and close to the core, is about self-actualization, determination, and power of action or ambition (Pahuus 1998). For modern individuals, the first element is associated with family and leisure, and the second with working life.

This profile of the good life is in agreement with my respondents' notions of a good life, which frequently emerged during our talks from problems in their present lives, though occasionally also from reflections on life as such. Asked how he felt about living in a modern society, Flemming, one of my interviewees, replied:

I kind of feel you're inquiring into my life. If I'm content with my life, somehow. And I have to say that I am. However harassed it may appear, the point of departure remains the family. And that we have all of this together. At times I feel things are just a little too much. . . . I admit that sometimes I could fancy myself moving into the country, to some green grass. Sometimes I do love my holiday and do not much look forward to going back to work. But then I'm also a person with an appetite for trying something new every now and then. The job does take up a lot of my everyday life, unbelievably so, so when I get to think of my quality of life, my job is really part of it too. I'm very much aware that my job needs to be right for me to thrive.

For Flemming, the family was the fixture, but work took up a lot of everyday life and therefore (also) became decisive in terms of feeling that he had a good life. In relation to the discussion of the good life, we may—like Flemming—have expectations (and often the experience) of family as the place where we find happiness, as an emotional state of contentment and equilibrium; that basically this is where spontaneity unfolds and life is lived, and that work is where one satisfies one's need for action and self-actualization. Like Faust, Flemming could not tarry in the moment. Later in the interview, he vented his concern with the time pressure at his work, and how it spilled over to his family and leisure. Flemming perceived the tension between work and leisure as a stress on the entire family, and one that could only be eased if he was sidetracked at work, or had himself sidetracked, or quit working altogether. He could not see or imagine anything like a blanket reduction of the pace, at work or in general.

In Flemming's view, it was beyond doubt that after all, family was his number one priority. Yet when asked the same question, the young respondents without children were less certain. Asked whether family or work was her first priority, Line, one of the young interviewees, answered:

I find that a tricky question. It does very much depend on the kind of person you are. But I believe that family does not mean anything as much as work, really. I think work has moved up and has taken a bigger place in people's life than family. Even though we would like family to be number one in our lives. But because we spend so much time working, we also have to renounce some of our family life. It's because we identify so much with our work, and we have to assert ourselves in society that way—so we no longer get our identity via the family.

I suppose that's the meaning of modern humans—being able to unite family and work. But I think that's very difficult to do, because one doesn't want to compromise, one neither wants to give up one thing nor the other. Plus, that it has become the economic security that we also need to have, that it has grown that important in our society, which it wasn't before, when the question was about surviving and living a good life. Now it's become so prestigious having a big car, a big house, or being able to give your children lots of things.

Thus, in the lives of modern individuals, the pressure often lies with the part constituting the core of the good life: namely, joie de vivre, spirits, and spontaneity. With everything scheduled and time at a premium, there is little room left for spontaneity and joie de vivre. But then, a modern life offers ample opportunity to take action, to come into character and prove oneself—which is the other part of the good life, and certainly part of the constant flows in modern life and society. This part could appear to have taken over, now prevailing over the core part that values life, spontaneity, and so forth. There has been a twisting of the good life, making it problematic and perhaps much less of a good life, since the time left for unfolding and spontaneity tends to be constrained. When everything is flowing or part of a flow, it can be difficult or even impossible to stand still and consider what life is all about.

## Yearning for Slowness

Everything in a modern society is mobile, everything is shifted around and shifts around to an ever-increasing extent and at an increasing rate. Especially over the last ten to fifteen years, following information technology developments, mobility has come to pervade all corners of community and everyday life. Mobility has become omnipresent.

The analysis on the previous pages has shown mobility to be inextricably interlocked with modern everyday life and how it is a core part of the flows in a networked society. This means that it is impossible to change mobility or solve the problems caused by transportation/mobility without parallel changes in modern everyday life and society. Moreover, this chapter has shown that mobility is an accessory to the ongoing acceleration of time, and hence to the time pressure burdening many modern individuals. In other words, mobility and the acceleration of time are part and parcel of our contemporary world.

The question is whether it is possible to direct or just control that development, or if we have arrived at a point where we are "no longer able to control the powers of the underworld" that have been called up (Marx and Engels [1848] 1964, 58). If we are to find solutions to the problems of mobility, we could for a start acknowledge the significance of modern mobility and the opportunities it creates. At the same time, we have to face the problems that follow, including the environmental ones, and try to find solutions to them. The respondents' yearning for more slowness, however, does not necessarily indicate that they would be eager for less mobility. On the contrary, mobility plays an important role in this yearning. During leisure time and holidays, modern people seek slowness far from the hectic urban life, and thereby often increase their mobility. This paradox has to be considered if we wish to contribute to solutions to the problems of mobility.

The results of my studies all point to something essential—namely, that the contemporary Faust character embodies some paradoxes: on the one hand, constant ambition, the quest for power, wealth (or work and career), and on the other hand, a longing for the simple life, love and peace of mind, children and partners. Modern people want everything; they do not want to renounce anything, and the only true constraint in their lives is time—of which they generally have too little.

Nevertheless, the tension springing from the disequilibrium of modern life and society, between the ever-accelerating pace and the dreams of more slowness, could perhaps give rise to changes. If such changes are to materialize as real solutions to our problems, however, we will need more than just a recognition and understanding of the forces driving such developments. We will also need ideas about and answers to where those changes are taking the individual and society—that is, how the good life can evolve into the good society. And the answers to that question are not simple or easy to find, and will require more time and space than afforded in this chapter.

## Notes

1. The view of modern society and the concept of modernity as such in this chapter is based on other authors who discuss this comprehensive topic (cf. Bauman 1989, 1991; Beck 1992; Berman 1997; Bourdieu 1994; Giddens 1990; Urry 2000b, 2003; Virilio 1994).

2. Commuting speed in metropolitan areas has stayed constant or even been reduced over the last decade or so, due to congestion, among other factors. But the *average* speed and travel distance are still increasing—see also the next footnote.

3. According to a report from the European Environment Agency, there is a still-growing transport volume in all EU member states; see <http://www.eea.eu.int/main_html>.

4. The examples are many: for instance, how the food culture came to change from boiled meals and several courses (requiring time and planning), to fried meals (which are faster to prepare and do not require extensive planning), to a fast-food culture (with take-out meals, which can be taken anytime, anywhere, with anyone, and require neither planning nor cooking). Including time in the analysis, one can also explain, say, the early retirement of many people: they might retire either because they never seem to quite catch up with the accelerating train of technology, or because they feel the time pressure at their workplace has grown so heavy that they can or will no longer put up with it. And time helps to reveal how the nature of financial markets has changed, from focusing on manufacturing to speculative currency and arbitrage operations in the circulation sphere—with all the implied uncertainties for individuals and society at large, because the velocity of buying and selling has increased so dramatically that every stir in the marketplace has a virtually instantaneous effect (see Castells 1996, 436).

5. Moreover, Rosa (2003, 10) also presents the underlying "motors" or social forces that drive the wheels of acceleration in contemporary societies.

6. According to *Statistisk Årbog* [*The yearbook of Statistics, Denmark*] (2000), 43 percent of Danish households owned a cell phone in 1997. In 1999, the figure was 59 percent—a 16 percent increase in two years—and in 2003, the number reached 85 percent (*Statistisk Årbog* 2004).

## References

Bauman, Z. 1989. *Modernity and the Holocaust.* Cambridge: Polity Press. Cambridge in association with Blackwell Publishers.

Bauman, Z. 1991. *Modernity and Ambivalence.* Cambridge: Polity Press.

Bauman, Z. 2000. *Liquid Modernity.* Cambridge: Polity Press.

Bech-Jørgensen, B. 1994. *Når hver dag bliver til hverdag.* [*When Every Day Becomes Everyday*]. Copenhagen: Akademisk Forlag.

Beck, U. 1992. *Risk Society: Towards a New Modernity.* London: Sage Publications.

Beckmann, J. 2000. Heavy Traffic: Paradoxes of a Modernity Mobility Nexus. Paper presented at Roskilde University, November.

Berge, G. 1997. *Livsstil, miljøbevissthet og transportatferd* [*Lifestyle, Environmental Awareness, and Transport Behavior*]. Oslo: Transportøkonomisk Institut.

Berman, M. 1997. *All That Is Solid Melts into Air: The Experience of Modernity.* London: Verso.

Bourdieu, P. 1994. *Distinction: A Social Critique of the Judgement of Taste.* Cambridge: Polity Press.

Castells, M. 1996. *The Rise of the Network Society.* Vol. 1 of *The Information Age: Economy, Society, and Culture.* Oxford: Blackwell Publishers.

Castells, M. 1998. *End of Millennium.* Vol. 3 of *The Information Age: Economy, Society, and Culture.* Oxford: Blackwell Publishers.

du Gay, P., S. Hall, L. Janes, H. Mackay, and K. Negus 1997, *Doing Cultural Studies: The story of the Sony Walkman.* London: Sage.

Giddens, A. 1990. *The Consequences of Modernity.* Cambridge: Polity Press.

Giddens, A. 1991. *Modernity and Self-Identity: Self and Society in the Late Modern Age.* Cambridge: Polity Press.

Halkier, B. 1999. *Miljø til daglig brug? Forbrugeres erfaringer med miljøhensyn i hverdagen* [*Environment for Everyday Use? Consumer Experiences in Everyday Environment-Conscious Behavior*]. Copenhagen: Forlaget Sociologi.

Hjorthol, R. 1998. *Hverdagslivets reiser: En analyse av kvinners og menns daglige reiser i Oslo* [*Everyday Travel: An Analysis of Women's and Men's Daily Travels in Oslo*]. Oslo: Transportøkonomisk Institut.

Hochschild, A. R. 1997. *The Time Bind: When Work Becomes Home and Home Becomes Work.* New York: Metropolitan Books.

Jensen, M. 1997a. *Benzin i blodet: Kvalitativ del* [*Speed in the Blood: Qualitative Part*]. Roskilde, Denmark: Danmarks Miljøundersøgelser.

Jensen, M. 1997b. *Benzin i blodet: Kvantitativ del* [*Speed in the Blood: Quantitative Part*]. Roskilde, Denmark: Danmarks Miljøundersøgelser.

Jensen, M. 2001. *Tendenser i tiden* [*Tendencies in Time*]. Copenhagen: Samfundslitteratur.

Klausen, S. H. 1997. *Metafysik: En grundbog* [*Metaphysics: A Basic Textbook*]. Copenhagen: Gyldendal.

Læssøe, J. 1999. *Mobilitetsbehov: kulturelle læreprocesser og bæredygtighed* [*Mobility Needs: Cultural Learning Processes and Sustainability*]. Copenhagen: Forlaget Sociologi.

Marx, K. and F. Engels. [1848] 1964. *Manifesto of the Communist Party.* London: Modern Reader.

Nowotny, H. 1996. *Time: The Modern and Postmodern Experience.* Cambridge: Polity Press.

Pahuus, M. 1998. *Det gode liv: Indføring i livsfilosofi* [*The Good Life: Introduction to a Philosophy of Life*]. Copenhagen: Gyldendal.

Rosa, H. 2003. Critical Theory of Speed Social Acceleration: Ethical and Political Consequences of a Desynchronized High-Speed Society. *Constellations* 10, no. 1:3–33.

Sennett, R. 1998. *The Corrosion of Character: The Personal Consequences of Work in the New Capitalism.* New York: W. W. Norton.

*Statistisk Årbog* (Statistical Yearbook). 2000. Available at <http://www.dst.dk>.

*Statistisk Årbog* (Statistical Yearbook). 2004. Available at <http://www.dst.dk>.

Shove, E. 2003. Converging Conventions of Comfort, Cleanliness, and Convenience. *Journal of Consumer Policy* 26, no. 3:395–418.

Urry, J. 2000a. Inhabiting the Car. Paper presented at Roskilde University, November.

Urry, J. 2000b. *Sociology beyond Societies.* London: Routledge.

Urry, J. 2003. *Global Complexity.* Cambridge: Polity Press.

Urry, J. 2004. The "System" of Automobility. *Theory, Culture, and Society* 21, no. 4/5:25–39.

Virilio, P. 1994. Et kontinent i afdrift [A Continent Adrift]. Petersen (eds.) In *Paul Virilio: krigen, byen og det politiske*, ed. N. Brügger and H. N. Petersen. Copenhagen: Forlaget politisk revy.

# 12

## Epilogue: Environmental Flows and Twenty-First-Century Environmental Social Sciences

Frederick H. Buttel, Gert Spaargaren, and Arthur P. J. Mol

It is exciting, but also sobering, to recognize that environmental sociology has arguably been transformed more over the past decade than it was during its initial two and a half decades. Within a few years after the emergence of U.S. environmental sociology in the late 1970s, the subdiscipline was largely characterized by the coexistence of neo-Marxist environmental sociology, particularly the treadmill-of-production theory, on the one hand, and the HEP-NEP perspective, on the other.[1] Virtually every review paper on environmental sociology prior to 2000 saw the field in these coexistent terms. Even quite recent review papers (Buttel and Gijswijt 2001; Buttel et al. 2002), which have given considerable play to the 1990s' debates over constructionism and ecological modernization while at the same time postulating the continued dominance of treadmill and HEP-NEP perspectives, already seem somewhat out of date, given the rapid changes in environmental sociology over the past few years.

Each of the major changes in environmental sociology has some significant connection with the themes brought forward in this volume on environmental flows. When analyzing the intellectual bases of the environmental flows perspective, it is helpful to discuss some of the linkages among the works of Urry, Castells, Spaargaren, and Mol. First, in some sense the environmental flows perspective can be regarded as a successor to or cousin of ecological modernization theory as proposed by Spaargaren and Mol. In this chapter, we will discuss some ways in which there is continuity from ecological modernization to environmental flows, and also some ways in which there are notable departures.

Second, to the degree that there is a kinship between environmental flows and ecological modernization theory, it is of importance to note that the birthing of the environmental flows perspective is occurring at the same time that ecological modernization has become subject to some intense criticism, especially in the United States. Global environmental flows should by no means be seen as merely a response to this criticism—particularly given that there are some critics of ecological modernization who will be satisfied only if ecological modernization becomes much more ecological in its focus, and far more pessimistic and foreboding in its prognoses about the future. A global environmental flows program will not satisfy these critics any more than ecological modernization was able to do.

Third, the environmental flows perspective is in some sense a culmination of the long-standing dissatisfaction with how environmental sociologists and political scientists have conceptualized the environment. Mainstream (that is to say, materialist, objectivist, and realist) environmental social scientists have tended to utilize concepts akin to Schnaiberg's (1980) notions of additions and withdrawals, and have also explicitly or implicitly conceptualized the environment in terms of Odum-style ecosystem biology. The environmental flows perspective is a soci(ologic)al and to some extent biophysical critique of both sets of concepts, as argued by us in chapters 2 and 6 (this volume). Many environmental sociologists—and less so political scientists—who are dissatisfied with the traditional conceptualization of the environment in the field have tended to move in the direction of what might be termed "nature-society talk": abstract epistemological discussions of the human or societal relationship to the natural world that tend not to lend themselves to research, and that carry a high risk of being teleological and nonfalsifiable (Grundmann and Stehr 2000). The global environmental flows perspective stresses the spatial specificity of flows—that there are movements of matter and energy, as well as wastes, money, information, capital, and so on, and that the origins, destinations, and sociospatial structures of these flows matter. This view is in contrast to the tendency for environmental social scientists to pay little attention, in particular, to the origins of raw materials and their movements over the worldwide social and ecological systems.

Finally, the environmental flows perspective should be seen as a quite fundamental critique of how environmental sociologists and political scientists have tended to conceptualize globalization. Traditionally, environmental sociologists and even more so environmental political scientists have thought of globalization from the vantage point of the national state, especially in terms of the extent to which the trend toward global economic, political, and cultural integration is leading to a diminution of the role or sovereignty of states. The flows perspective rejects the notion that globalization should be understood from the standpoint of (nation-)states primarily and exclusively.

We will analyze each of these contexts of the environmental flows perspective in more detail and discuss one of the more notable conclusions that derive from this volume—that the environmental flows perspective is not an entirely integrated one—by noting that there exist two rather different tendencies for dealing with flows in the environmental social sciences. One tendency is to de-privilege governance and "nuance" the role of nation-states as managers of environmental change, while the opposite tendency is to stress the new nature and challenges of environmental governance (also by states), given the highly interdependent twenty-first-century world that is characterized by highly structured, but often invisible, patterns of flows and fluids. We will briefly discuss how several of the chapters in this collection relate to these two tendencies within the environmental flows perspective, partly also reflecting disciplinary traditions. Finally, we will look at some of the potential risks and opportunities of embracing and further developing an environmental flows perspective in the environmental social sciences.

## The Lineages of the Environmental Flows Perspective

The theoretical chapters in this volume show that the notion of environmental flows derives closely from the work of Castells and Urry, although an effort is also made to "rematerialize" the work of Castells and Urry on networks, flows, fluids, and scapes. As far as the contribution by Mol and Spaargaren is concerned, the question arises why ecological modernization theorists would venture into these territories of scapes, networks, and flows. There are, however, several rationales for this evolution. Three of these reasons are particularly germane to this section.

First, Urry's recourse to concepts of "complex systems" and "post-disciplinarity," and his advocacy of blending social and biophysical explanatory schemes, is highly compatible with the historic (anti-"social facts") thrust of Western environmental sociology. Urry's advocacy of the notion that "agents are not just humans but will be a variety of human and non-human actants that constitute the typical mobile, roaming hybrids" (2000a, 196), accords well with the environmental-sociological promotion of the need to de-emphasize purely social explanations of social phenomena, as well as its need to stress the reciprocal relations between the social and the biophysical. In the opening chapter to this volume, Urry's notion of hybrid systems is embraced to emphasize the blending of the social and the material, particularly in the era of globalization.

Second, and perhaps the most important of the reasons for ecological modernization theory morphing into environmental flows, is that the flows perspective is highly compatible with the globalization imagery of ecological modernization, especially that advanced by Mol (2001). Urry's conception of flows can be viewed as his own (essentially postmodern) response to globalization phenomena. Following Beck (1997; Beck and Wilms 2004) in this respect, Urry's (2003) analysis is anchored in a commitment to the notion that a high priority for the social sciences is the need to reassess its traditional conviction that society is the self-evident unit of analysis, and to scrutinize the notion that society, the nation-state, national culture, and national identity are coterminous or coincident. Basically, the most fundamental legacy of the classical and twentieth-century sociological and political science traditions was the presumption that societies and culture were national. This shorthand of national society enabled social scientists to avoid having to examine the complex iterative processes that underlie social systems and structures. Social change in "structured" systems was analyzed with the help of the concept of agency. Although the notion that system change can be seen to result (only) from human agency was already misleading forty years ago, present-day globalization cast conclusive doubt on this sociological reductionism (Urry 2000a, 196).

A third rationale for ecological modernization theorists venturing into the conceptual world of flows and fluids is arguably the fact that Mol and Spaargaren felt the need to present a clearer or more nuanced image of governance in the modern world, partly in response to critics who read into ecological modernization a twentieth-century, essentialist, political-science-type, decision-making-centered logic. What ecological modernization theory in fact tried to establish—following Jänicke's early work in this respect—was a more abstract, institutional perspective on policymaking, governance, and the changing role of the nation-state. Complexity theory and flows analysis of the sort pioneered by Urry and Castells accord reasonably well with this broad type of institutional analysis that the ecological modernizationists intended to promote. The Castells-Urry view of governance perhaps places more stress on the highly circumscribed capacities of national states and international regimes (the "power of flows," in Castells's terminology) than ecological modernizationists (of the sort represented by Jänicke, for example) would prefer, but the commitment—shown throughout this volume—to work from the power of flows assumption is a considerable antidote to what some critics have tended to read from ecological modernization works.

## The Nation-State and Global Governance

The flows perspective is rooted in a critique of the notion that most economic and social problems or risks are produced by, and soluble at the level of, the individual society through national policies. This did occur to some degree from the 1930s until the 1970s or so by way of the development and expansion of the social insurance state, which was able to identify and respond to the "risks of organized capitalism" in perhaps "a dozen or so societies of the North Atlantic rim" (Urry 2000a, 190). Even then, this "societal model" was a limited one because the remainder of the world was subject to the domination of this handful of North Atlantic developed countries. But global mobilities have rendered the societal model increasingly irrelevant (Urry 2000b).

To understand globalization requires one to recognize the complex flows and fluids organized through networks and scapes that are embedded

within and across different societies. Urry has argued specifically against
the appropriateness of the concept of structure since it "implies a centre,
a concentration of power, vertical hierarchy and a formal or informal
constitution" (1998, 3). The Mol-Spaargaren notion of environmental
flows appears to be an extension of the Urry concept of fluids.

The flows idea and perspective also involve resisting conceptualizing
globalization from the viewpoint of the nation-state—that is, in terms of
whether there is or is not a decline in national sovereignty or "stateness."
At the same time, the flows perspective is a sharp response to functionalist and conspiratorial views of globalization. In the flows perspective,
the complexity of these global flows leads the national state and international regimes to struggle to deal with "deterritorialized and decen-
tred mobilities of the global system. States have increasingly shifted to a
regulative rather than direct production/employment function, partly
facilitated by new forms for information gathering, storage and
retrieval" (Urry 1999, 313–314). And as Castells notes repeatedly in his
*The Rise of the Network Society* (1996), the power of flows takes analytic precedence over the flows of power.

Globalization further exacerbates the limits on national state power:
under conditions of globalization, states have lost the ability and willingness to detail the patterns, regularities, and order of societies, and
increasingly turn to regulating mobilities and ensuring the conditions for
a favorable interaction between processes and flows. As remarked by
Mol and Spaargaren in this volume, Urry (2000b) sets forth the EU as
the prototypical example of a gamekeeper state—a relatively small
bureaucracy regulating activities and mobilities via computer-based
information. The thrust of the analysis is thus to stress the reactivity and
limited incapacities of these gamekeeper national states and international
regimes. As Beck would have it, the "container view" of power as characteristic of the first phase of modernity is no longer adequate to describe
the role of the nation-state in second, reflexive modernity.

In Urry's early work on flows, he made the case that while global
processes restructure social inequalities and transform many states into
" 'regulators' of such flows" (1999, 314), the appearance of an enhanced
regulatory role of states may be more an indicator of their limited capacities than of their stateness. In a similar vein, Castells argues that in the

network society, states have been transformed from sovereign subjects into strategic actors, who foster the productivity and competitiveness of their economies by allying themselves closely with economic interests structured by global rules favorable to capital flows. In Urry's most recent work, *Global Complexity* (2003), however, the state seems to become even more irrelevant and is almost absent in analyses of global modernity. In this later work, GINs and especially global fluids are hardly touched by activities of nation-states, nor do the scapes seem to have any specific relation to nation-states. The environmental flows adherents whose works are featured in this volume strike a middle ground between the 1990s' writings of Urry and Castells and the more elaborated (and sociologically rambunctious) *Global Complexity* book.

In a nutshell, then, the notion of environmental flows is an ambitious attempt to capture the complexity of the global environment, and to do so in a way that grapples innovatively with the new realities of globalization. Environmental flows is a materialized take on Urry's notion of fluids. To be sure, Urry provides some environmental or environmentally relevant examples of fluids in his *Global Complexity* ("automobility," "environmental and health hazards," and the "world's oceans"), but the thrust of his contention is to stress the higher-order commonalities between (rather than the distinctive properties of) environmentally relevant fluids, on the one hand, and the predominantly social instances of fluids emphasized in the bulk of the analysis, on the other hand. The environmental flows notion is an extension of the stress on globalization in recent versions of ecological modernization. The flows perspective à la Urry and Castells is a post-postmodernist, post–political economy, and poststructural perspective that resists structural-causal reasoning and reductionism. Finally, the environmental flows perspective is a reaction to the political-decision-centered (mis)interpretation of ecological modernization by some of its critics.

## Environmental Flows and Ecological Modernization

One obvious point of departure for understanding the intellectual significance of the global environmental flows perspective is to point to the fact that this notion is put forward by two authors—Mol and

Spaargaren—who are known as ecological modernization theorists. Almost by definition, then, environmental flows concepts share some kinship with ecological modernization ideas.

There are several key continuities between the ecological modernization and environmental flows perspectives, some of which may not be entirely obvious. Both ecological modernization and global environmental flows are disjunctural-transformational perspectives in that they hold that the late twentieth to early twenty-first centuries represent a watershed period in the development of industrial capitalism. As noted several times above, both perspectives also stress the role of globalization. Third, there is continuity between ecological modernization (especially its more recent versions; see Mol and Spaargaren 2004) and global environmental flows in the emphasis that each places on consumption as well as production. Finally, and perhaps least self-evident but very important, there is a great deal of continuity between the two in their commitment to "nonapocalyptic" views of the environment and environmental quality conditions.

That said, there are two particularly noteworthy departures between ecological modernization theory and global environmental flows. First, while ecological modernization is solidly modernist—albeit "reflexively modernist"—in its ontology, the environmental flows perspective tries to confront some of the "postmodern" challenges as discussed by Urry and Castells. Second, the two perspectives differ in their treatment of governance. As pointed out earlier by Buttel (2003), ecological modernization can be interpreted as, at root, a theory of political modernization. It presupposes the increasingly autonomous institutional centrality of the environment, and looks at the principles of decentralization and the related arrangements that facilitate public and private decision making that reinforces the autonomy of "the environmental." By contrast, the global environmental flows perspective tends to downplay the obviously crucial character of governance, at least when limited to the level of nation-states. Not only does the environmental flows perspective suggest the limited or bounded significance of nation-state-driven policymaking but it also tends to de-emphasize the importance of global regime governance as viewed from a "games" perspective on the role of national states.

Global environmental flows should be viewed not only as a new perspective deriving from ecological modernization. Just as critical as the ontological convergences between the two perspectives is the fact that the environmental flows standpoint has been developed in a context of enhanced debates and criticism on ecological modernization theory. While there has been a critique of ecological modernization theory almost from the outset of the first publications in English, the early criticism (e.g., Murphy 1996; Blowers 1997; Blühdorn 1997, 2000; Boland 1994) came from different—mostly European—sources and tended to be rather fragmented. The recent—U.S.-based—criticism as developed by a relatively new grouping of scholars, who may be referred to as the neohuman ecologists, is more fierce and shrill than the earlier versions (York et al. 2002, 2003; York and Rosa 2003; York 2003). Indeed, the increased visibility and persuasiveness of the neohuman ecologists has itself been one of the most far-reaching—and unexpected—trends in U.S. and to a lesser extent international environmental sociology since 2000. Neohuman ecology is essentially an adaptation of the neo-Malthusian Impact Population Affluence Technology (IPAT) model of Paul Ehrlich (for details on its most recent reincarnation, see Holdren and Ehrlich [1971]; York et al. [2003]).[2] Contemporary ("STIRPAT") neohuman ecology (York et al. 2003) has added a layer of technical sophistication to the IPAT model while retaining and building on the three major components of neo-Malthusian reasoning. First, there is a stress on consumption, resulting in the corresponding tendency to reconceptualize issues involving production institutions as consumption issues. Second, it works with "social-morphological" causality, meaning that the emphasis is on the broad, mostly empirical categories of the "drivers" of consumption such as income growth, the economy, and urbanization. Third, it has a characteristic emphasis on population and demographic factors such as population size, density, growth, and so on.

Although only in the United States has the revival of neo-Malthusianism resulted in a direct confrontation with ecological modernization theory, the "footprint" social sciences have gained considerable weight in Europe over the recent past. When trying to respond to some of the—empirical, indicator-related—criticisms, ecological modernization theorists will have to venture more explicitly into the natural sciences concepts and literatures that are so strongly represented in the footprint approaches. The environmental flows perspective in this respect can be seen as an effort to incorporate some natural sciences–based concepts and dynamics into the environmental social sciences in a way explored by Urry and others.

## Governing Global Environmental Flows: Drawing the Balance of the Book

The critics of ecological modernization may not be any more satisfied with the global environmental flows perspective than they were with ecological modernization, but the flows perspective's departures from ecological modernization—especially from the critics' views of what ecological modernization is—will mean that the environmental social sciences are in for an entirely new set of debates. One of the axes of debate—also included in this volume—will likely concern whether there is or ought to be a clear or unitary view within environmental flows about how to think about governance and the regulation of environmental flows/fluids. One of the major results of this book is to demonstrate that the environmental and social sciences interest in the notions of environmental flows is occurring despite—and perhaps because of—the fact that there remains a considerable diversity of viewpoints about the place that the analysis of governance and regulation should play in this perspective.

The thrust of the Mol and Spaargaren chapter, "Toward a Sociology of Environmental Flows," has been to typify the postpositivist, intentionally nondeterministic, de-privileging, and institutionally oriented view—or in other words, a largely Urry- and Castells-driven perspective—on governance and regulation. That is to say, Mol and Spaargaren concur with the basic position of Urry's and Castells's work about why one should not privilege the realm of state (and state-related) decision making as the explanation for either environmental degradation or its changing forms or mitigation. At the same time, many of the environmental social scientists who are attracted to the flows concept feel that way because it sheds new light on how to think about governance and regulation. The (relative) diversity within the environmental flows community is nicely illustrated by the chapters in this collection. In this section, we will comment on several of these chapters from the vantage point of the implications of the flows perspective for understanding environmental governance.

Four chapters that represent the de-privileging, institutionally oriented view of governance are the Mol and Spaargaren one; the van Koppen chapter "Governing Nature?"; the one by Peter Oosterveer, "Environmental Governance of Global Food Flows"; and the chapter by Presas and Mol, "Greening Transnational Buildings."

In his chapter, van Koppen analyzes how biodiversity conservation changes through globalization, and how these new conservation configurations can be identified and understood using a flows perspective. State centrality and place boundedness in conservation has made room for new hybrid arrangements, transboundary flows, and hybrid networks.

The Oosterveer chapter on labeling as a mechanism for regulating global flows of food is another instance of the de-privileging, institutionally oriented view of governance. Oosterveer, like Presas and Mol, works particularly closely from Castells's views about the space of flows increasingly replacing the space of places. He sees his case study of the global flows of food as being particularly appropriate for exploring Castells's arguments; while agri-food capitals and networks—especially in their global financial aspect—may appear to be increasingly disembedded and footloose, agriculture remains the quintessentially locally embedded process because of the tie of most food production to the land resource. Oosterveer looks at the WTO's SPS Agreement, and especially its implications for labeling with respect to fair-trade coffee and MSC fish, in order to understand the scope and prospects of labeling as an alternative food system regulatory practice. He finds that food labeling has a certain promise as an alternative practice for regulating the negative environmental aspects of the modern food production system. At the same time, however, alternative food labeling must be understood as having considerable limits because it is also a product of an increasingly globalized, footloose agri-food system.

The essence of the Presas and Mol chapter, from a governance point of view, is set forth in the introductory section in which the authors note that "we are less concerned with quantifying the actual improvements in the buildings' environmental performance, but rather with developing a conceptual understanding of the mechanisms and dynamics instigating their environmental restructuring." This goal, and disclaimer, harks back to the comments made earlier about some of the ways in which the environmental flows perspective is aimed at transcending the political-decision-driven interpretations of many of the critics of ecological modernization. The remainder of the chapter 10 consists of elaborating a Castells-oriented model of how the greening of transnational corporations' buildings is codetermined by an interaction between the global and local management of environmental flows. Global management basically involves the corporate quest to meet a variety of goals—"to attract clients, satisfy customers, and neutralize critics"—even as the ultimate parameter of how and to what extent corporate buildings will undergo greening remains that of maximizing profits and ensuring the continuity of a firm. At the local end are local environmental policies, which themselves are subject to transnationalization. Presas and Mol lay out preliminary case studies of four corporations in three metropolises, and demonstrate the interaction between global management and local regulation in shaping how buildings are greened.

It should also be mentioned that the van Koppen and Oosterveer, and Presas and Mol chapters are essential reading for those who want to understand in a more concrete sense the ontology and epistemology of global environmental flows. The Mol and Spaargaren chapter, as useful and necessary as it is in laying out the theoretical rationale for a flows and fluids view of environmental phenomena, nonetheless conveys relatively little about how "environmental flows practitioners" would identify concrete research problems and work through these research problems. The three empirical chapters that lie very close to Mol and Spaargaren's theoretical chapter nicely illustrate global environmental flows from the perspective of problem identification, research design, and methodology.

By contrast to this type of chapters, there are chapters that represent a somewhat different tendency: employing the notion of environmental flows in order to provide a *deeper understanding* of governance. Political scientists seem to be more strongly represented in this category than in the former type. Here, we will say very little about this second category of chapters except to point out *how* they put different emphases on governance compared to the environmental governance perspective that has been advanced by Mol and Spaargaren in their theoretical chapter. This second category—which contains, for instance, chapters by Jänicke, Stevis and Bruyninckx, Buttel and Fischhendler—partly departs from the full-blown flows ontology and epistemology set forth in the Mol and Spaargaren chapter in one or both of two respects. One such departure from the ideal-typical flows perspective is that of retaining an emphasis on the nature and role of environmental governance from a national state viewpoint; the chapters by Jänicke, Buttel, and Fischhendler are largely based on the national state as a major unit of analysis. The second type of departure is to retain a relatively more positivist-causal perspective on governance than is implied in the works of Urry, Castells, Spaargaren, and Mol. The chapters by Jänicke, Stevis and Bruyninckx, and Buttel lie somewhat apart from the more institutional and causally indeterminate view of governance that is advanced by the Mol and Spaargaren chapter in this volume.

One additional chapter that warrants comment in terms of the diversity of approaches that are now emerging on environmental flows and governance is Gille's "Detached Flows or Grounded Place-Making Projects?" The thrust of this chapter is that, on the one hand, Gille applauds environmental flows analysts for taking globalization and phenomenological perspectives seriously in terms of transcending the national and nation-state unit of analysis, recognizing the two-way patterns of causality between the local and the global, and calling attention to the need for environmental sociologists to recognize the significance of what she calls material circulation. On the other hand, Gille wishes to see environmental flows scholars adopt a perspective on globalization that goes beyond what she dubs the bird's-eye views that are "written from the outside, or from above"—a "view-of-everywhere, yet a view from the nowhere." In contrast to Castells's and Urry's views on globalization and the global, she advocates a global ethnography position that is simultaneously more political, economic (à la Massey 1994), and phenomenological (à la Goldman 2001), as well as being locally rooted and less bird's-eye in its unit of analysis. Arguably, in analyzing (auto)mobility patterns Jensen applies such a locally rooted, ethnographic, structural perspective of flows, in which local citizen-consumers seem to be caught in, but also try to resist the space of mobility flows.

The diversity of views as to what is most significant and appealing about the global environmental flows perspective indicates that it is unlikely to move relatively rapidly toward closure, as did the ecological modernization perspective. Some will lament this state of affairs as signaling the lack of coherence in global environmental flows theorizing. This situation is by no means a negative one, however. Global environmental flows scholarship may well develop in an ecumenical manner and avoid attracting premature polemics because of its diversity, and because the perspective will not lend itself to caricaturization.

### Concluding Remarks and Some Challenges for the Future

In this chapter, we have been reflecting on both the newly developing field of scholarship on environmental flows while also taking into account the status and prospects of the larger enterprise of environmental sociology and political science. The big picture is that global environmental flows is yet one more dimension of how environmental sociology and political science across the world have become highly diversified, perhaps even fragmented. As just noted, some will lament this state of affairs, but on the whole it has a lot to commend it.

There are, however, some potential risks and challenges to the global environmental flows perspective that deserve consideration and attention. Perhaps the major risk regarding environmental flows is that the perspective departs so much from mainstream—especially U.S.—sociological and political science scholarship that there will for a considerable time be a comprehension barrier.[3] This is not only an issue with regard to the appropriation by the environmental social sciences of the global environmental flows notions but also with regard to sociology and political science as a whole, and their U.S. branches in particular. While U.S. sociology has become somewhat more attuned to cultural sociology and phenomenology, and—together with U.S. political science—has become more "Continental" in recent years, the U.S. social sciences community—and especially its environmental branches—retains a fairly strong commitment to a relatively positivist and causal ontology.[4] The global environmental flows research program is unlikely to witness the same bandwagon effect that ecological modernization did because of the fact that flows in general, and global environmental flows in particular, clearly do not lend themselves well to an intellectual shorthand—of, say, one page in an entry-level text—that can be transcribed in positivist-causal terms. Again, this is not a bad thing; witness the fact that the deceptive ease with which ecological modernization could be caricatured no doubt contributed to its present contestedness in the United States.

A further challenge concerning global environmental flows is that its practitioners should take some care to ensure that the concepts of flows and fluids do not lapse into a highly abstract, nonempirical, metaphoric, and ultimately dematerialized view of the environment. The environmental flows notion is an agenda to selectively *materialize* the imagery of flows, fluids, and networks that derives from the works of Urry and Castells. But the fact remains that intrinsic to Castells's position is that he finds relatively little about the material world and environment that is of interest or importance. And for Urry, the examples provided of environmental-type flows/fluids are scarcely distinguished from the more clearly social types of flows/fluids. Urry thus implicitly suggests that all kinds of flows and fluids are essentially homologous, with none regarded as being in principle more predominant or significant, or of a qualitatively different character, than others. A related, but somewhat different reason that environmental flows scholars need to avoid a basically metaphoric view of environmental flows has to do with the imperative of environmental flows theorists to appeal to environmental sociologists and political scientists. Environmental social scientists as a group are predisposed to materialist, realist, and objectivist ontologies and epistemologies, and the flows perspective is something of a challenge to all three postures. Thus, while we are more than sympathetic to the view that environmental sociology and political science stand in need of the kind of methodological diversification that the flows perspective can provide, environmental flows scholars do have to take the sensibilities of environmental sociologists and political scientists into account as they elaborate their views about the social and biophysical nature of flows and fluids.

Yet another crucial issue is the one raised by Gille, Buttel, and others in this volume, though for the present purposes we will couch it in somewhat different terms. The works of the flows and network theorists come perilously close at times to denying that there is anything like a social structure out there. Sociologists, political scientists, and all others who look to these social sciences to contribute to a cumulative understanding of how the social world works—and yes, how it is structured—will resist the radical indeterminacy that characterizes Urry's and Castells's writings in some respects. There *is* a political-economic bedrock to the globe's environmental dynamics, even if that political economy is more complicated than that portrayed in standard political-economic accounts. Global environmental flows practitioners not only need to maintain a nontrivial commitment to considering the materiality of flows and fluids; they also need to entertain the notion that there is some flow to history, and that this is in principle knowable. Otherwise, environmental flows may suffer the fate that befell Latourian actor network scholarship, for example. There is an emerging consensus that ACT is particularly radically indeterminate as a perspective, and that instead of being a theory, it is merely a "way of looking at the world," and one that does not lead to cumulative, replicable knowledge but rather tends toward holistic paralysis. The ultimate threat is teleology; if one posits that the world is an ensemble of hybrids, one will tend to find hybrids everywhere. The Mol and Spaargaren interpretation and reformulation of the general flows sociology shows much awareness of the dangers of such indeterminacy and teleology.

Finally, an environmental flows perspective also offers new opportunities through coalitions and linkages between schools and research traditions that have been operating rather separately for some time. This volume supplies evidence of the strong interdependency of environmental sociology and environmental political science, on the one hand, with the mother disciplines, on the other. The drawing on, and at the same time feeding back into, the mother disciplines by the environmental subdisciplines seems to take a new turn with the advancement of the environmental flows perspective, and the discussions and debates it brings with it. This book also illustrates that bringing together environmental sociologists and environmental political scientists on the issue of governing environmental flows opens up new debates on the role of states and international (state-based) regimes, as we argued above. Further, a global environmental flows perspective seems to enable stronger interrelations between WST scholars who have recently (re)discovered the environment and those ecological modernizationists who are more inclined to include global, political economy perspectives.[5] And finally, a flows perspective facilitates links between the environmental social sciences and the more integrative environmental (footprint) studies contributions (cf. industrial ecology, environmental flows analysis, and environmental system analysis), but now on the conditions set by the former rather than the latter.

## Notes

The core of this chapter was designed and written by Fred Buttel as the first and principle author. Due to Fred's untimely death, the other editors adapted and completed this chapter, following the suggestions of reviewers.

1. As noted in some detail elsewhere (Buttel 2004), the treadmill-of-production theory is a neo-Marxist theory (only) in a very particular sense. Buttel developed a typology of major neo-Marxist environmental sociologies, which distinguishes among "early," "late," and "plain" Marxisms, and between those that stress only transformative nonfarm industry or transformative industry plus the "ecoregulatory" sectors (such as agriculture, forestry, and fisheries).

2. IPAT is also often referred to as the "Paul Ehrlich equation" or the "consumption equation." The IPAT equation is presented as: $I = P * A * T$, where:

I is the impact on the environment resulting from consumption

P is the population number

A is the consumption per capita (affluence)

T is the technology factor

The relationship between population, consumption, and environmental impact can be described in approximate terms by an equation first proposed by Holdren and Ehrlich (1971):

$$TEI = P \times UC/hp \times EE - 1,$$

where:

TEI is the total environmental impact

P is the population

UC/hp is the (average) units of the consumption of products and services per head of the population

EE is the environmental efficiency of the production, use, and disposal of those units

3. An example of what we are referring to here concerns the historical one of Beck (1992) and risk society theory. Beck's work is not easy to grasp, and for this reason the vast majority of U.S. environmental sociologists were completely unaware of Beck and risk society theory until the late 1990s, when certain (and sometimes oversimplifying) secondary accounts were published.

4. Thus, in Kiel's (2003) review of Urry (2003) in the *American Journal of Sociology*, he is respectful of Urry's work but admonishes the prospective reader in two ways. First, he warns the prospective reader that few will have the background in the "sciences of complexity" to permit a "full understanding" of what Urry has to say. Second, Kiel basically makes the case that Urry's views about globalization, flows, and fluids will not have much impact on sociology without a full-blown Kuhnian paradigmatic revolution. Most sociologists are not so ambitious or imaginative.

5. Note the emerging number of environmentally oriented pieces recently in, for instance, the *Journal of World-Systems Research* (including both occasional articles as well as periodic special issues on environmental topics, such as the fall 1997 and summer 2003 issues).

# References

Beck, U. 1992. *Risk Society*. London: Sage.

Beck, U. 1997. *Was ist Globalisierung?* Frankfurt am Main: Suhrkamp Verlag.

Beck, U., and J. Wilms. 2004. *Conversations with Ulrich Beck*. Cambridge: Polity Press.

Blowers, A. 1997. Environmental Policy: Ecological Modernization and the Risk Society? *Urban Studies* 34, nos. 5–6:845–871.

Blühdorn, I. 1997. A Theory of Post-Ecologist Politics. *Environmental Politics* 6:125–147.

Blühdorn, I. 2000. *Post-Ecologist Politics*. London: Routledge.

Boland, J. 1994. Ecological Modernization. *Capitalism-Nature-Socialism* 5:135–141.

Buttel, F. H. 2003. Environmental Sociology and the Explanation of Environmental Reform. *Organization and Environment* 16:306–344.

Buttel, F. H. 2004. The Treadmill of Production: An Appreciation, Assessment, and Agenda for Research. *Organization and Environment* 17:323–336.

Buttel, F. H., P. Dickens, R. E. Dunlap, and A. Gijswijt. 2002. Sociological Theory and the Environment: An Overview and Introduction. In *Sociological Theory and the Environment: Classical Foundations, Contemporary Insights*, ed. R. E. Dunlap, P. Dickens, F. H. Buttel, and A. Gijswijt, 3–32. Lanham, MD: Rowman and Littlefield.

Buttel, F. H., and A. Gijswijt. 2001. Emerging Trends in Environmental Sociology. In *Blackwell Companion to Sociology*, ed. J. R. Blau, 43–70. Oxford: Blackwell.

Castells, M. 1996. *The Rise of the Network Society.* Vol. 1 of *The Information Age: Economy, Society, and Culture.* Oxford: Blackwell.

Goldman, M. 2001. Constructing an Environmental State: Eco-Governmentality and Other Transnational Practices of a "Green" World Bank. *Social Problems* 48:499–523.

Grundmann, R., and N. Stehr. 2000. Social Science and the Absence of Nature: Uncertainty and the Reality of Extremes. *Social Science Information* 39:155–179.

Holdren, J. P., and P. R. Ehrlich. 1971. Impact of Population Growth. *Science* 171:1211–1217.

Kiel, L. D. 2003. Review of John Urry, *Global Complexity. American Journal of Sociology* 109:755–756.

Massey, D. 1994. *Space, Place, and Gender.* Minneapolis: University of Minnesota Press.

Mol, A. P. J. 2001. *Globalization and Environmental Reform.* Cambridge: MIT Press.

Mol, A. P. J., and G. Spaargaren. 2004. Ecological Modernization and Consumption: A Reply. *Society and Natural Resources* 17:261–266.

Murphy, R. 1996. *Sociology and Nature.* Boulder, CO: Westview Press.

Schnaiberg, A. 1980. *The Environment.* New York: Oxford University Press.

Urry, J. 1998. Locating HE in the Global Landscape. <http://www.comp.lancs.ac.uk/sociology/papers/urry-locating-he.pdf>.

Urry, J. 1999. Globalization and Citizenship. *Journal of World-Systems Research* 5:311–324.

Urry, J. 2000a. Mobile Sociology. *British Journal of Sociology* 51:185–203.

Urry, J. 2000b. *Sociology beyond Societies.* London: Routledge.

Urry, J. 2003. *Global Complexity.* Cambridge: Polity Press.

York, R. 2003. Cross-National Variation in the Size of Passenger Car Fleets: A Study in Environmentally Significant Consumption. *Population and Environment* 25:119–140.

York, R., and E. A. Rosa. 2003. Key Challenges to Ecological Modernization: Institutional Efficacy, Case Study Evidence, Units of Analysis, and the Pace of Eco-Efficiency. *Organization and Environment* 16:273–288.

York, R., E. A. Rosa, and T. Dietz. 2002. Bridging Environmental Science with Environmental Policy: The Plasticity of Population, Affluence, and Technology. *Social Science Quarterly* 83:18–34.

York, R., E. A. Rosa, and T. Dietz. 2003. Footprints on the Earth: The Environmental Consequences of Modernity. *American Sociological Review* 68:279–300.

# Index